HIDEYUKI FURUHASHI

I attended Napoli Comic-Con
this past spring, and then,
in September, I was invited
to an event called Manga
Festival in Bangkok. It was a
ton of fun!

BETTEN COURT

In volume 7 I mentioned
going to Napoli Comic-Con,
and just the other day, I
was a special guest at an
event in Bangkok! This one
was a blast too, so now
I'm wondering how to turn
attending overseas autograph
sessions into a career...

D0110845

MY HERO ACADEMIA VIGILANTES

VOLUME 8
SHONEN JUMP Manga Edition

STORY: HIDEYUKI FURUHASHI
ART: BETTEN COURT
ORIGINAL CONCEPT: KOHEI HORIKOSHI

Translation & English Adaptation/Caleb Cook
Touch-Up Art & Lettering/John Hunt
Designer/Julian [JR] Robinson
Editor/Mike Montesa

VIGILANTE -BOKU NO HERO ACADEMIA ILLEGALS-
© 2016 by Hideyuki Furuhashi, Betten Court, Kohei Horikoshi
All rights reserved.
First published in Japan in 2016 by SHUEISHA Inc., Tokyo.
English translation rights arranged by SHUEISHA Inc.

The stories, characters and incidents mentioned in this publication
are entirely fictional.

Printed in the U.S.A.

Published by VIZ Media, LLC
P.O. Box 77010
San Francisco, CA 94107

10 9 8 7 6 5 4 3 2 1
First printing, November 2020

viz.com

shonenjump.com

PARENTAL ADVISORY
MY HERO ACADEMIA: VIGILANTES is rated
T for Teen and is recommended for ages
13 and up. This volume contains fantasy
violence.

MY HERO ACADEMIA
VIGILANTES

Writer / Letterer
Hideyuki Furuhashi

Penciller / Colorist
Betten Court

Original Concept
Kohei Horikoshi

【deus ex machina】

noun | de · us ex ma · chi · na
: a plot device that literally means "god from the machine," used in the plays of ancient Greece;
or : an overly convenient contrivance in a story that forcibly resolves the conflict

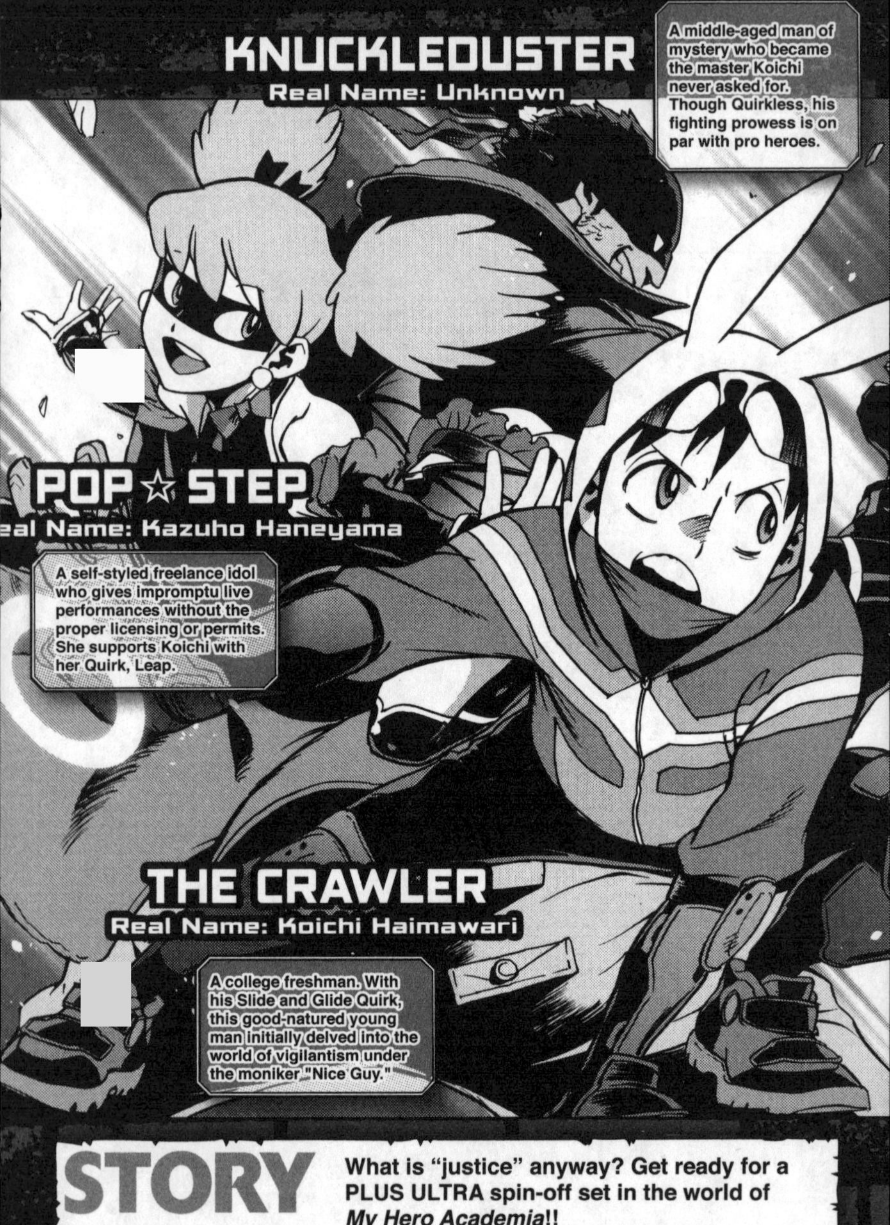
KNUCKLEDUSTER
Real Name: Unknown
A middle-aged man of mystery who became the master Koichi never asked for. Though Quirkless, his fighting prowess is on par with pro heroes.
POP☆STEP
eal Name: Kazuho Haneyama
A self-styled freelance idol who gives impromptu live performances without the proper licensing or permits. She supports Koichi with her Quirk, Leap.
THE CRAWLER
Real Name: Koichi Haimawari
A college freshman. With his Slide and Glide Quirk, this good-natured young man initially delved into the world of vigilantism under the moniker "Nice Guy."

STORY

What is "justice" anyway? Get ready for a PLUS ULTRA spin-off set in the world of *My Hero Academia*!!

Heroes. The chosen ones who, with explicit government permission, use their natural talents, or Quirks, to aid society. However, not everyone can be chosen, and some take action of their own accord, becoming illegal heroes. What does justice mean to them? And can we really call them heroes? This story takes to the streets in order to follow the exploits of those known as *vigilantes*.

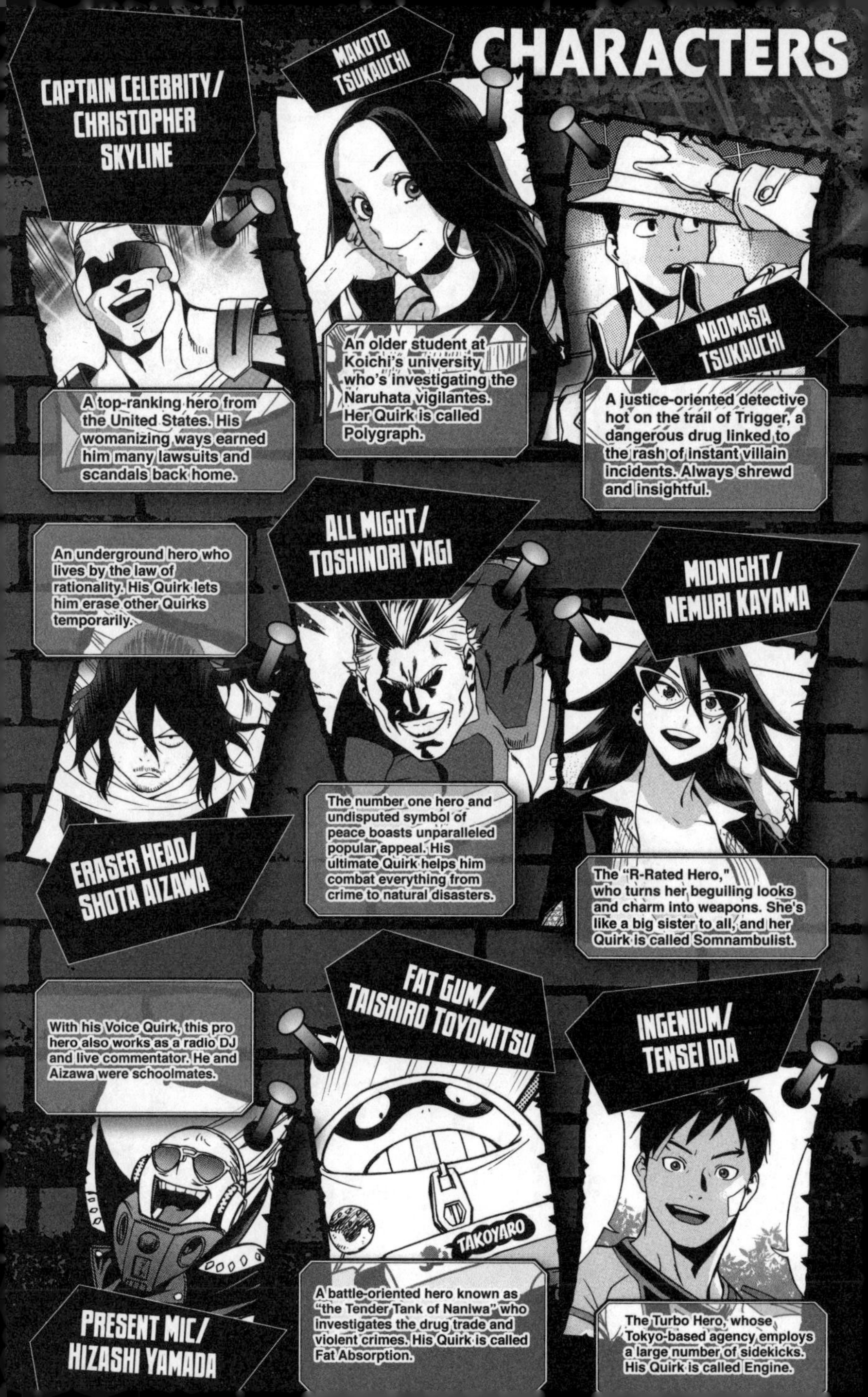
CHARACTERS
NAOMASA TSUKAUCHI
A justice-oriented detective hot on the trail of Trigger, a dangerous drug linked to the rash of instant villain incidents. Always shrewd and insightful.
MAKOTO TSUKAUCHI
An older student at Koichi's university who's investigating the Naruhata vigilantes. Her Quirk is called Polygraph.
CAPTAIN CELEBRITY/ CHRISTOPHER SKYLINE
A top-ranking hero from the United States. His womanizing ways earned him many lawsuits and scandals back home.
MIDNIGHT/ NEMURI KAYAMA
The "R-Rated Hero," who turns her beguiling looks and charm into weapons. She's like a big sister to all, and her Quirk is called Somnambulist.
ALL MIGHT/ TOSHINORI YAGI
The number one hero and undisputed symbol of peace boasts unparalleled popular appeal. His ultimate Quirk helps him combat everything from crime to natural disasters.
ERASER HEAD/ SHOTA AIZAWA
An underground hero who lives by the law of rationality. His Quirk lets him erase other Quirks temporarily.
INGENIUM/ TENSEI IDA
The Turbo Hero, whose Tokyo-based agency employs a large number of sidekicks. His Quirk is called Engine.
FAT GUM/ TAISHIRO TOYOMITSU
TAKOYARO
A battle-oriented hero known as "the Tender Tank of Naniwa" who investigates the drug trade and violent crimes. His Quirk is called Fat Absorption.
PRESENT MIC/ HIZASHI YAMADA
With his Voice Quirk, this pro hero also works as a radio DJ and live commentator. He and Aizawa were schoolmates.

MY HERO ACADEMIA VIGILANTES

8

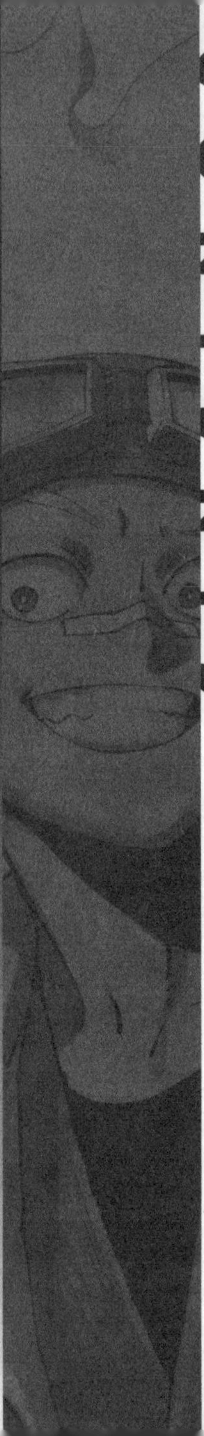

CONTENTS

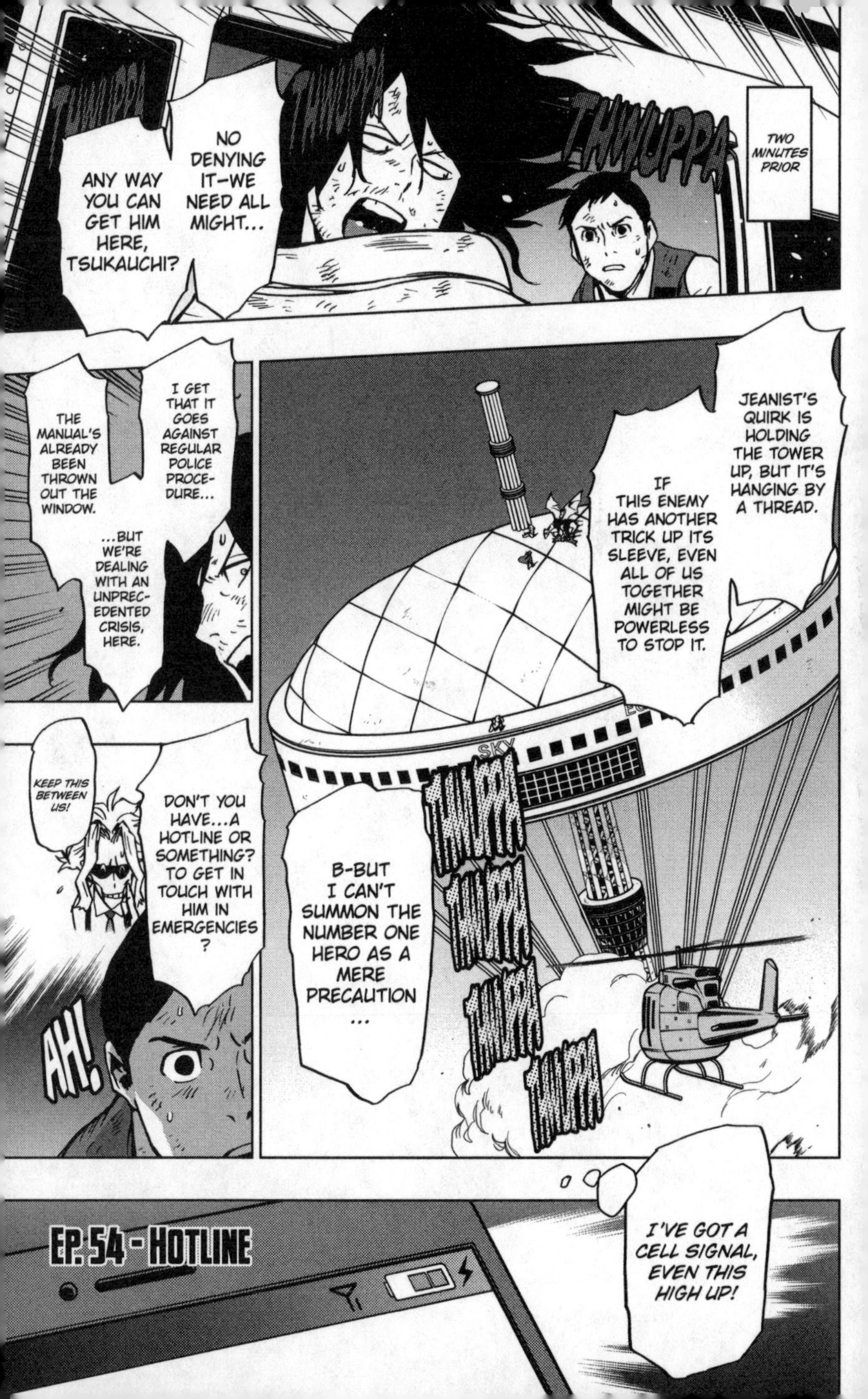
TWO MINUTES PRIOR
THWUPPA
NO DENYING IT—WE NEED ALL MIGHT...
ANY WAY YOU CAN GET HIM HERE, TSUKAUCHI?
JEANIST'S QUIRK IS HOLDING THE TOWER UP, BUT IT'S HANGING BY A THREAD.
IF THIS ENEMY HAS ANOTHER TRICK UP ITS SLEEVE, EVEN ALL OF US TOGETHER MIGHT BE POWERLESS TO STOP IT.
SKY
B-BUT I CAN'T SUMMON THE NUMBER ONE HERO AS A MERE PRECAUTION...
I GET THAT IT GOES AGAINST REGULAR POLICE PROCEDURE...
...BUT WE'RE DEALING WITH AN UNPRECEDENTED CRISIS, HERE.
THE MANUAL'S ALREADY BEEN THROWN OUT THE WINDOW.
DON'T YOU HAVE...A HOTLINE OR SOMETHING? TO GET IN TOUCH WITH HIM IN EMERGENCIES?
KEEP THIS BETWEEN US!
AH!
I'VE GOT A CELL SIGNAL, EVEN THIS HIGH UP!
EP. 54 - HOTLINE

EP. 54 - HOTLINE

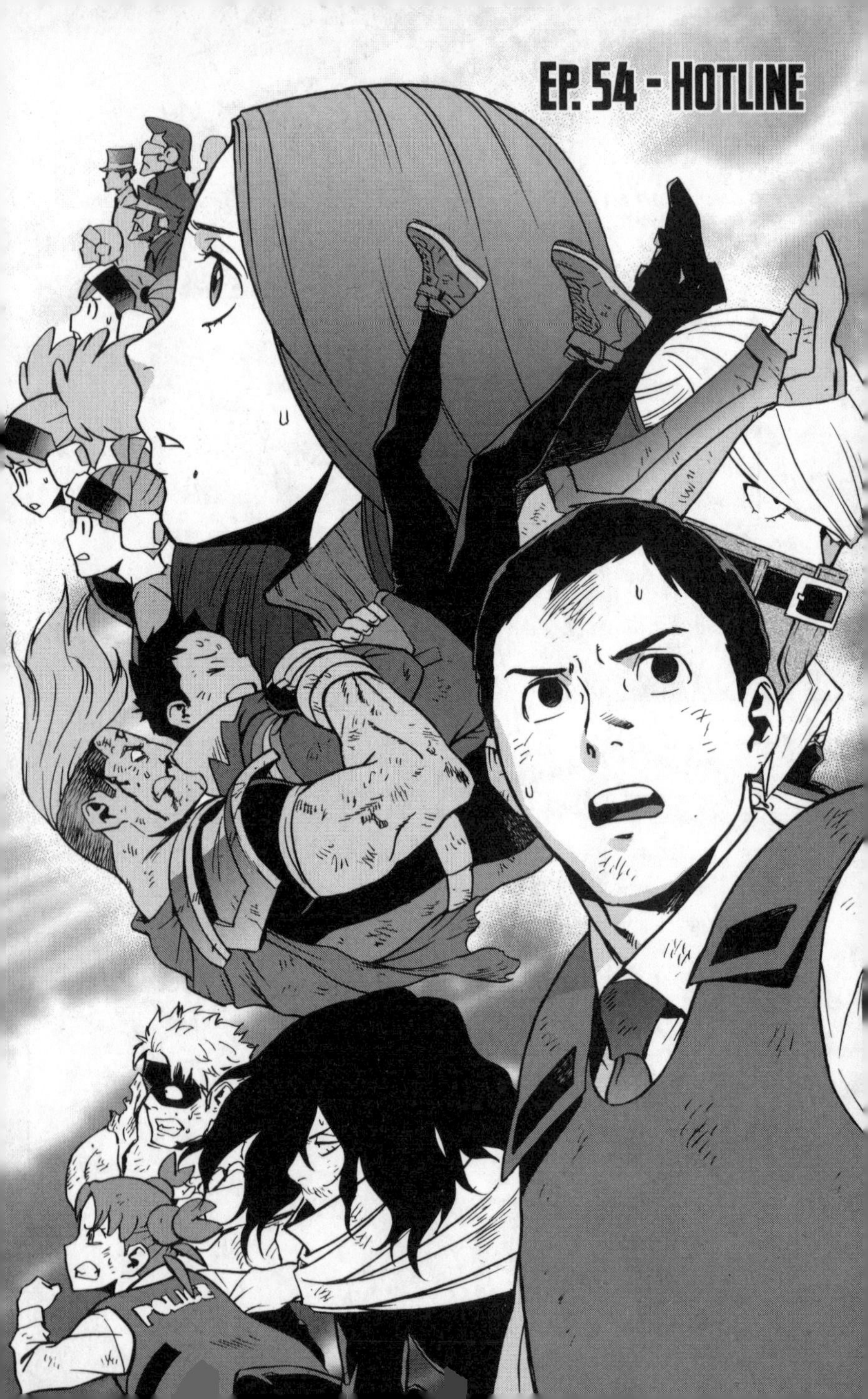

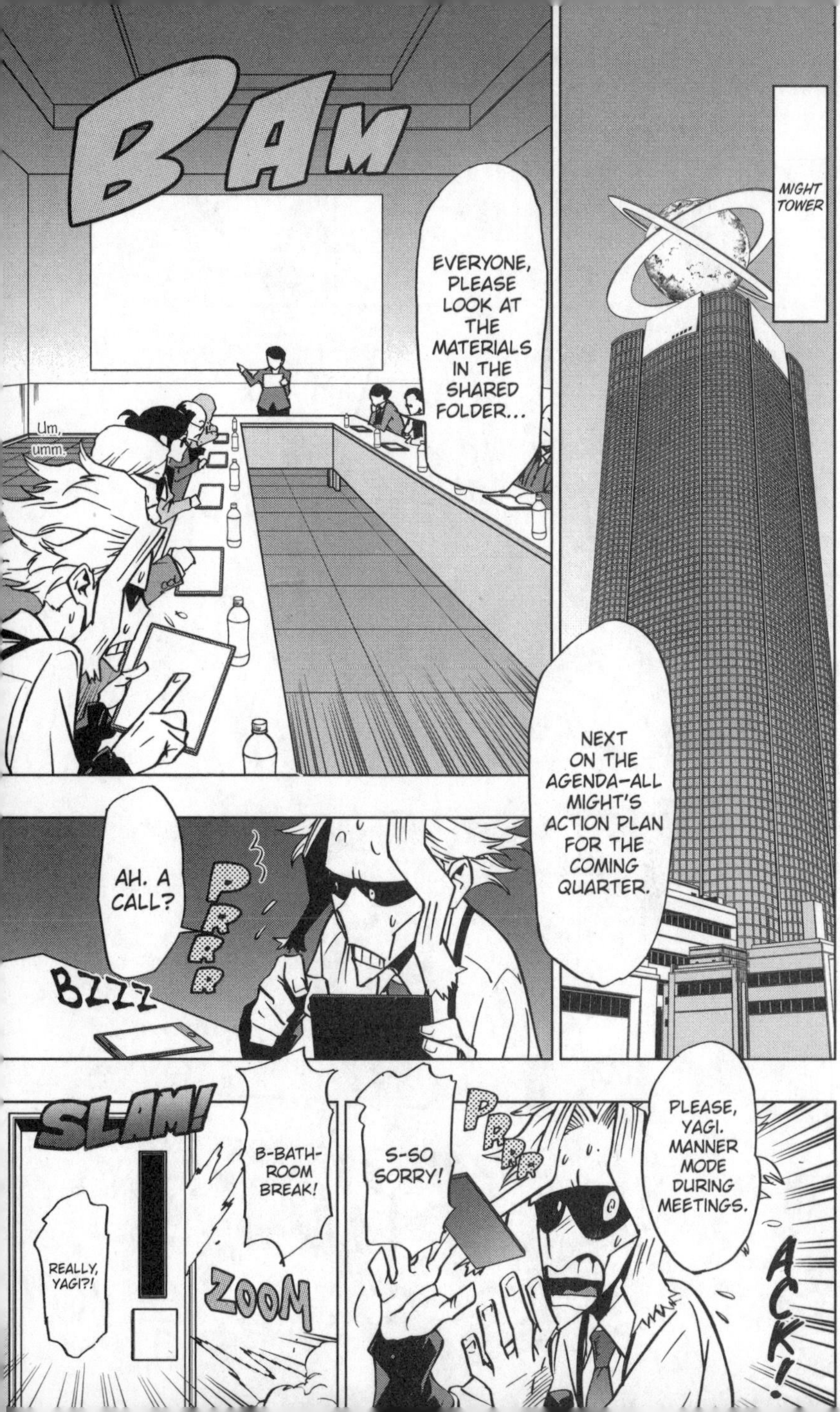
MIGHT TOWER
NEXT ON THE AGENDA—ALL MIGHT'S ACTION PLAN FOR THE COMING QUARTER.
BAM
EVERYONE, PLEASE LOOK AT THE MATERIALS IN THE SHARED FOLDER...
Um, umm.
AH. A CALL?
PRRRR
BZZZ
PRRRR
PLEASE, YAGI. MANNER MODE DURING MEETINGS.
ACK!
S-SO SORRY!
B-BATHROOM BREAK!
ZOOM
SLAM!
REALLY, YAGI?!

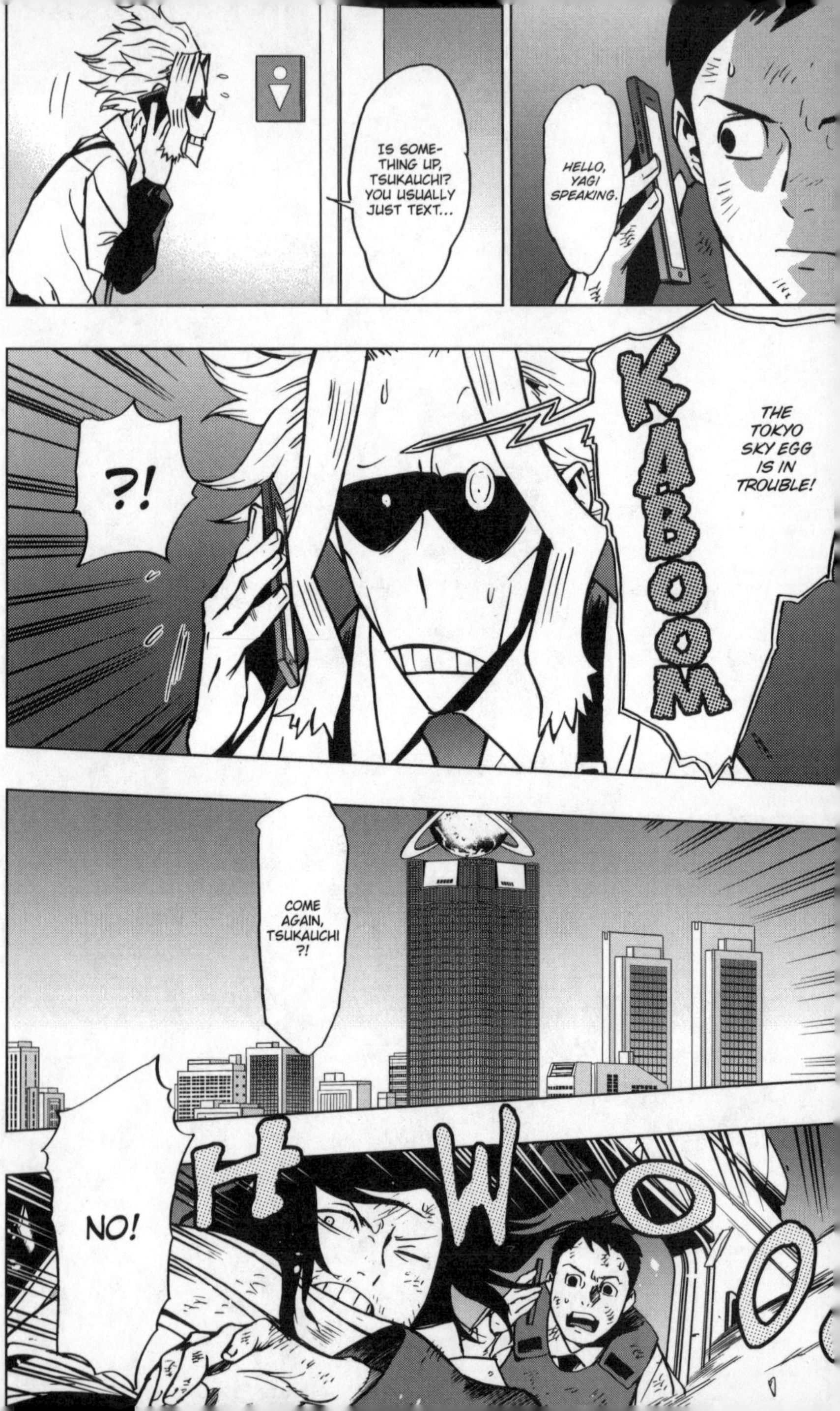
HELLO, YAGI SPEAKING.
IS SOME-THING UP, TSUKAUCHI? YOU USUALLY JUST TEXT...
THE TOKYO SKY EGG IS IN TROUBLE!
KABOOM
?!
COME AGAIN, TSUKAUCHI?!
HWOO
NO!

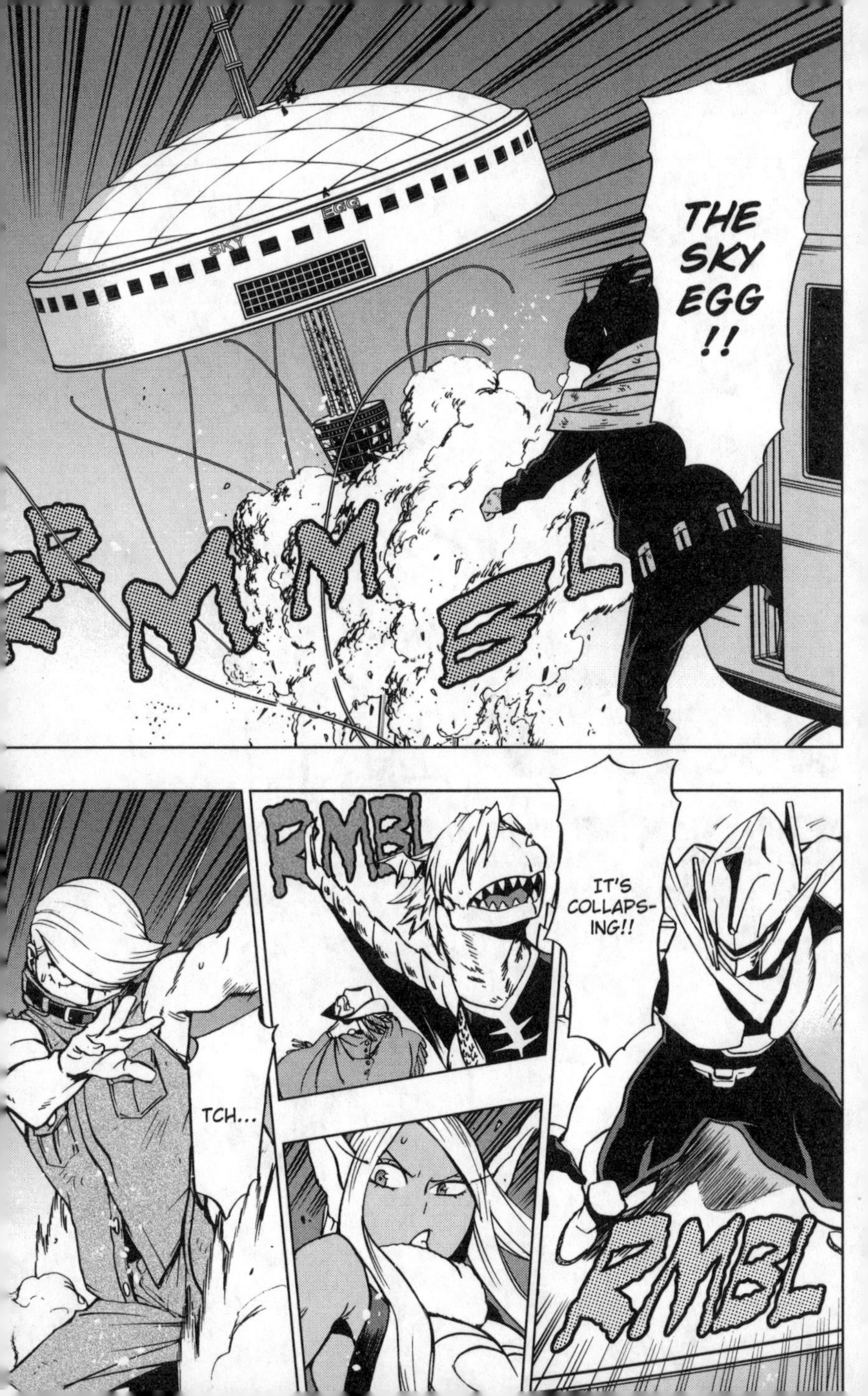
THE SKY EGG !!
SKY EGG
RRMMBL
IT'S COLLAPSING!!
RMBL
RMBL
TCH...

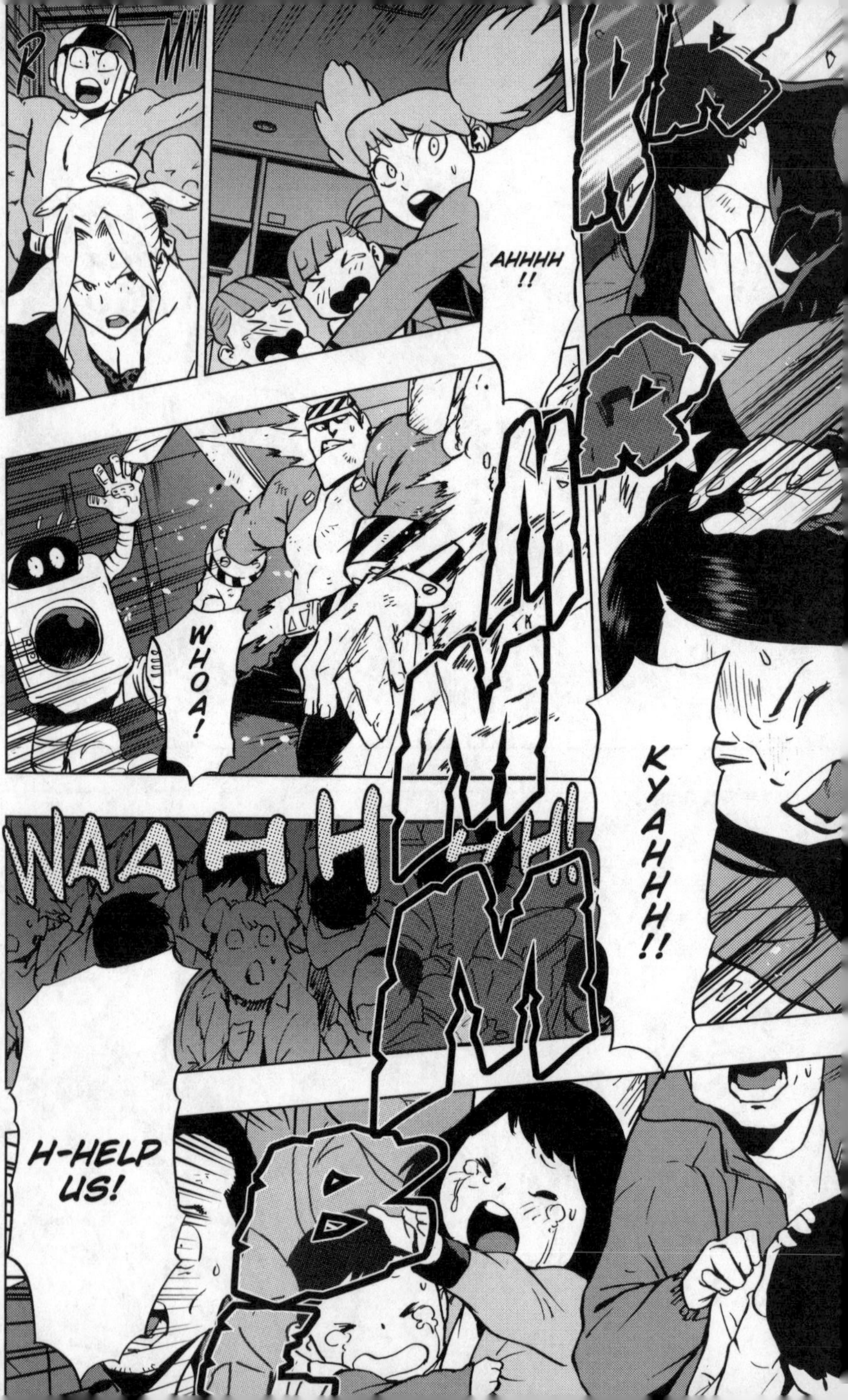
AHHHH!!
WHOA!
KYAHHHH!!
WAAHHHH!
H-HELP US!

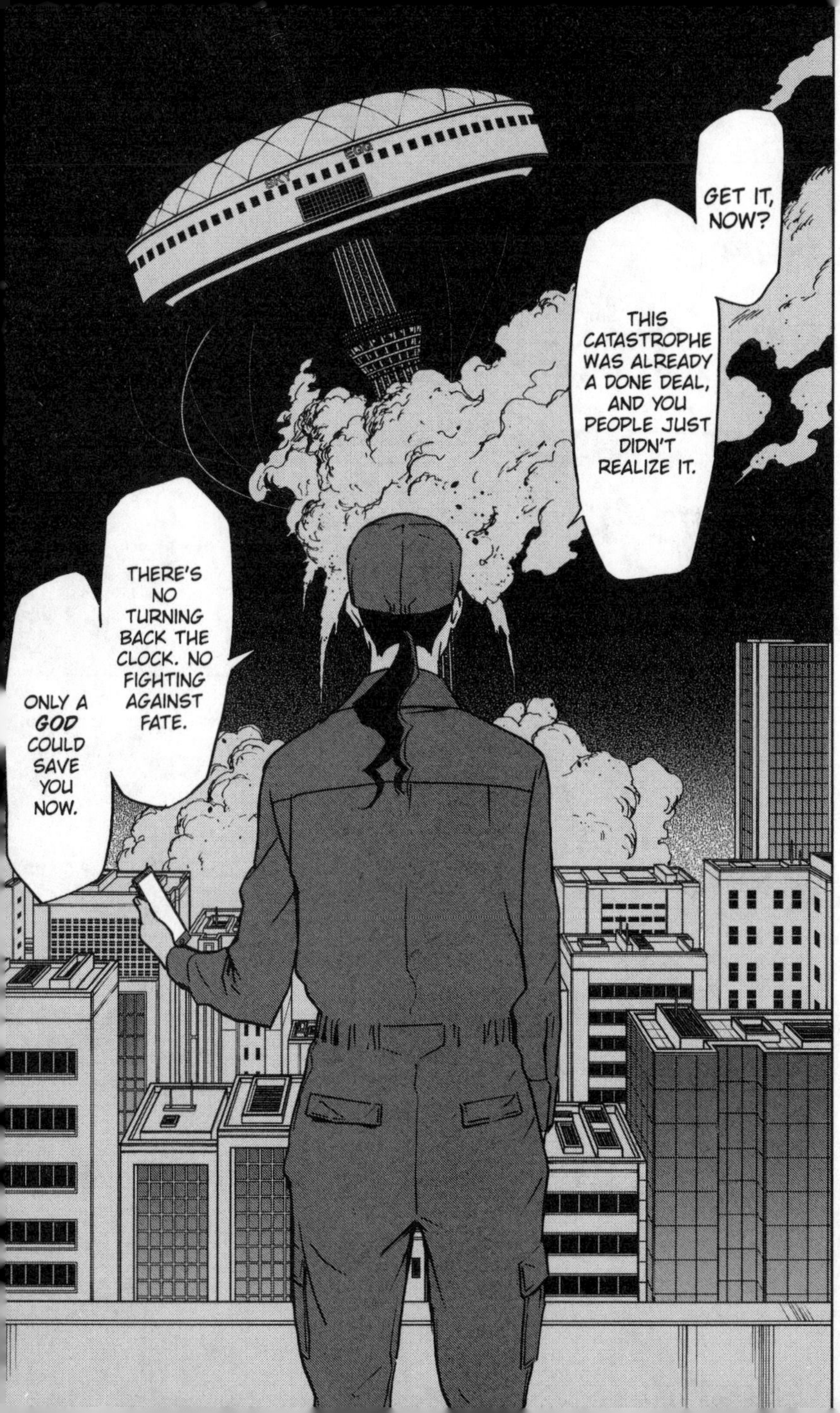
SKY EGG
GET IT, NOW?
THIS CATASTROPHE WAS ALREADY A DONE DEAL, AND YOU PEOPLE JUST DIDN'T REALIZE IT.
THERE'S NO TURNING BACK THE CLOCK. NO FIGHTING AGAINST FATE.
ONLY A *GOD* COULD SAVE YOU NOW.

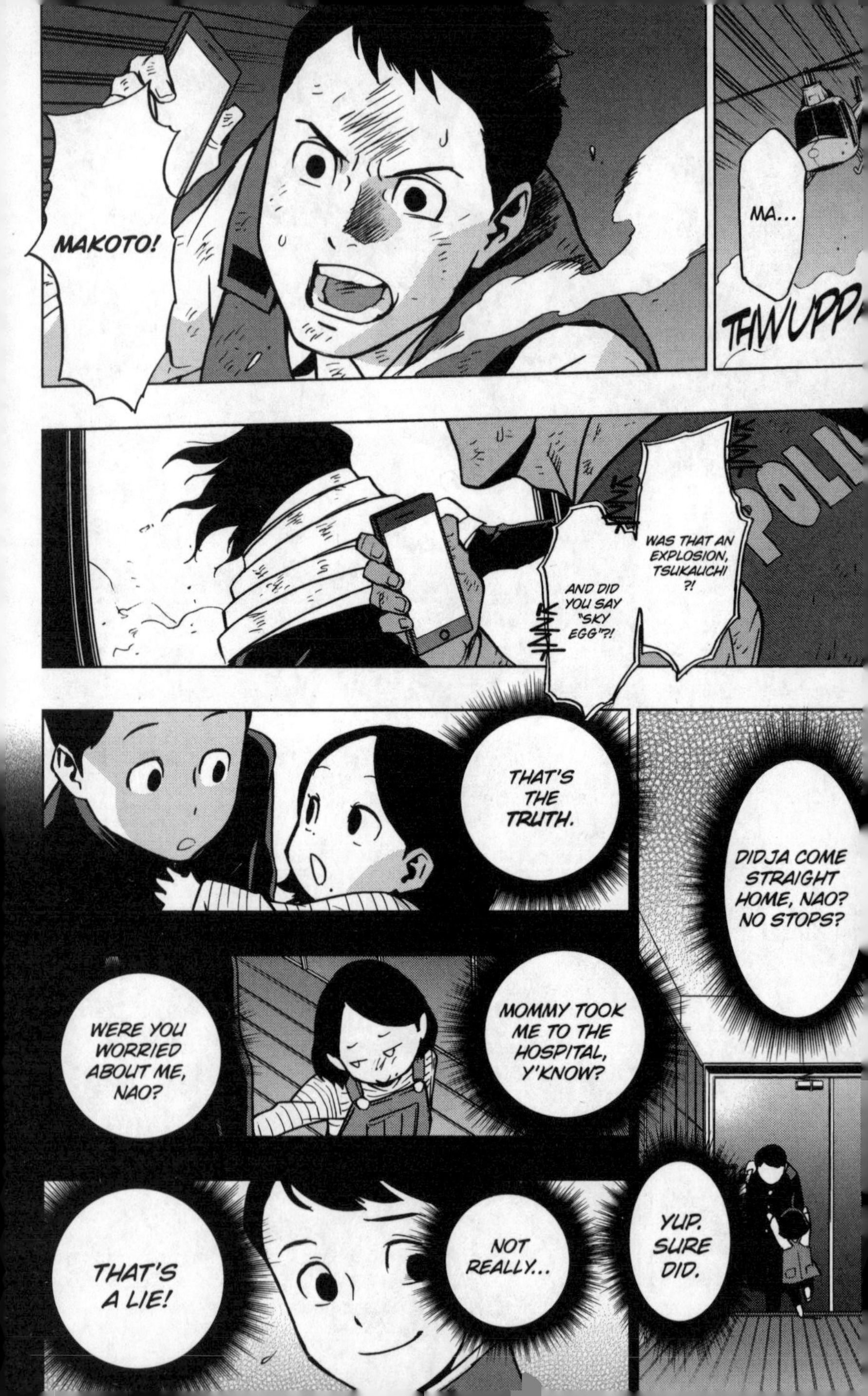
MA...
THWUPP
MAKOTO!
WAS THAT AN EXPLOSION, TSUKAUCHI?!
AND DID YOU SAY "SKY EGG"?!
DIDJA COME STRAIGHT HOME, NAO? NO STOPS?
YUP. SURE DID.
THAT'S THE TRUTH.
MOMMY TOOK ME TO THE HOSPITAL, Y'KNOW?
WERE YOU WORRIED ABOUT ME, NAO?
NOT REALLY...
THAT'S A LIE!

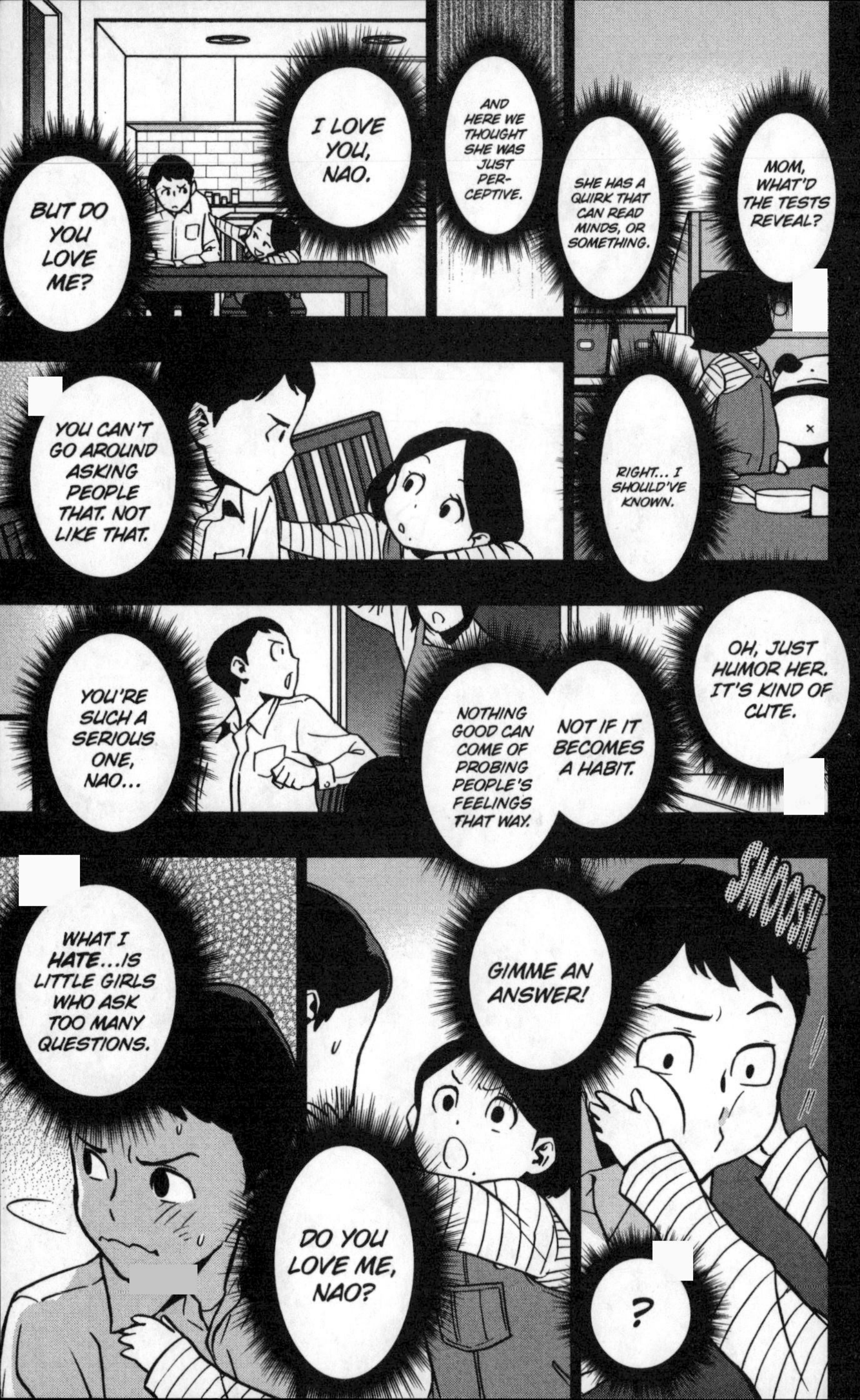
MOM, WHAT'D THE TESTS REVEAL?
SHE HAS A QUIRK THAT CAN READ MINDS, OR SOMETHING.
RIGHT... I SHOULD'VE KNOWN.
AND HERE WE THOUGHT SHE WAS JUST PER-CEPTIVE.
I LOVE YOU, NAO.
BUT DO YOU LOVE ME?
YOU CAN'T GO AROUND ASKING PEOPLE THAT. NOT LIKE THAT.
OH, JUST HUMOR HER. IT'S KIND OF CUTE.
NOT IF IT BECOMES A HABIT.
NOTHING GOOD CAN COME OF PROBING PEOPLE'S FEELINGS THAT WAY.
YOU'RE SUCH A SERIOUS ONE, NAO...
SHOOSH
GIMME AN ANSWER!
?
DO YOU LOVE ME, NAO?
WHAT I HATE...IS LITTLE GIRLS WHO ASK TOO MANY QUESTIONS.

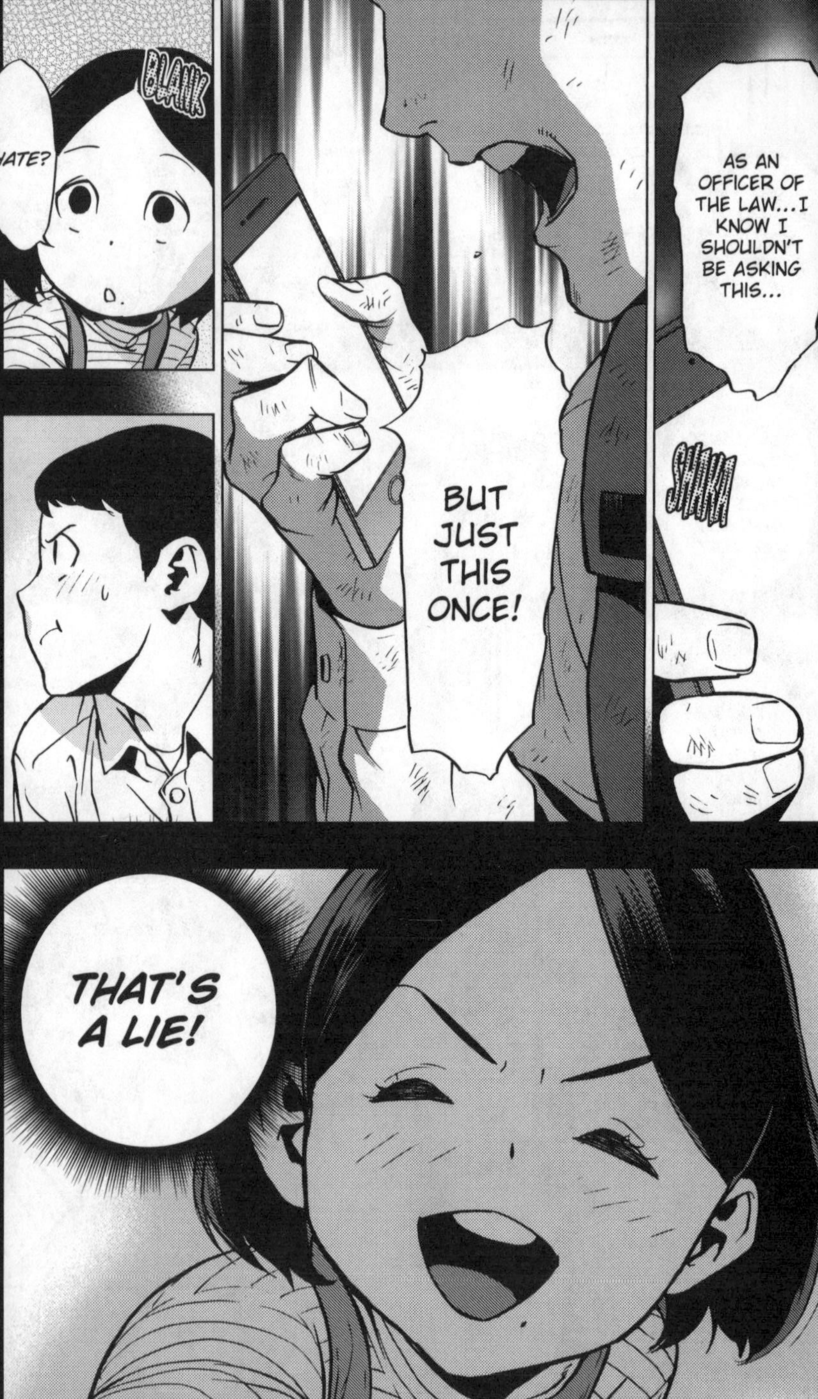
AS AN OFFICER OF THE LAW...I KNOW I SHOULDN'T BE ASKING THIS...
SHAKA
BUT JUST THIS ONCE!
BLANK
HATE?
THAT'S A LIE!

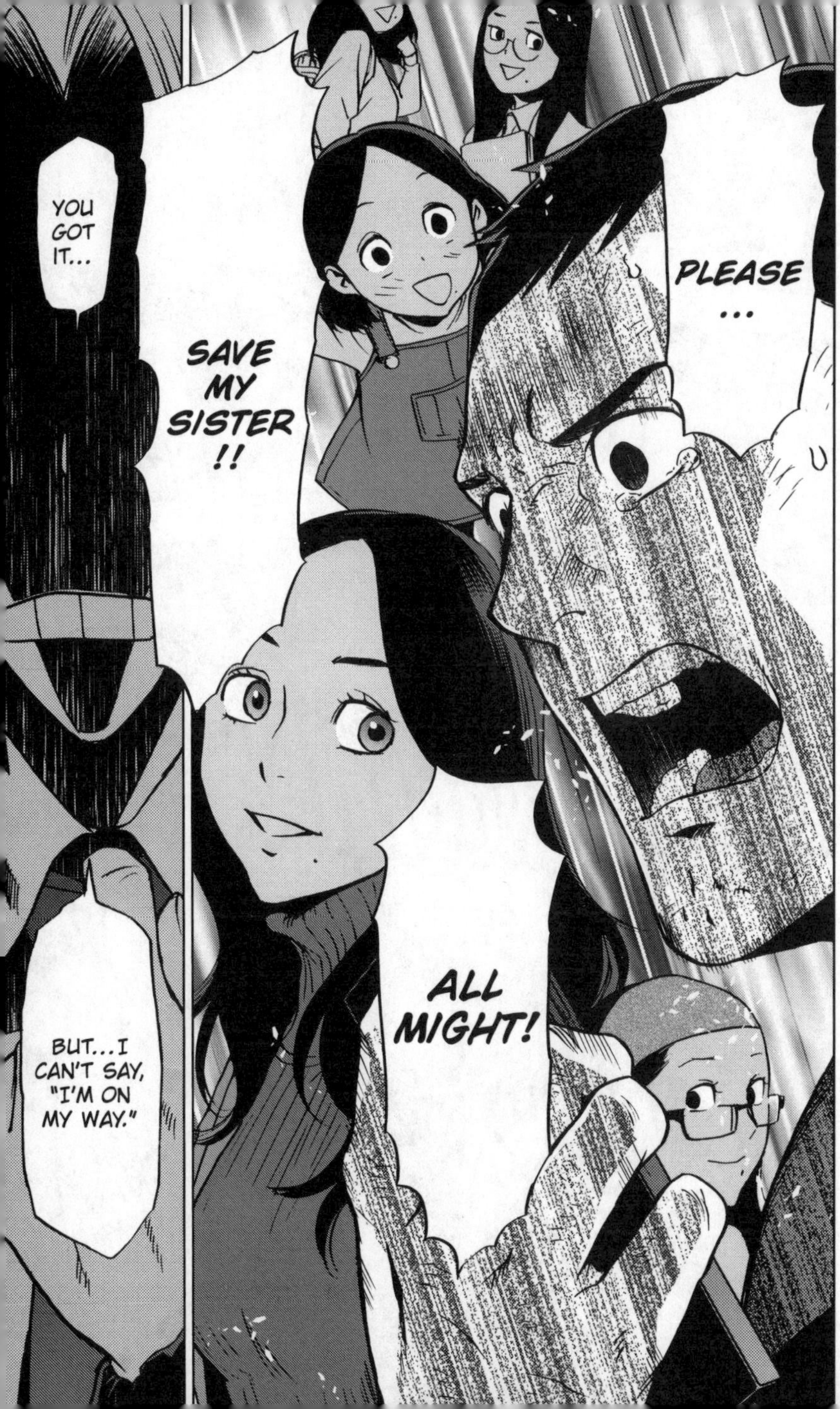
PLEASE...
SAVE MY SISTER!!
ALL MIGHT!
YOU GOT IT...
BUT...I CAN'T SAY, "I'M ON MY WAY."

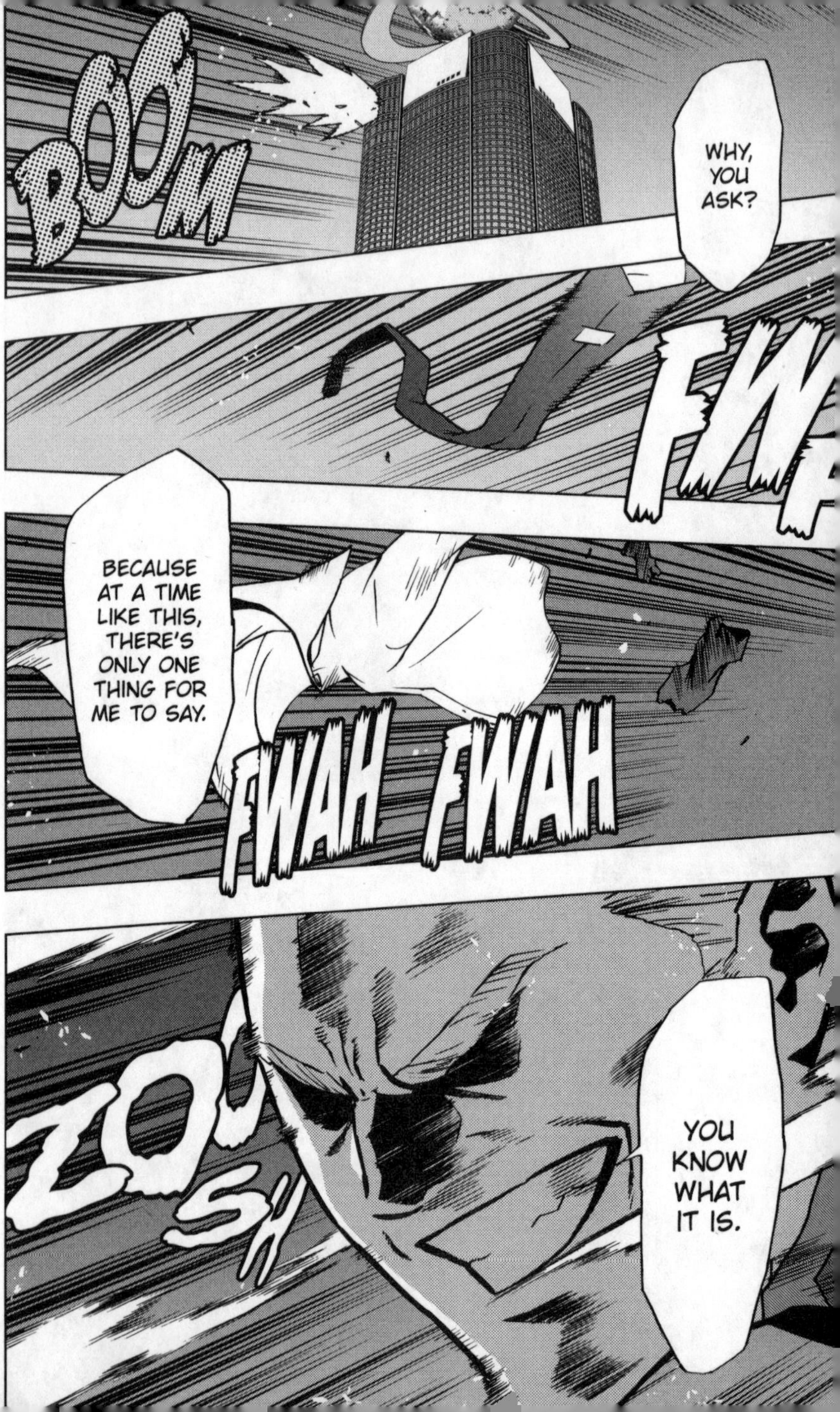
WHY, YOU ASK?
BOOM
FW
BECAUSE AT A TIME LIKE THIS, THERE'S ONLY ONE THING FOR ME TO SAY.
FWAH FWAH
YOU KNOW WHAT IT IS.
ZOOSH

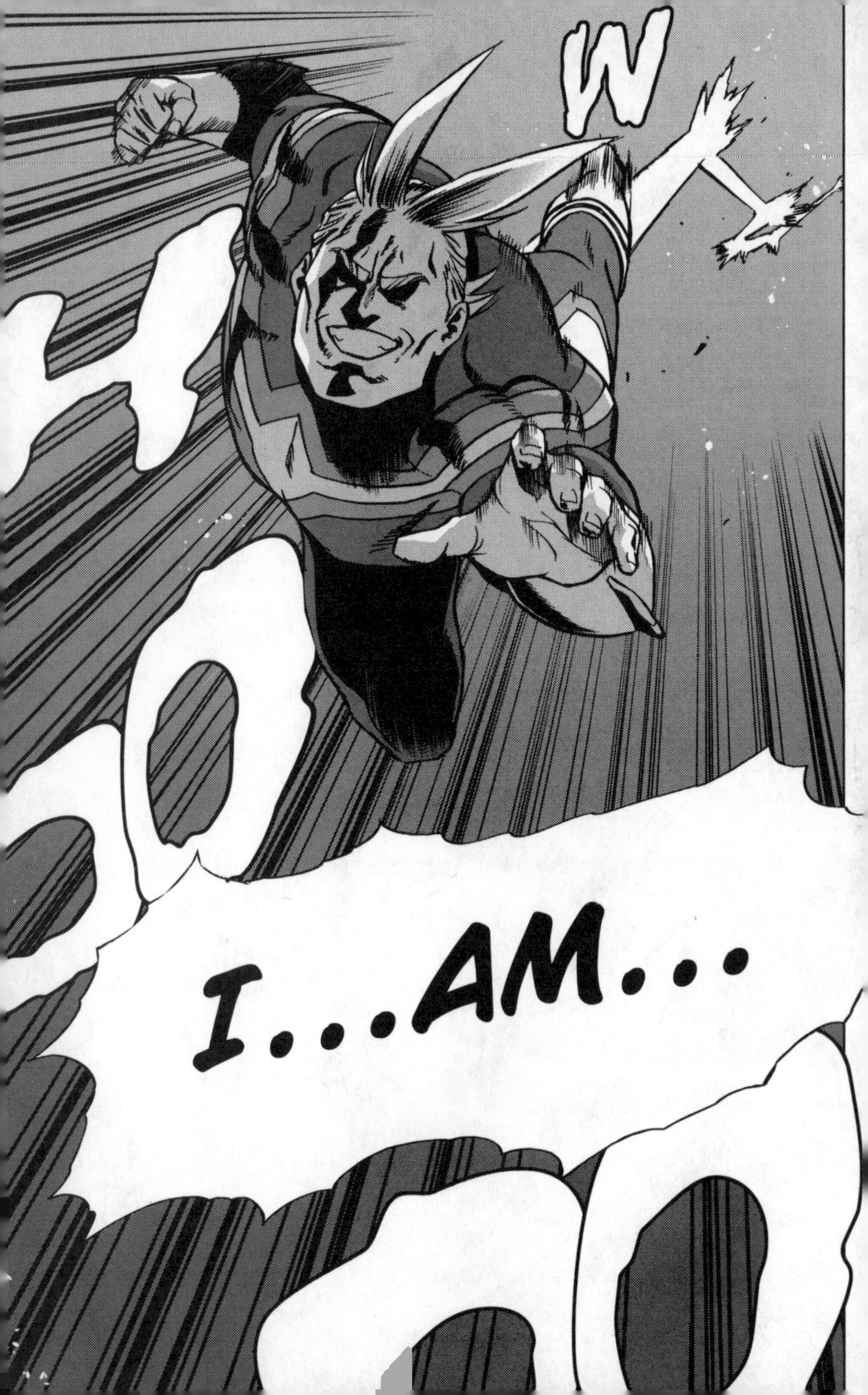
W
I...AM...

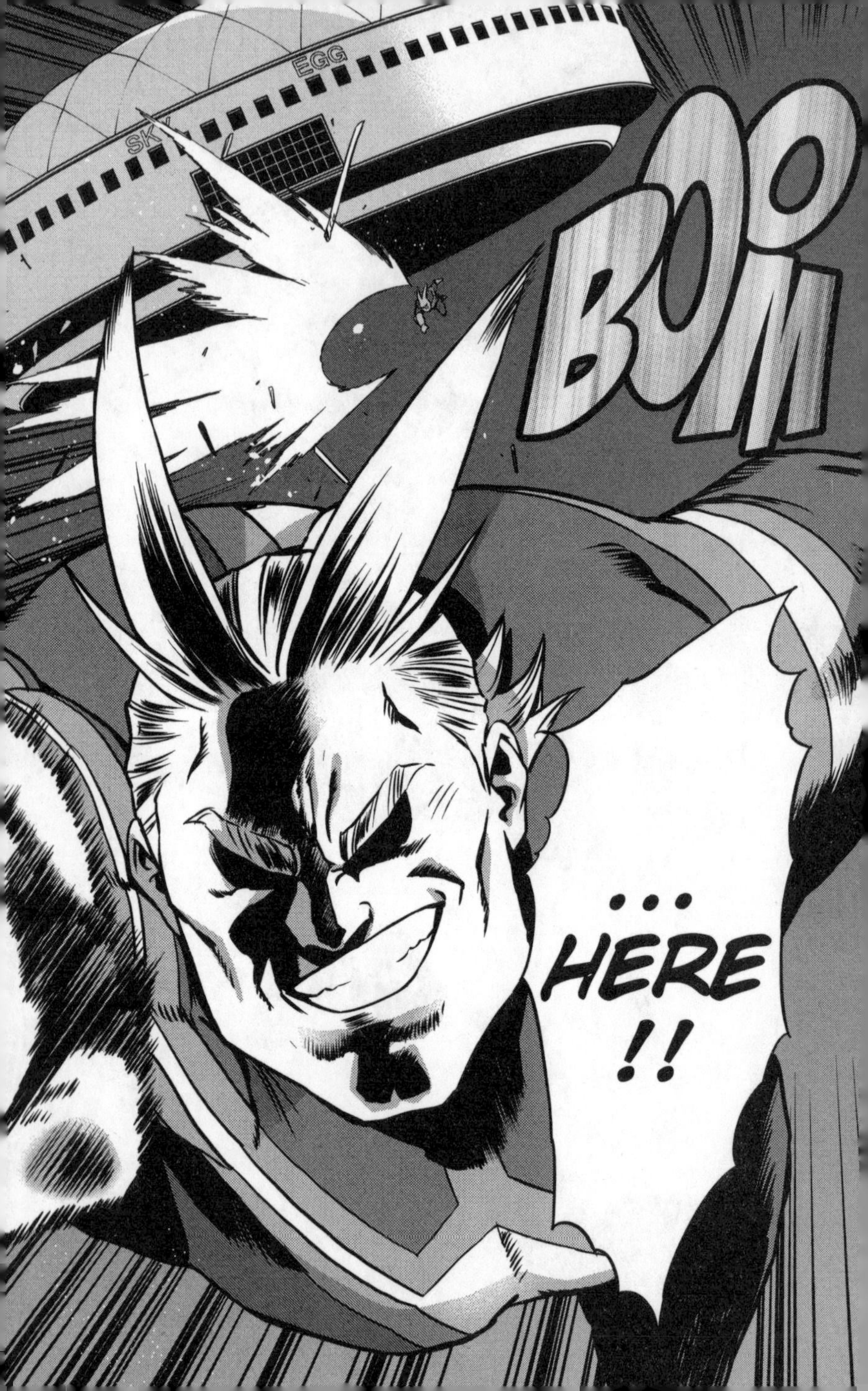
SKY EGG
BOOM
...HERE!!

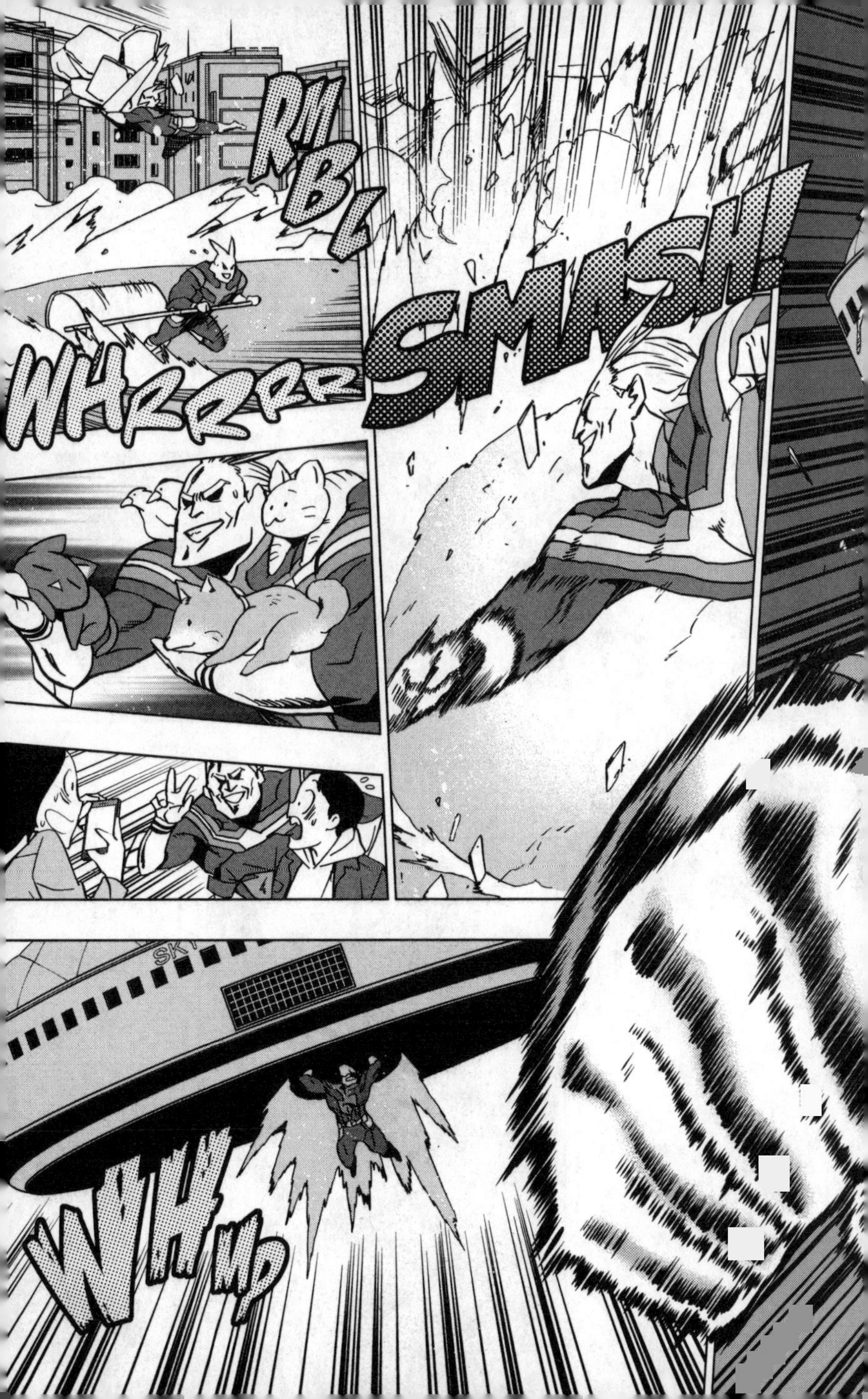
SMASH!!
RMBL
WHRRRRR
WHMP

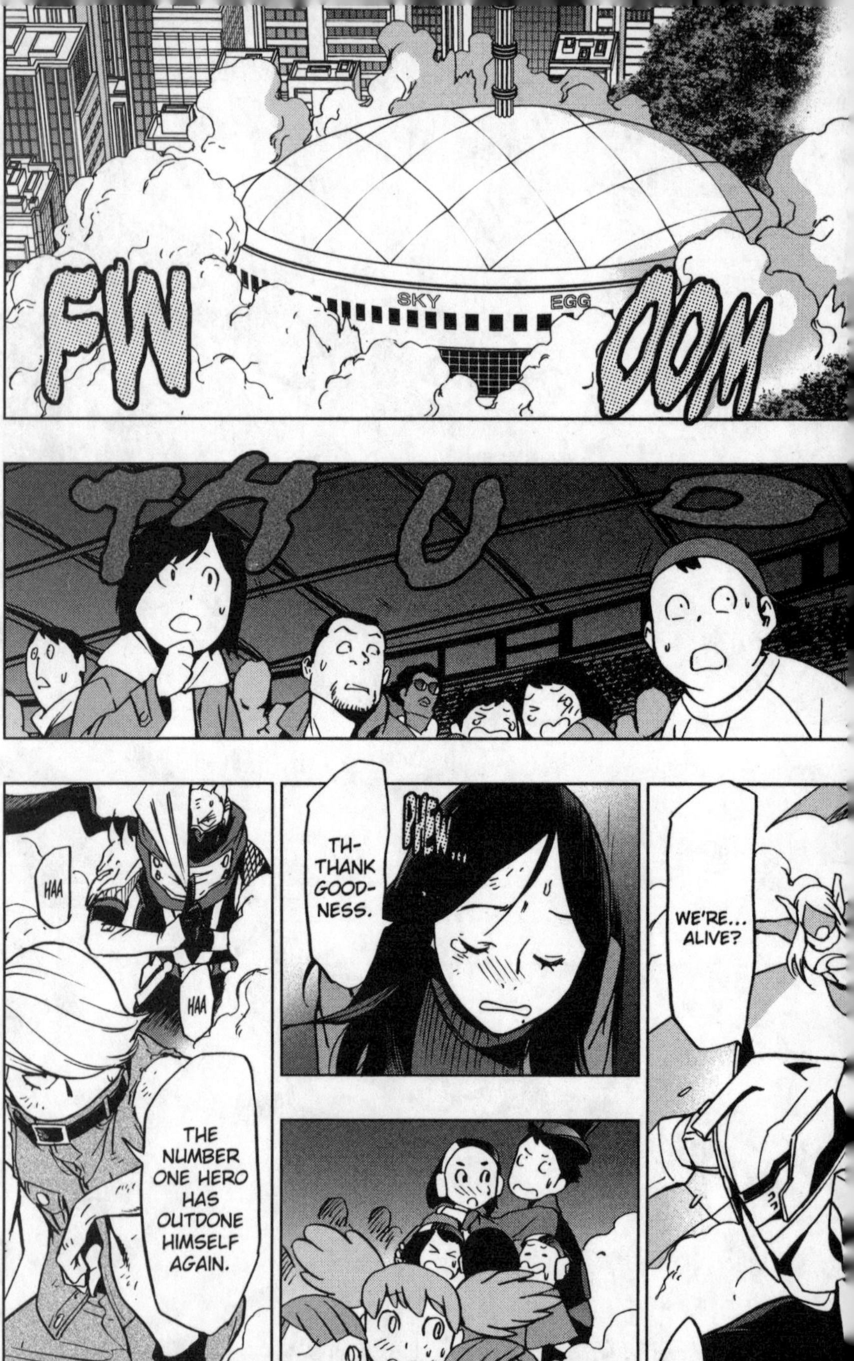
SKY EGG
FWOOM
THUD
WE'RE... ALIVE?
PHEW...
TH- THANK GOODNESS.
HAA
HAA
THE NUMBER ONE HERO HAS OUTDONE HIMSELF AGAIN.

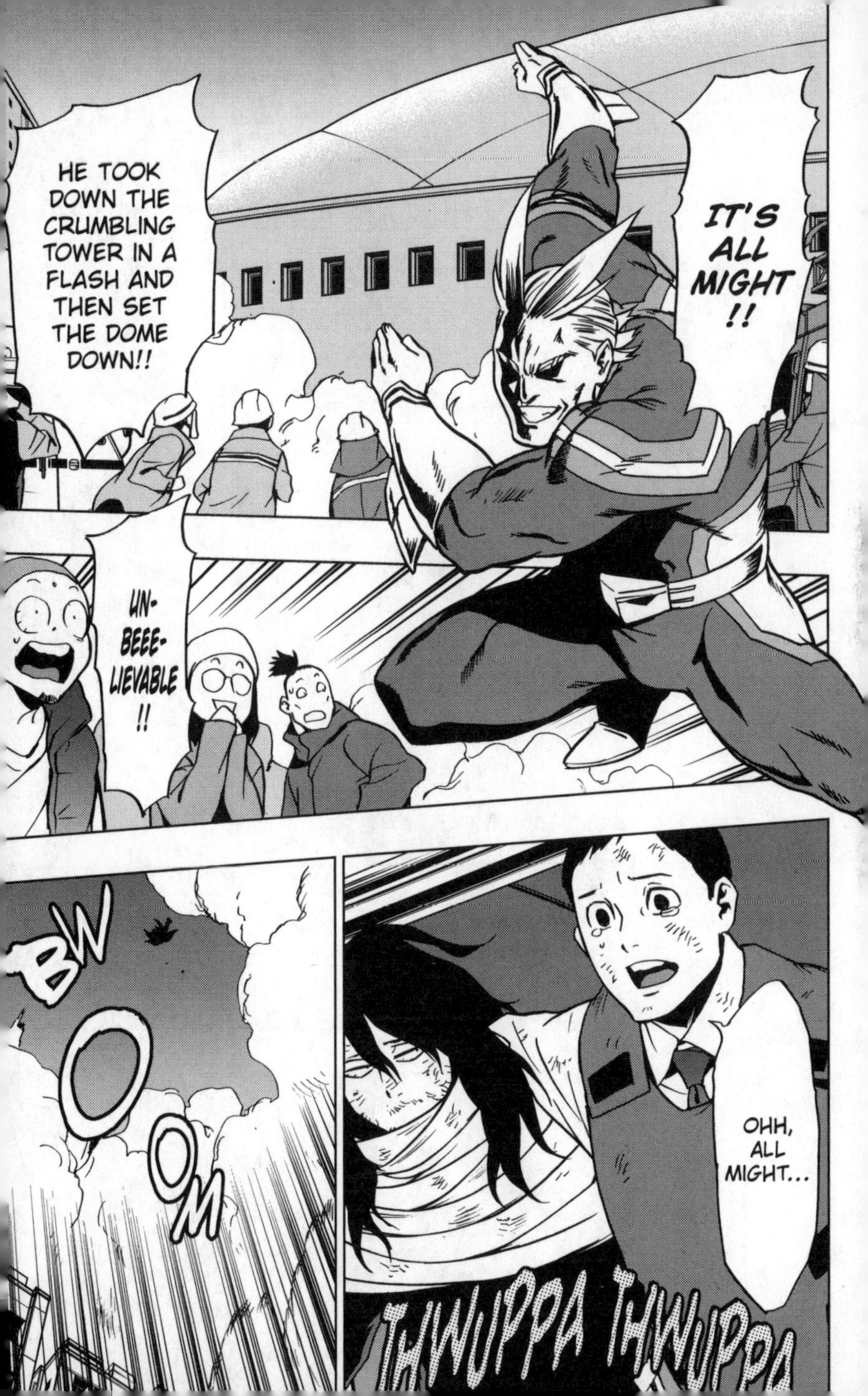
IT'S ALL MIGHT!!
HE TOOK DOWN THE CRUMBLING TOWER IN A FLASH AND THEN SET THE DOME DOWN!!
UN-BEEEE-LIEVABLE!!
OHH, ALL MIGHT...
THWUPPA THWUPPA
BWOOM

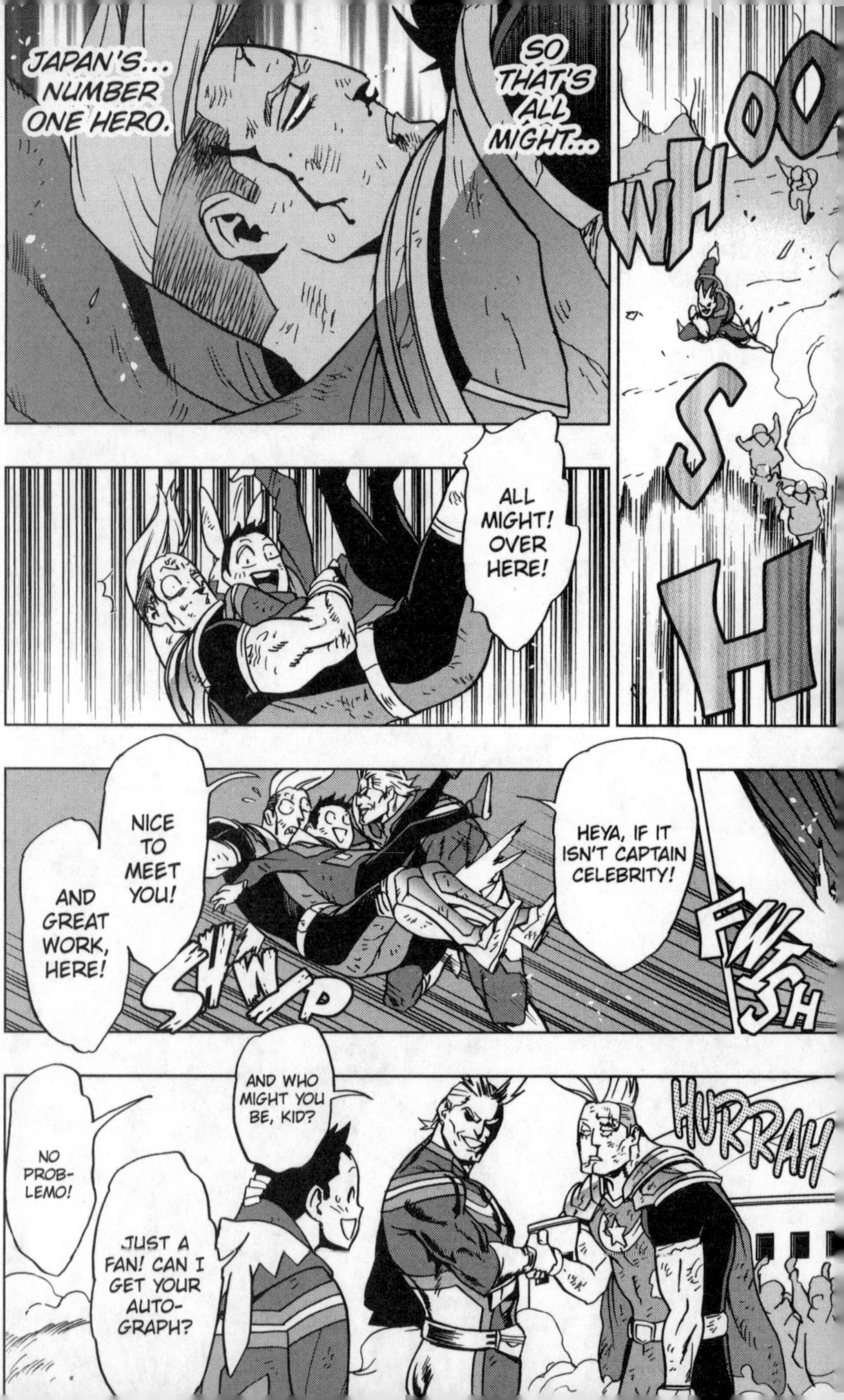
WHOOOSH
SO THAT'S ALL MIGHT...
JAPAN'S... NUMBER ONE HERO.
ALL MIGHT! OVER HERE!
FWISH
HEYA, IF IT ISN'T CAPTAIN CELEBRITY!
NICE TO MEET YOU!
AND GREAT WORK, HERE!
SHWIP
HURRAH
AND WHO MIGHT YOU BE, KID?
JUST A FAN! CAN I GET YOUR AUTO-GRAPH?
NO PROB-LEMO!

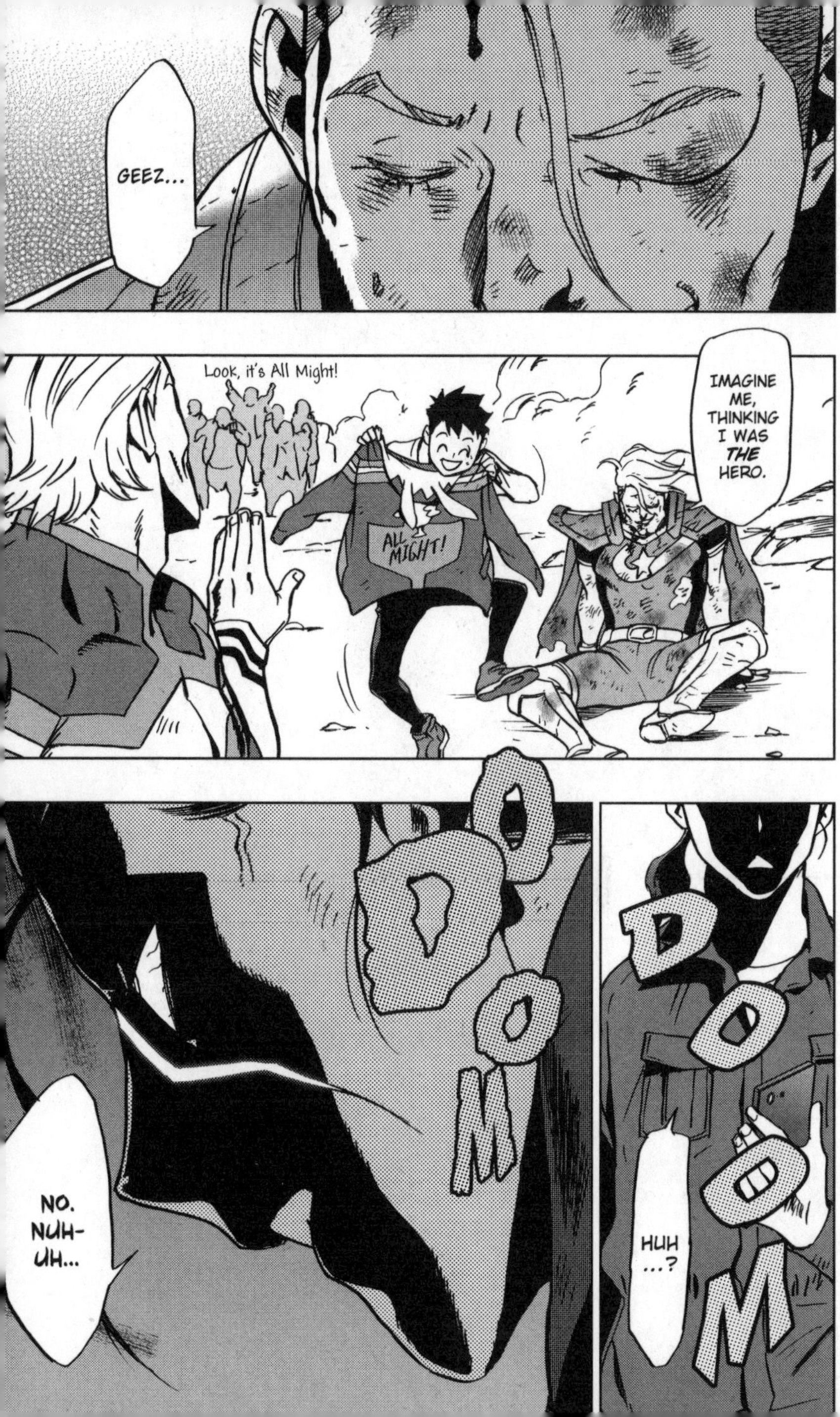
GEEZ...
IMAGINE ME, THINKING I WAS *THE* HERO.
Look, it's All Might!
ALL MIGHT!
DOOM
HUH ...?
DOOM
NO. NUH-UH...

TSUKAUCHI SIBLINGS

THE ROUGH DESIGN

(Young) Tsukauchi Siblings

Nao

A serious-looking lad

Mako

BEHIND THE SCENES

The ultimate hero is moved to action by a personal cause!

That was a theme I'd wanted to tackle for a while, and we'd been portraying scenes with the Tsukauchi siblings since way back. By the way, Makoto's self-confidence was born from her unshakable faith in her brother's love for her. She pretty much takes it for granted at this point, which is why she treats him so flippantly.

—Furuhashi

I made a strong push for portraying Naomasa in a school uniform instead of a blazer, since that was something I personally wanted to see. (LOL) I really thought that flashback was great, and I wish I could've drawn more of it.

—Betten

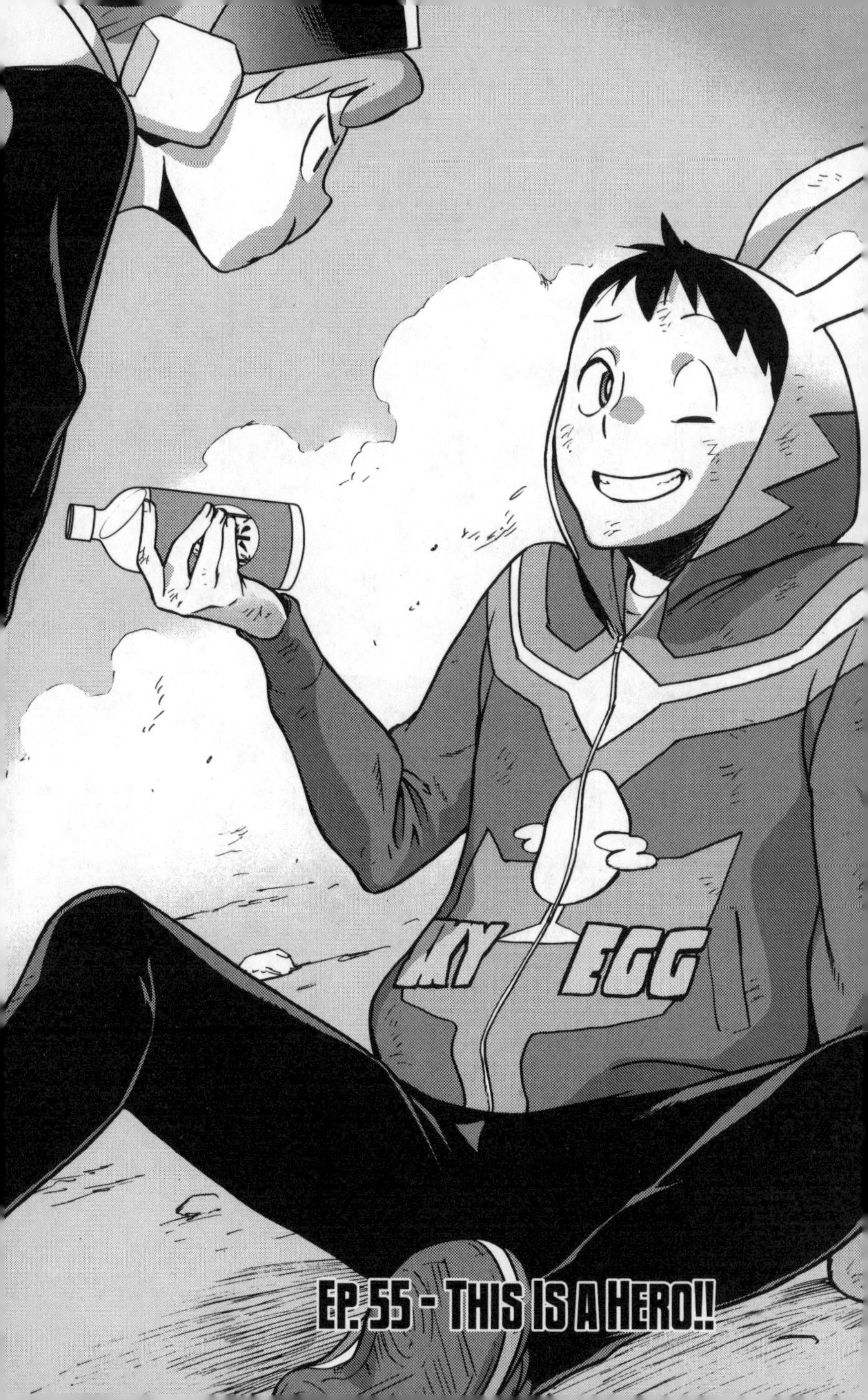
MY EGG
EP. 55 - THIS IS A HERO!!

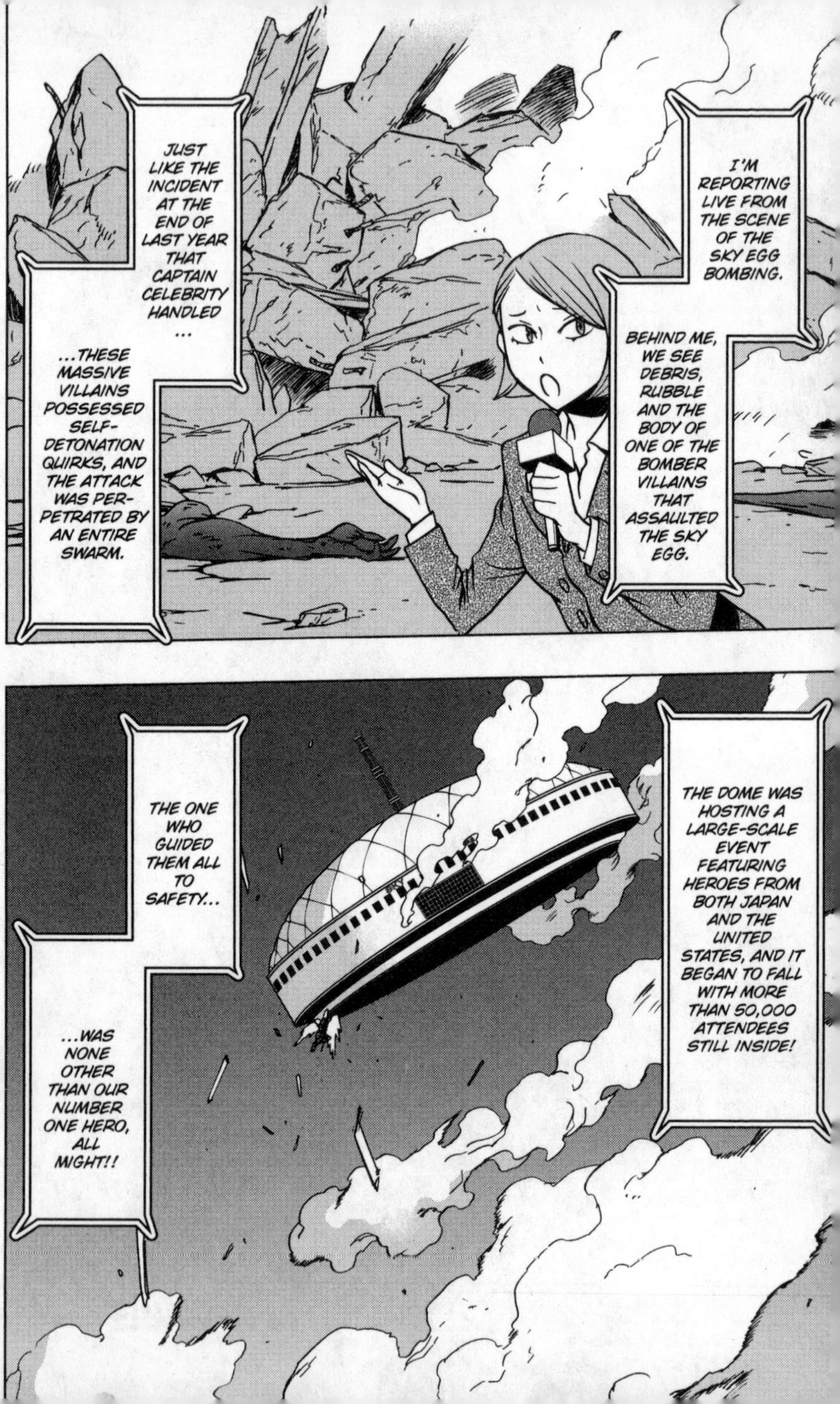
I'M REPORTING LIVE FROM THE SCENE OF THE SKY EGG BOMBING.
BEHIND ME, WE SEE DEBRIS, RUBBLE AND THE BODY OF ONE OF THE BOMBER VILLAINS THAT ASSAULTED THE SKY EGG.
JUST LIKE THE INCIDENT AT THE END OF LAST YEAR THAT CAPTAIN CELEBRITY HANDLED ...
...THESE MASSIVE VILLAINS POSSESSED SELF-DETONATION QUIRKS, AND THE ATTACK WAS PER-PETRATED BY AN ENTIRE SWARM.
THE DOME WAS HOSTING A LARGE-SCALE EVENT FEATURING HEROES FROM BOTH JAPAN AND THE UNITED STATES, AND IT BEGAN TO FALL WITH MORE THAN 50,000 ATTENDEES STILL INSIDE!
THE ONE WHO GUIDED THEM ALL TO SAFETY...
...WAS NONE OTHER THAN OUR NUMBER ONE HERO, ALL MIGHT!!

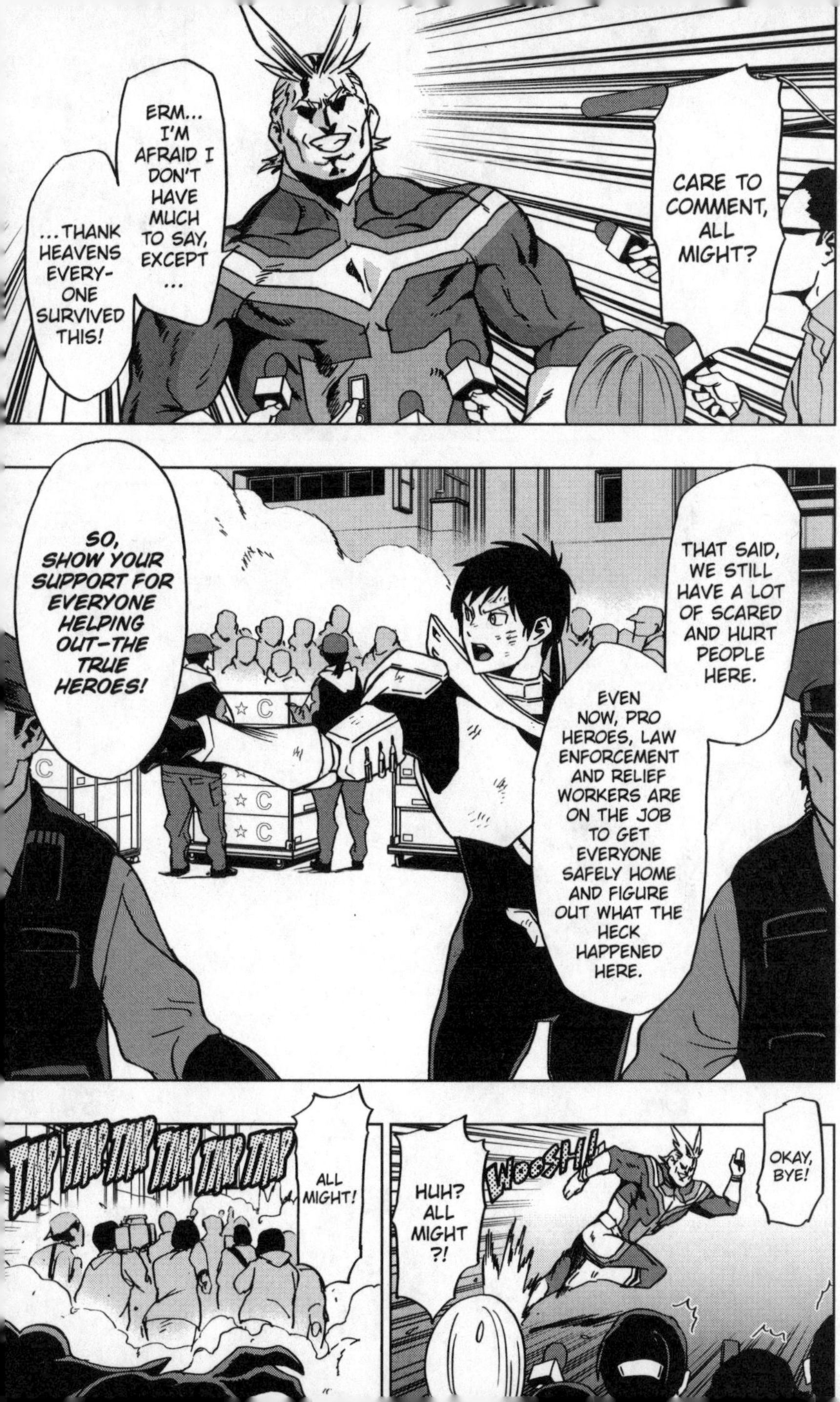
CARE TO COMMENT, ALL MIGHT?
ERM... I'M AFRAID I DON'T HAVE MUCH TO SAY, EXCEPT ...
...THANK HEAVENS EVERYONE SURVIVED THIS!
THAT SAID, WE STILL HAVE A LOT OF SCARED AND HURT PEOPLE HERE.
EVEN NOW, PRO HEROES, LAW ENFORCEMENT AND RELIEF WORKERS ARE ON THE JOB TO GET EVERYONE SAFELY HOME AND FIGURE OUT WHAT THE HECK HAPPENED HERE.
SO, SHOW YOUR SUPPORT FOR EVERYONE HELPING OUT—THE TRUE HEROES!
OKAY, BYE!
WOOSH!!
HUH? ALL MIGHT ?!
ALL MIGHT!
TMP TMP TMP TMP TMP TMP

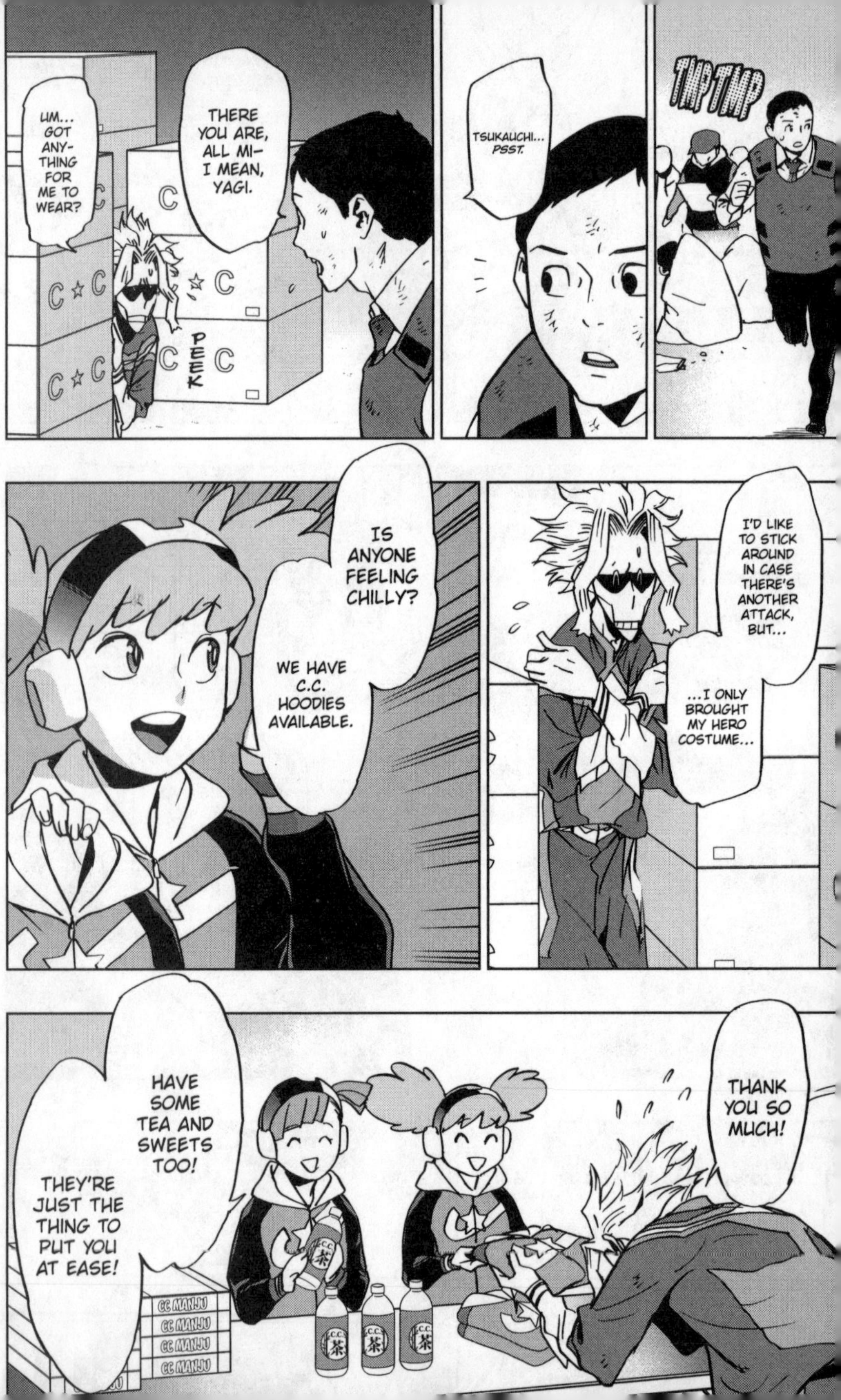
TMP TMP
TSUKAUCHI... PSST.
THERE YOU ARE, ALL MI— I MEAN, YAGI.
UM... GOT ANYTHING FOR ME TO WEAR?
PEEK
I'D LIKE TO STICK AROUND IN CASE THERE'S ANOTHER ATTACK, BUT...
...I ONLY BROUGHT MY HERO COSTUME...
IS ANYONE FEELING CHILLY?
WE HAVE C.C. HOODIES AVAILABLE.
THANK YOU SO MUCH!
HAVE SOME TEA AND SWEETS TOO!
THEY'RE JUST THE THING TO PUT YOU AT EASE!
CC MANJU
CC MANJU
CC MANJU
CC MANJU

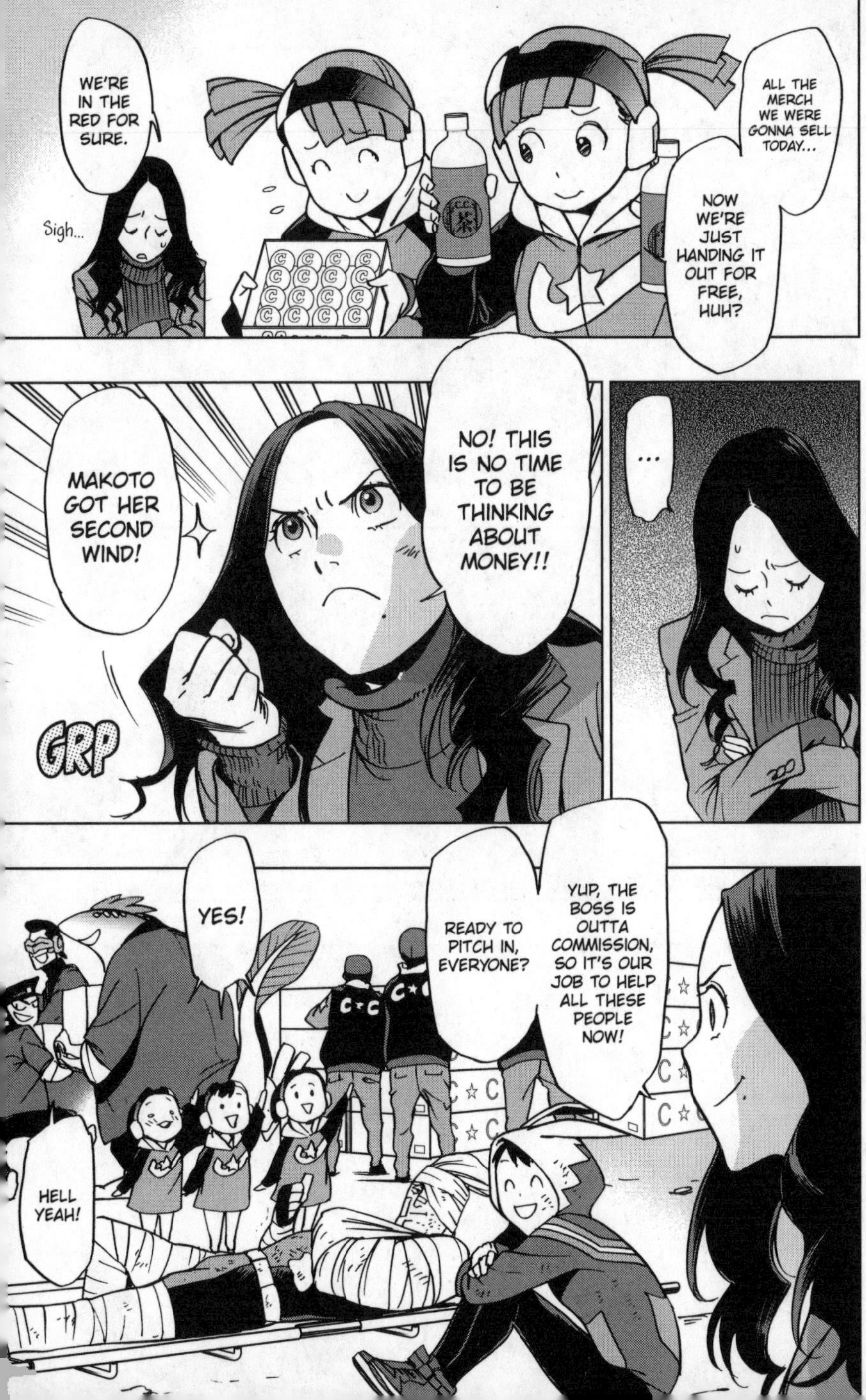
ALL THE MERCH WE WERE GONNA SELL TODAY...
NOW WE'RE JUST HANDING IT OUT FOR FREE, HUH?
WE'RE IN THE RED FOR SURE.
Sigh...
...
NO! THIS IS NO TIME TO BE THINKING ABOUT MONEY!!
MAKOTO GOT HER SECOND WIND!
GRP
YUP, THE BOSS IS OUTTA COMMISSION, SO IT'S OUR JOB TO HELP ALL THESE PEOPLE NOW!
READY TO PITCH IN, EVERYONE?
YES!
HELL YEAH!

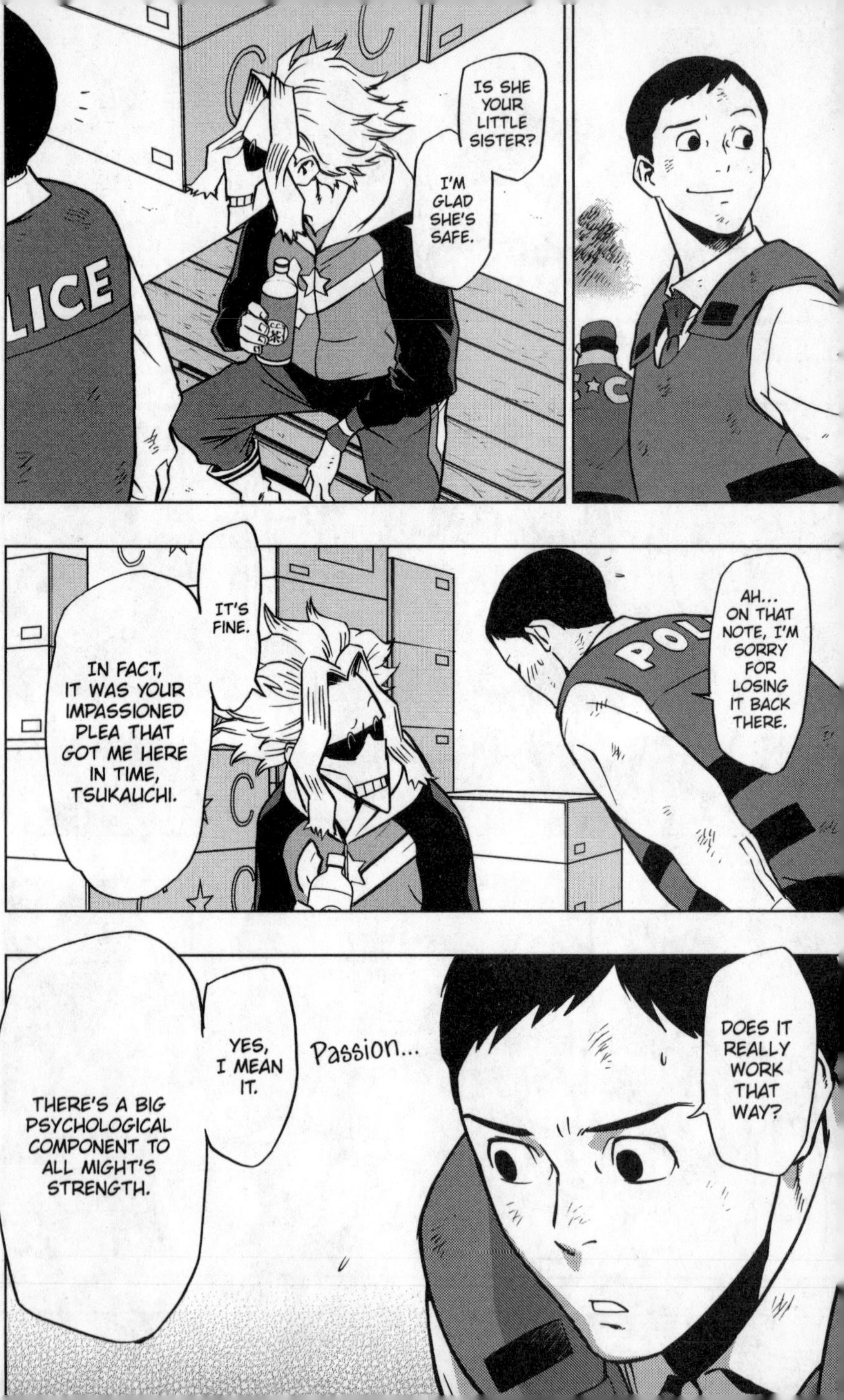
IS SHE YOUR LITTLE SISTER?
I'M GLAD SHE'S SAFE.
AH... ON THAT NOTE, I'M SORRY FOR LOSING IT BACK THERE.
IT'S FINE.
IN FACT, IT WAS YOUR IMPASSIONED PLEA THAT GOT ME HERE IN TIME, TSUKAUCHI.
DOES IT REALLY WORK THAT WAY?
Passion...
YES, I MEAN IT.
THERE'S A BIG PSYCHOLOGICAL COMPONENT TO ALL MIGHT'S STRENGTH.

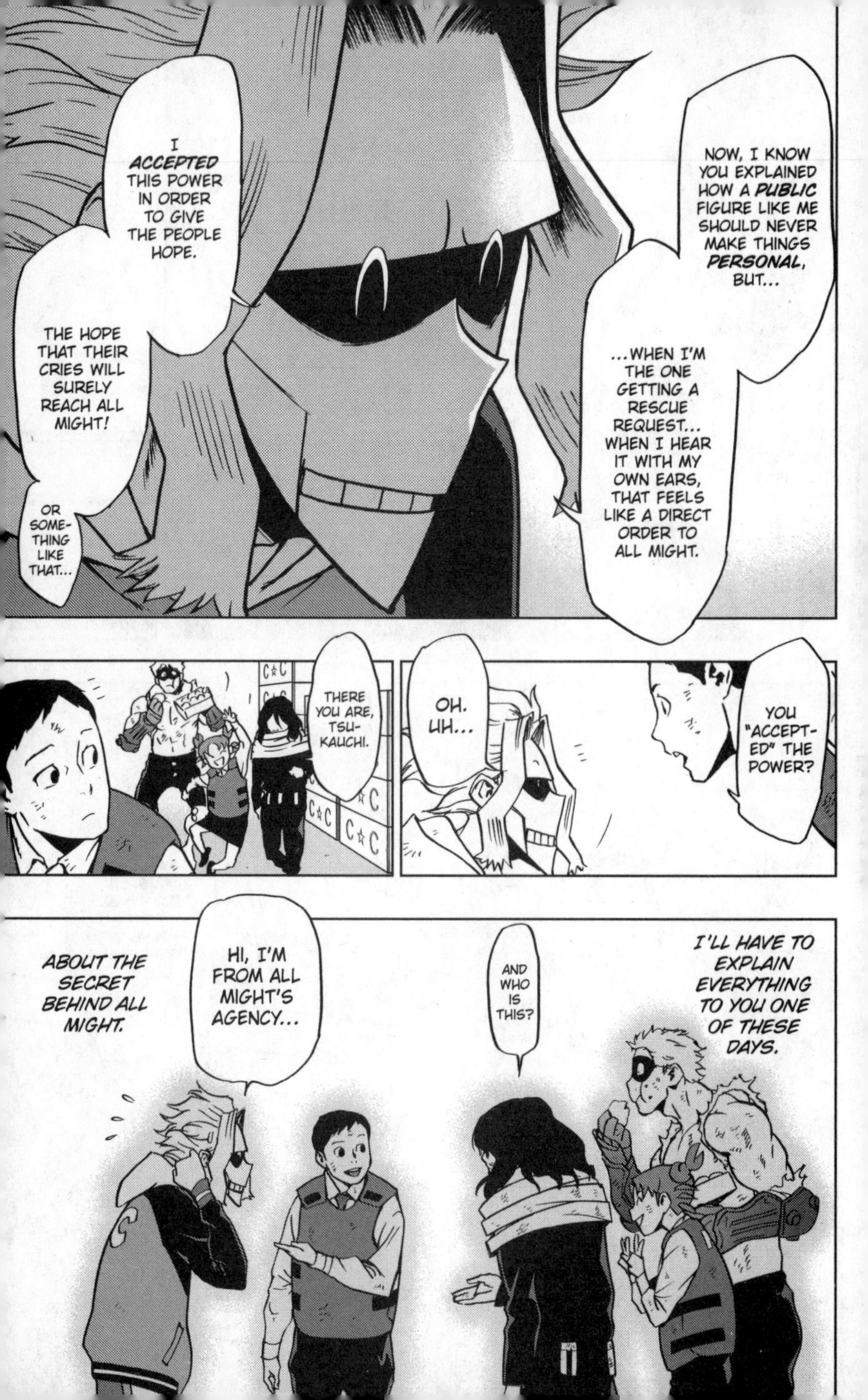
NOW, I KNOW YOU EXPLAINED HOW A PUBLIC FIGURE LIKE ME SHOULD NEVER MAKE THINGS PERSONAL, BUT...
...WHEN I'M THE ONE GETTING A RESCUE REQUEST... WHEN I HEAR IT WITH MY OWN EARS, THAT FEELS LIKE A DIRECT ORDER TO ALL MIGHT.
I ACCEPTED THIS POWER IN ORDER TO GIVE THE PEOPLE HOPE.
THE HOPE THAT THEIR CRIES WILL SURELY REACH ALL MIGHT!
OR SOMETHING LIKE THAT...
YOU "ACCEPTED" THE POWER?
OH. UH...
THERE YOU ARE, TSUKAUCHI.
I'LL HAVE TO EXPLAIN EVERYTHING TO YOU ONE OF THESE DAYS.
AND WHO IS THIS?
HI, I'M FROM ALL MIGHT'S AGENCY...
ABOUT THE SECRET BEHIND ALL MIGHT.

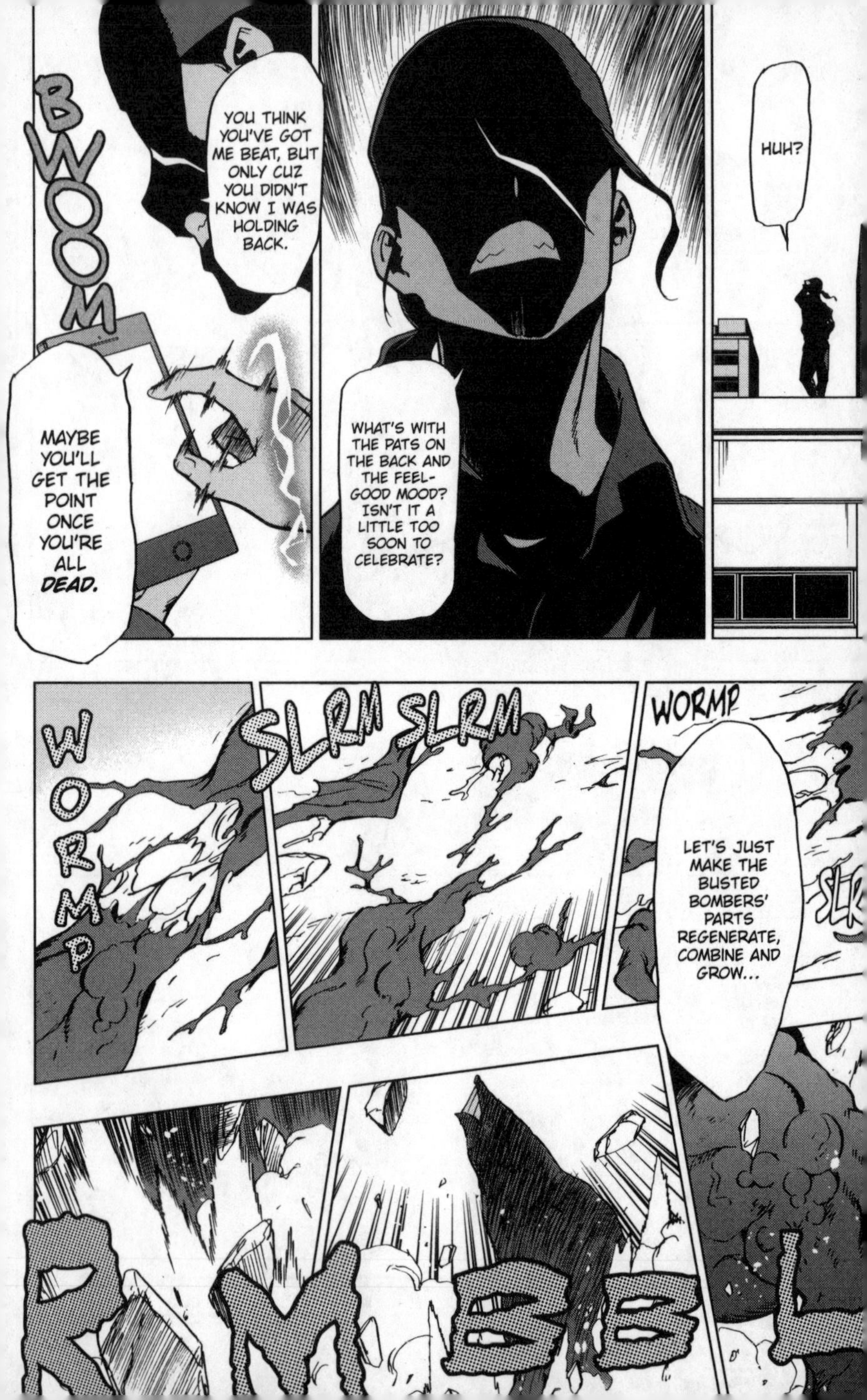
HUH?
WHAT'S WITH THE PATS ON THE BACK AND THE FEEL-GOOD MOOD? ISN'T IT A LITTLE TOO SOON TO CELEBRATE?
YOU THINK YOU'VE GOT ME BEAT, BUT ONLY CUZ YOU DIDN'T KNOW I WAS HOLDING BACK.
BWOOM
MAYBE YOU'LL GET THE POINT ONCE YOU'RE ALL *DEAD.*
WORMP
LET'S JUST MAKE THE BUSTED BOMBERS' PARTS REGENERATE, COMBINE AND GROW...
SLRM SLRM
WORMP

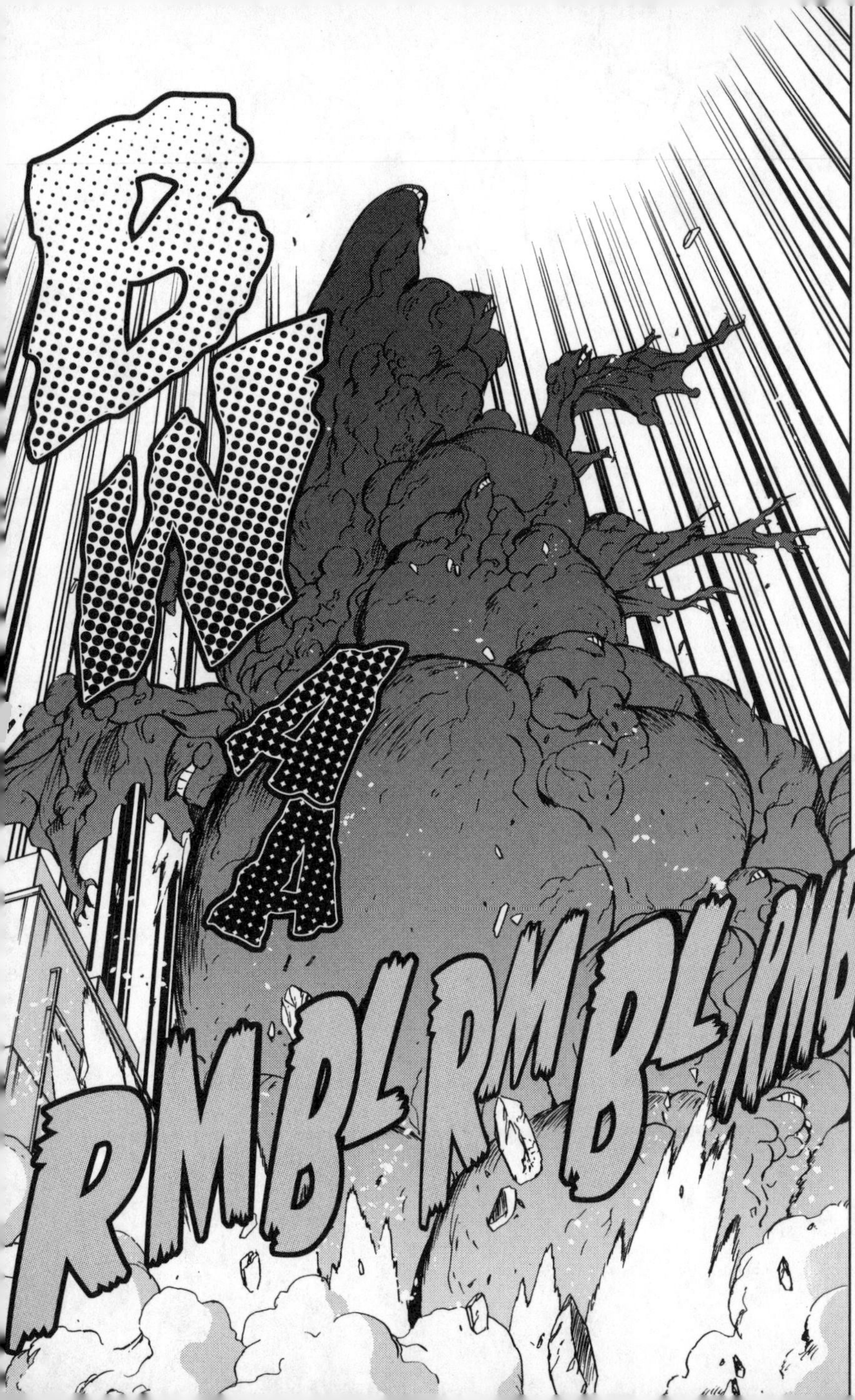
BWA
RMBL RMBL

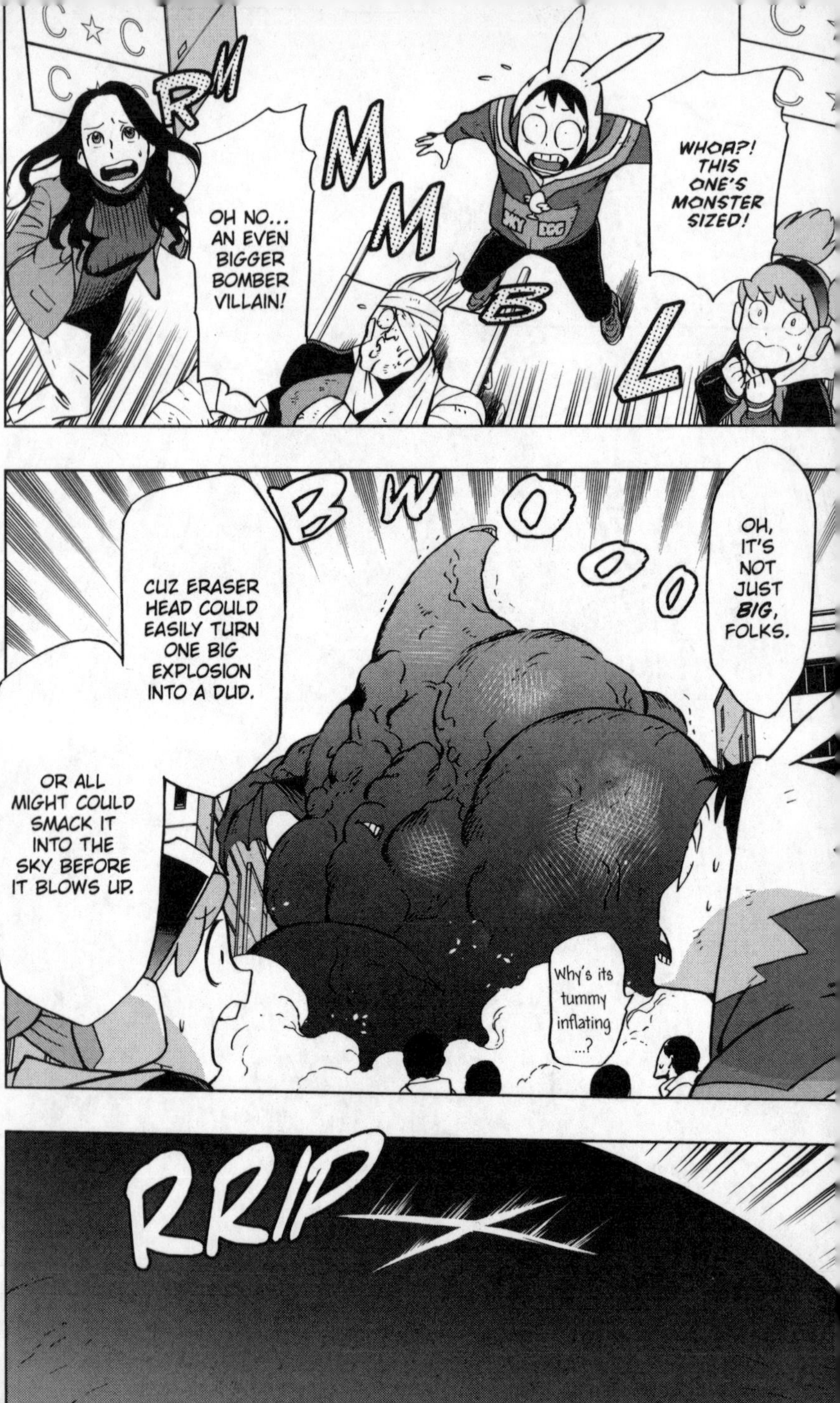
WHOA?! THIS ONE'S MONSTER SIZED!
CRMMBL
OH NO... AN EVEN BIGGER BOMBER VILLAIN!
OH, IT'S NOT JUST *BIG*, FOLKS.
BWOOOO
Why's its tummy inflating ...?
CUZ ERASER HEAD COULD EASILY TURN ONE BIG EXPLOSION INTO A DUD.
OR ALL MIGHT COULD SMACK IT INTO THE SKY BEFORE IT BLOWS UP.
RRIP

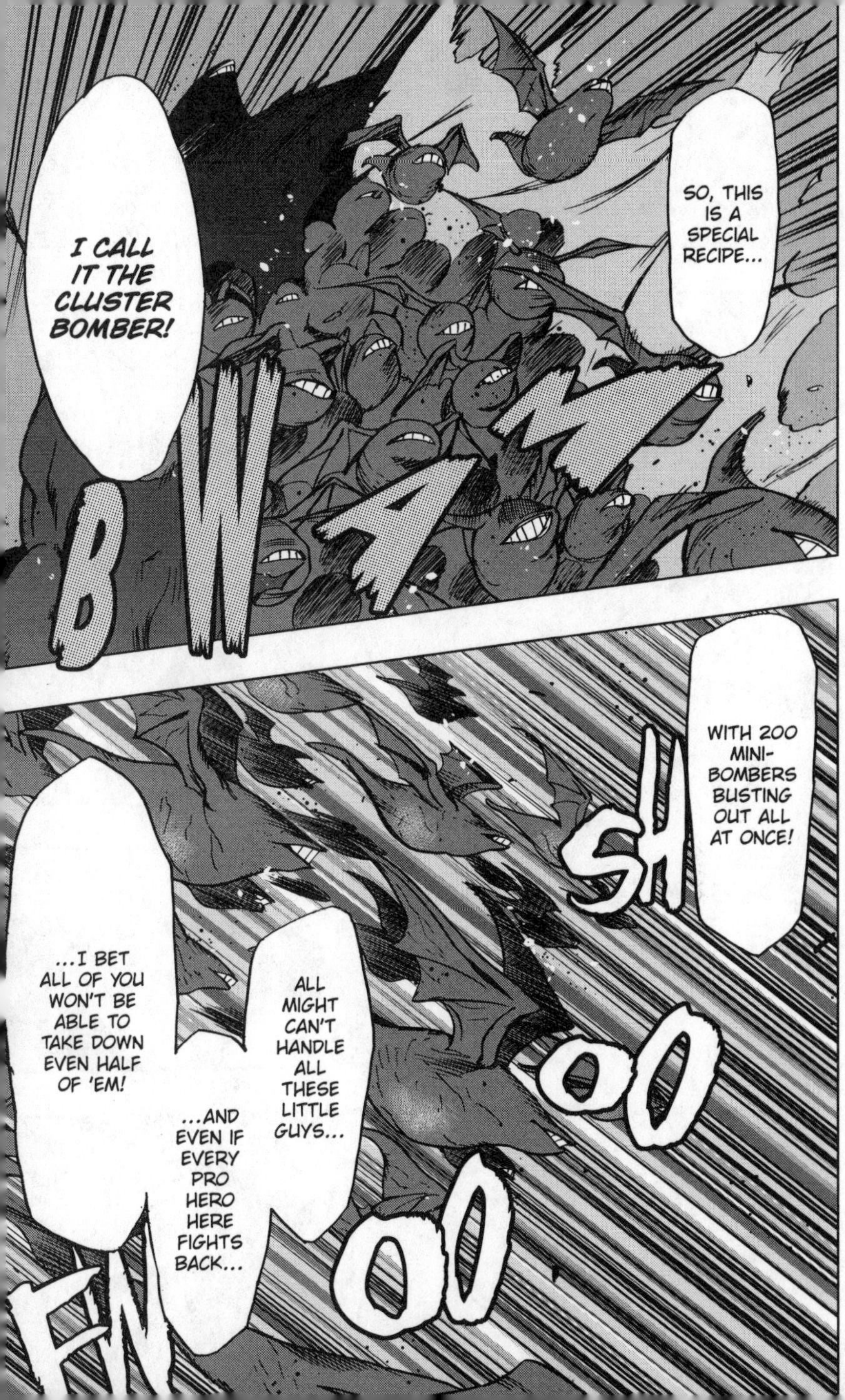
SO, THIS IS A SPECIAL RECIPE...
I CALL IT THE CLUSTER BOMBER!
BWAM
WITH 200 MINI-BOMBERS BUSTING OUT ALL AT ONCE!
SHOO
ALL MIGHT CAN'T HANDLE ALL THESE LITTLE GUYS...
...AND EVEN IF EVERY PRO HERO HERE FIGHTS BACK...
...I BET ALL OF YOU WON'T BE ABLE TO TAKE DOWN EVEN HALF OF 'EM!

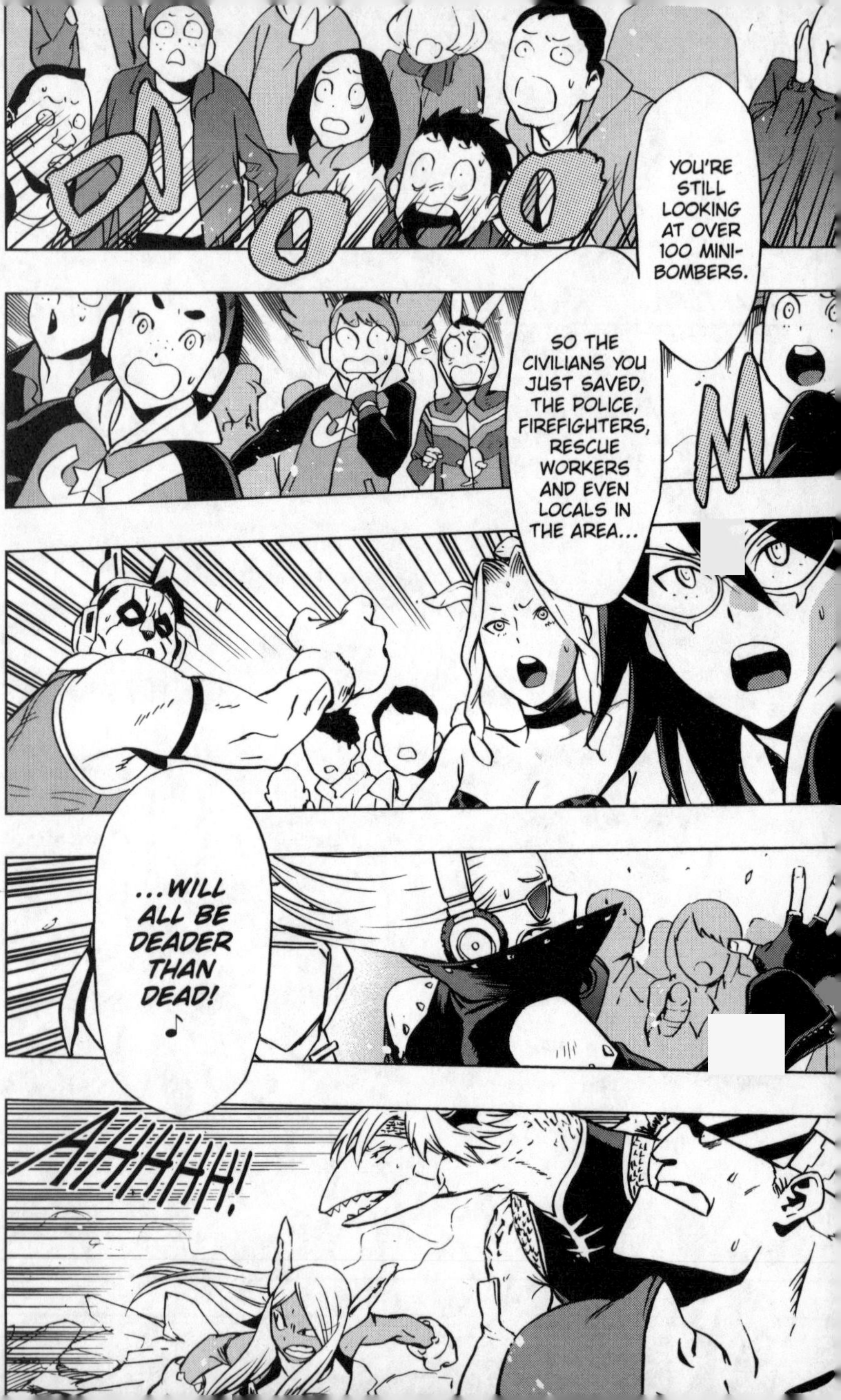
YOU'RE STILL LOOKING AT OVER 100 MINI-BOMBERS.
DOOO
M
SO THE CIVILIANS YOU JUST SAVED, THE POLICE, FIREFIGHTERS, RESCUE WORKERS AND EVEN LOCALS IN THE AREA...
...WILL ALL BE DEADER THAN DEAD! ♪
AHHHH!

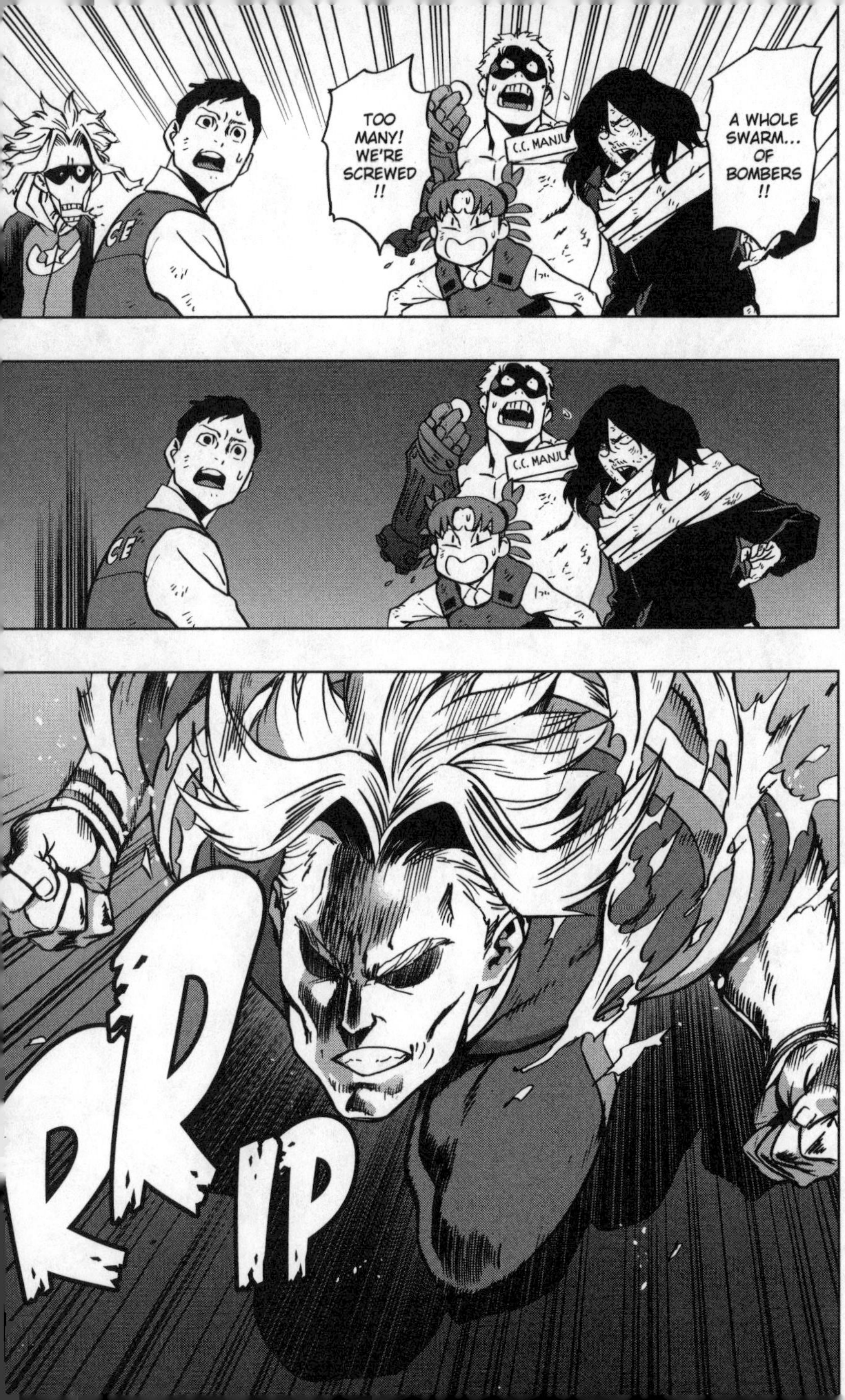
A WHOLE SWARM... OF BOMBERS !!
C.C. MANJU
TOO MANY! WE'RE SCREWED !!
C.C. MANJU
RRIP

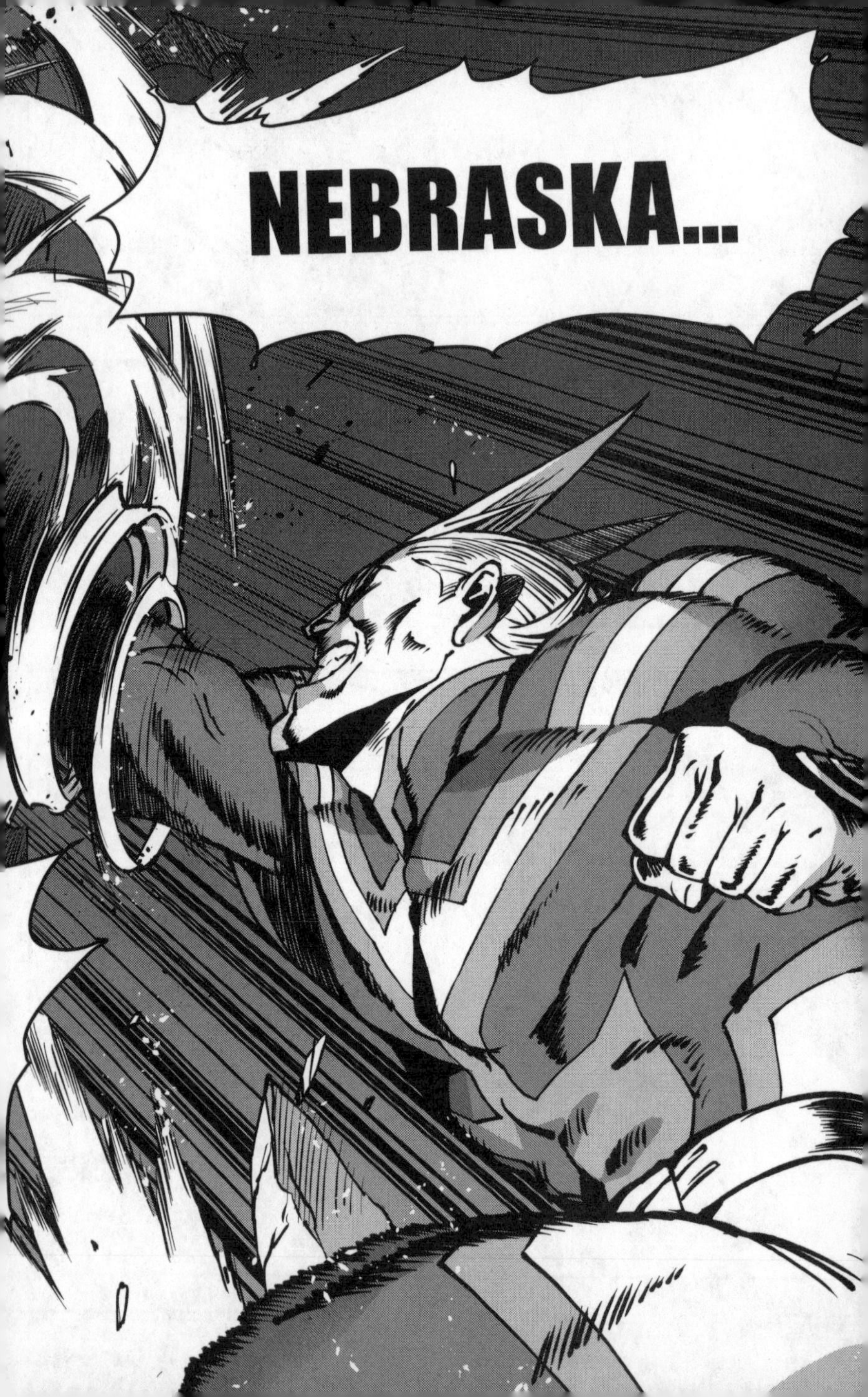
NEBRASKA...

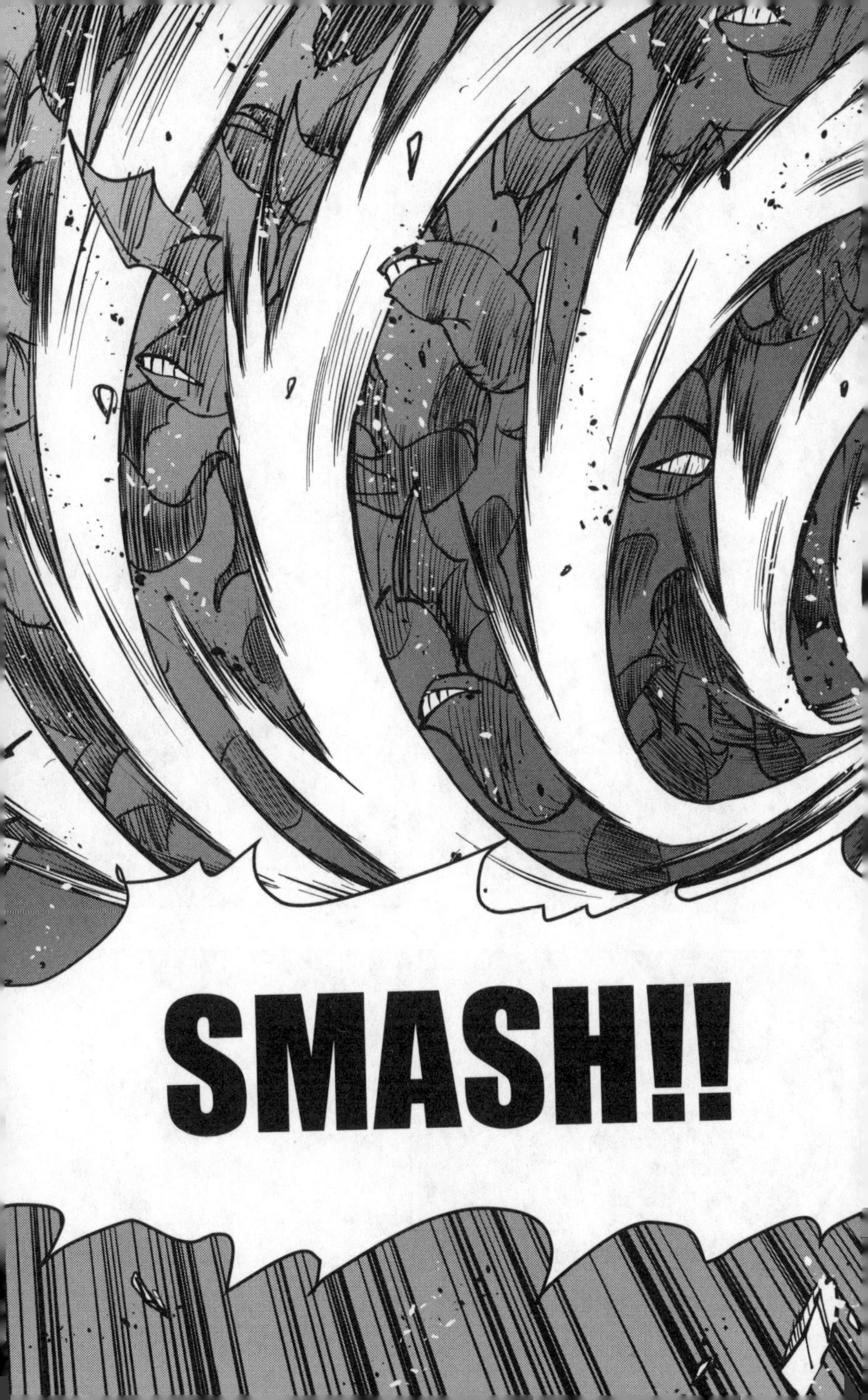
SMASH!!

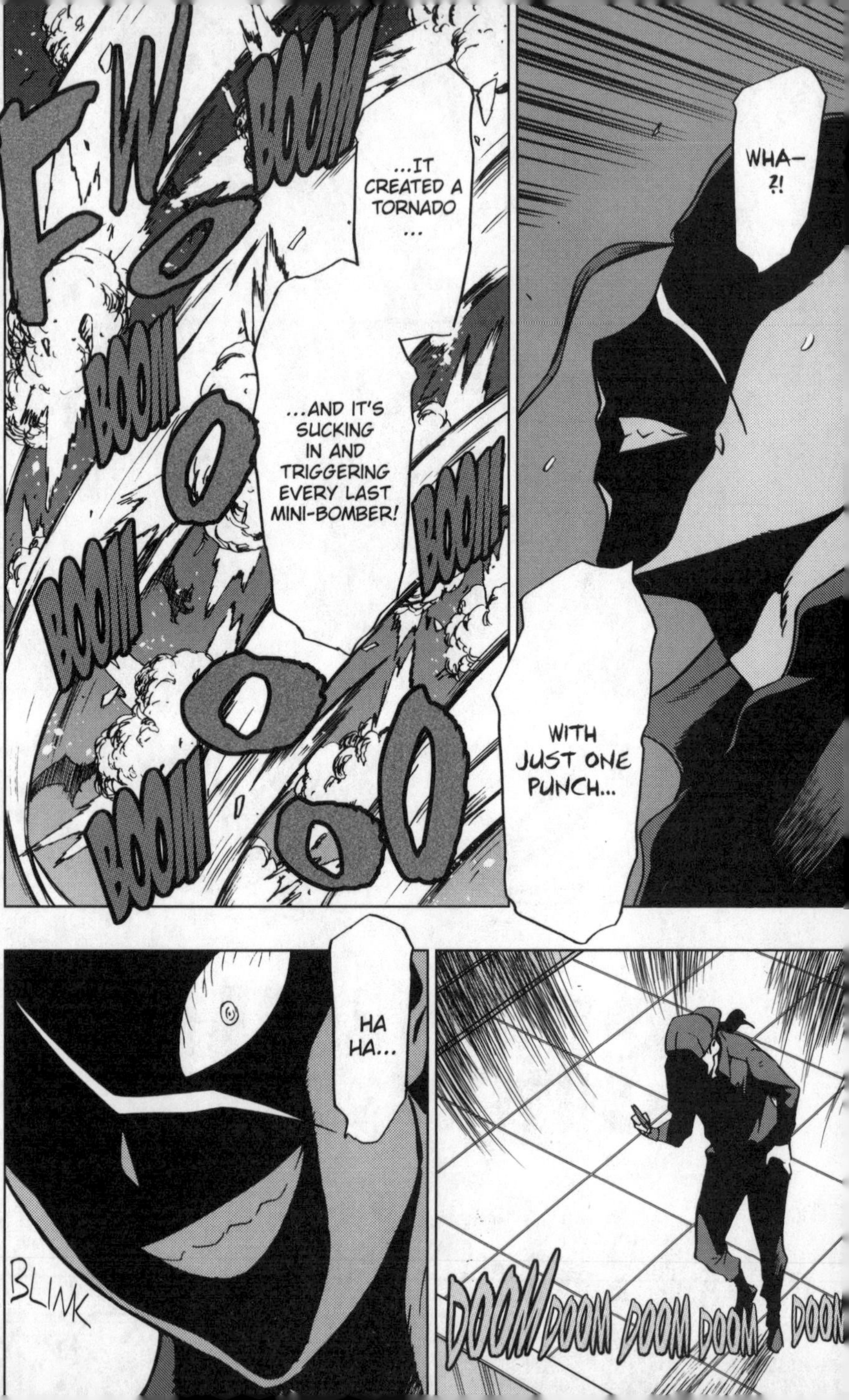
WHA-?!
WITH JUST ONE PUNCH...
FWOOM
BOOM
...IT CREATED A TORNADO...
...AND IT'S SUCKING IN AND TRIGGERING EVERY LAST MINI-BOMBER!
BOOM
BOOM
BOOM
BOOM
DOOM DOOM DOOM DOOM DOOM
HA HA...
BLINK

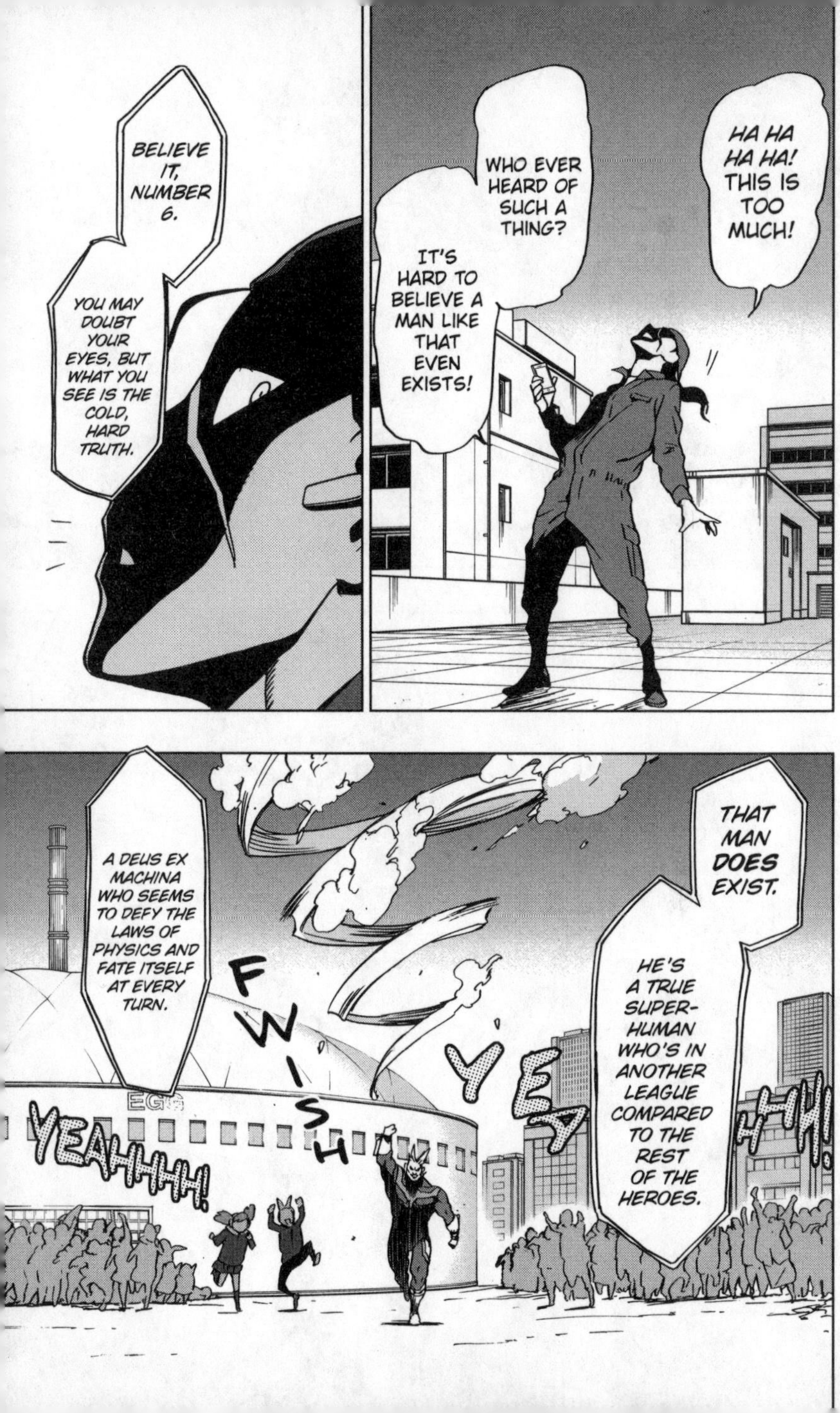

HA HA HA HA! THIS IS TOO MUCH!
WHO EVER HEARD OF SUCH A THING?
IT'S HARD TO BELIEVE A MAN LIKE THAT EVEN EXISTS!
BELIEVE IT, NUMBER 6.
YOU MAY DOUBT YOUR EYES, BUT WHAT YOU SEE IS THE COLD, HARD TRUTH.
THAT MAN DOES EXIST.
HE'S A TRUE SUPER-HUMAN WHO'S IN ANOTHER LEAGUE COMPARED TO THE REST OF THE HEROES.
YEAHHH!
FWISH
A DEUS EX MACHINA WHO SEEMS TO DEFY THE LAWS OF PHYSICS AND FATE ITSELF AT EVERY TURN.
EGG
YEAHHHHH!

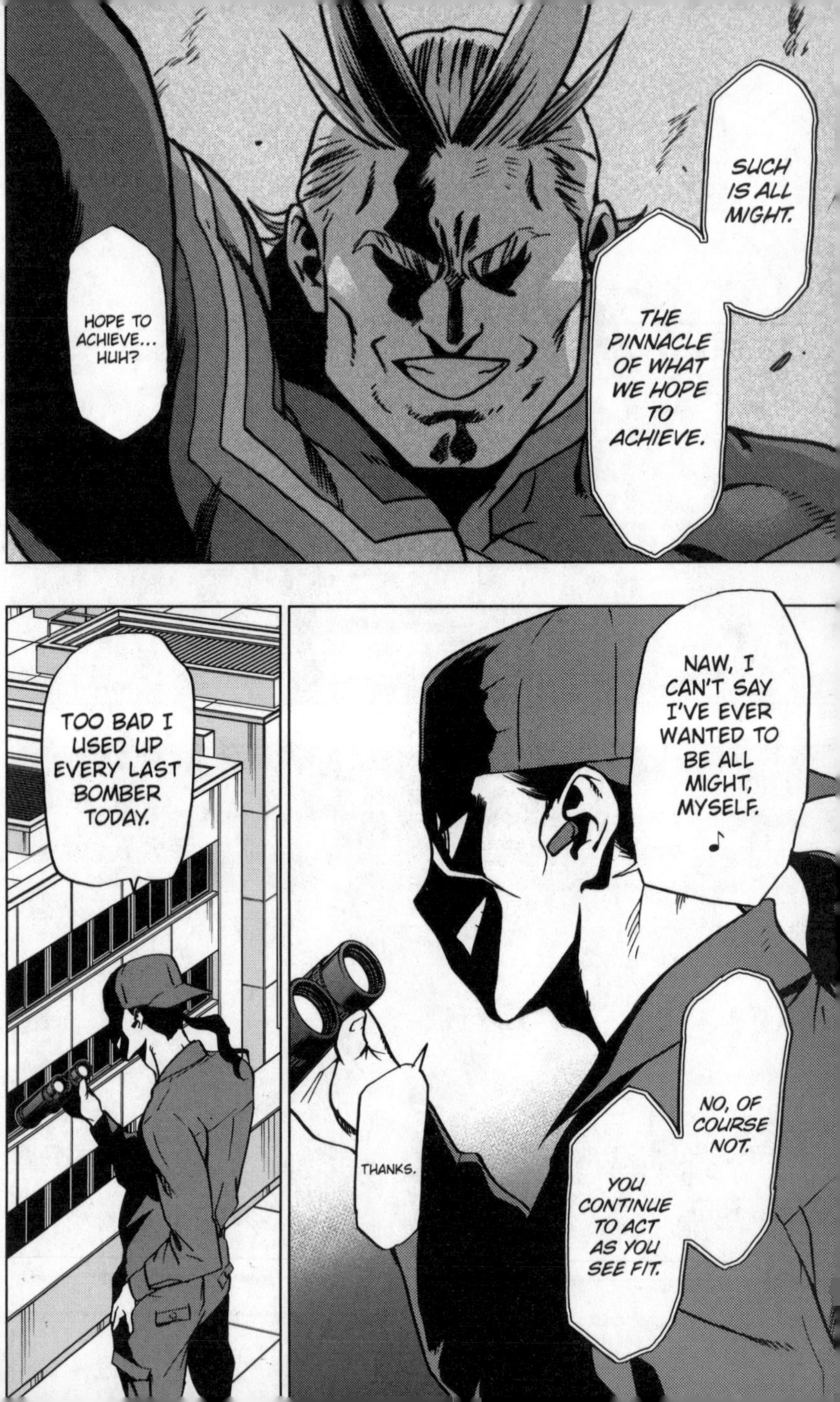
SUCH IS ALL MIGHT.
THE PINNACLE OF WHAT WE HOPE TO ACHIEVE.
HOPE TO ACHIEVE... HUH?
NAW, I CAN'T SAY I'VE EVER WANTED TO BE ALL MIGHT, MYSELF. ♪
NO, OF COURSE NOT.
YOU CONTINUE TO ACT AS YOU SEE FIT.
THANKS.
TOO BAD I USED UP EVERY LAST BOMBER TODAY.

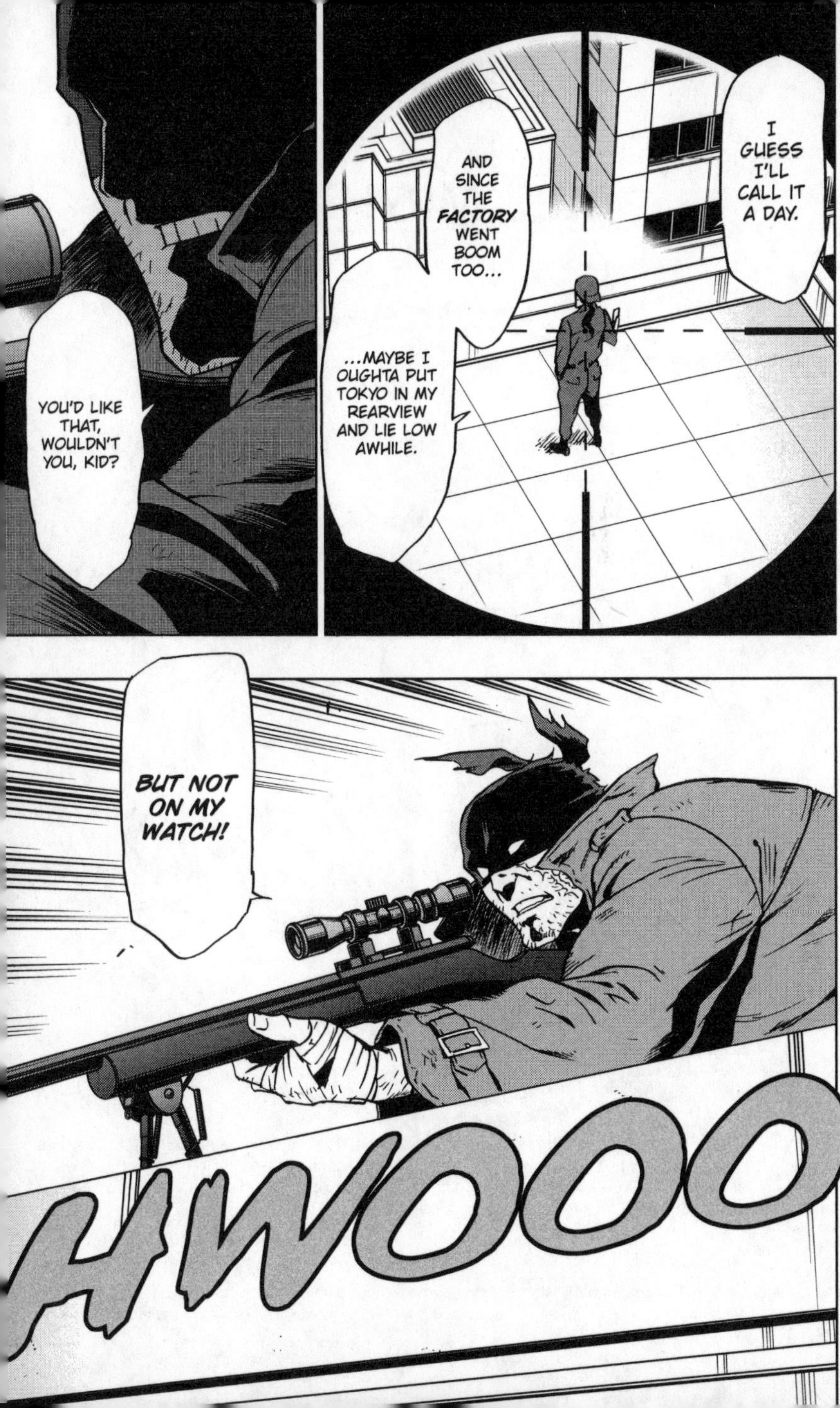
I GUESS I'LL CALL IT A DAY.
AND SINCE THE *FACTORY* WENT BOOM TOO...
...MAYBE I OUGHTA PUT TOKYO IN MY REARVIEW AND LIE LOW AWHILE.
YOU'D LIKE THAT, WOULDN'T YOU, KID?
BUT NOT ON MY WATCH!
HWOOO

THE COLUMN

ALL MIGHT

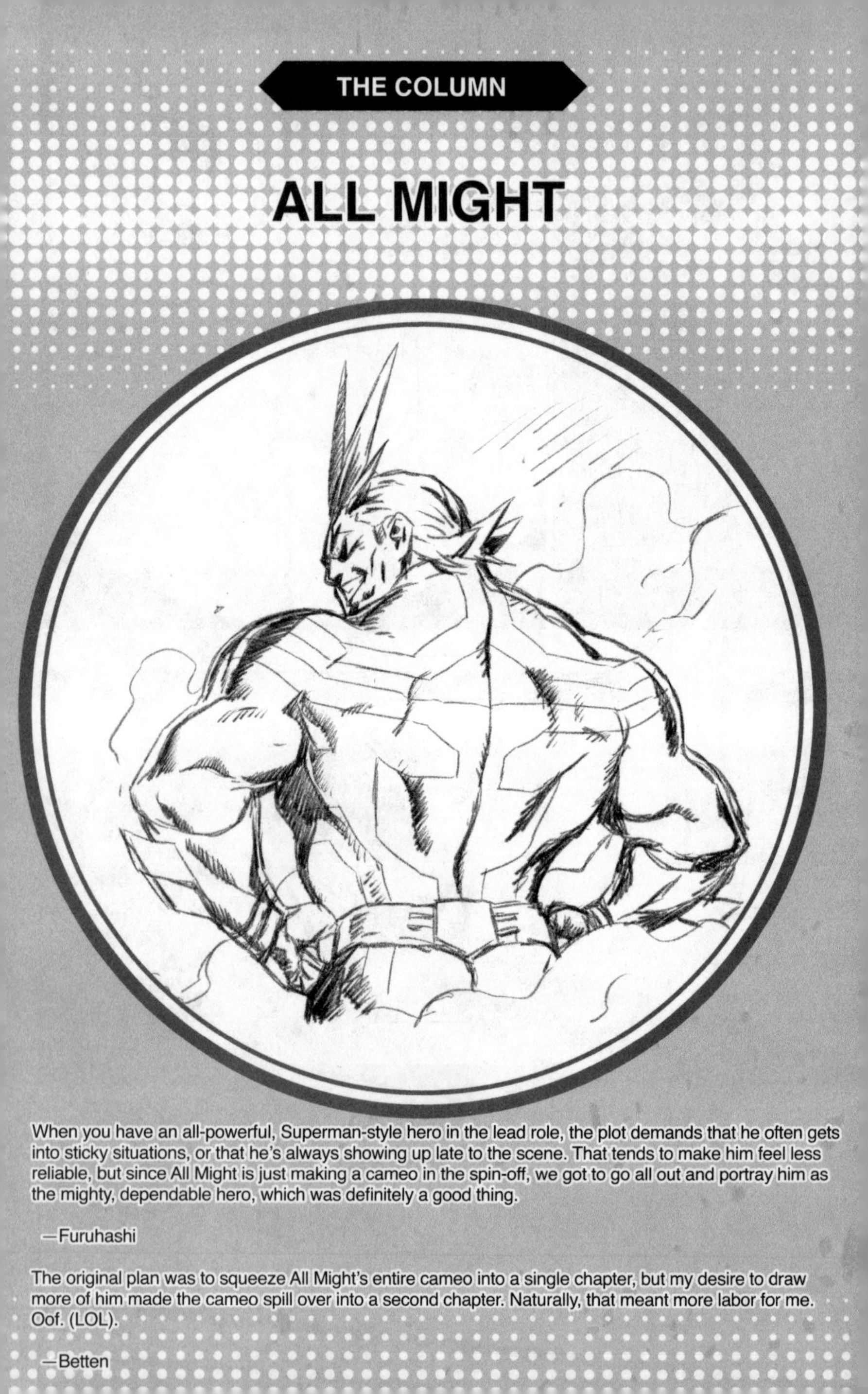

When you have an all-powerful, Superman-style hero in the lead role, the plot demands that he often gets into sticky situations, or that he's always showing up late to the scene. That tends to make him feel less reliable, but since All Might is just making a cameo in the spin-off, we got to go all out and portray him as the mighty, dependable hero, which was definitely a good thing.

—Furuhashi

The original plan was to squeeze All Might's entire cameo into a single chapter, but my desire to draw more of him made the cameo spill over into a second chapter. Naturally, that meant more labor for me. Oof. (LOL).

—Betten

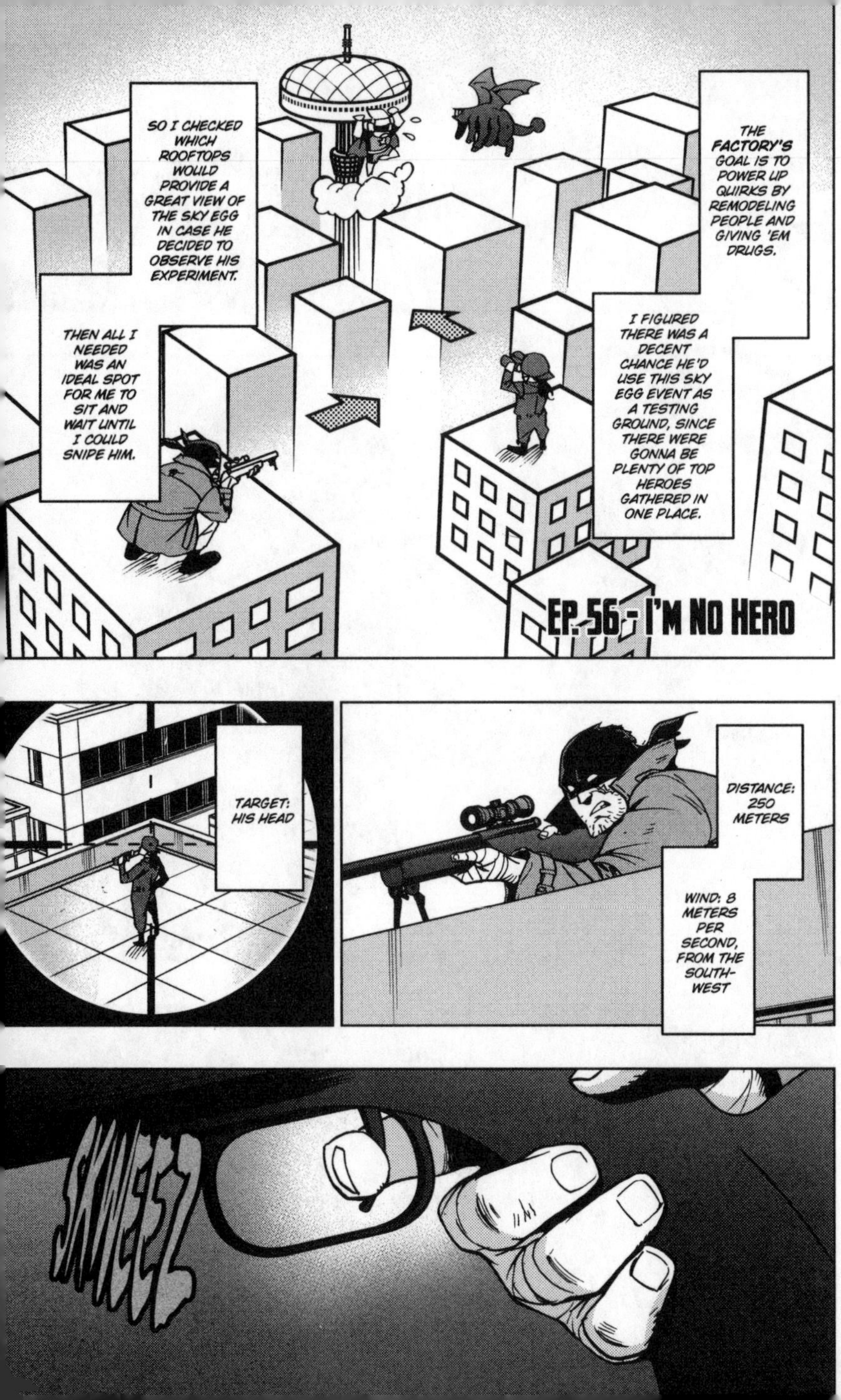
THE FACTORY'S GOAL IS TO POWER UP QUIRKS BY REMODELING PEOPLE AND GIVING 'EM DRUGS.
I FIGURED THERE WAS A DECENT CHANCE HE'D USE THIS SKY EGG EVENT AS A TESTING GROUND, SINCE THERE WERE GONNA BE PLENTY OF TOP HEROES GATHERED IN ONE PLACE.
SO I CHECKED WHICH ROOFTOPS WOULD PROVIDE A GREAT VIEW OF THE SKY EGG IN CASE HE DECIDED TO OBSERVE HIS EXPERIMENT.
THEN ALL I NEEDED WAS AN IDEAL SPOT FOR ME TO SIT AND WAIT UNTIL I COULD SNIPE HIM.
EP. 56 - I'M NO HERO
DISTANCE: 250 METERS
WIND: 8 METERS PER SECOND, FROM THE SOUTH-WEST
TARGET: HIS HEAD
SKWEEZ

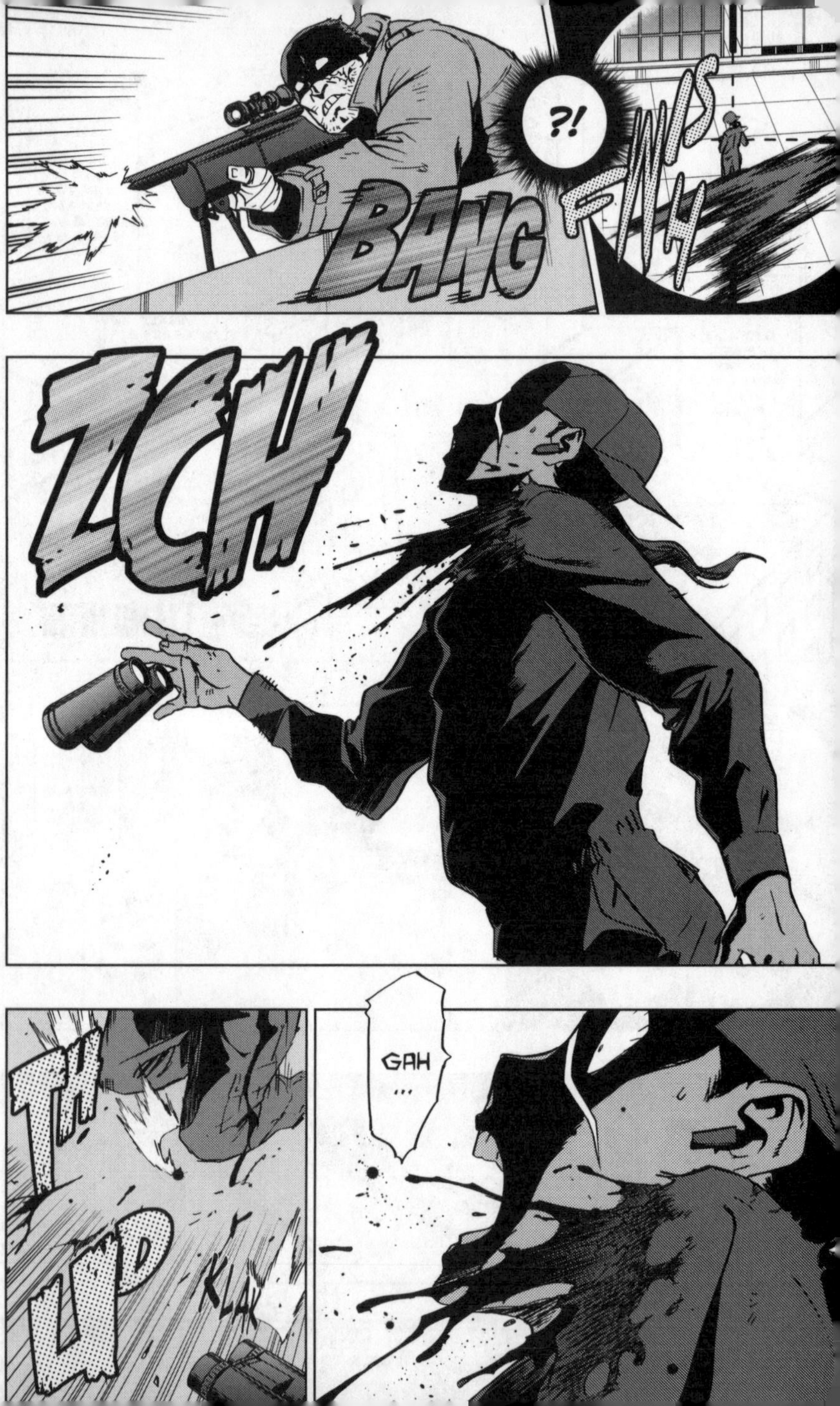
?!
BANG
ZCH
GAH ...
THUD
KLAK

EP. 56 - I'M NO HERO

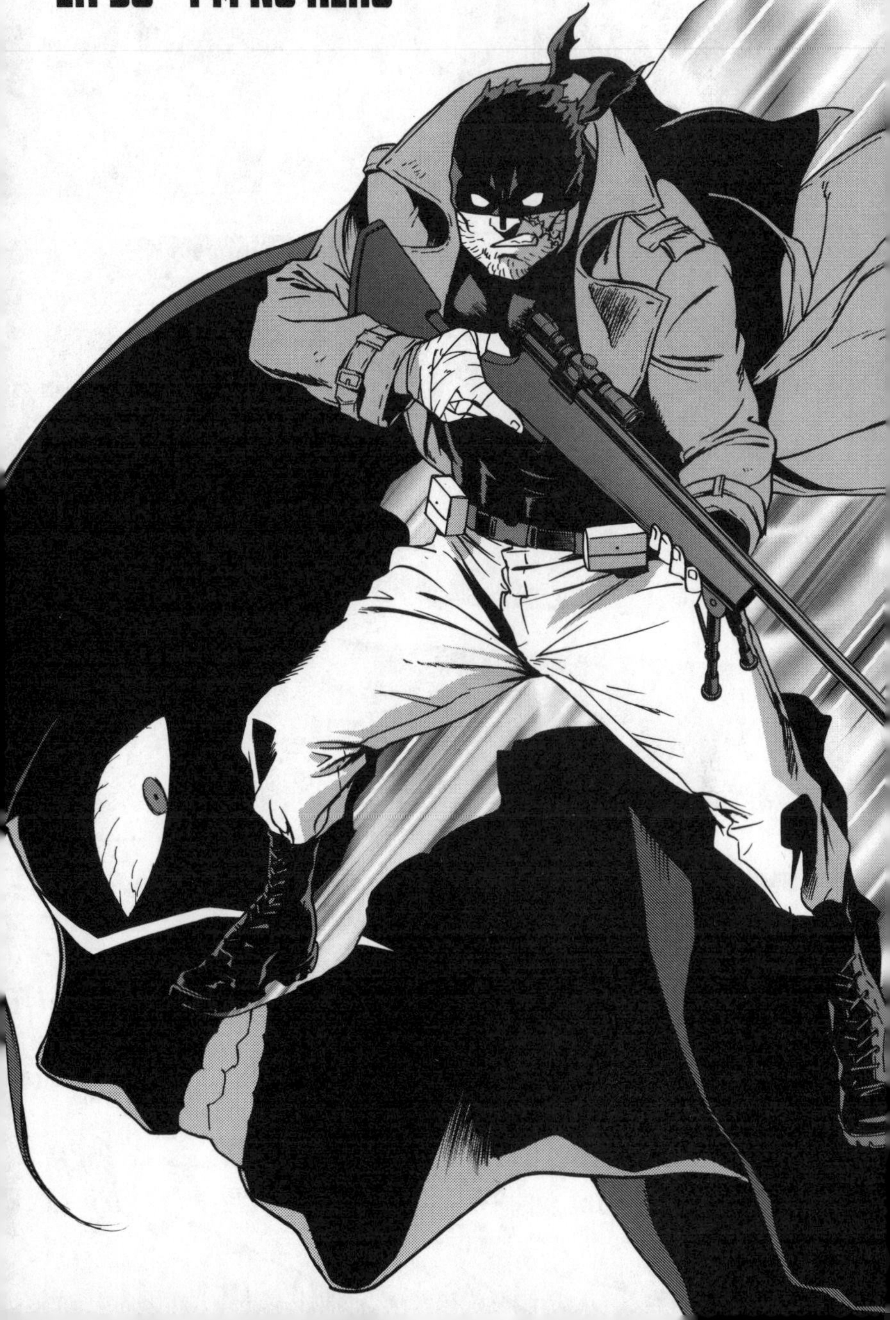

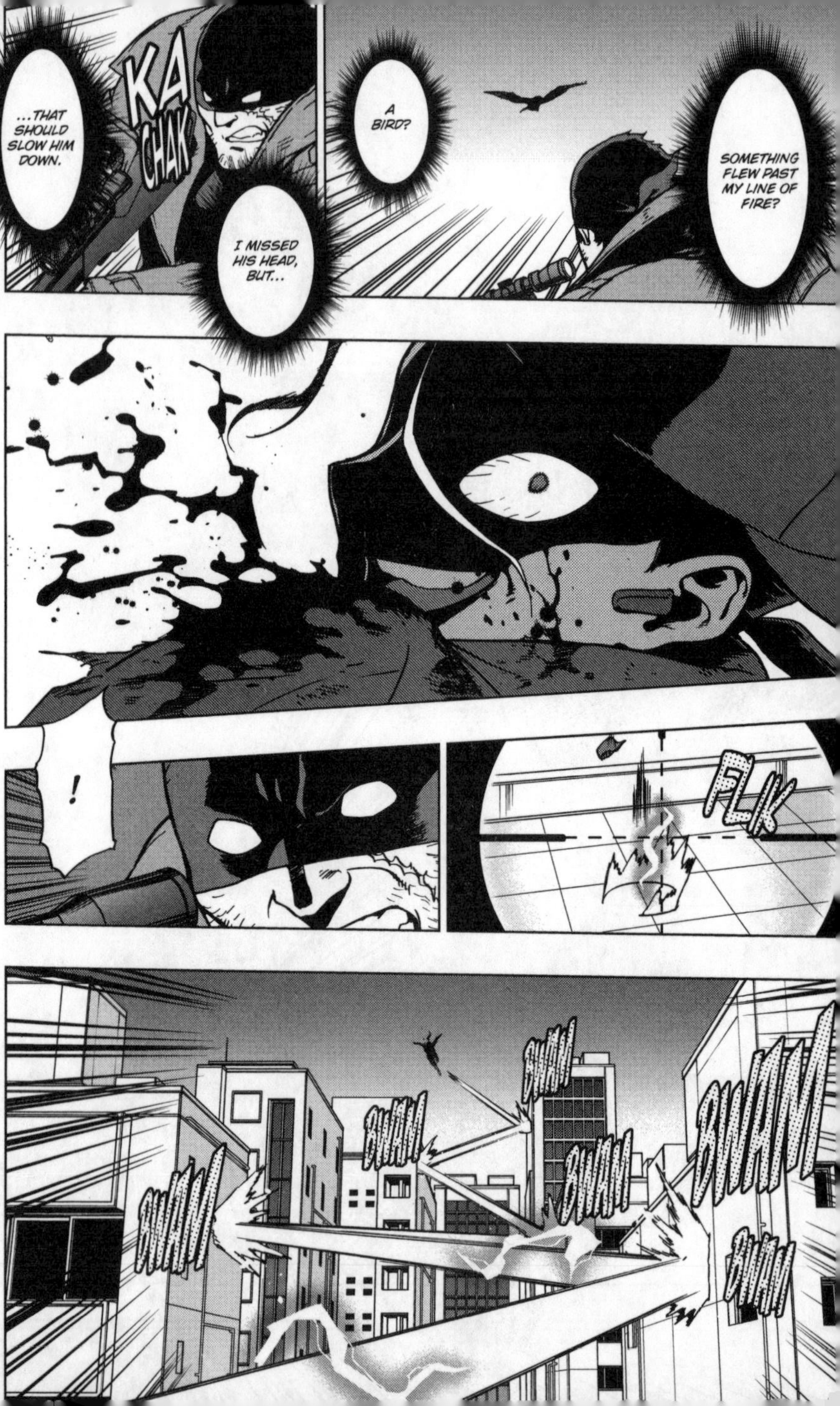

SOMETHING FLEW PAST MY LINE OF FIRE?
A BIRD?
KA CHAK
I MISSED HIS HEAD, BUT...
...THAT SHOULD SLOW HIM DOWN.
FLIK
!
BWAM
BWAM
BWAM
BWAM
BWAM
BWAM
BWAM

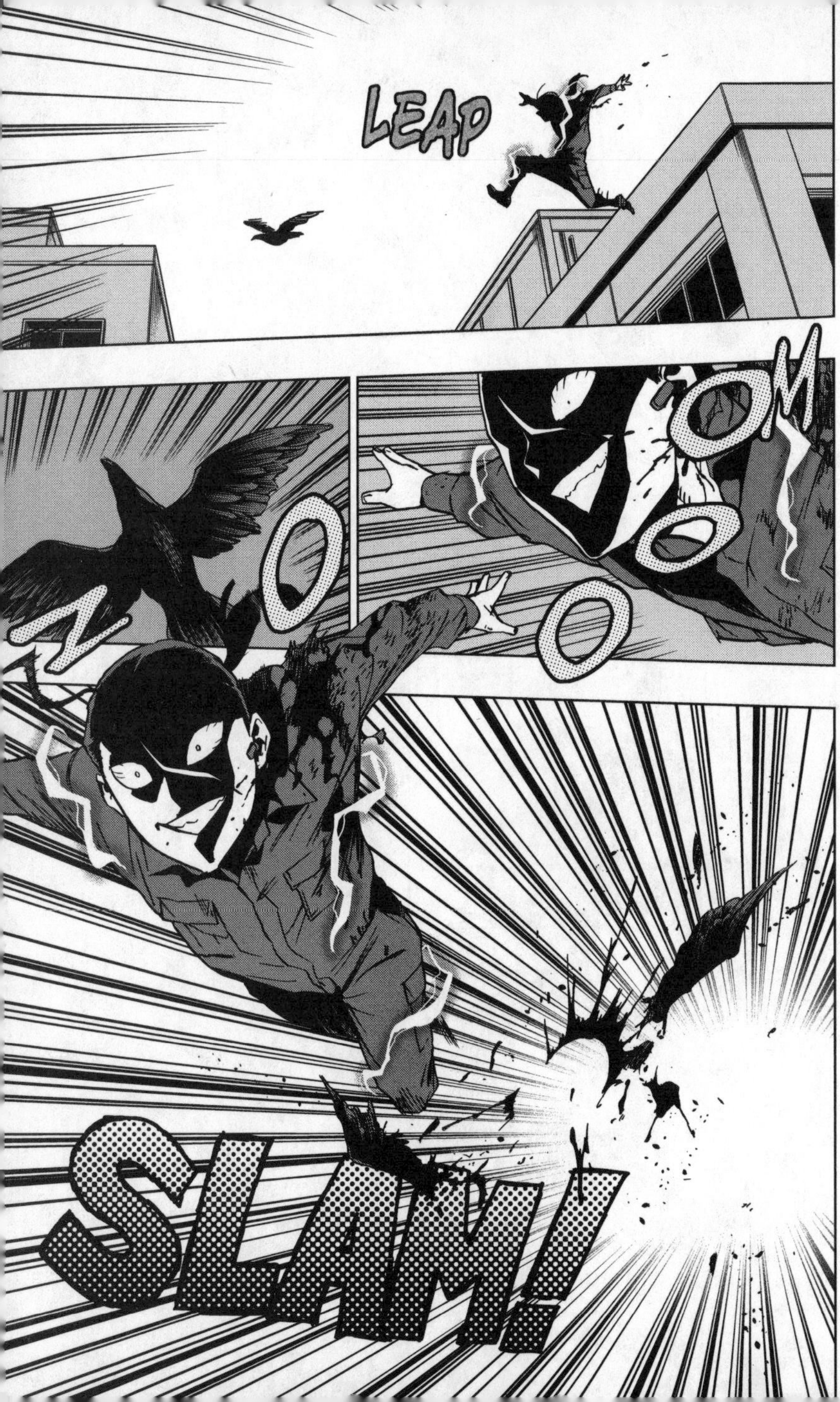
LEAP
WHOOOOOOM
SLAM!

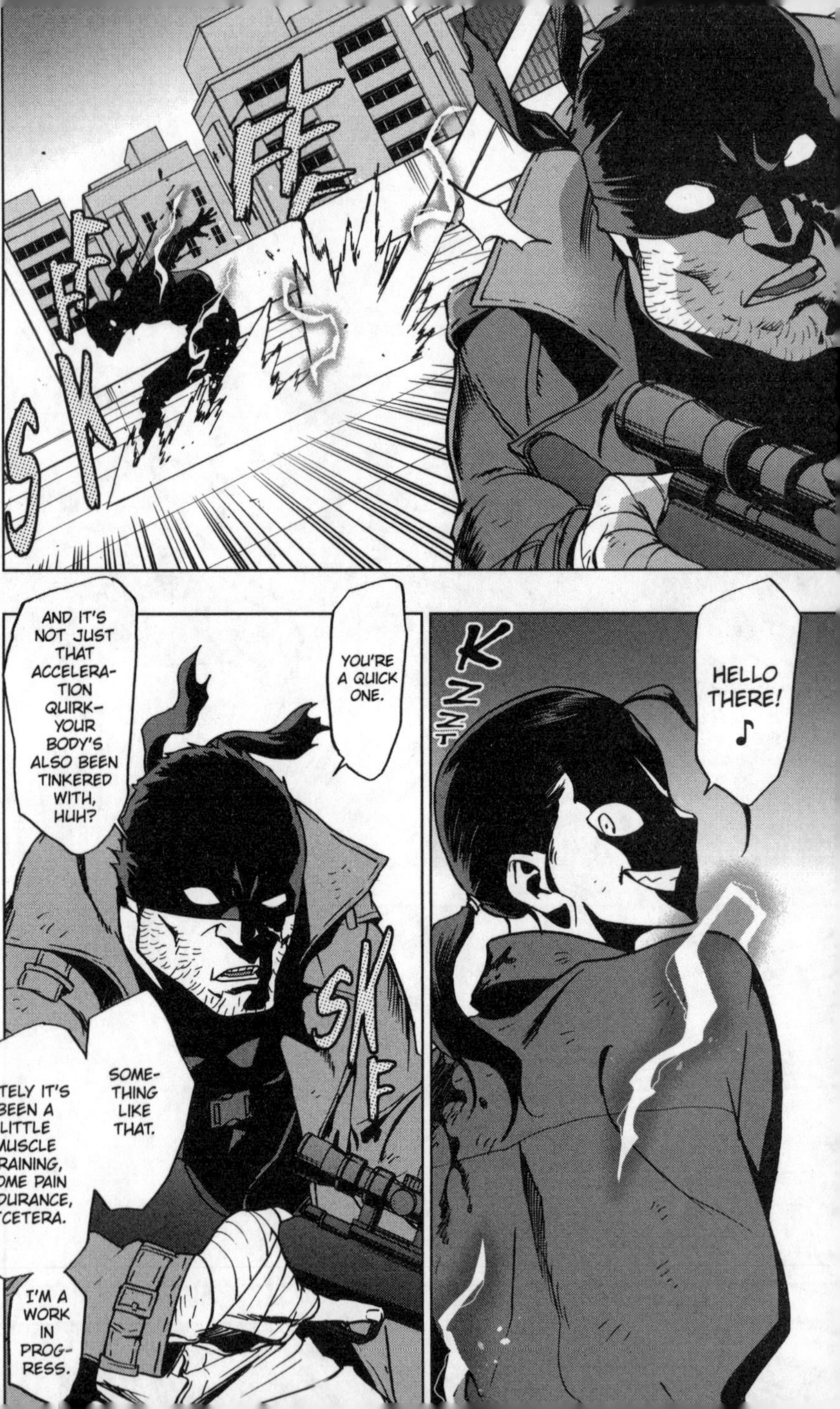
HELLO THERE! ♪
YOU'RE A QUICK ONE.
AND IT'S NOT JUST THAT ACCELERATION QUIRK—YOUR BODY'S ALSO BEEN TINKERED WITH, HUH?
SKF
SOMETHING LIKE THAT.
LATELY IT'S BEEN A LITTLE MUSCLE TRAINING, SOME PAIN ENDURANCE, ETCETERA.
I'M A WORK IN PROGRESS.

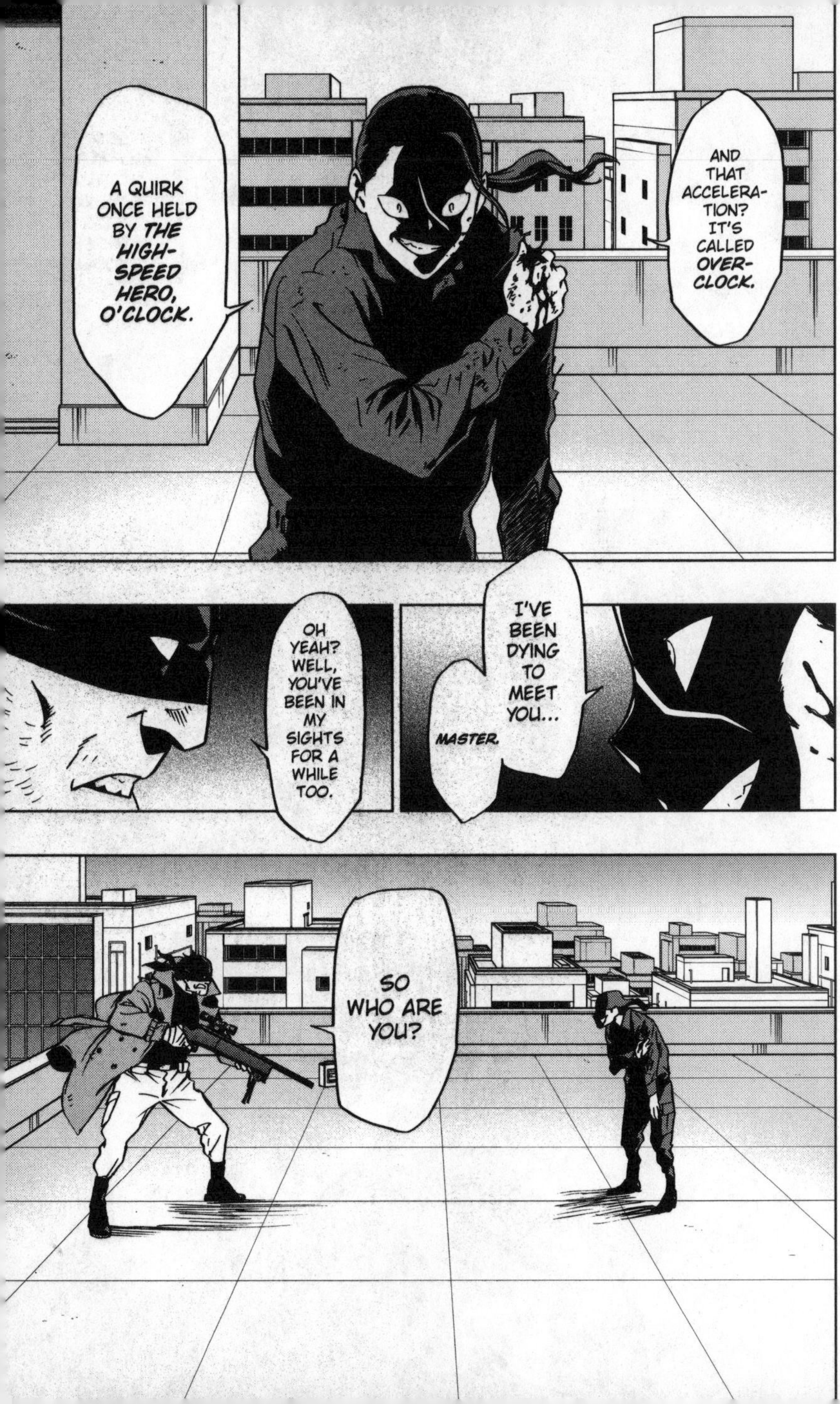
AND THAT ACCELERATION? IT'S CALLED OVERCLOCK.
A QUIRK ONCE HELD BY THE HIGH-SPEED HERO, O'CLOCK.
I'VE BEEN DYING TO MEET YOU...
MASTER.
OH YEAH? WELL, YOU'VE BEEN IN MY SIGHTS FOR A WHILE TOO.
SO WHO ARE YOU?

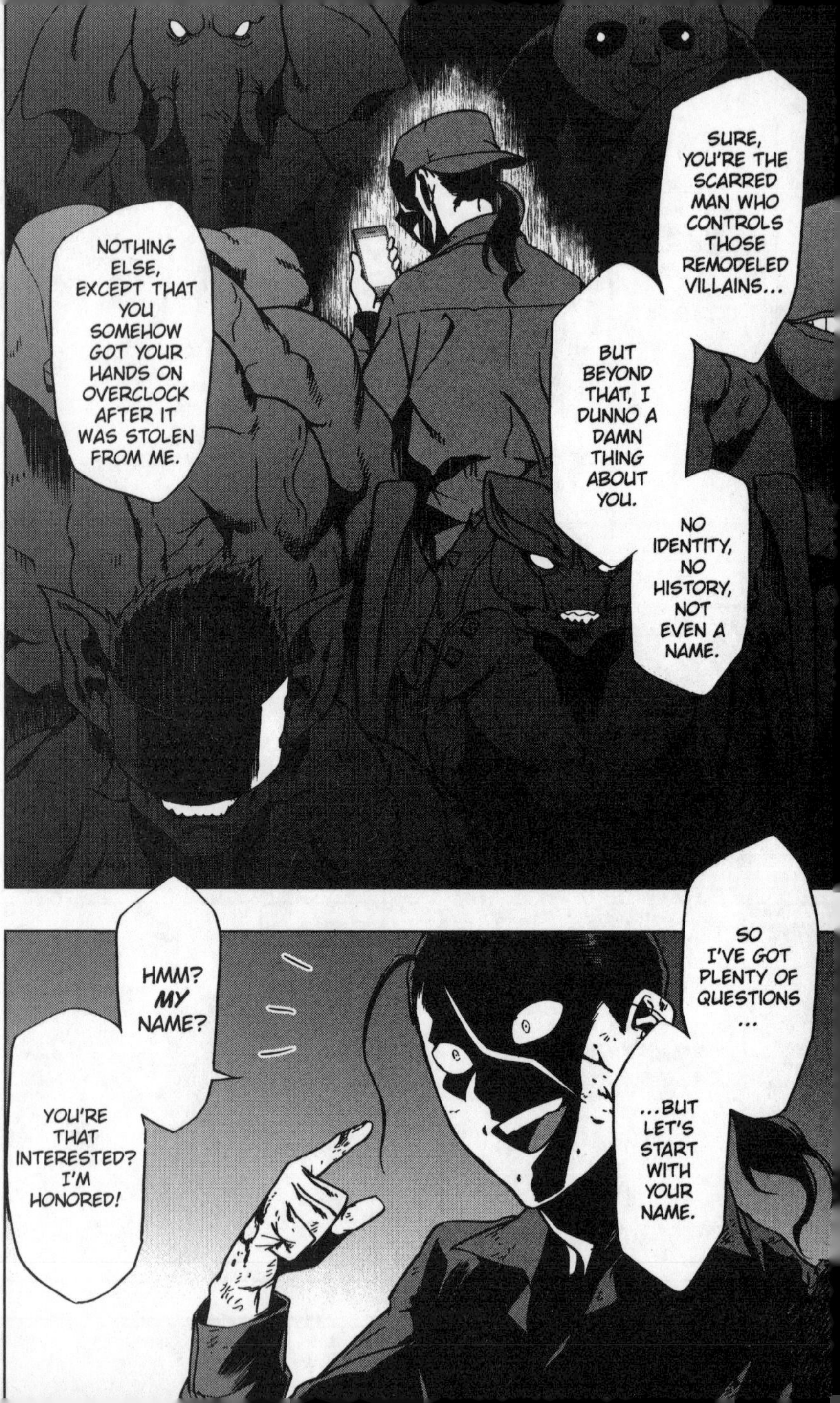
SURE, YOU'RE THE SCARRED MAN WHO CONTROLS THOSE REMODELED VILLAINS...
BUT BEYOND THAT, I DUNNO A DAMN THING ABOUT YOU.
NO IDENTITY, NO HISTORY, NOT EVEN A NAME.
NOTHING ELSE, EXCEPT THAT YOU SOMEHOW GOT YOUR HANDS ON OVERCLOCK AFTER IT WAS STOLEN FROM ME.
SO I'VE GOT PLENTY OF QUESTIONS...
...BUT LET'S START WITH YOUR NAME.
HMM? *MY* NAME?
YOU'RE THAT INTERESTED? I'M HONORED!

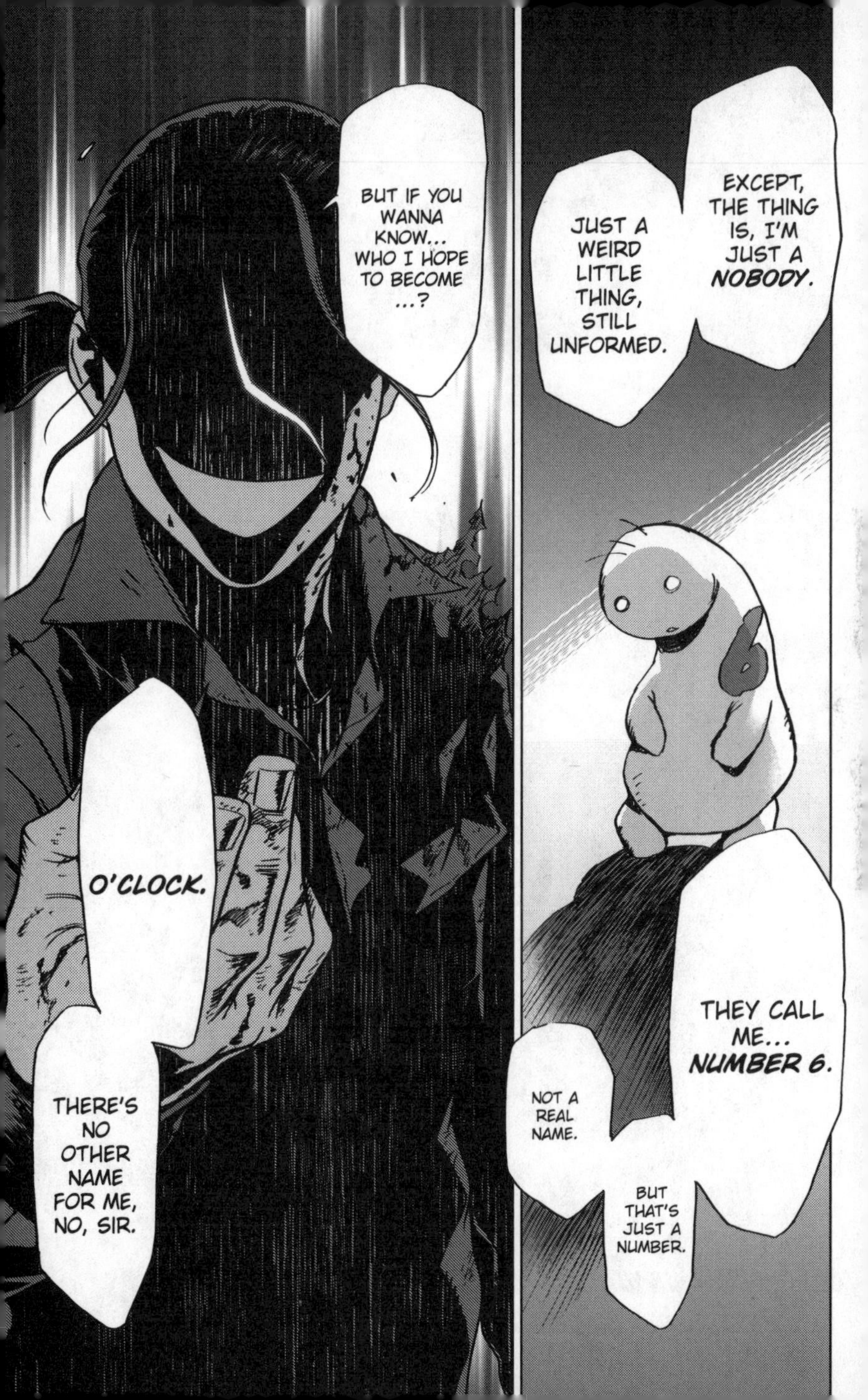
EXCEPT, THE THING IS, I'M JUST A ***NOBODY***.
JUST A WEIRD LITTLE THING, STILL UNFORMED.
THEY CALL ME... ***NUMBER 6***.
NOT A REAL NAME.
BUT THAT'S JUST A NUMBER.
BUT IF YOU WANNA KNOW... WHO I HOPE TO BECOME ...?
O'CLOCK.
THERE'S NO OTHER NAME FOR ME, NO, SIR.

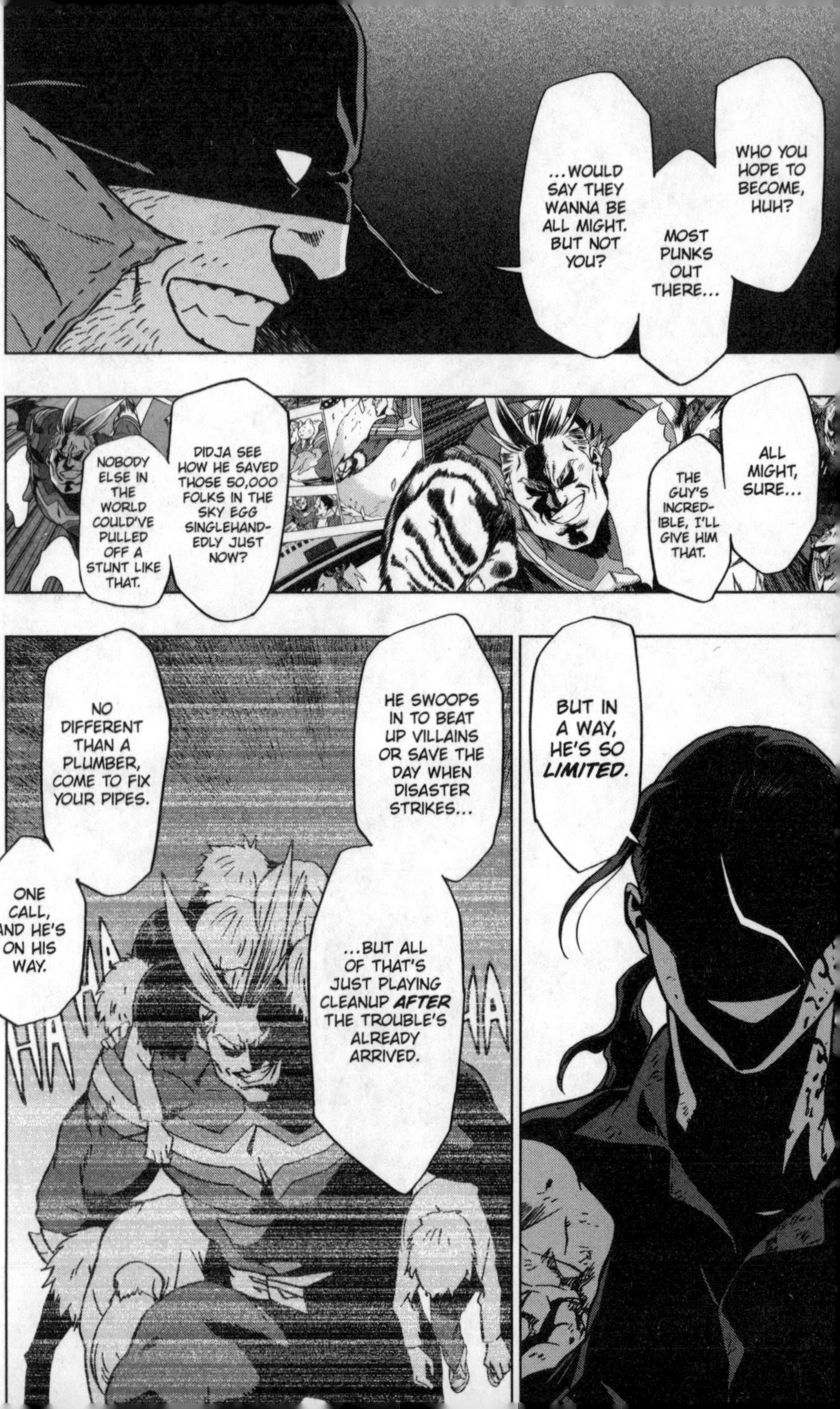
WHO YOU HOPE TO BECOME, HUH?
MOST PUNKS OUT THERE...
...WOULD SAY THEY WANNA BE ALL MIGHT. BUT NOT YOU?
ALL MIGHT, SURE...
THE GUY'S INCRED-IBLE, I'LL GIVE HIM THAT.
DIDJA SEE HOW HE SAVED THOSE 50,000 FOLKS IN THE SKY EGG SINGLEHAND-EDLY JUST NOW?
NOBODY ELSE IN THE WORLD COULD'VE PULLED OFF A STUNT LIKE THAT.
BUT IN A WAY, HE'S SO ***LIMITED***.
HE SWOOPS IN TO BEAT UP VILLAINS OR SAVE THE DAY WHEN DISASTER STRIKES...
...BUT ALL OF THAT'S JUST PLAYING CLEANUP ***AFTER*** THE TROUBLE'S ALREADY ARRIVED.
NO DIFFERENT THAN A PLUMBER, COME TO FIX YOUR PIPES.
ONE CALL, AND HE'S ON HIS WAY.

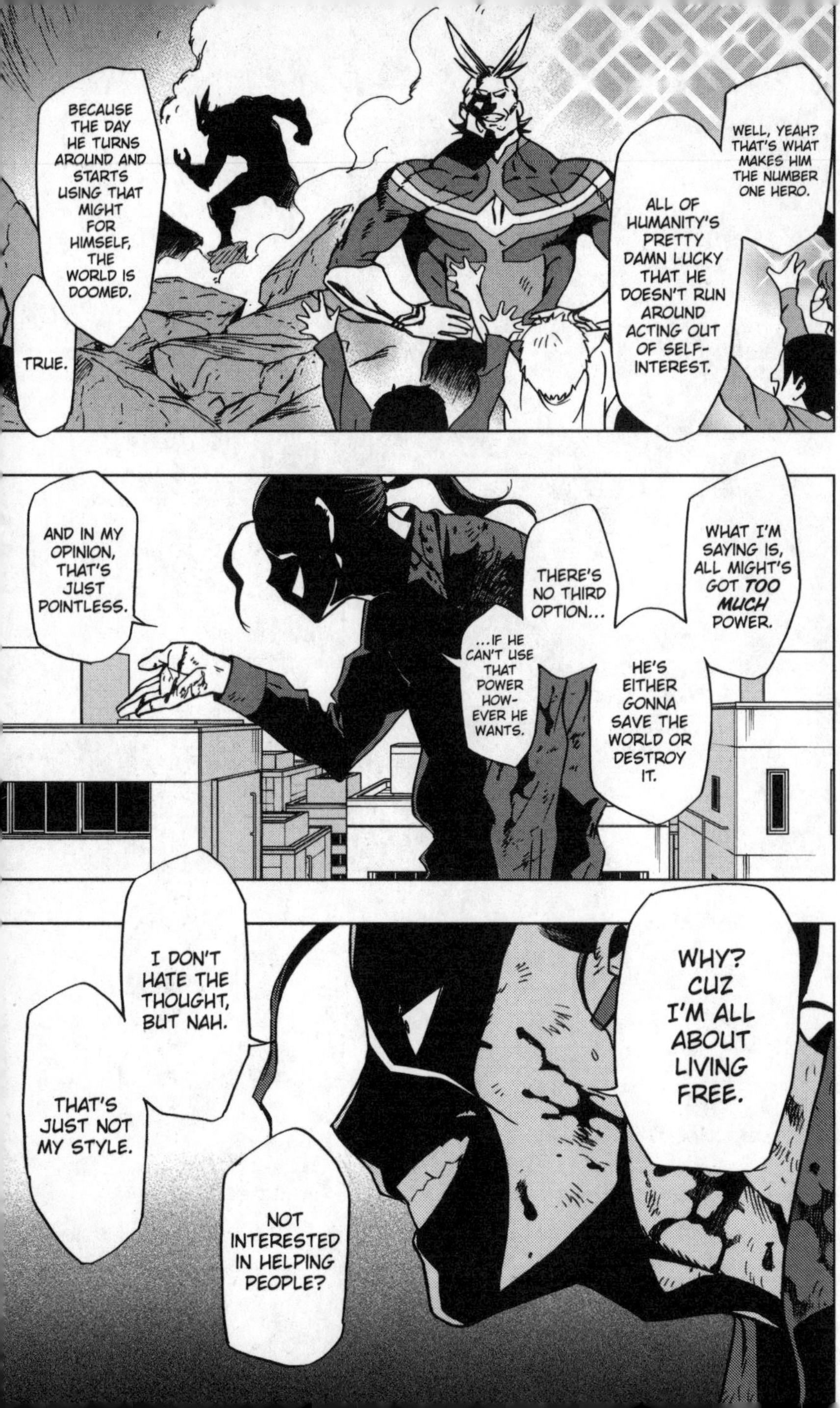
WELL, YEAH? THAT'S WHAT MAKES HIM THE NUMBER ONE HERO.
ALL OF HUMANITY'S PRETTY DAMN LUCKY THAT HE DOESN'T RUN AROUND ACTING OUT OF SELF-INTEREST.
BECAUSE THE DAY HE TURNS AROUND AND STARTS USING THAT MIGHT FOR HIMSELF, THE WORLD IS DOOMED.
TRUE.
WHAT I'M SAYING IS, ALL MIGHT'S GOT *TOO MUCH* POWER.
HE'S EITHER GONNA SAVE THE WORLD OR DESTROY IT.
THERE'S NO THIRD OPTION...
...IF HE CAN'T USE THAT POWER HOWEVER HE WANTS.
AND IN MY OPINION, THAT'S JUST POINTLESS.
WHY? CUZ I'M ALL ABOUT LIVING FREE.
I DON'T HATE THE THOUGHT, BUT NAH.
THAT'S JUST NOT MY STYLE.
NOT INTERESTED IN HELPING PEOPLE?

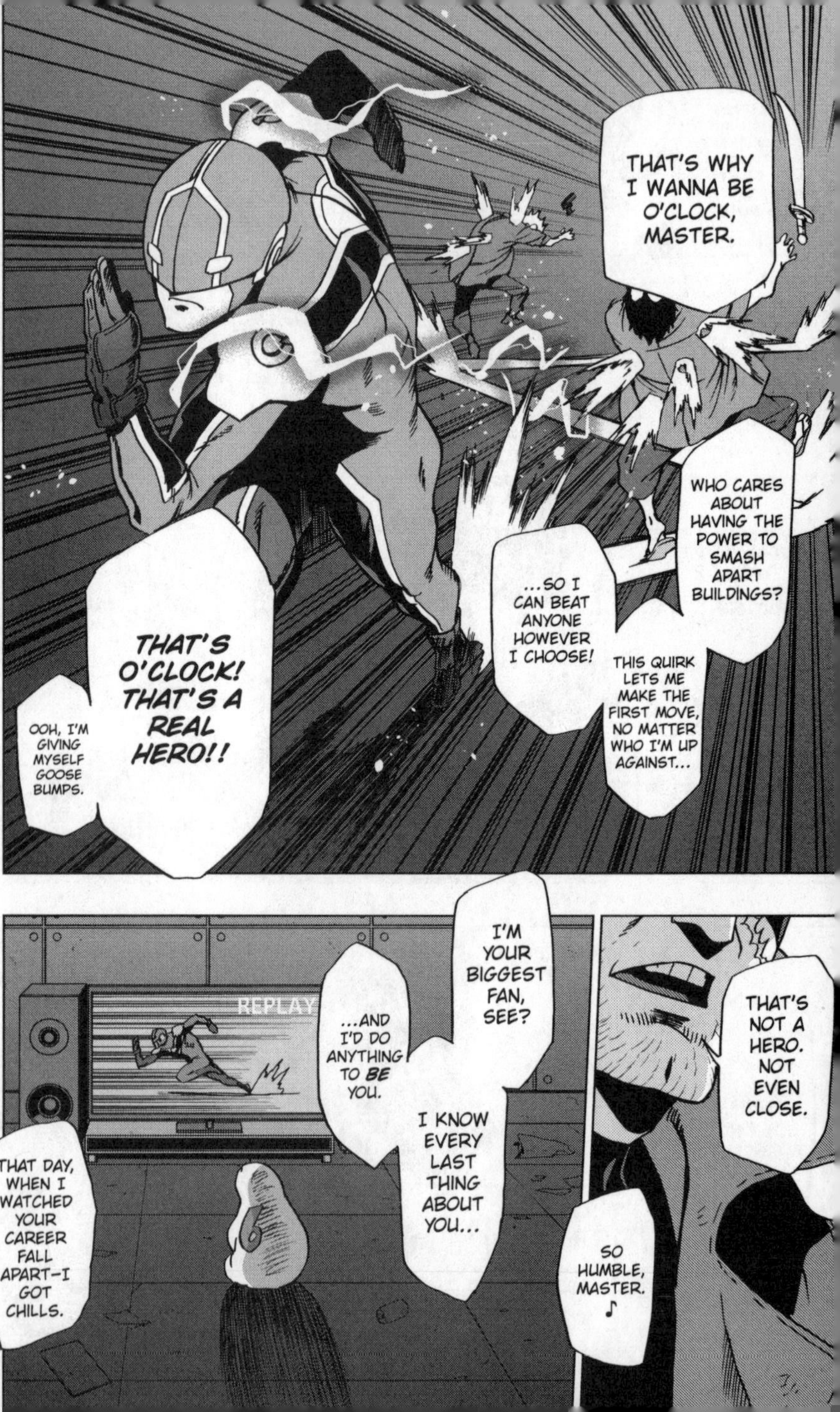
THAT'S WHY I WANNA BE O'CLOCK, MASTER.
WHO CARES ABOUT HAVING THE POWER TO SMASH APART BUILDINGS?
THIS QUIRK LETS ME MAKE THE FIRST MOVE, NO MATTER WHO I'M UP AGAINST...
...SO I CAN BEAT ANYONE HOWEVER I CHOOSE!
THAT'S O'CLOCK! THAT'S A REAL HERO!!
OOH, I'M GIVING MYSELF GOOSE BUMPS.
THAT'S NOT A HERO. NOT EVEN CLOSE.
SO HUMBLE, MASTER. ♪
I'M YOUR BIGGEST FAN, SEE?
...AND I'D DO ANYTHING TO *BE* YOU.
REPLAY
I KNOW EVERY LAST THING ABOUT YOU...
THAT DAY, WHEN I WATCHED YOUR CAREER FALL APART—I GOT CHILLS.

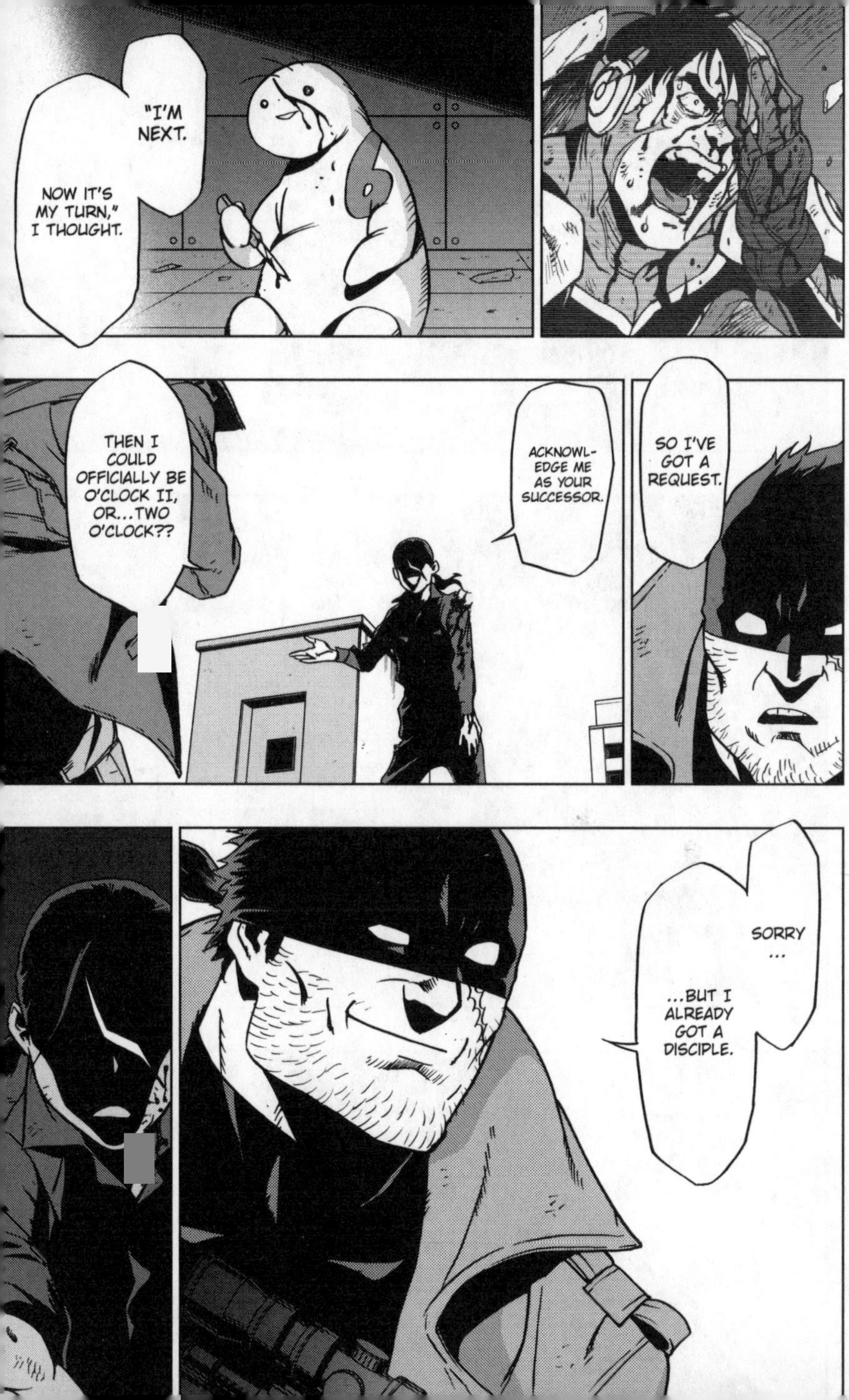
"I'M NEXT.
NOW IT'S MY TURN," I THOUGHT.
SO I'VE GOT A REQUEST.
ACKNOWL-EDGE ME AS YOUR SUCCESSOR.
THEN I COULD OFFICIALLY BE O'CLOCK II, OR...TWO O'CLOCK??
SORRY ...
...BUT I ALREADY GOT A DISCIPLE.

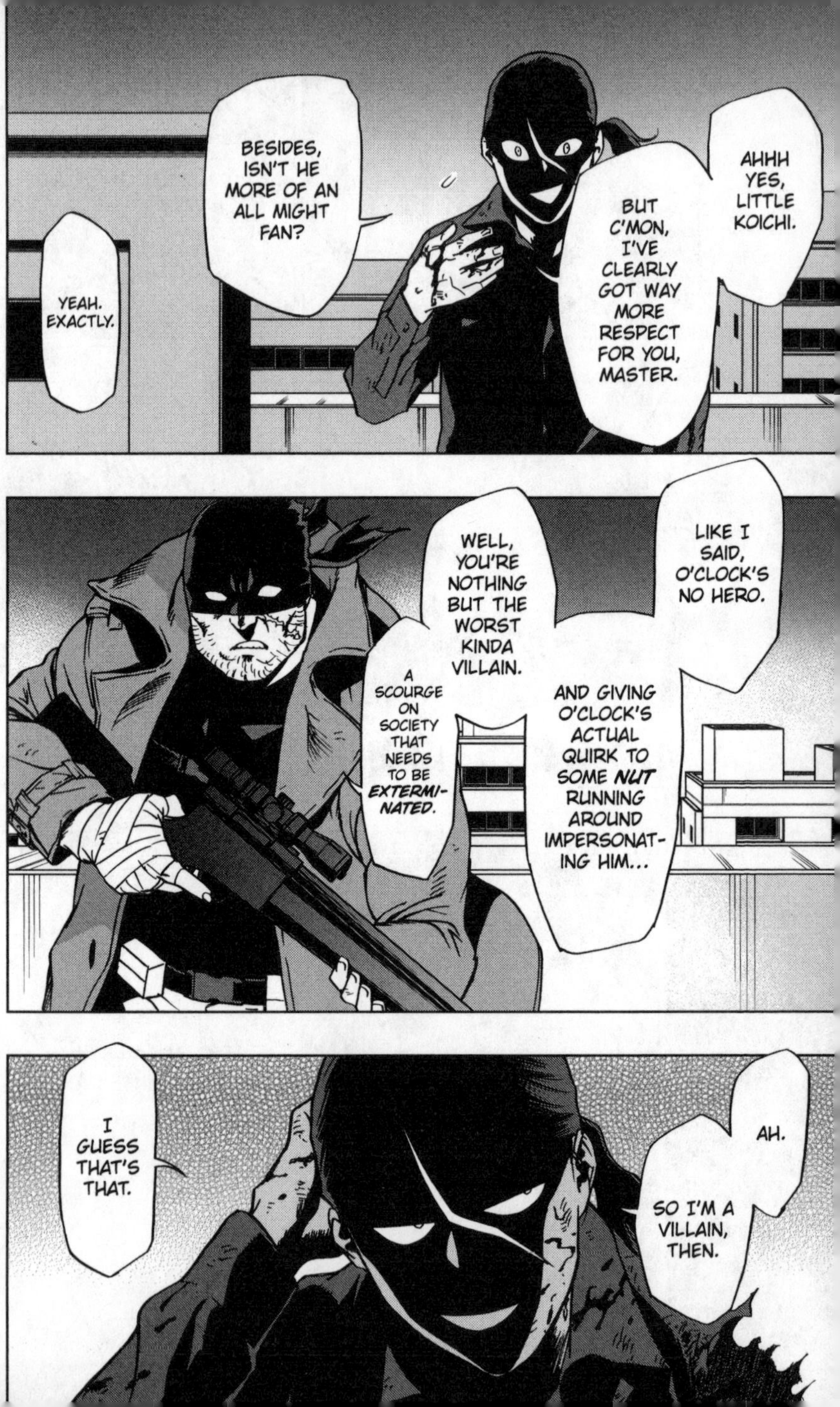
AHHH YES, LITTLE KOICHI.
BUT C'MON, I'VE CLEARLY GOT WAY MORE RESPECT FOR YOU, MASTER.
BESIDES, ISN'T HE MORE OF AN ALL MIGHT FAN?
YEAH. EXACTLY.
LIKE I SAID, O'CLOCK'S NO HERO.
AND GIVING O'CLOCK'S ACTUAL QUIRK TO SOME *NUT* RUNNING AROUND IMPERSONATING HIM...
WELL, YOU'RE NOTHING BUT THE WORST KINDA VILLAIN.
A SCOURGE ON SOCIETY THAT NEEDS TO BE *EXTERMINATED*.
AH.
SO I'M A VILLAIN, THEN.
I GUESS THAT'S THAT.

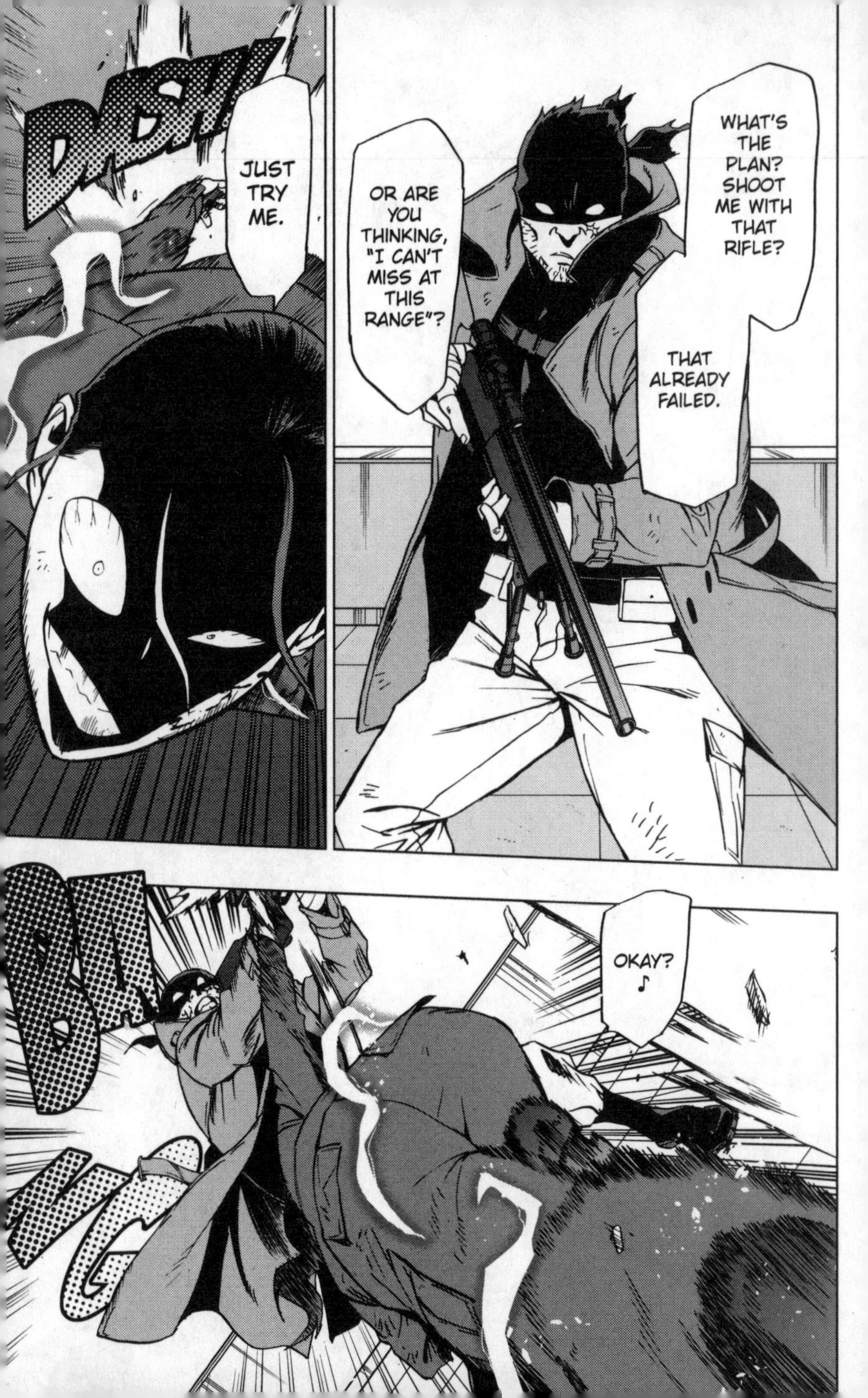
WHAT'S THE PLAN? SHOOT ME WITH THAT RIFLE?
THAT ALREADY FAILED.
OR ARE YOU THINKING, "I CAN'T MISS AT THIS RANGE"?
DASH!!
JUST TRY ME.
OKAY? ♪

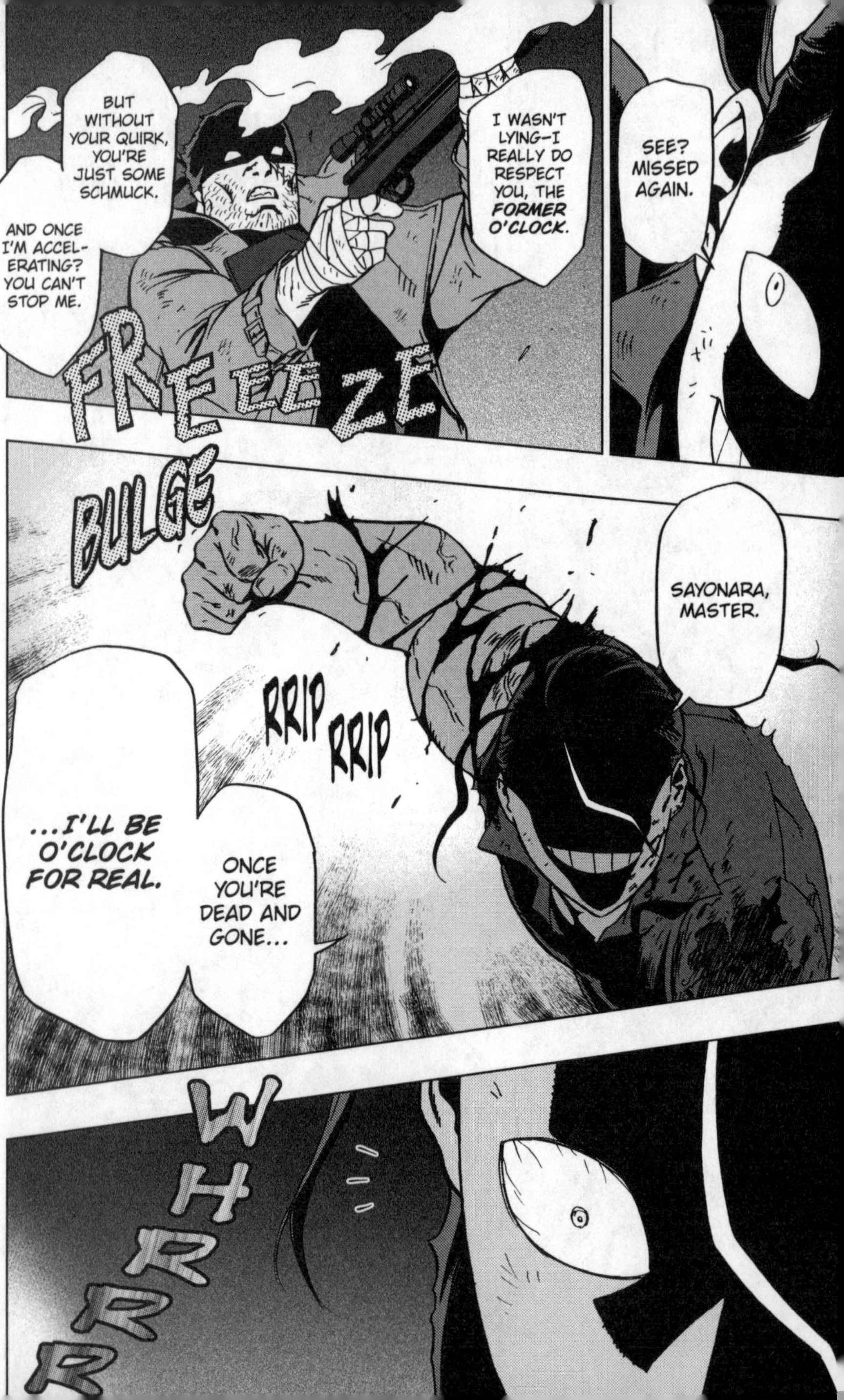
SEE? MISSED AGAIN.
I WASN'T LYING—I REALLY DO RESPECT YOU, THE FORMER O'CLOCK.
BUT WITHOUT YOUR QUIRK, YOU'RE JUST SOME SCHMUCK.
AND ONCE I'M ACCELERATING? YOU CAN'T STOP ME.
FREEZE
SAYONARA, MASTER.
BULGE
RRIP RRIP
ONCE YOU'RE DEAD AND GONE...
...I'LL BE O'CLOCK FOR REAL.
WHRRRR

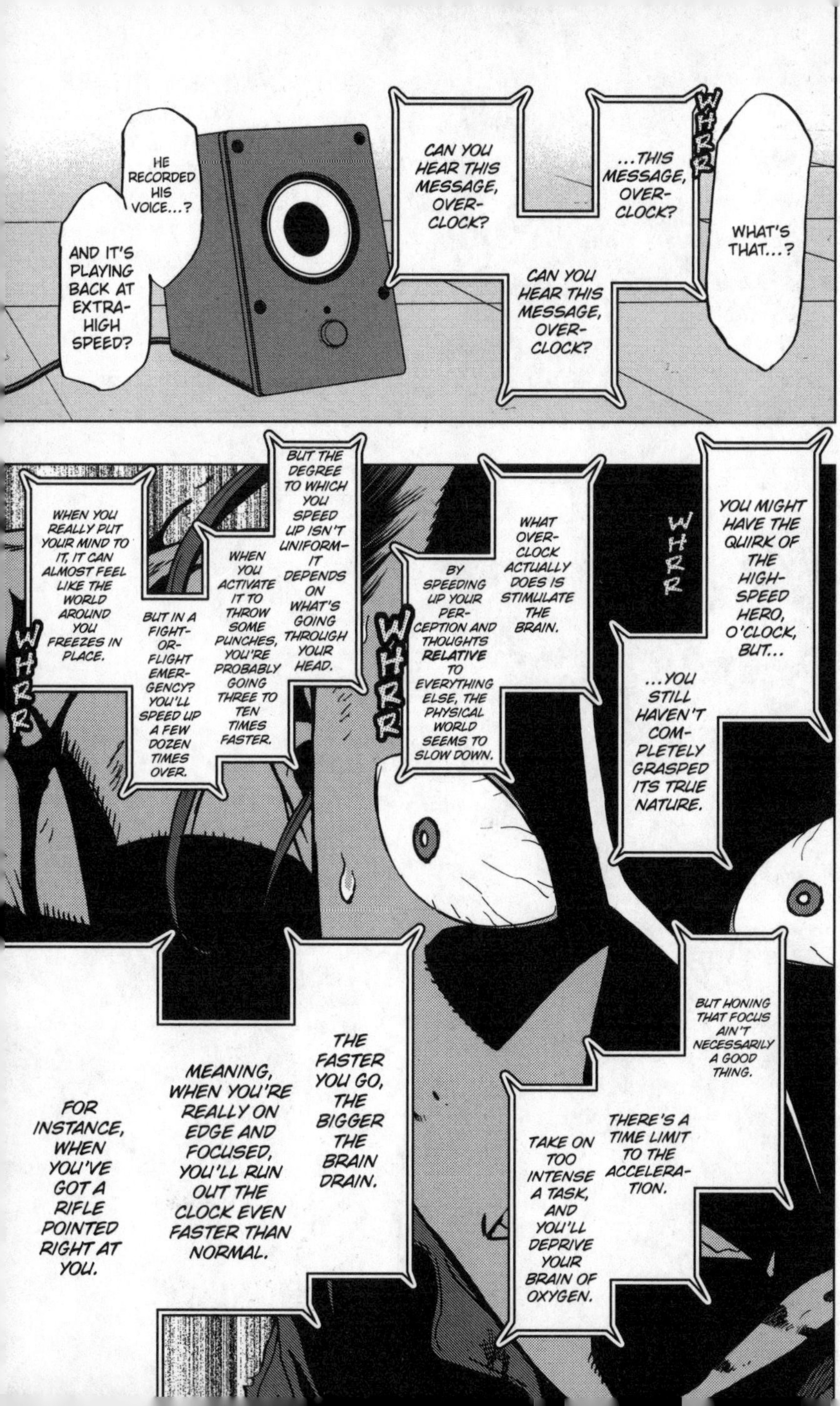
WHAT'S THAT...?
WHRR
...THIS MESSAGE, OVER-CLOCK?
CAN YOU HEAR THIS MESSAGE, OVER-CLOCK?
CAN YOU HEAR THIS MESSAGE, OVER-CLOCK?
HE RECORDED HIS VOICE...?
AND IT'S PLAYING BACK AT EXTRA-HIGH SPEED?
YOU MIGHT HAVE THE QUIRK OF THE HIGH-SPEED HERO, O'CLOCK, BUT...
...YOU STILL HAVEN'T COMPLETELY GRASPED ITS TRUE NATURE.
WHRR
WHAT OVER-CLOCK ACTUALLY DOES IS STIMULATE THE BRAIN.
BY SPEEDING UP YOUR PERCEPTION AND THOUGHTS **RELATIVE** TO EVERYTHING ELSE, THE PHYSICAL WORLD SEEMS TO SLOW DOWN.
WHRR
BUT THE DEGREE TO WHICH YOU SPEED UP ISN'T UNIFORM—IT DEPENDS ON WHAT'S GOING THROUGH YOUR HEAD.
WHEN YOU ACTIVATE IT TO THROW SOME PUNCHES, YOU'RE PROBABLY GOING THREE TO TEN TIMES FASTER.
BUT IN A FIGHT-OR-FLIGHT EMERGENCY? YOU'LL SPEED UP A FEW DOZEN TIMES OVER.
WHEN YOU REALLY PUT YOUR MIND TO IT, IT CAN ALMOST FEEL LIKE THE WORLD AROUND YOU FREEZES IN PLACE.
WHRR
BUT HONING THAT FOCUS AIN'T NECESSARILY A GOOD THING.
THERE'S A TIME LIMIT TO THE ACCELERATION.
TAKE ON TOO INTENSE A TASK, AND YOU'LL DEPRIVE YOUR BRAIN OF OXYGEN.
THE FASTER YOU GO, THE BIGGER THE BRAIN DRAIN.
MEANING, WHEN YOU'RE REALLY ON EDGE AND FOCUSED, YOU'LL RUN OUT THE CLOCK EVEN FASTER THAN NORMAL.
FOR INSTANCE, WHEN YOU'VE GOT A RIFLE POINTED RIGHT AT YOU.

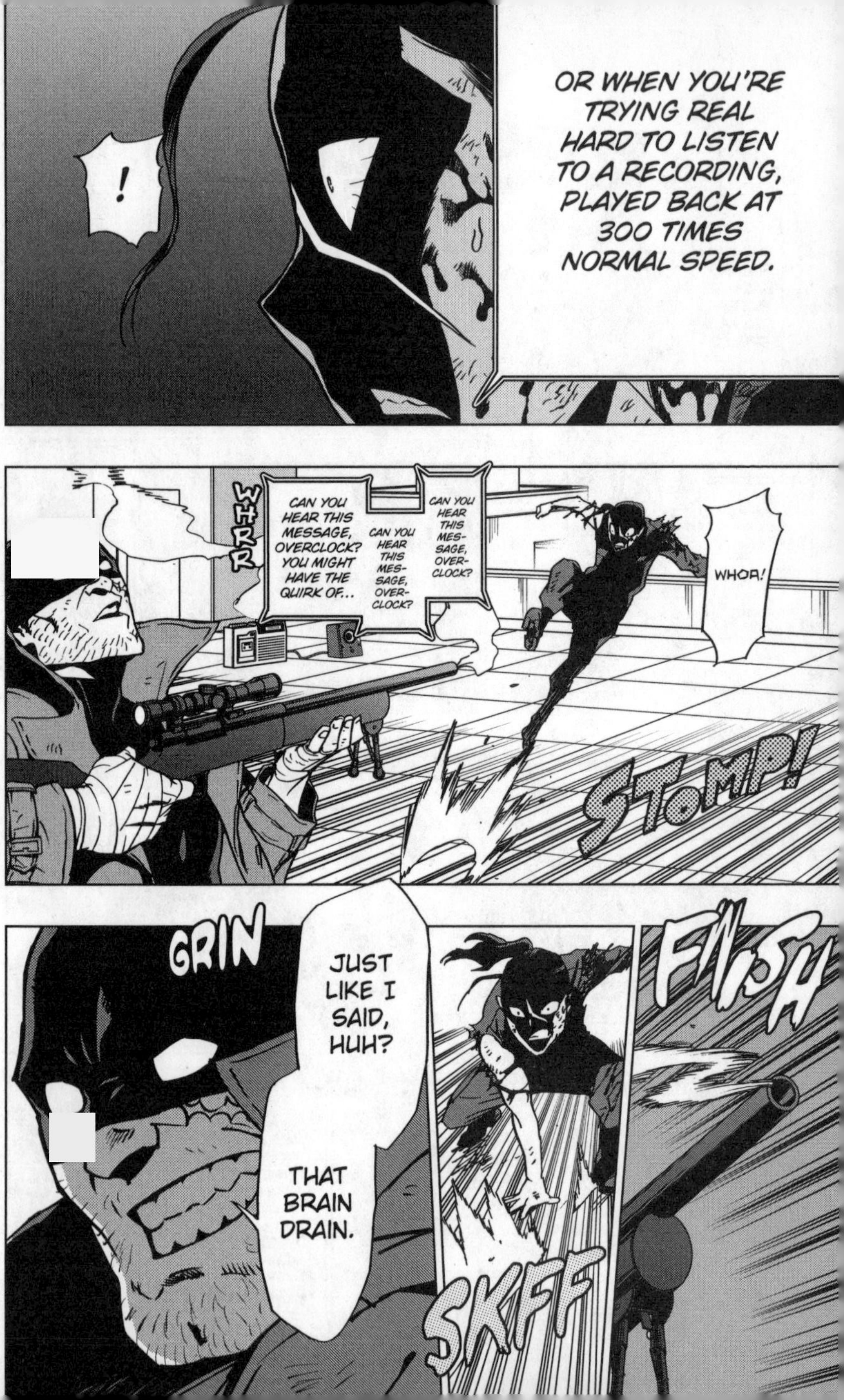

OR WHEN YOU'RE TRYING REAL HARD TO LISTEN TO A RECORDING, PLAYED BACK AT 300 TIMES NORMAL SPEED.
!
WHOA!
STOMP!
CAN YOU HEAR THIS MES-SAGE, OVER-CLOCK?
CAN YOU HEAR THIS MES-SAGE, OVER-CLOCK?
CAN YOU HEAR THIS MESSAGE, OVERCLOCK? YOU MIGHT HAVE THE QUIRK OF...
WHRR
FWSH
SKFF
GRIN
JUST LIKE I SAID, HUH?
THAT BRAIN DRAIN.

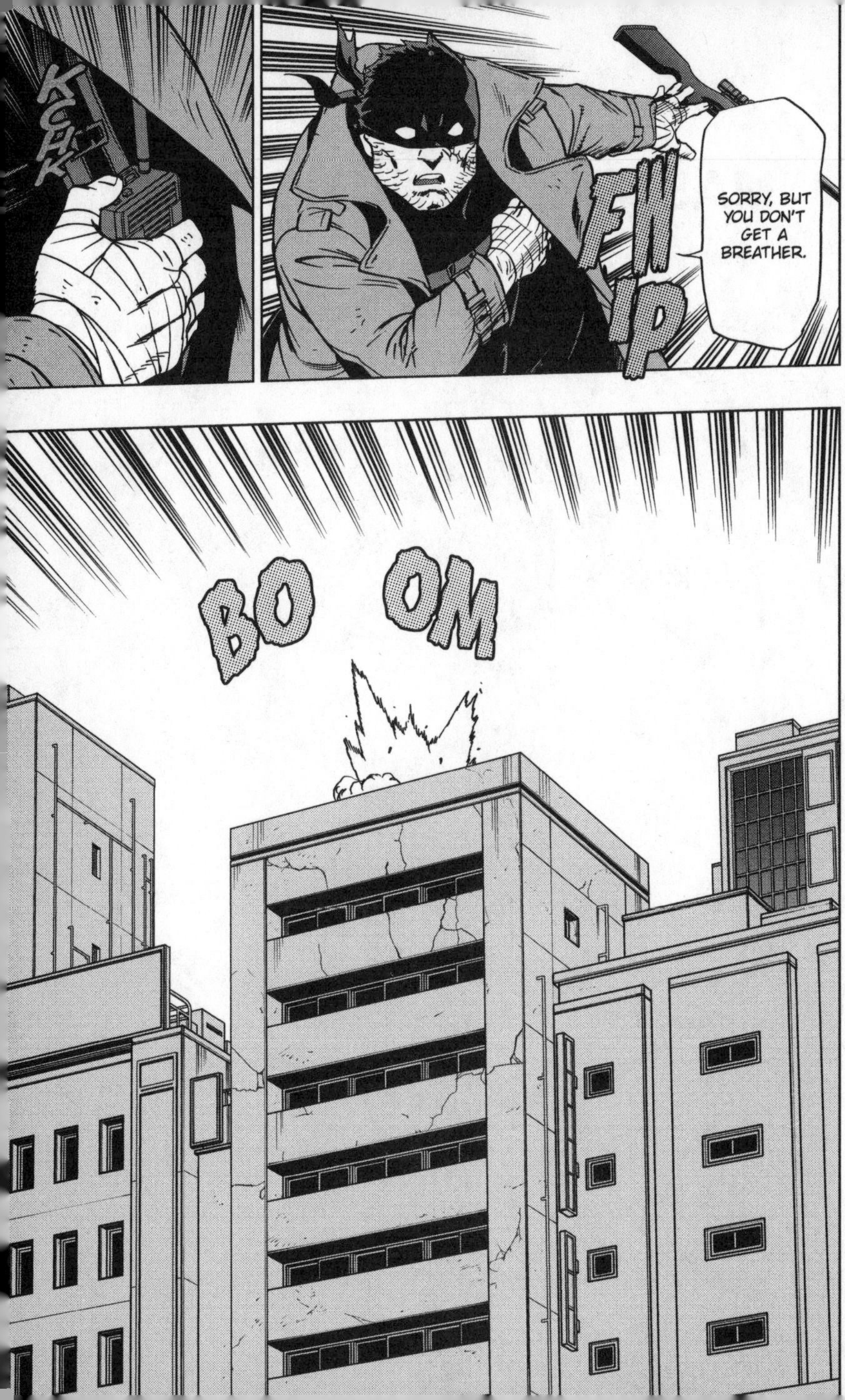
SORRY, BUT YOU DON'T GET A BREATHER.
FWIP
KCHK
BOOM

THE COLUMN

MASTER VS. NUMBER 6

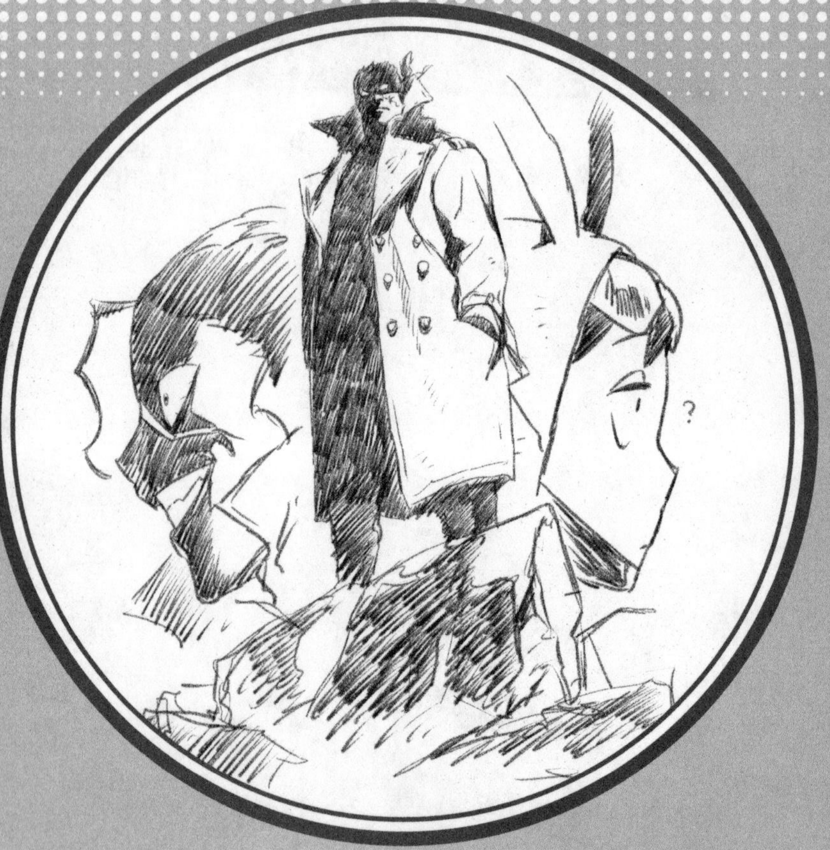

The master/student relationship between Knuckleduster and Koichi is a key through line in *Vigilantes*, so Number 6 is a villain who adds to that theme… That said, there's still plenty we can't reveal yet.

—Furuhashi

Whenever I draw Master, I get that distinct, "Ahh I'm drawing *Vigilantes*" sensation. When I draw Number 6, all I can think is, "I'm all out of tricks and contrivances to keep his face hidden in shadow." (LOL)

—Betten

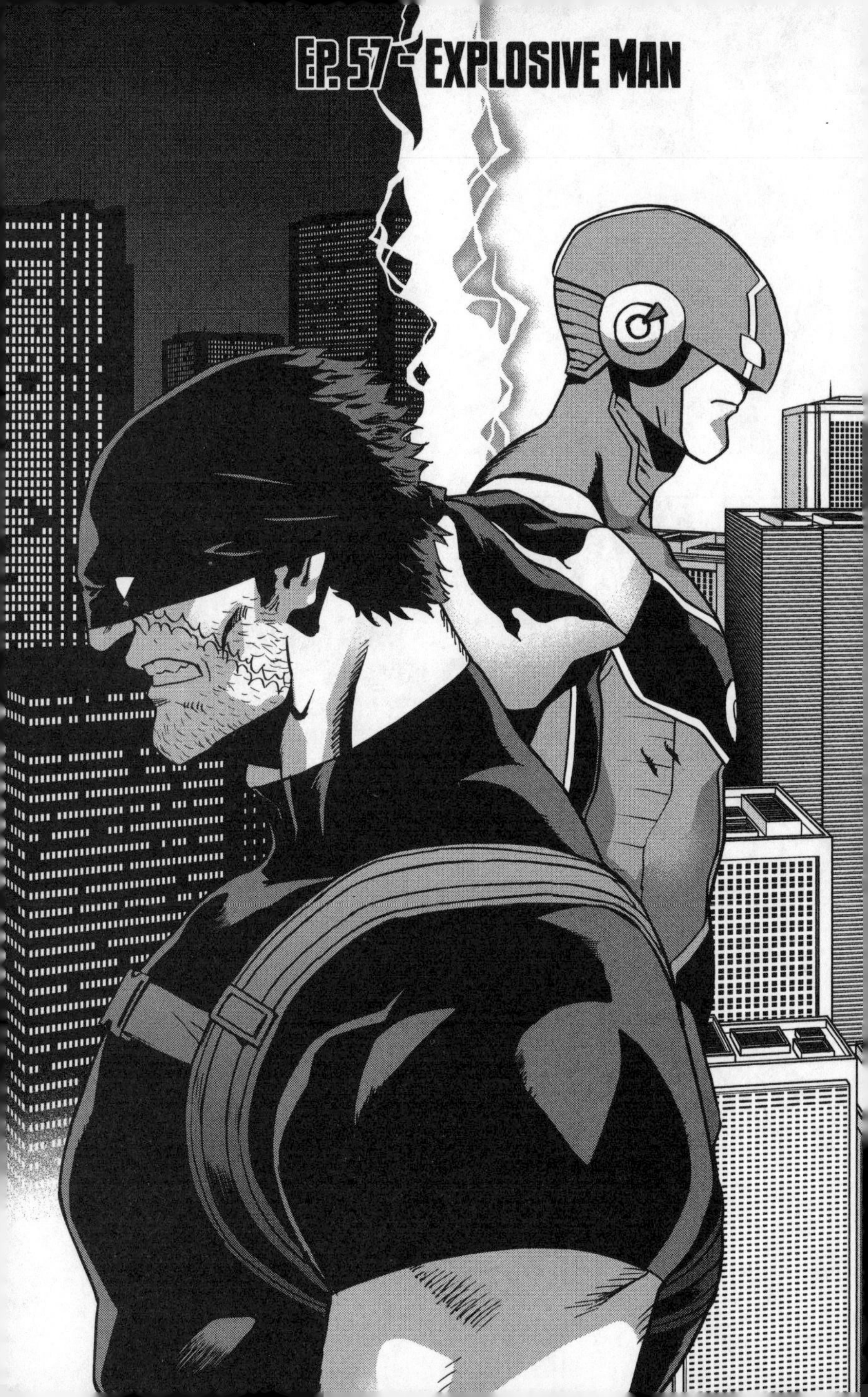
EP. 57 - EXPLOSIVE MAN

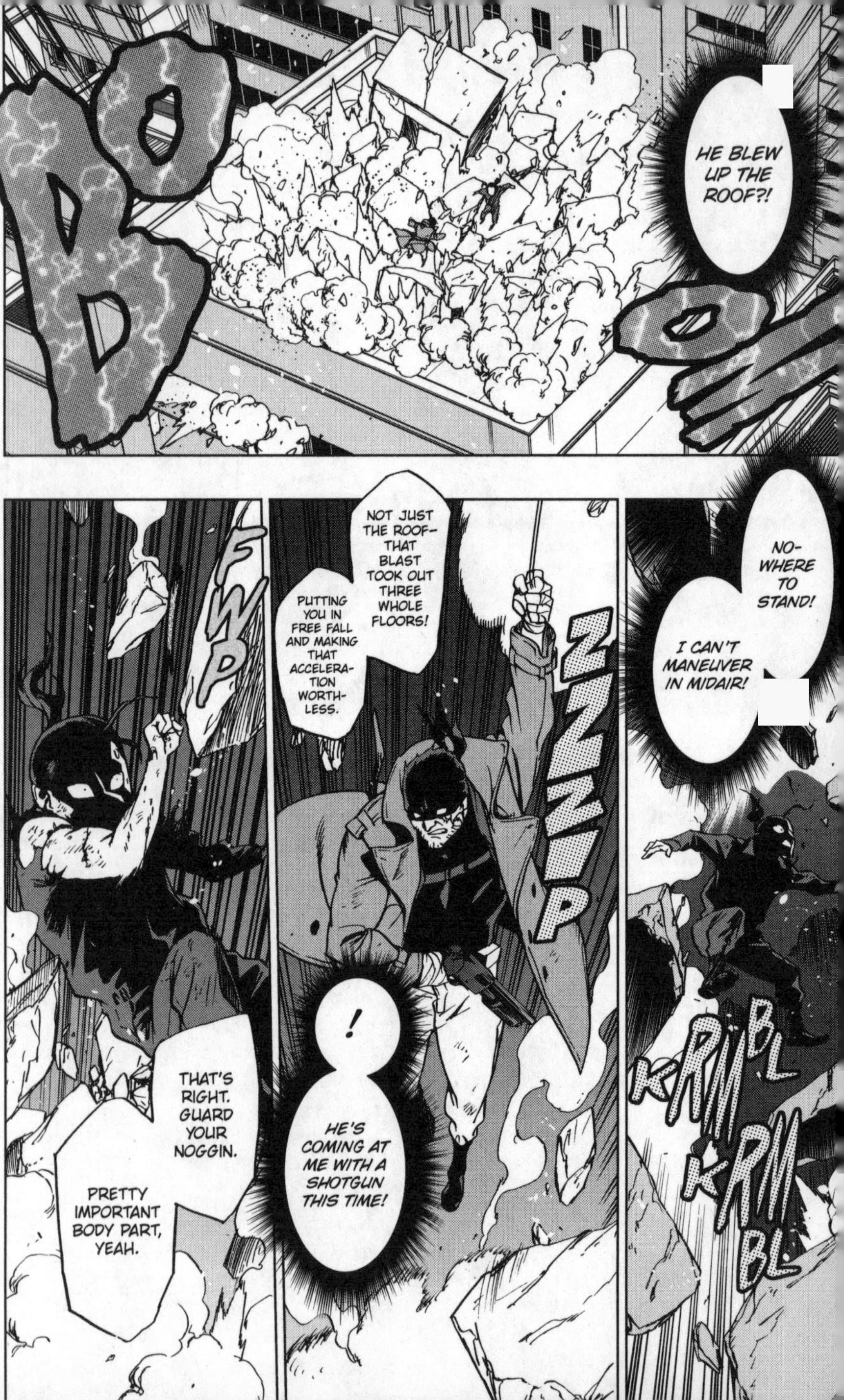
HE BLEW UP THE ROOF?!
NO-WHERE TO STAND!
I CAN'T MANEUVER IN MIDAIR!
KRMBL KRMBL
NOT JUST THE ROOF—THAT BLAST TOOK OUT THREE WHOLE FLOORS!
PUTTING YOU IN FREE FALL AND MAKING THAT ACCELERA-TION WORTH-LESS.
!
HE'S COMING AT ME WITH A SHOTGUN THIS TIME!
FWP
THAT'S RIGHT. GUARD YOUR NOGGIN.
PRETTY IMPORTANT BODY PART, YEAH.

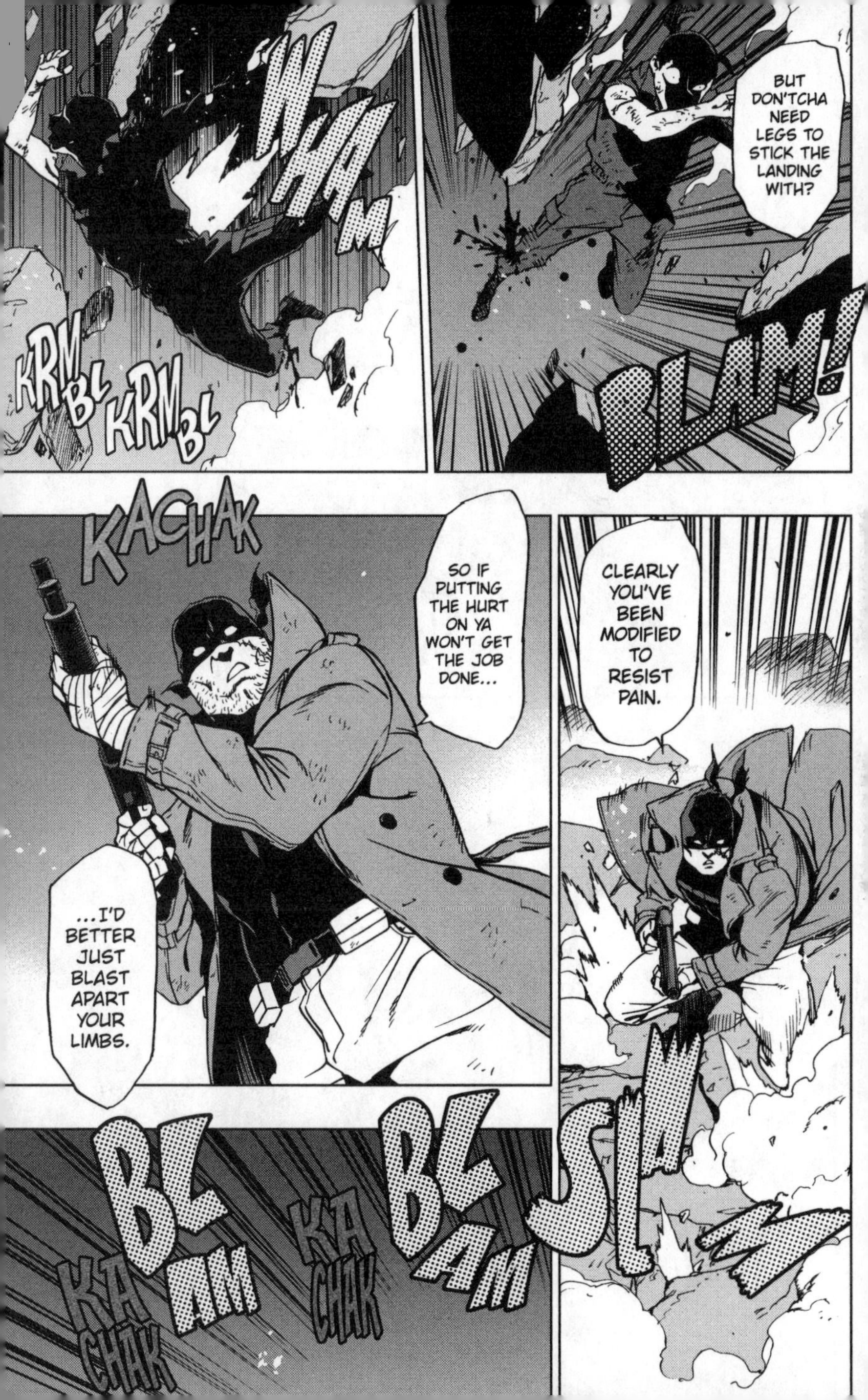
BUT DON'TCHA NEED LEGS TO STICK THE LANDING WITH?
BLAM!
WHAM
KRMBL KRMBL
CLEARLY YOU'VE BEEN MODIFIED TO RESIST PAIN.
KACHAK
SO IF PUTTING THE HURT ON YA WON'T GET THE JOB DONE...
...I'D BETTER JUST BLAST APART YOUR LIMBS.
SLAM
BLAM
KACHAK
BLAM
KACHAK

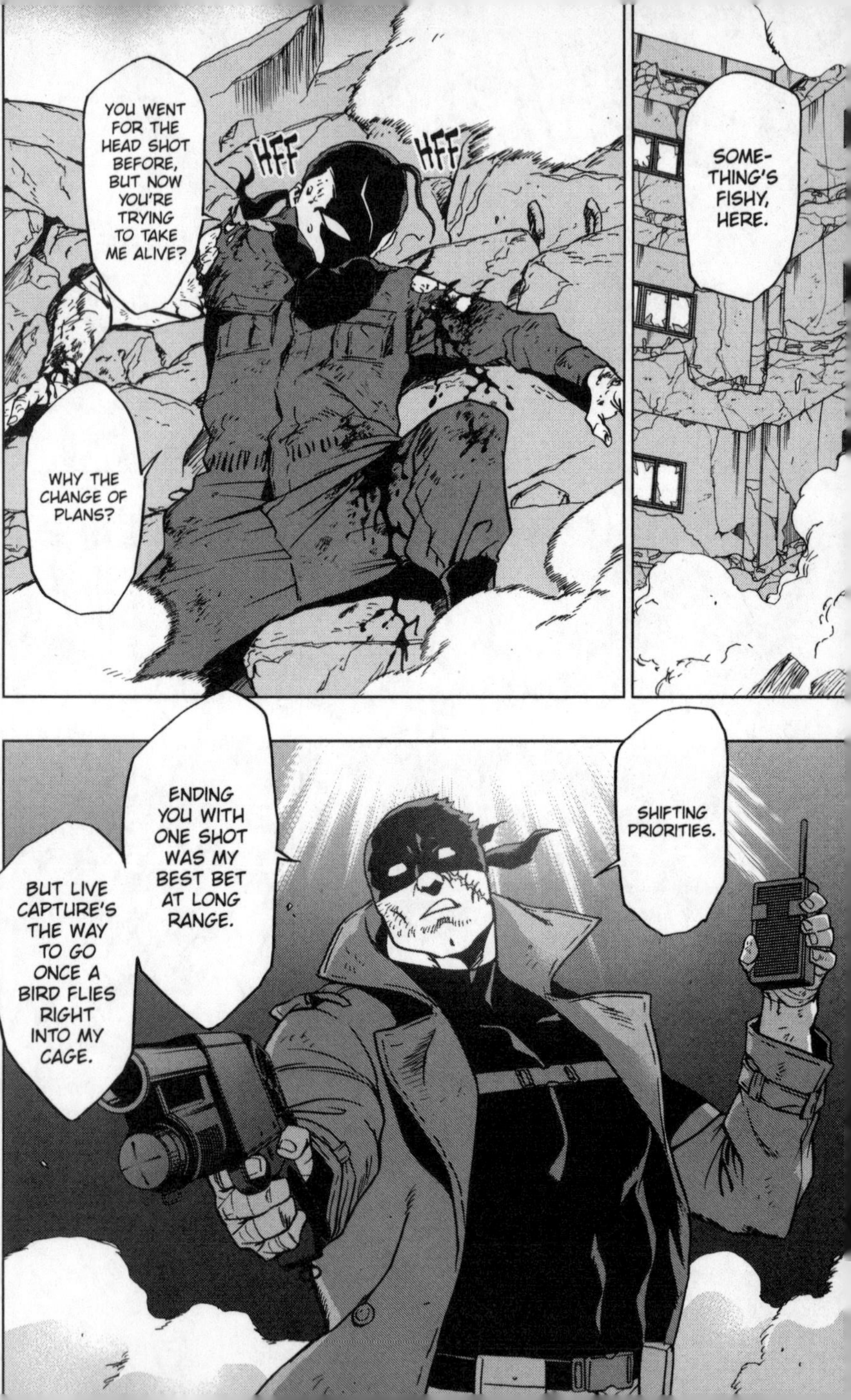
SOME-THING'S FISHY, HERE.
HFF
HFF
YOU WENT FOR THE HEAD SHOT BEFORE, BUT NOW YOU'RE TRYING TO TAKE ME ALIVE?
WHY THE CHANGE OF PLANS?
SHIFTING PRIORITIES.
ENDING YOU WITH ONE SHOT WAS MY BEST BET AT LONG RANGE.
BUT LIVE CAPTURE'S THE WAY TO GO ONCE A BIRD FLIES RIGHT INTO MY CAGE.

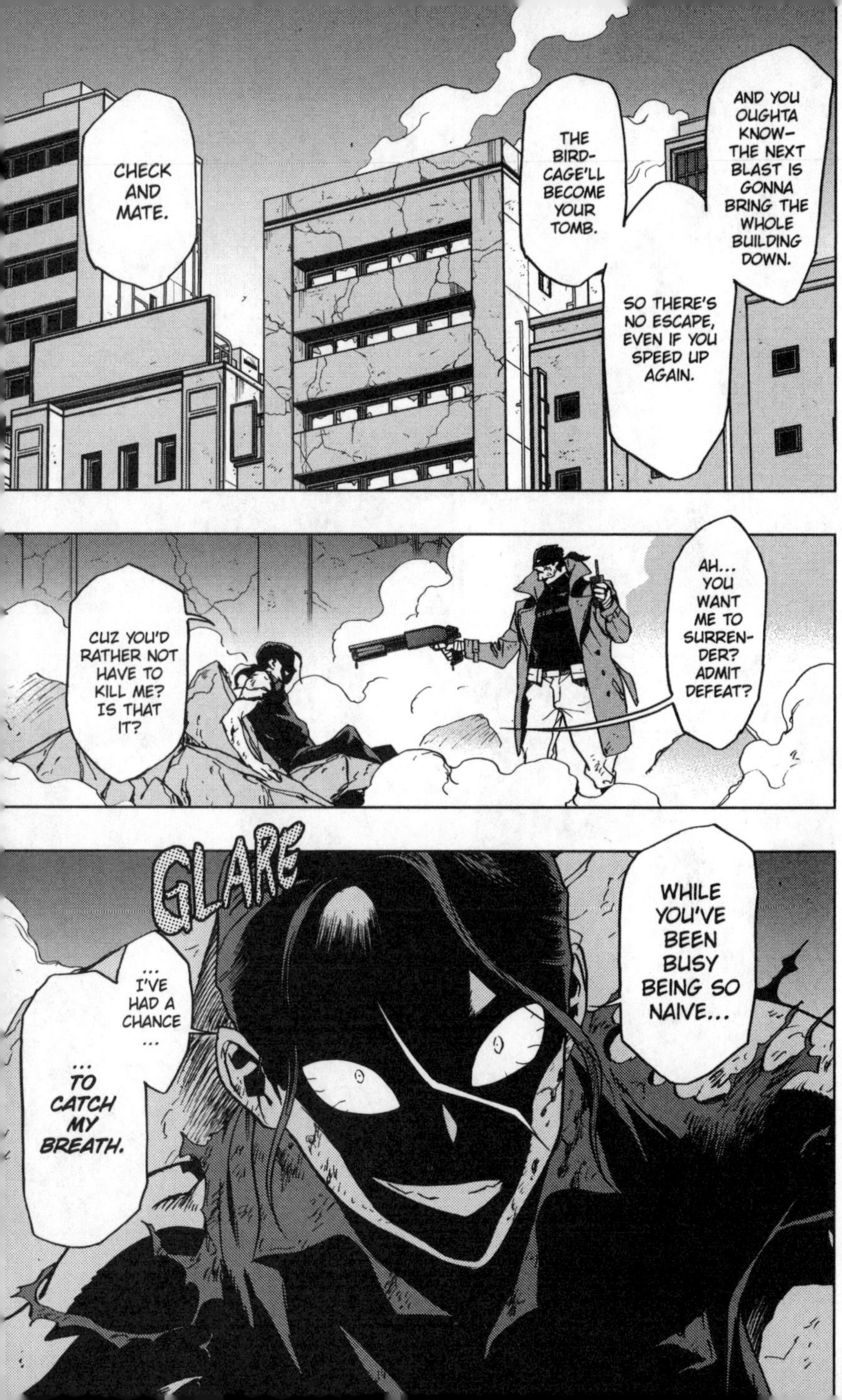
AND YOU OUGHTA KNOW— THE NEXT BLAST IS GONNA BRING THE WHOLE BUILDING DOWN.
THE BIRD-CAGE'LL BECOME YOUR TOMB.
SO THERE'S NO ESCAPE, EVEN IF YOU SPEED UP AGAIN.
CHECK AND MATE.
AH... YOU WANT ME TO SURREN-DER? ADMIT DEFEAT?
CUZ YOU'D RATHER NOT HAVE TO KILL ME? IS THAT IT?
GLARE
WHILE YOU'VE BEEN BUSY BEING SO NAIVE...
... I'VE HAD A CHANCE ...
... TO CATCH MY BREATH.

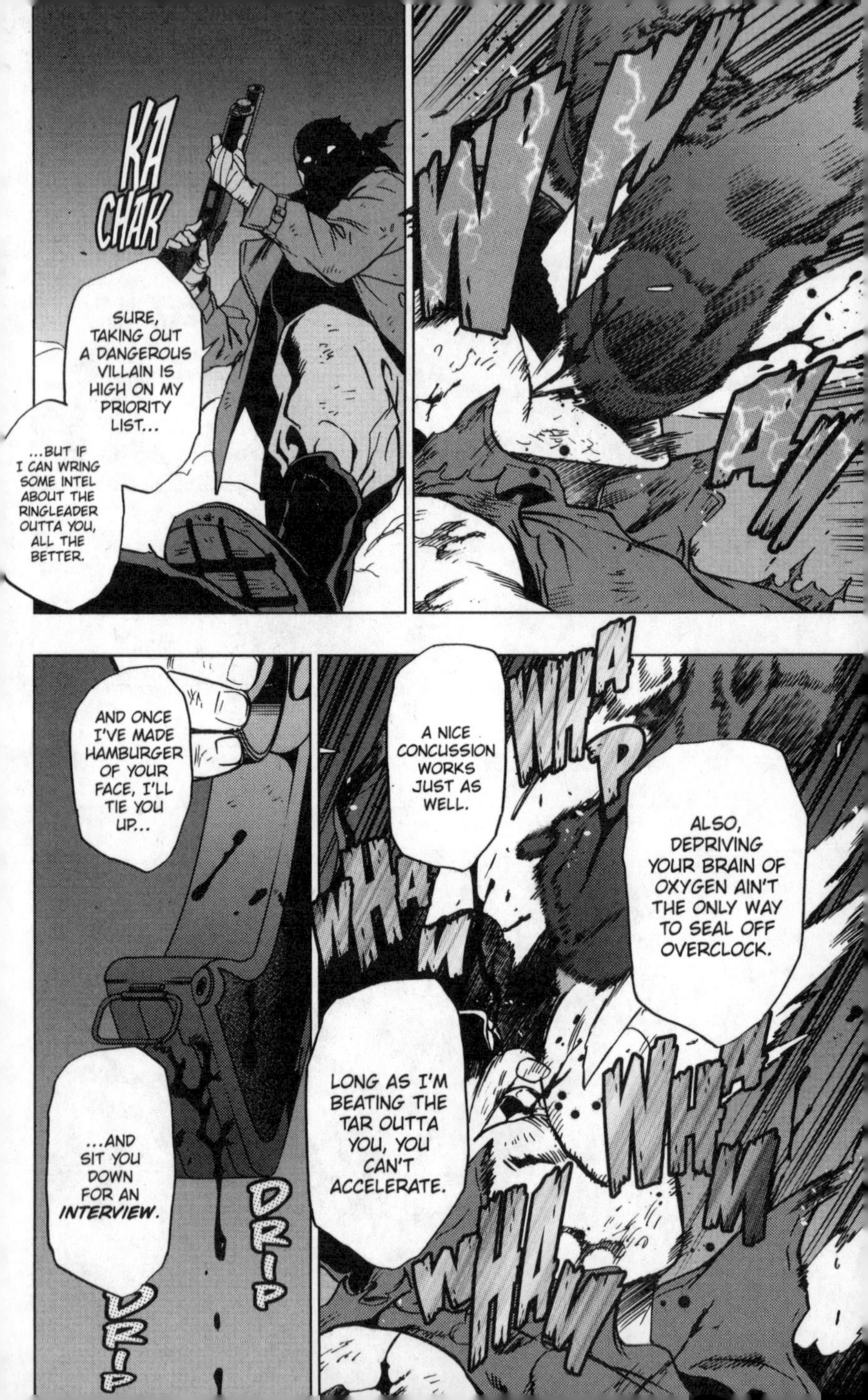
WHAM
KA CHAK
SURE, TAKING OUT A DANGEROUS VILLAIN IS HIGH ON MY PRIORITY LIST...
...BUT IF I CAN WRING SOME INTEL ABOUT THE RINGLEADER OUTTA YOU, ALL THE BETTER.
WHAP
A NICE CONCUSSION WORKS JUST AS WELL.
ALSO, DEPRIVING YOUR BRAIN OF OXYGEN AIN'T THE ONLY WAY TO SEAL OFF OVERCLOCK.
WHAM
LONG AS I'M BEATING THE TAR OUTTA YOU, YOU CAN'T ACCELERATE.
WHAM
AND ONCE I'VE MADE HAMBURGER OF YOUR FACE, I'LL TIE YOU UP...
...AND SIT YOU DOWN FOR AN *INTERVIEW*.
DRIP
DRIP

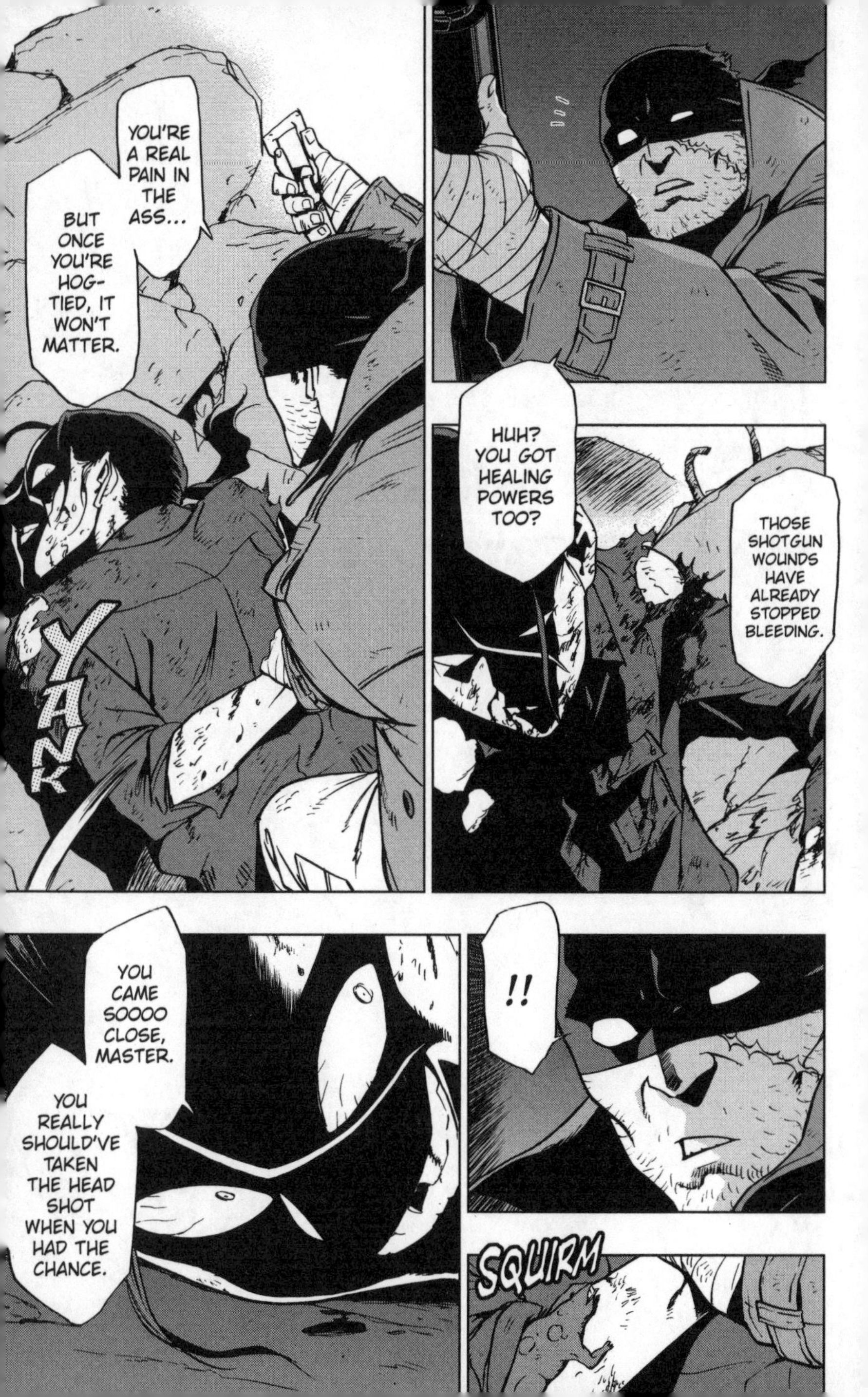
THOSE SHOTGUN WOUNDS HAVE ALREADY STOPPED BLEEDING.
HUH? YOU GOT HEALING POWERS TOO?
YOU'RE A REAL PAIN IN THE ASS...
BUT ONCE YOU'RE HOG-TIED, IT WON'T MATTER.
YANK
!!
SQUIRM
YOU CAME SOOOO CLOSE, MASTER.
YOU REALLY SHOULD'VE TAKEN THE HEAD SHOT WHEN YOU HAD THE CHANCE.

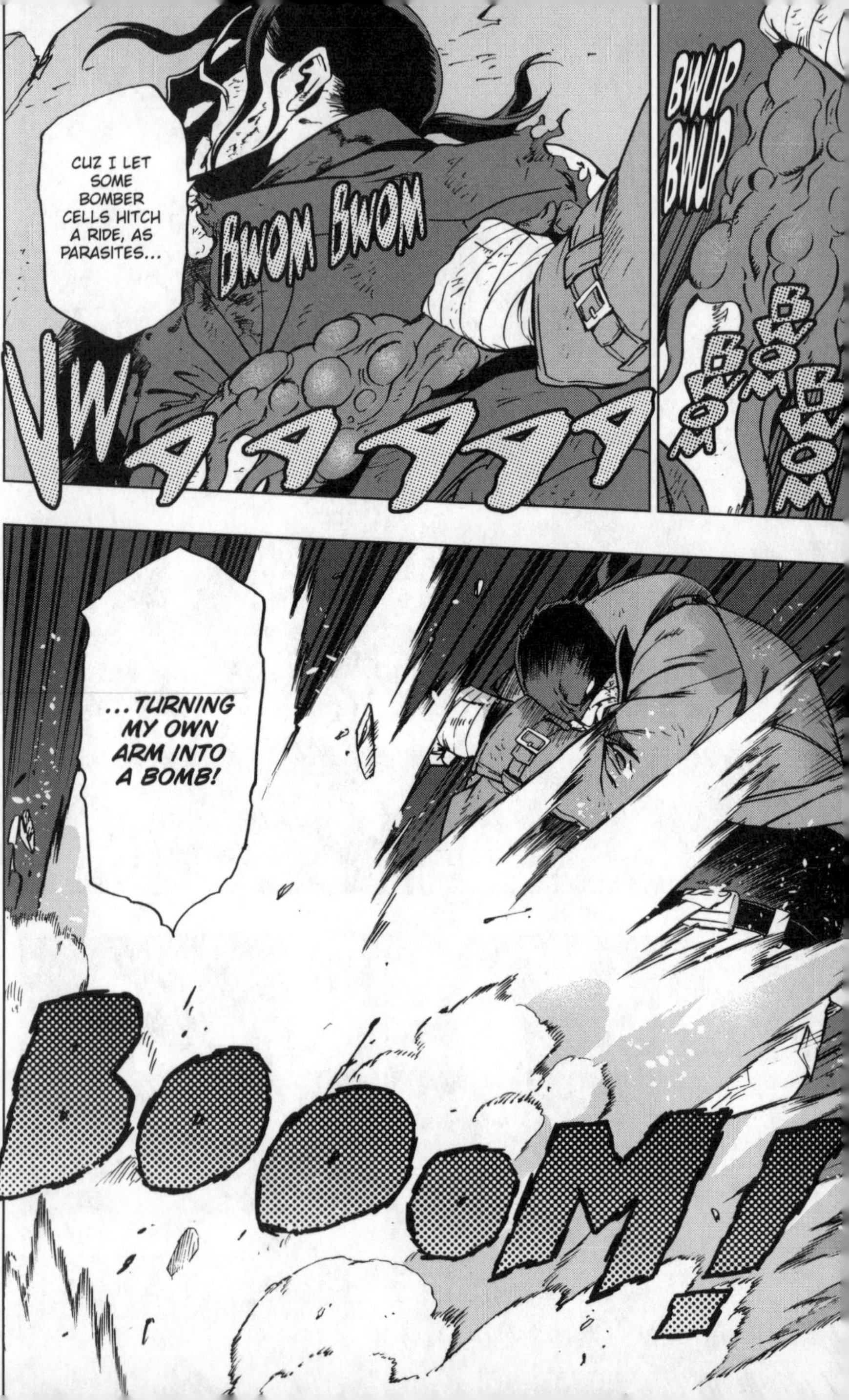
BWUP BWUP
CUZ I LET SOME BOMBER CELLS HITCH A RIDE, AS PARASITES...
BWOM BWOM
VWAAAAA
...TURNING MY OWN ARM INTO A BOMB!
BOOOOM!!

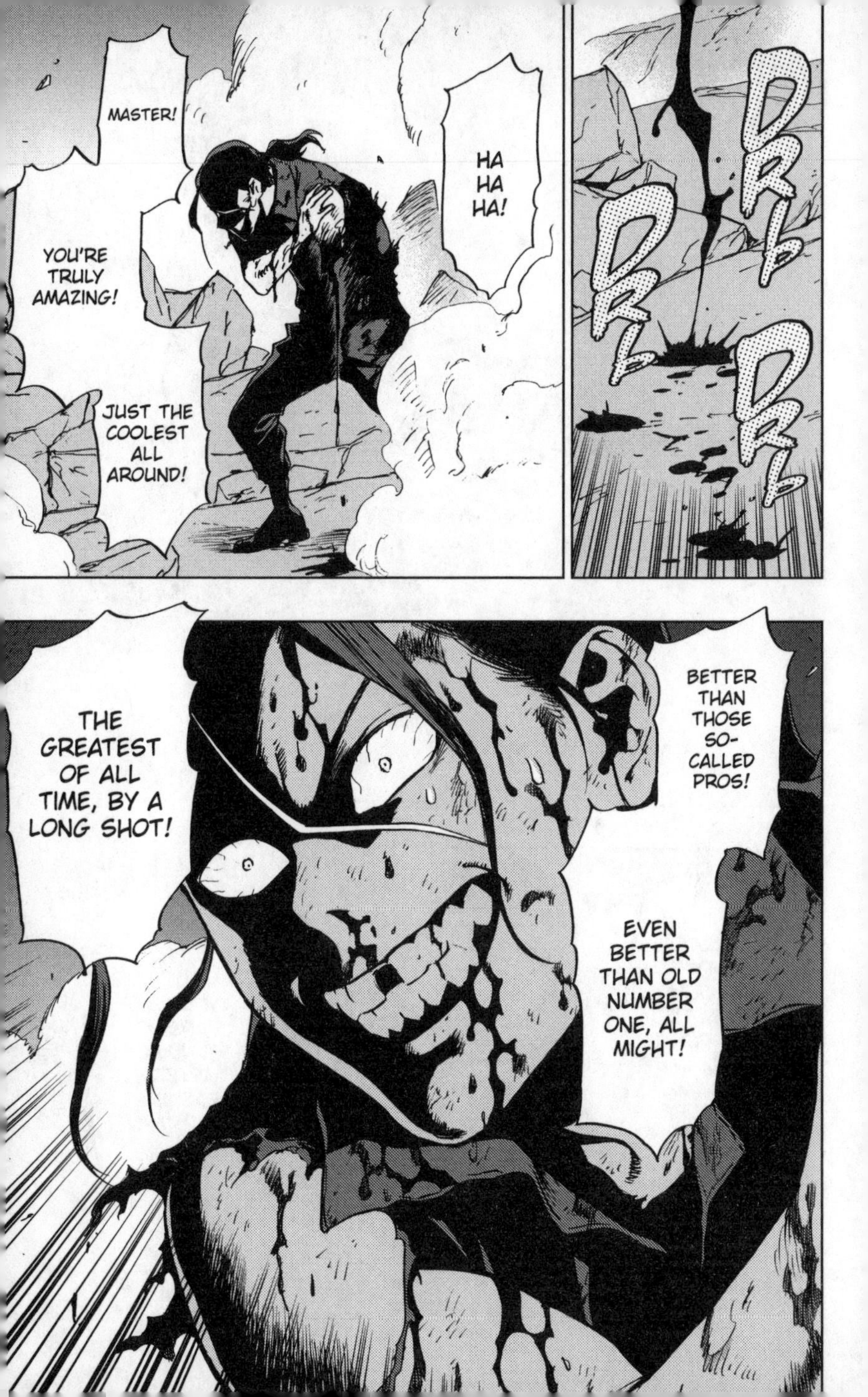
DRB
DRB
HA HA HA!
MASTER!
YOU'RE TRULY AMAZING!
JUST THE COOLEST ALL AROUND!
BETTER THAN THOSE SO-CALLED PROS!
THE GREATEST OF ALL TIME, BY A LONG SHOT!
EVEN BETTER THAN OLD NUMBER ONE, ALL MIGHT!

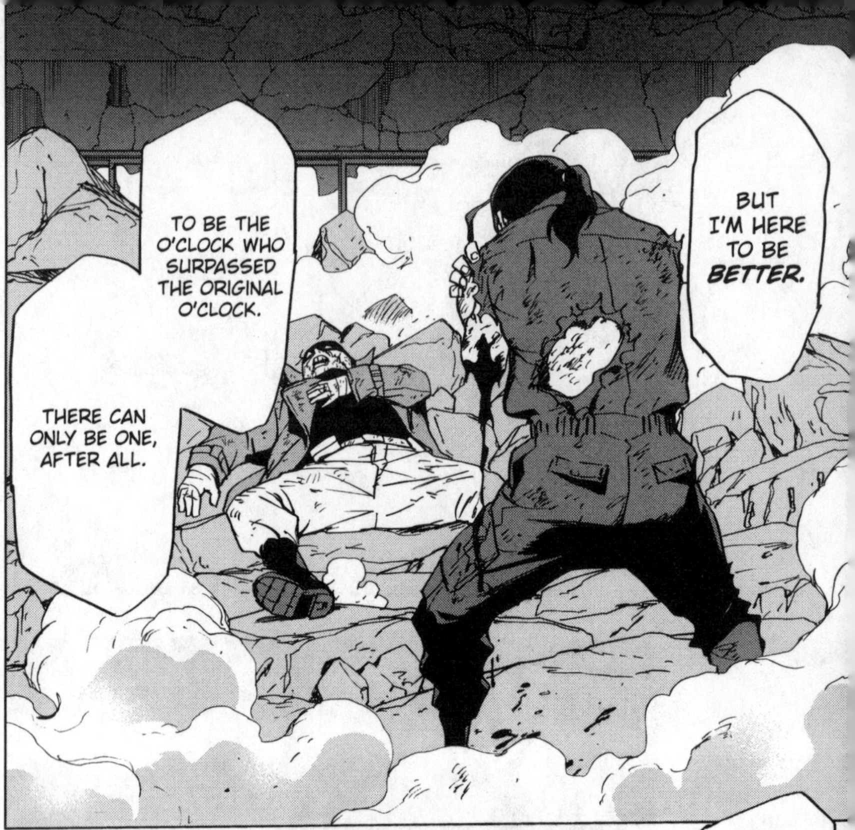
BUT I'M HERE TO BE ***BETTER.***
TO BE THE O'CLOCK WHO SURPASSED THE ORIGINAL O'CLOCK.
THERE CAN ONLY BE ONE, AFTER ALL.
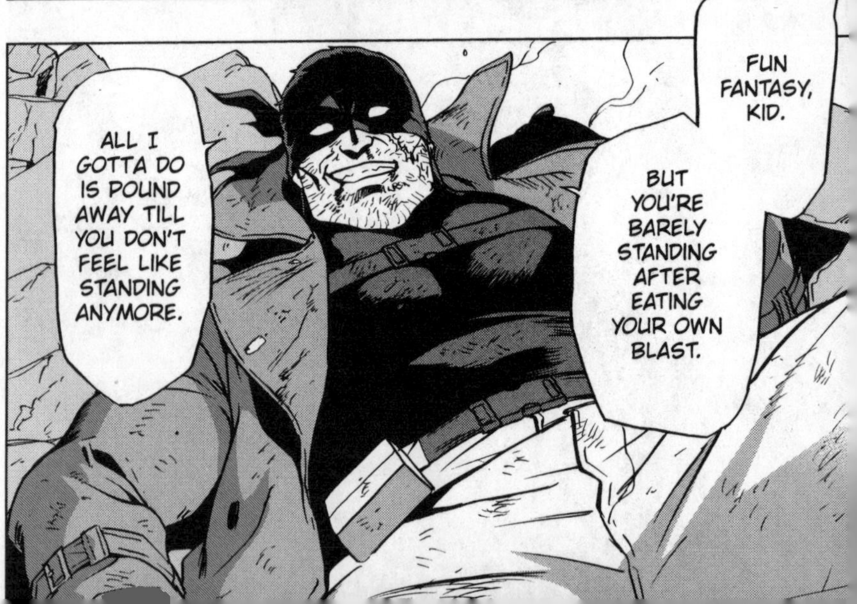
FUN FANTASY, KID.
BUT YOU'RE BARELY STANDING AFTER EATING YOUR OWN BLAST.
ALL I GOTTA DO IS POUND AWAY TILL YOU DON'T FEEL LIKE STANDING ANYMORE.

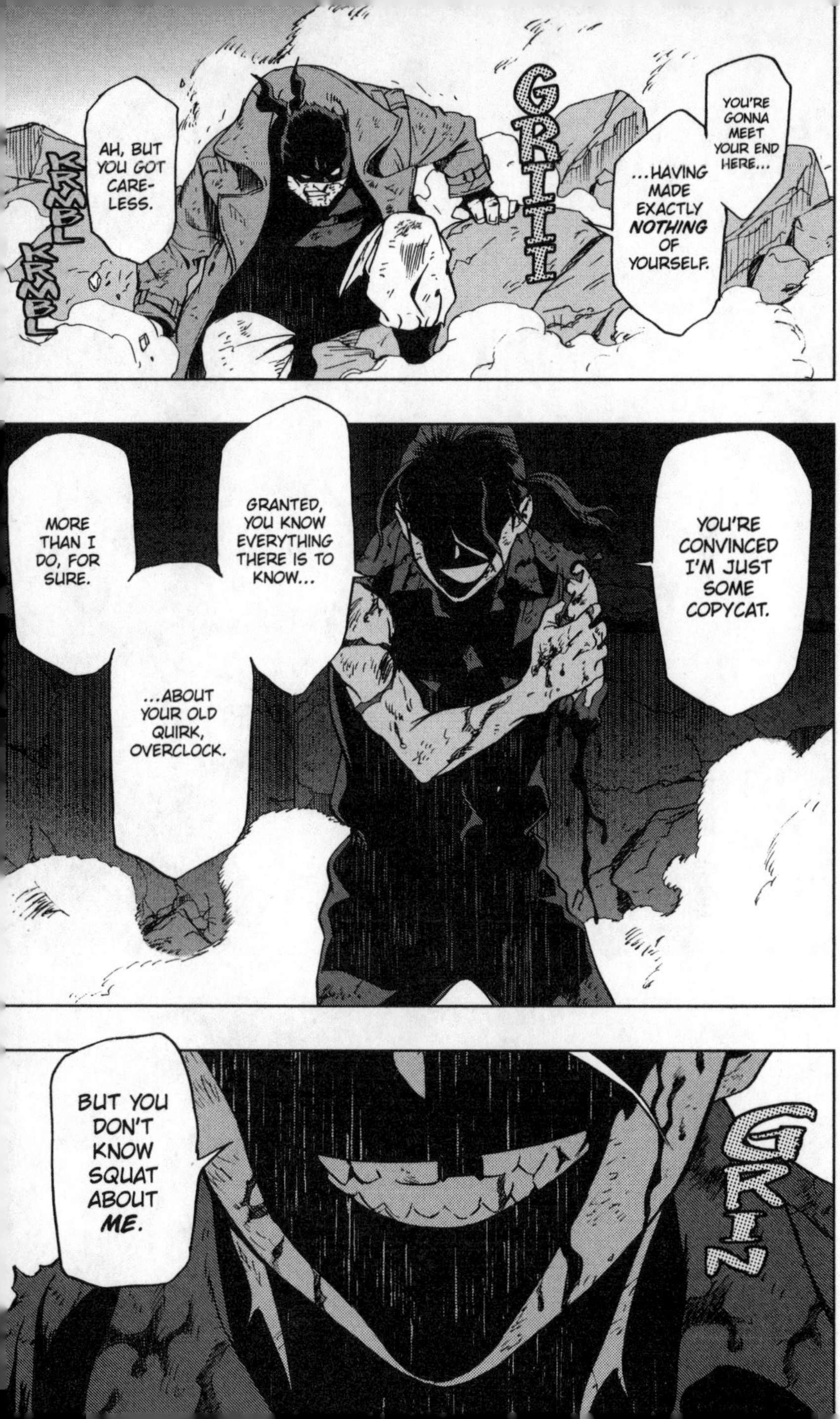
YOU'RE GONNA MEET YOUR END HERE...
...HAVING MADE EXACTLY *NOTHING* OF YOURSELF.
GRIIII
AH, BUT YOU GOT CARE-LESS.
KRMBL KRMBL
YOU'RE CONVINCED I'M JUST SOME COPYCAT.
GRANTED, YOU KNOW EVERYTHING THERE IS TO KNOW...
MORE THAN I DO, FOR SURE.
...ABOUT YOUR OLD QUIRK, OVERCLOCK.
GRIN
BUT YOU DON'T KNOW SQUAT ABOUT *ME*.

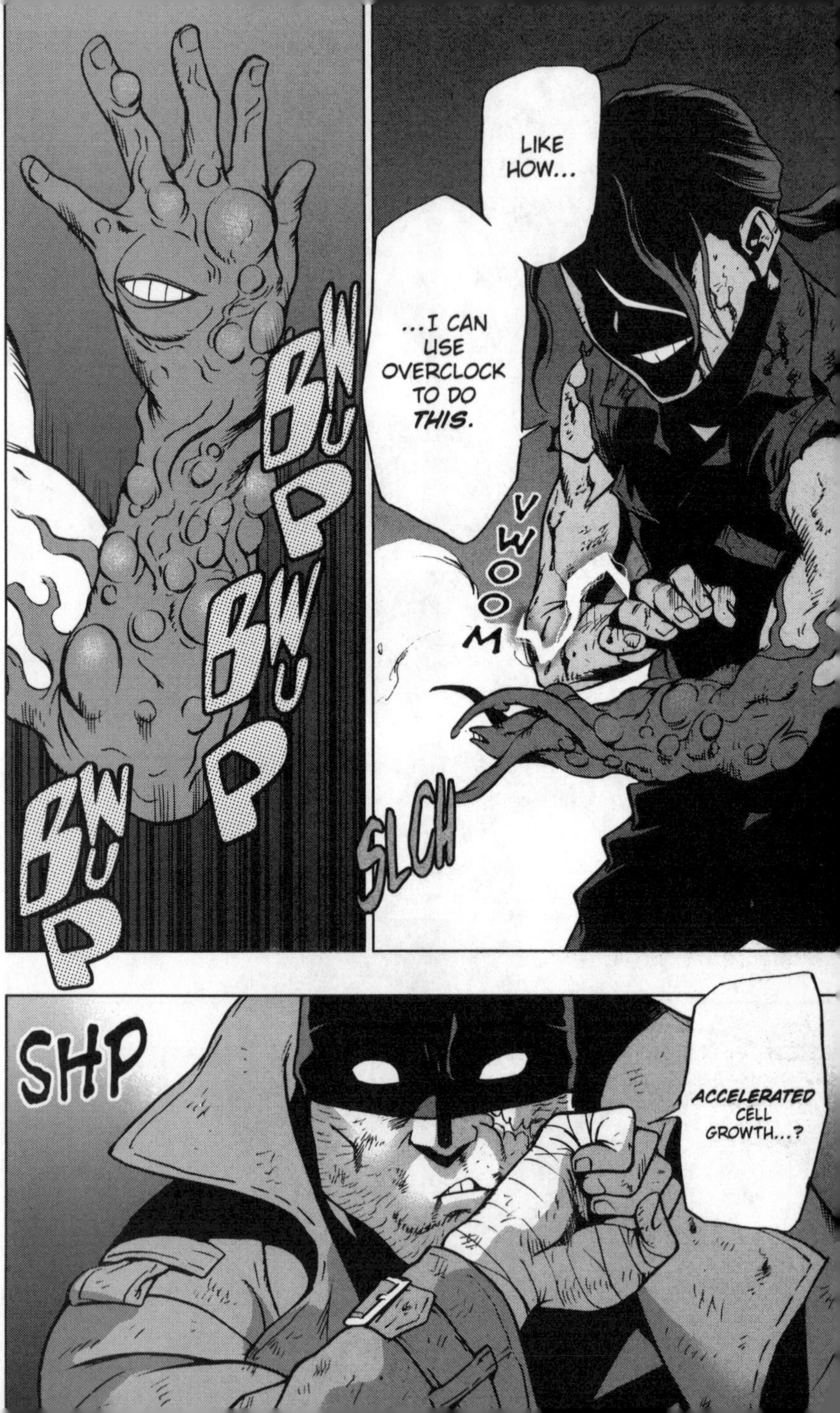
LIKE HOW...
...I CAN USE OVERCLOCK TO DO *THIS*.
VWOOOM
SLCH
BWUP
BWUP
BWUP
ACCELERATED CELL GROWTH...?
SHP

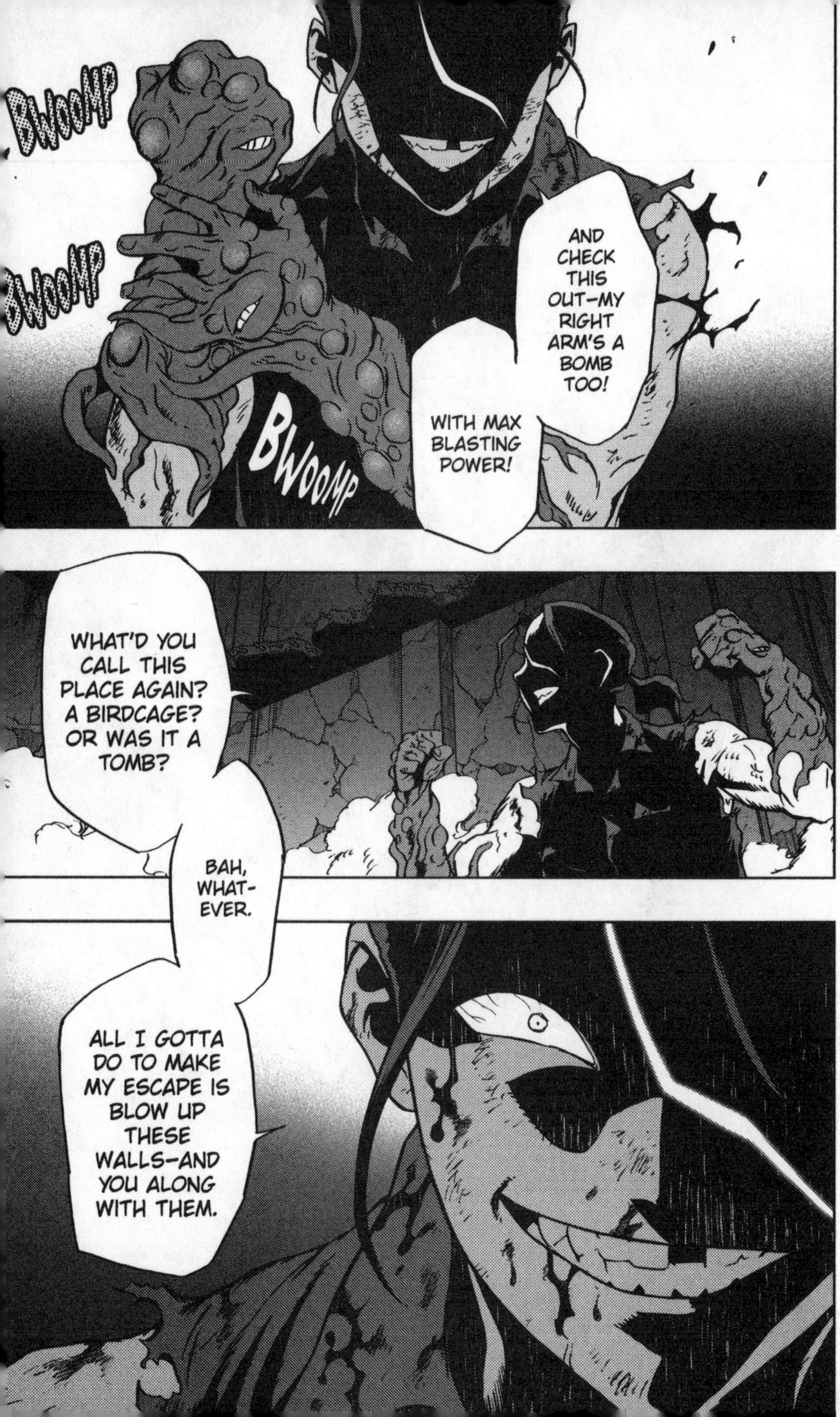
AND CHECK THIS OUT—MY RIGHT ARM'S A BOMB TOO!
WITH MAX BLASTING POWER!
BWOOMP
BWOOMP
BWOOMP
WHAT'D YOU CALL THIS PLACE AGAIN? A BIRDCAGE? OR WAS IT A TOMB?
BAH, WHAT-EVER.
ALL I GOTTA DO TO MAKE MY ESCAPE IS BLOW UP THESE WALLS—AND YOU ALONG WITH THEM.

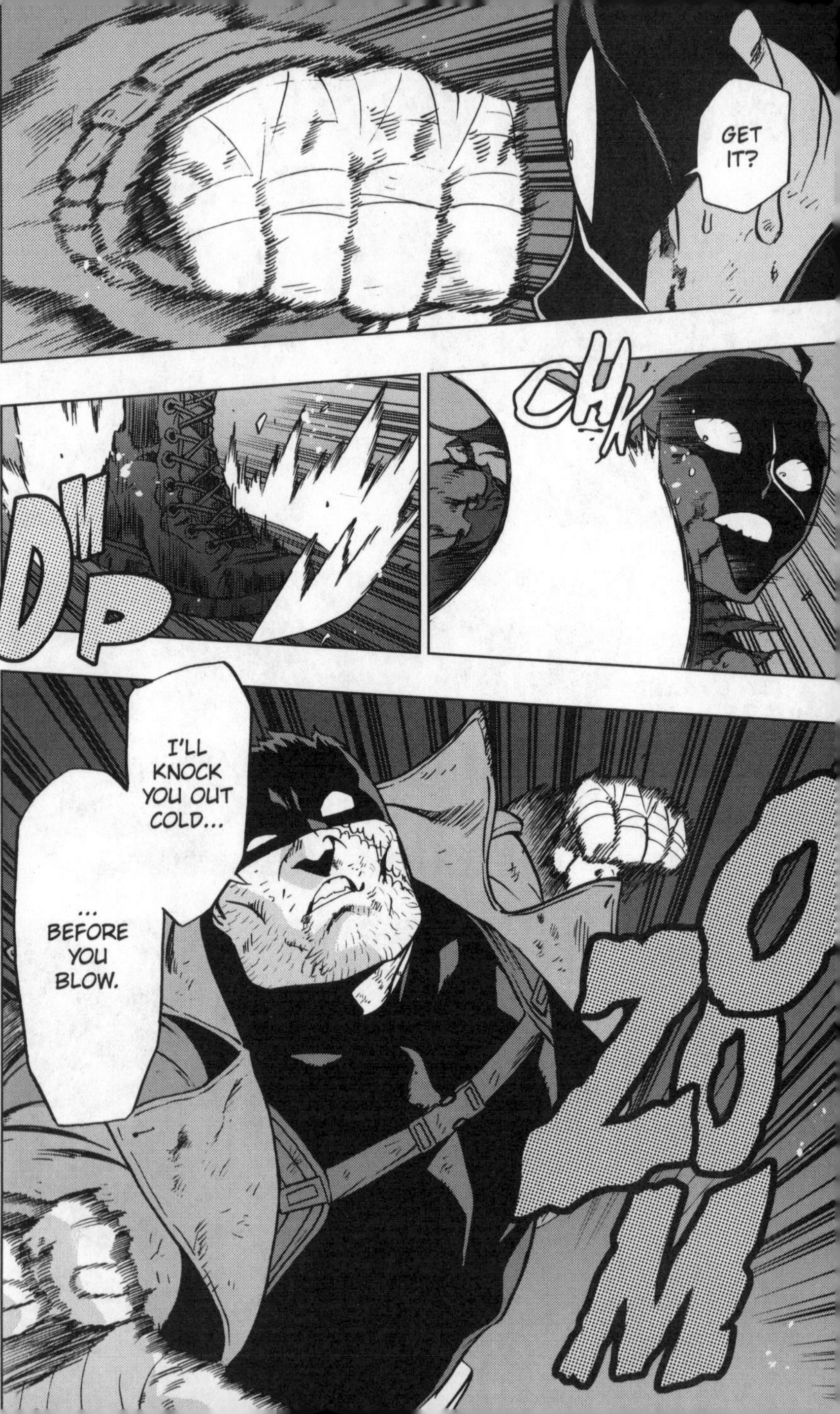
GET IT?
CHK
I'LL KNOCK YOU OUT COLD...
... BEFORE YOU BLOW.
ZOOM

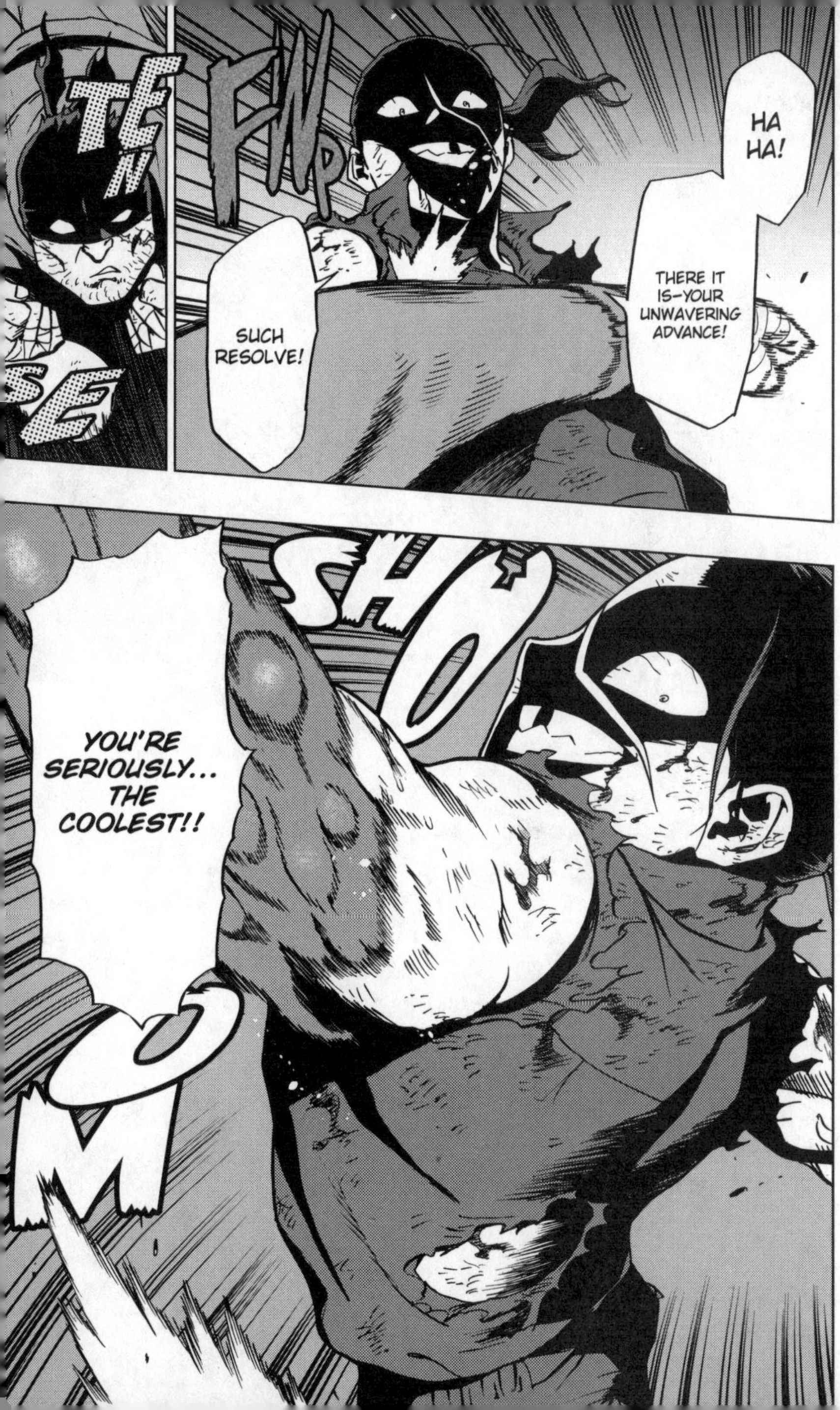
HA HA!
THERE IT IS—YOUR UNWAVERING ADVANCE!
SUCH RESOLVE!
YOU'RE SERIOUSLY... THE COOLEST!!

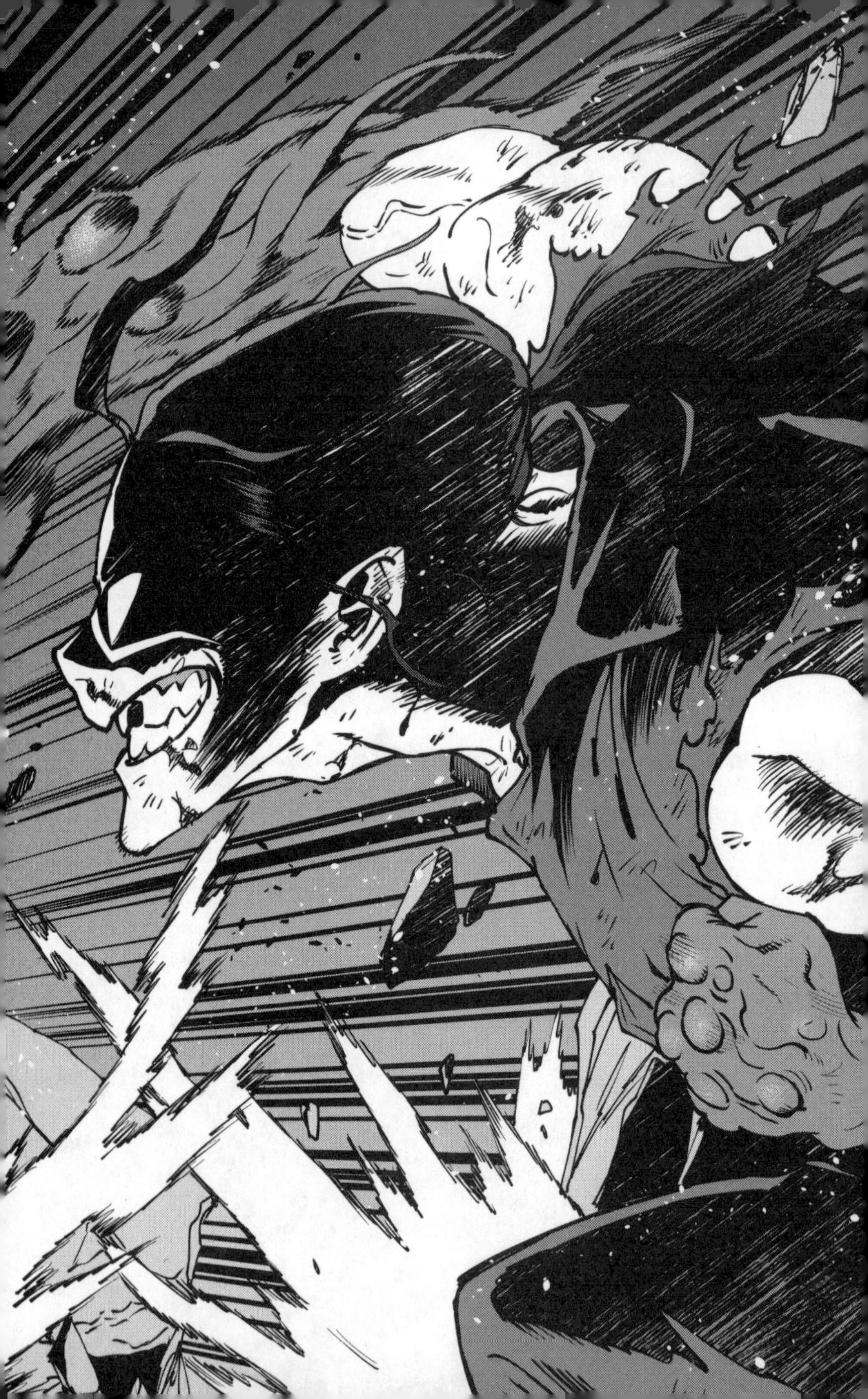

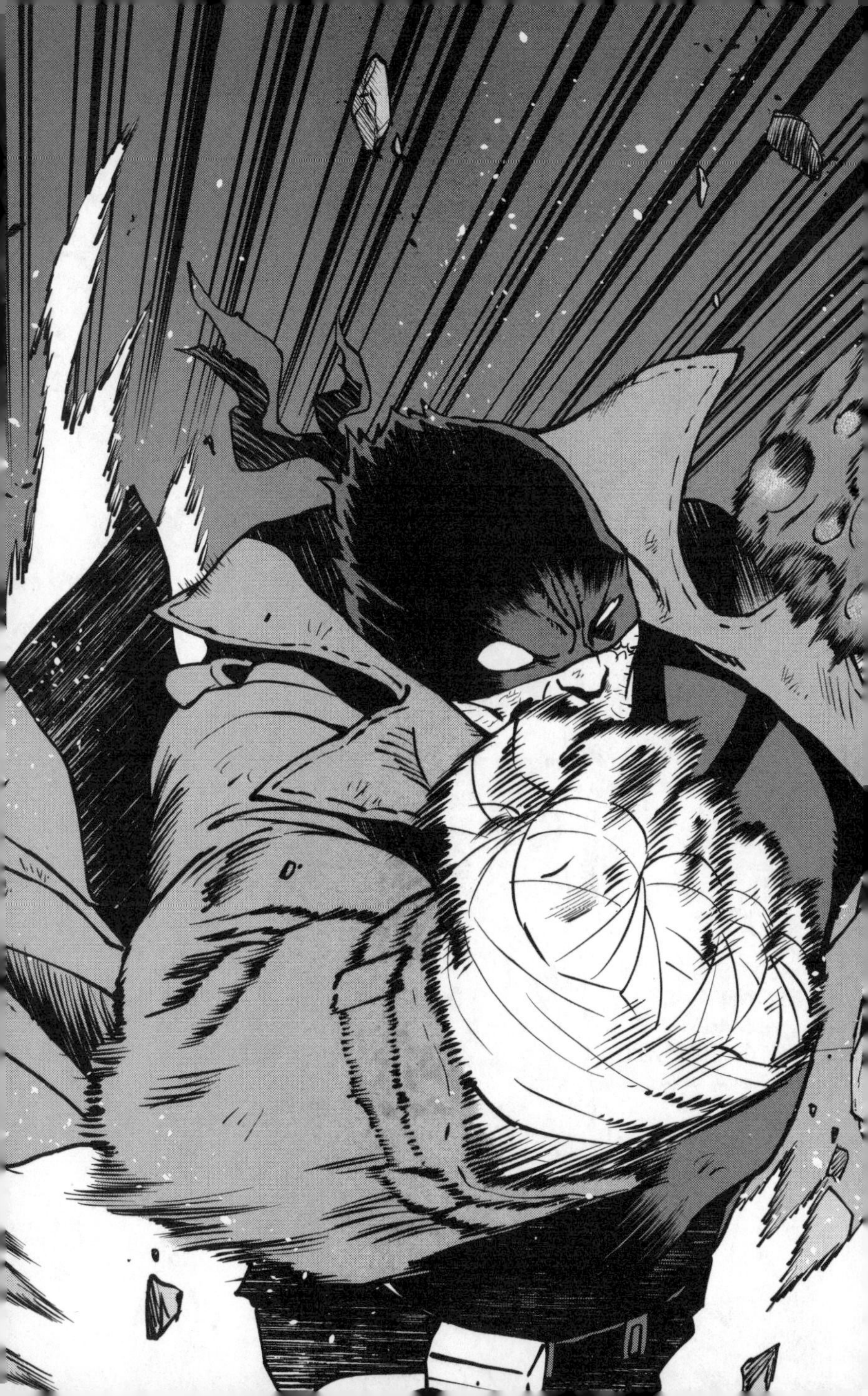

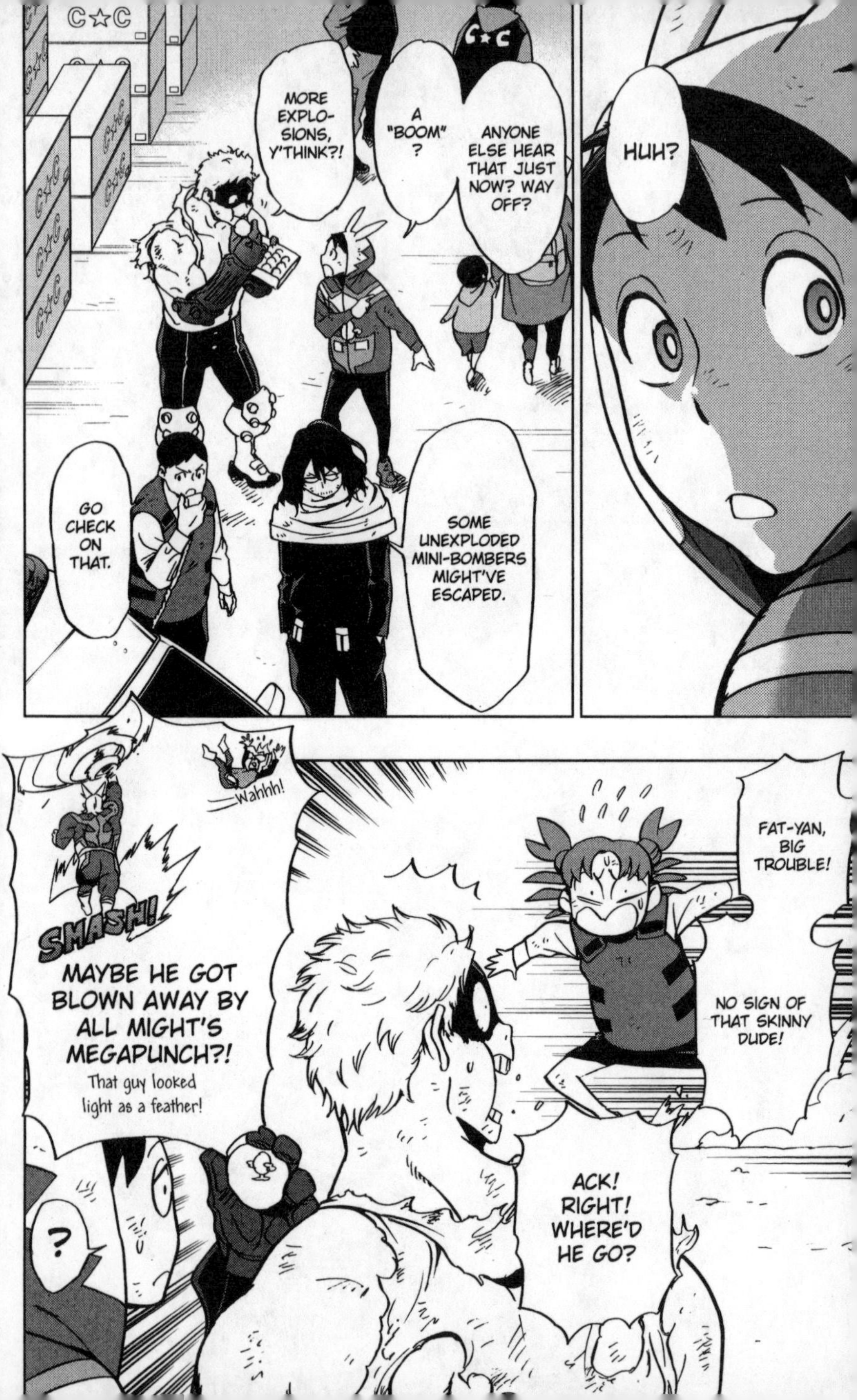
HUH?
C☆C
ANYONE ELSE HEAR THAT JUST NOW? WAY OFF?
A "BOOM"?
MORE EXPLOSIONS, Y'THINK?!
SOME UNEXPLODED MINI-BOMBERS MIGHT'VE ESCAPED.
GO CHECK ON THAT.
FAT-YAN, BIG TROUBLE!
NO SIGN OF THAT SKINNY DUDE!
ACK! RIGHT! WHERE'D HE GO?
Wahhh!
SMASH!
MAYBE HE GOT BLOWN AWAY BY ALL MIGHT'S MEGAPUNCH?!
That guy looked light as a feather!
?

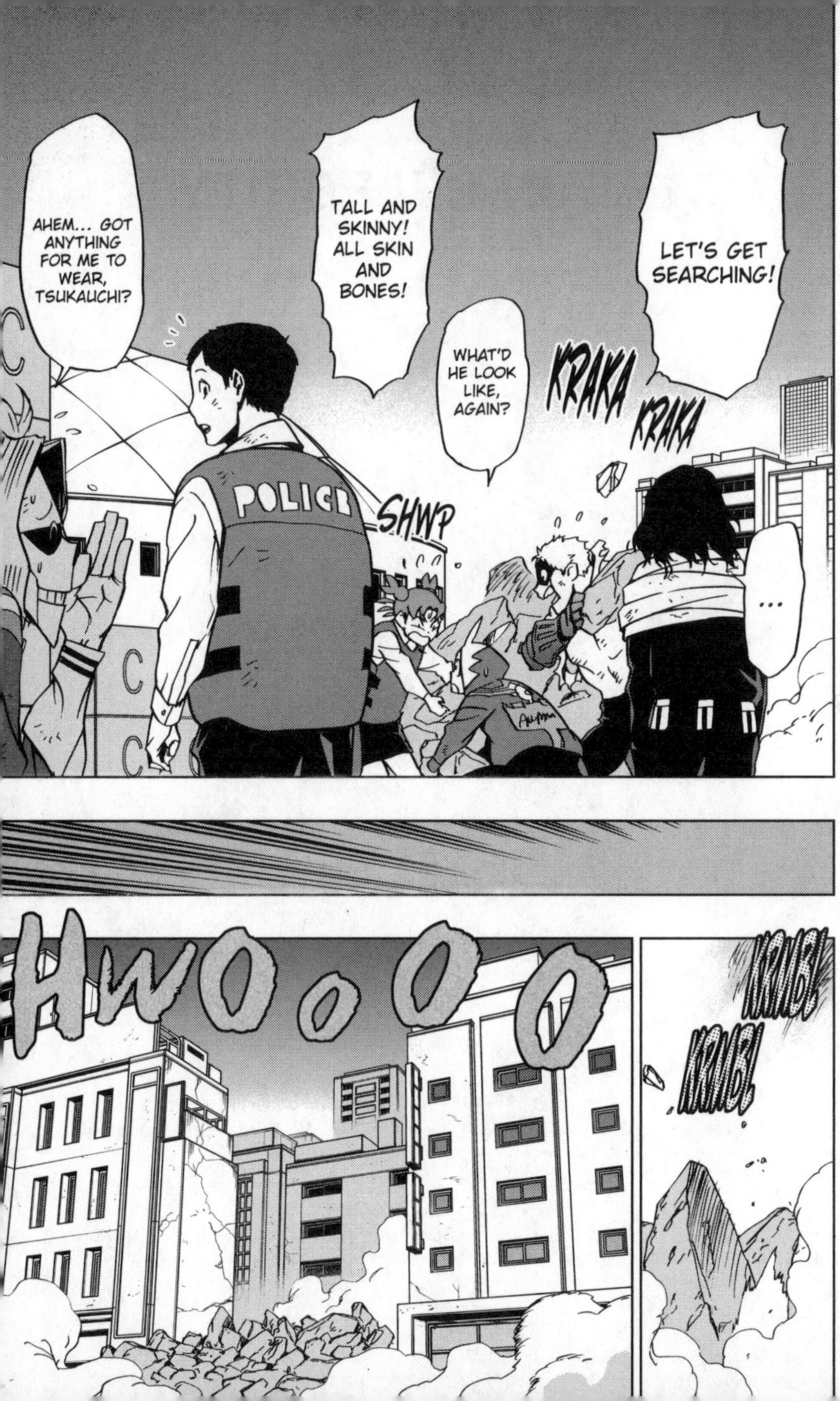
LET'S GET SEARCHING!
KRAKA KRAKA
...
WHAT'D HE LOOK LIKE, AGAIN?
TALL AND SKINNY! ALL SKIN AND BONES!
SHWP
AHEM... GOT ANYTHING FOR ME TO WEAR, TSUKAUCHI?
POLICE
KRMBL! KRMBL!
HWOOOO

THE COLUMN

CAPTAIN CELEBRITY

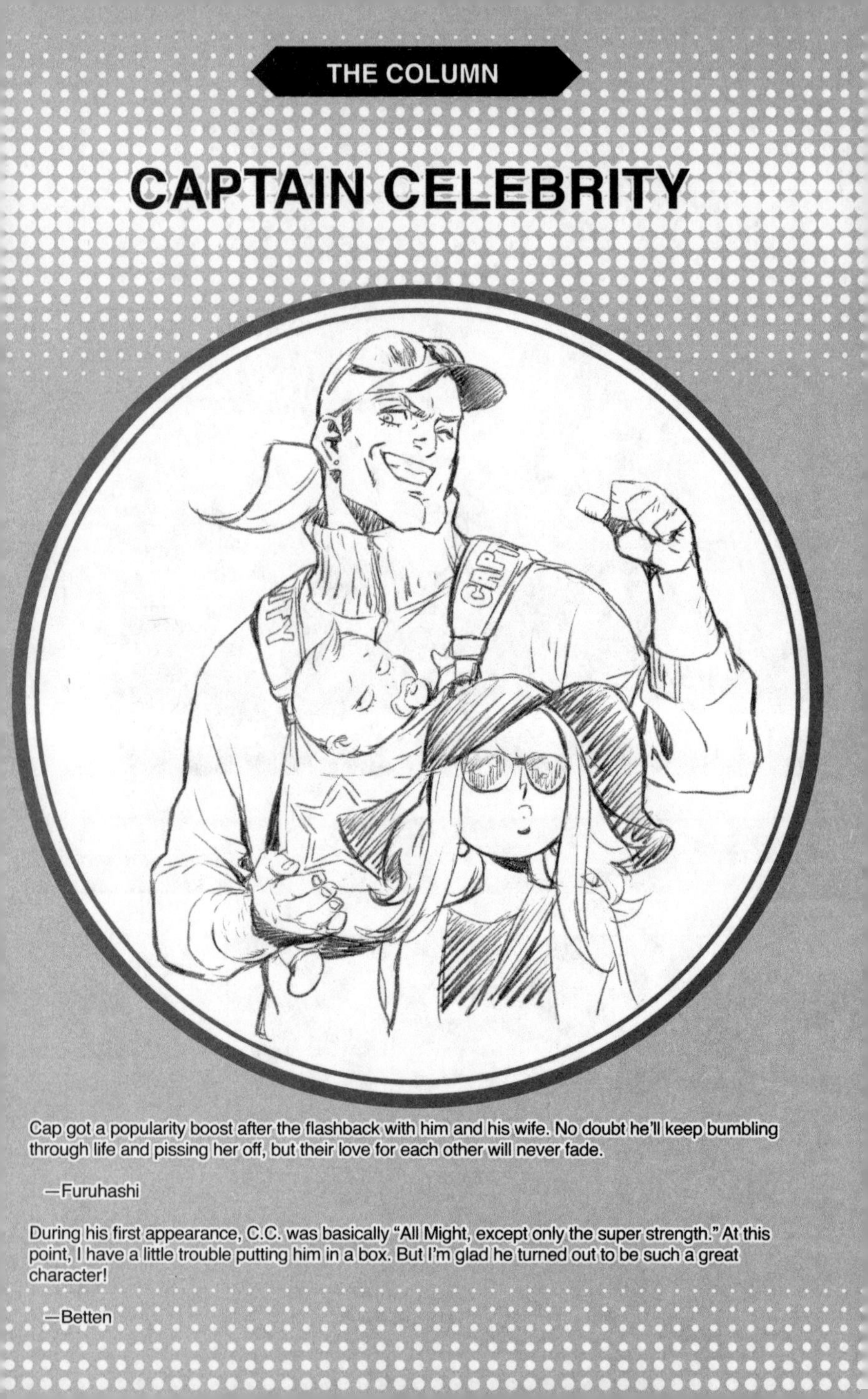
CAPT
ITY

Cap got a popularity boost after the flashback with him and his wife. No doubt he'll keep bumbling through life and pissing her off, but their love for each other will never fade.

—Furuhashi

During his first appearance, C.C. was basically "All Might, except only the super strength." At this point, I have a little trouble putting him in a box. But I'm glad he turned out to be such a great character!

—Betten

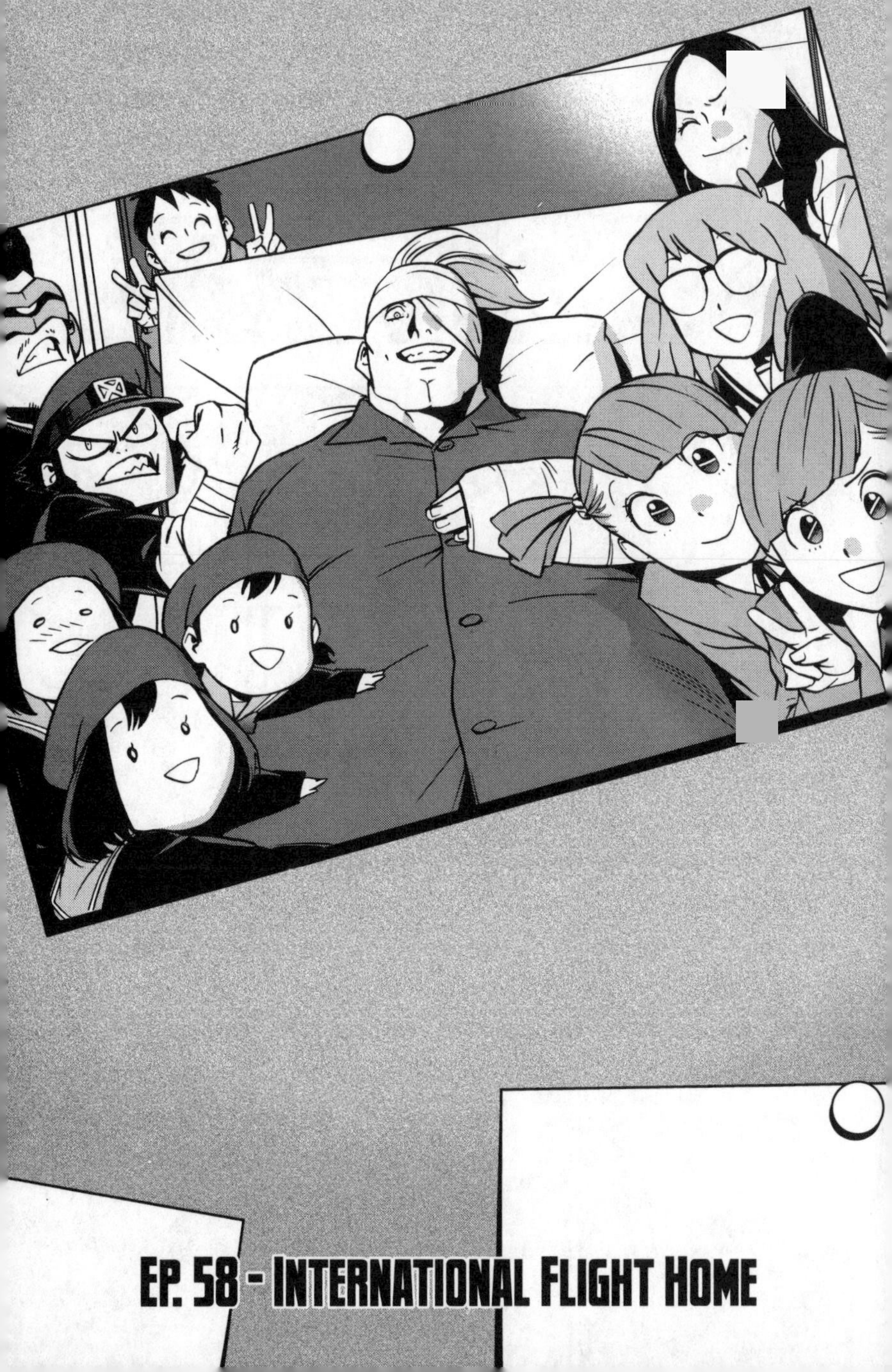

EP. 58 - INTERNATIONAL FLIGHT HOME

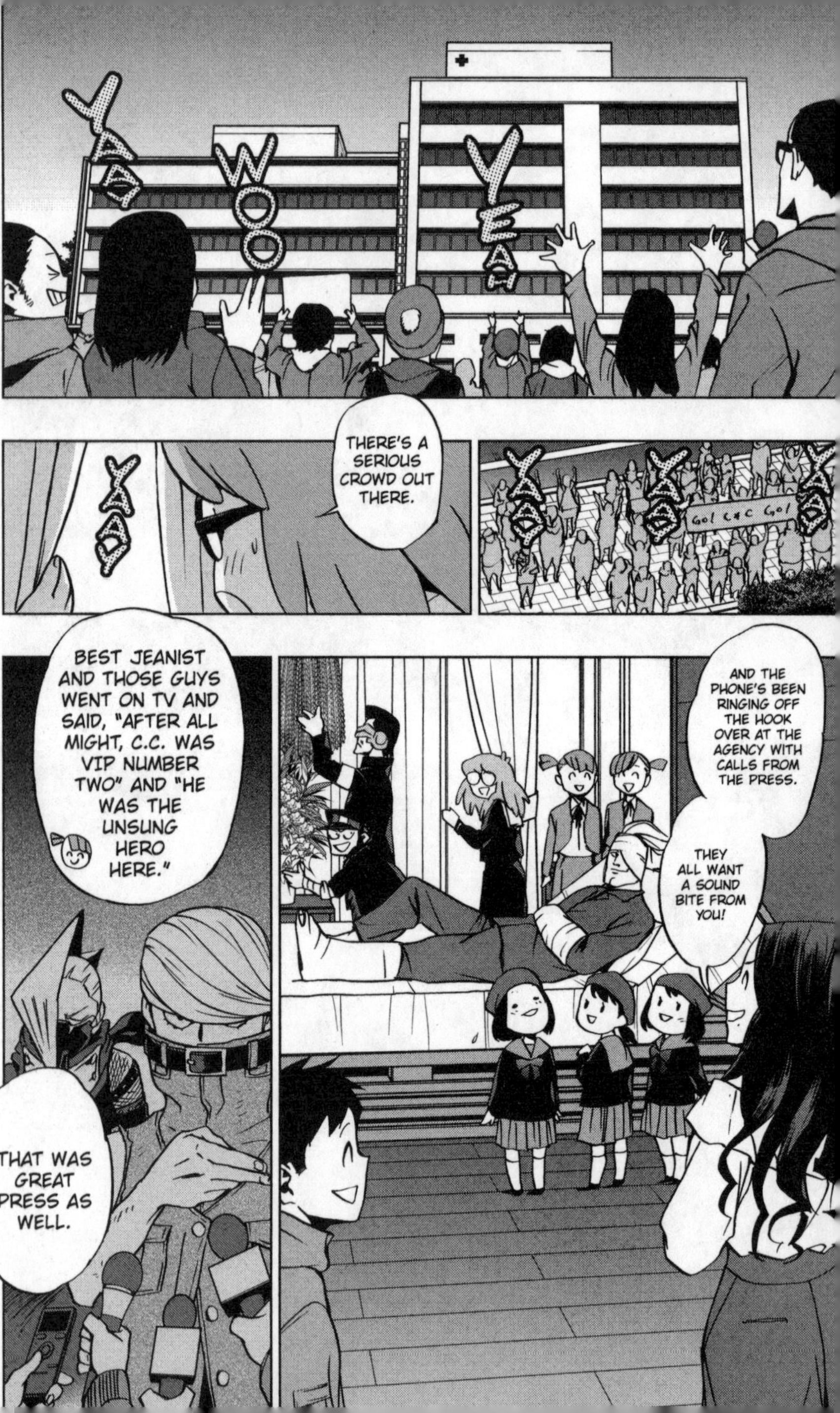
YEAH
WOO
YAY
YAY
YAY
YAY
GO! C&C GO!
THERE'S A SERIOUS CROWD OUT THERE.
YAY
AND THE PHONE'S BEEN RINGING OFF THE HOOK OVER AT THE AGENCY WITH CALLS FROM THE PRESS.
THEY ALL WANT A SOUND BITE FROM YOU!
BEST JEANIST AND THOSE GUYS WENT ON TV AND SAID, "AFTER ALL MIGHT, C.C. WAS VIP NUMBER TWO" AND "HE WAS THE UNSUNG HERO HERE."
THAT WAS GREAT PRESS AS WELL.

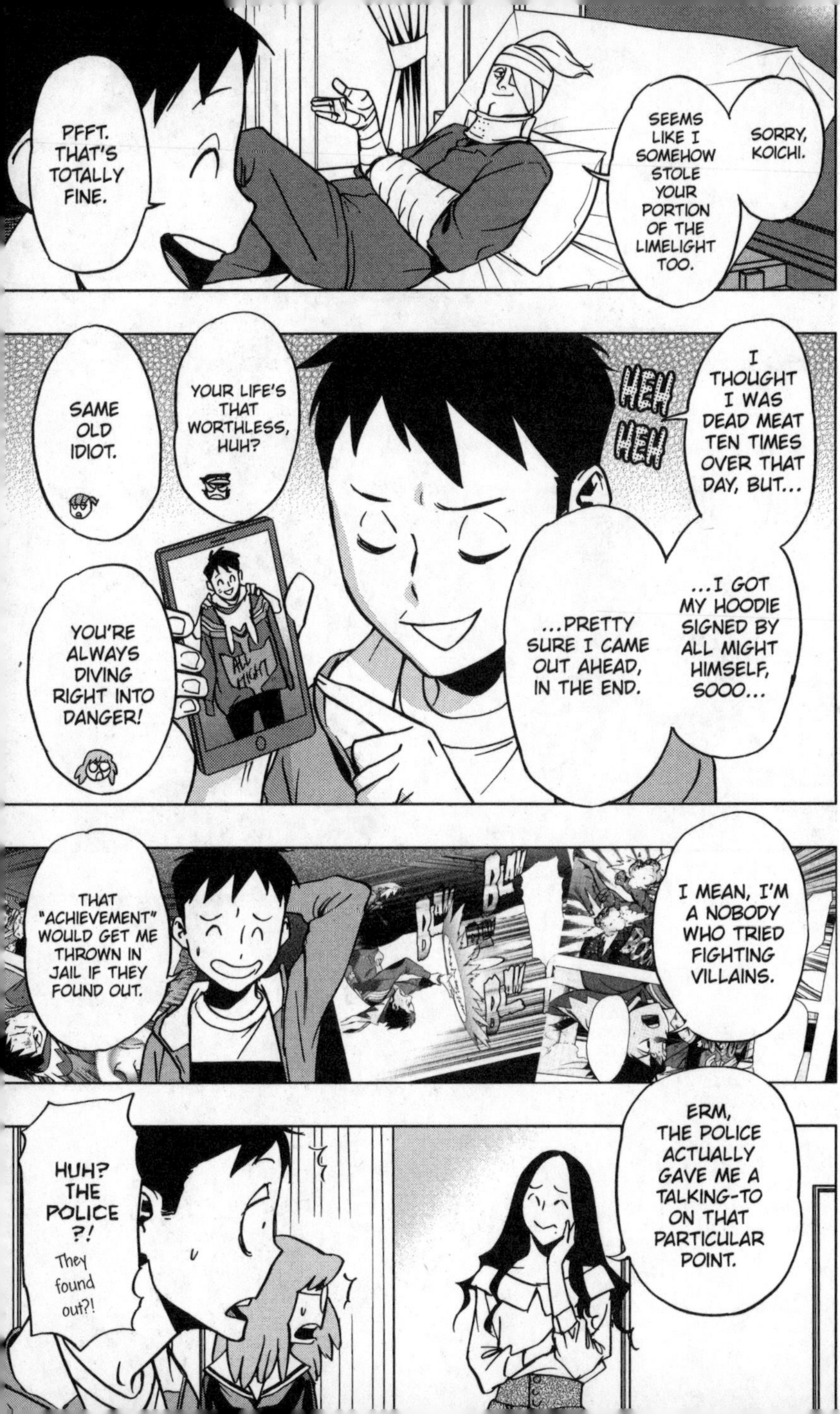
SORRY, KOICHI.
SEEMS LIKE I SOMEHOW STOLE YOUR PORTION OF THE LIMELIGHT TOO.
PFFT. THAT'S TOTALLY FINE.
I THOUGHT I WAS DEAD MEAT TEN TIMES OVER THAT DAY, BUT...
HEH HEH
...I GOT MY HOODIE SIGNED BY ALL MIGHT HIMSELF, SOOO...
...PRETTY SURE I CAME OUT AHEAD, IN THE END.
YOUR LIFE'S THAT WORTHLESS, HUH?
SAME OLD IDIOT.
ALL MIGHT
YOU'RE ALWAYS DIVING RIGHT INTO DANGER!
I MEAN, I'M A NOBODY WHO TRIED FIGHTING VILLAINS.
THAT "ACHIEVEMENT" WOULD GET ME THROWN IN JAIL IF THEY FOUND OUT.
ERM, THE POLICE ACTUALLY GAVE ME A TALKING-TO ON THAT PARTICULAR POINT.
HUH? THE POLICE?!
They found out?!

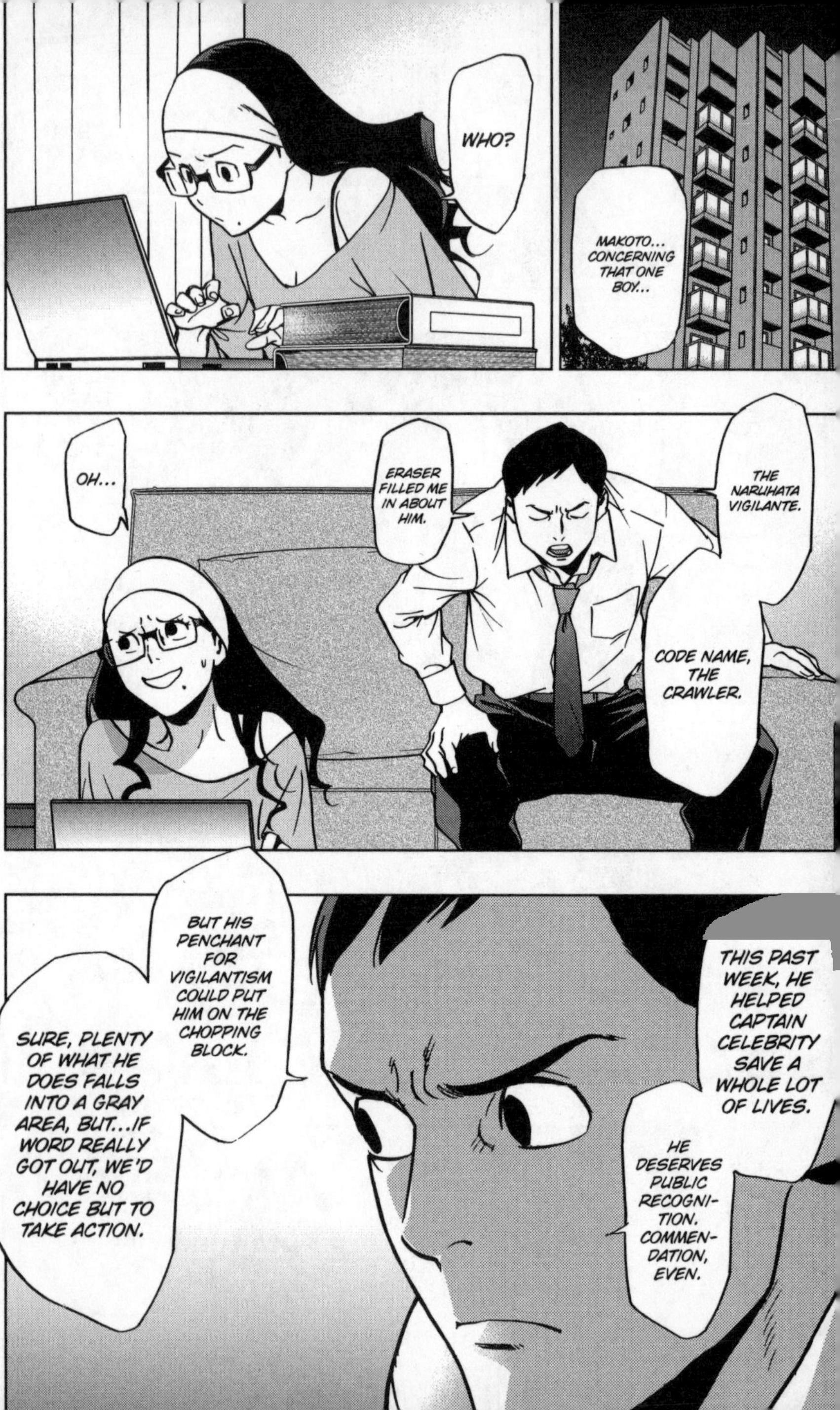
MAKOTO... CONCERNING THAT ONE BOY...
WHO?
THE NARUHATA VIGILANTE.
CODE NAME, THE CRAWLER.
ERASER FILLED ME IN ABOUT HIM.
OH...
THIS PAST WEEK, HE HELPED CAPTAIN CELEBRITY SAVE A WHOLE LOT OF LIVES.
HE DESERVES PUBLIC RECOGNITION. COMMENDATION, EVEN.
BUT HIS PENCHANT FOR VIGILANTISM COULD PUT HIM ON THE CHOPPING BLOCK.
SURE, PLENTY OF WHAT HE DOES FALLS INTO A GRAY AREA, BUT...IF WORD REALLY GOT OUT, WE'D HAVE NO CHOICE BUT TO TAKE ACTION.

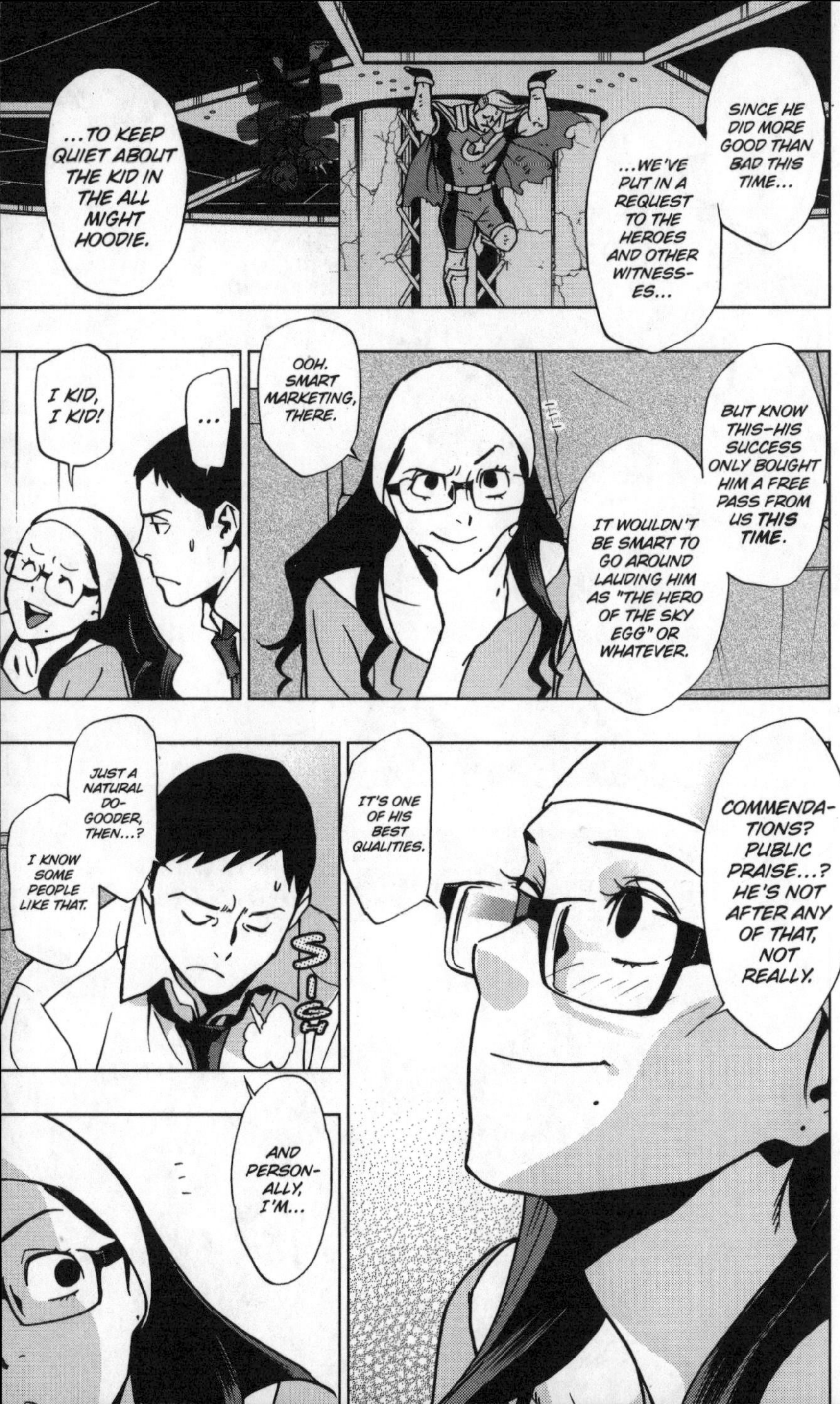
SINCE HE DID MORE GOOD THAN BAD THIS TIME...
...WE'VE PUT IN A REQUEST TO THE HEROES AND OTHER WITNESSES...
...TO KEEP QUIET ABOUT THE KID IN THE ALL MIGHT HOODIE.
BUT KNOW THIS—HIS SUCCESS ONLY BOUGHT HIM A FREE PASS FROM US THIS TIME.
IT WOULDN'T BE SMART TO GO AROUND LAUDING HIM AS "THE HERO OF THE SKY EGG" OR WHATEVER.
OOH. SMART MARKETING, THERE.
...
I KID, I KID!
COMMENDATIONS? PUBLIC PRAISE...? HE'S NOT AFTER ANY OF THAT, NOT REALLY.
IT'S ONE OF HIS BEST QUALITIES.
JUST A NATURAL DO-GOODER, THEN...?
I KNOW SOME PEOPLE LIKE THAT.
SIGH
AND PERSONALLY, I'M...

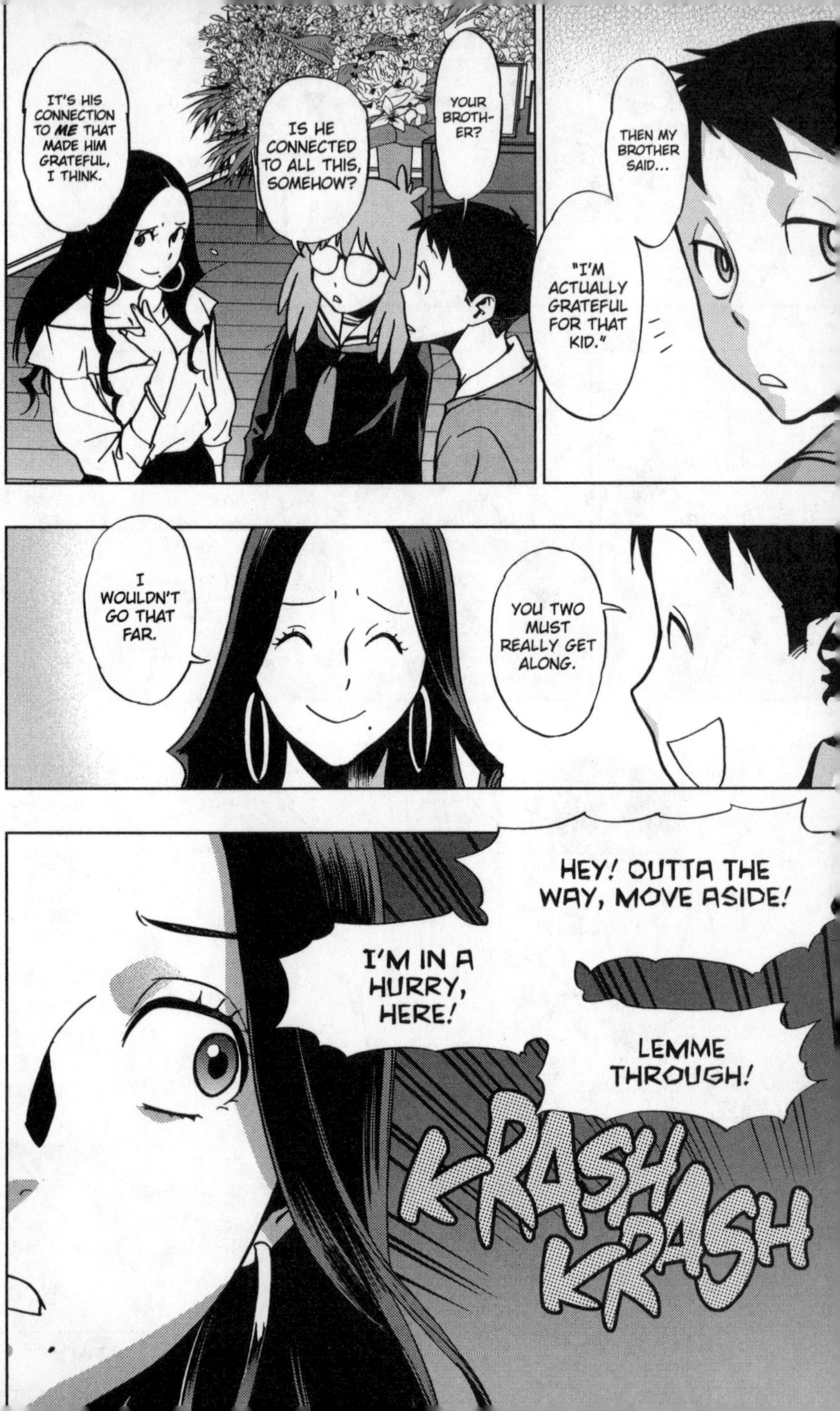
THEN MY BROTHER SAID...
"I'M ACTUALLY GRATEFUL FOR THAT KID."
YOUR BROTH-ER?
IS HE CONNECTED TO ALL THIS, SOMEHOW?
IT'S HIS CONNECTION TO ME THAT MADE HIM GRATEFUL, I THINK.
YOU TWO MUST REALLY GET ALONG.
I WOULDN'T GO THAT FAR.
HEY! OUTTA THE WAY, MOVE ASIDE!
I'M IN A HURRY, HERE!
LEMME THROUGH!
KRASH KRASH

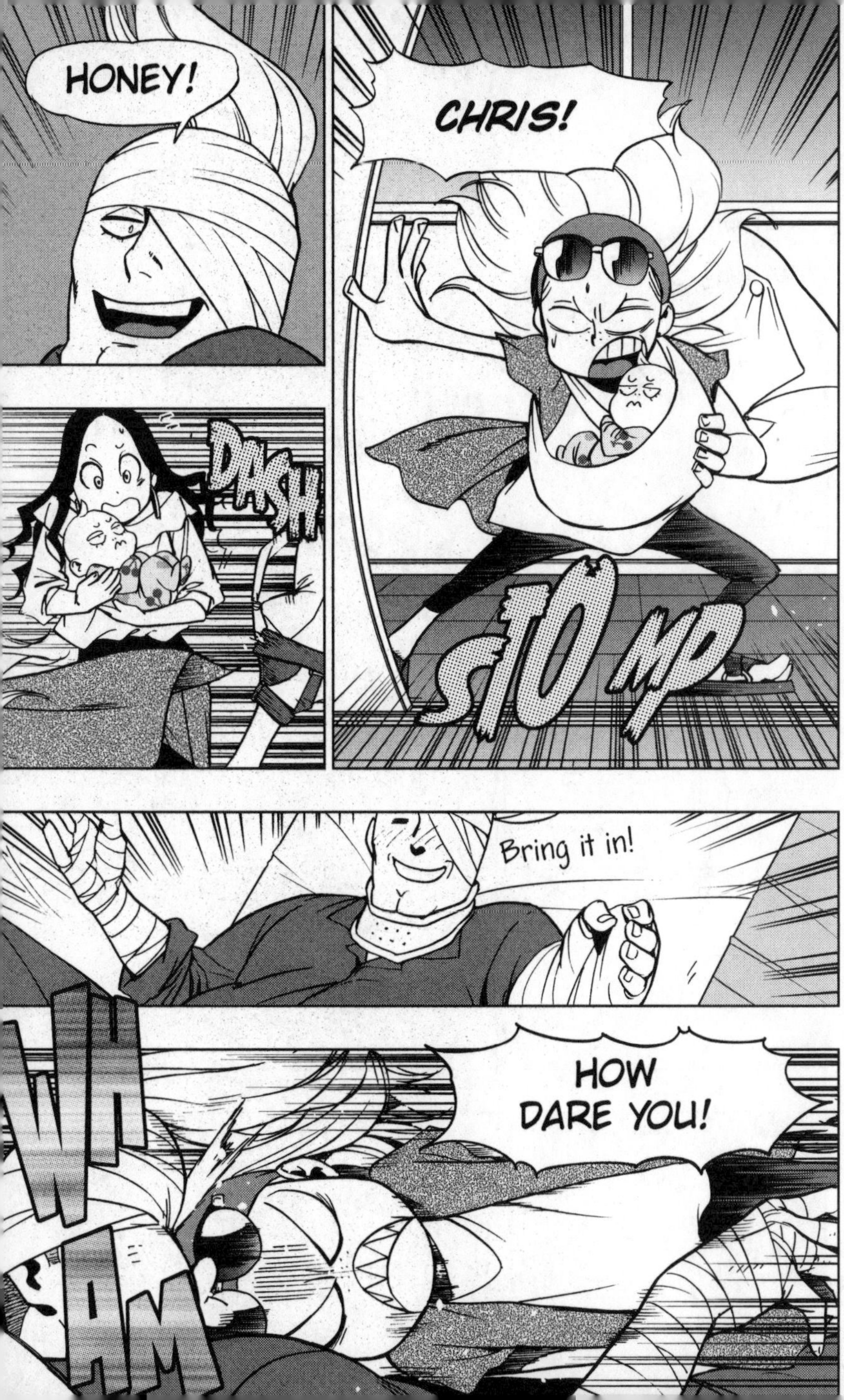
CHRIS!
STOMP
HONEY!
DASH
Bring it in!
HOW DARE YOU!
WHAM

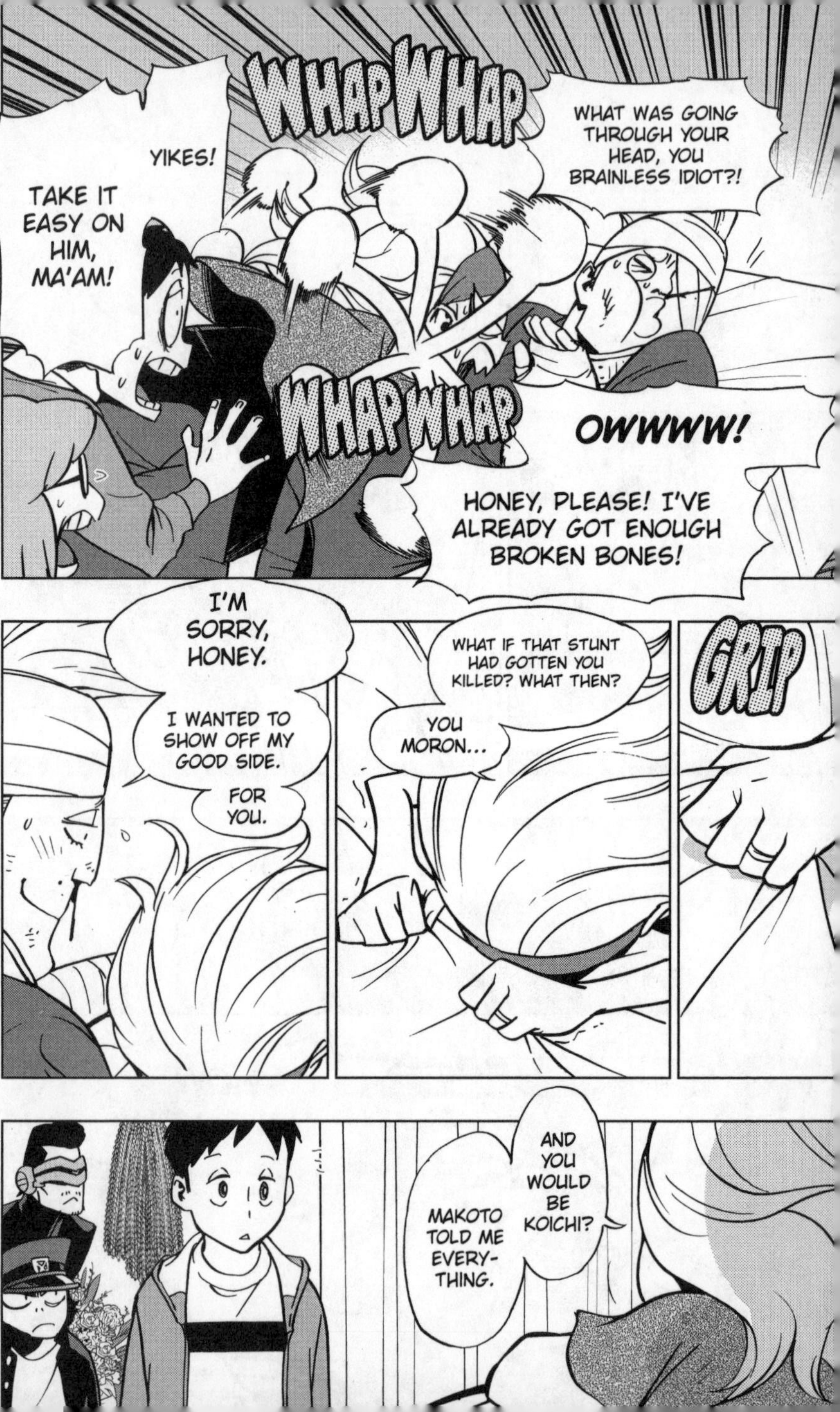
WHAT WAS GOING THROUGH YOUR HEAD, YOU BRAINLESS IDIOT?!
WHAP WHAP
YIKES!
TAKE IT EASY ON HIM, MA'AM!
OWWWW!
HONEY, PLEASE! I'VE ALREADY GOT ENOUGH BROKEN BONES!
WHAP WHAP
GRIP
WHAT IF THAT STUNT HAD GOTTEN YOU KILLED? WHAT THEN?
YOU MORON...
I'M SORRY, HONEY.
I WANTED TO SHOW OFF MY GOOD SIDE.
FOR YOU.
AND YOU WOULD BE KOICHI?
MAKOTO TOLD ME EVERY-THING.

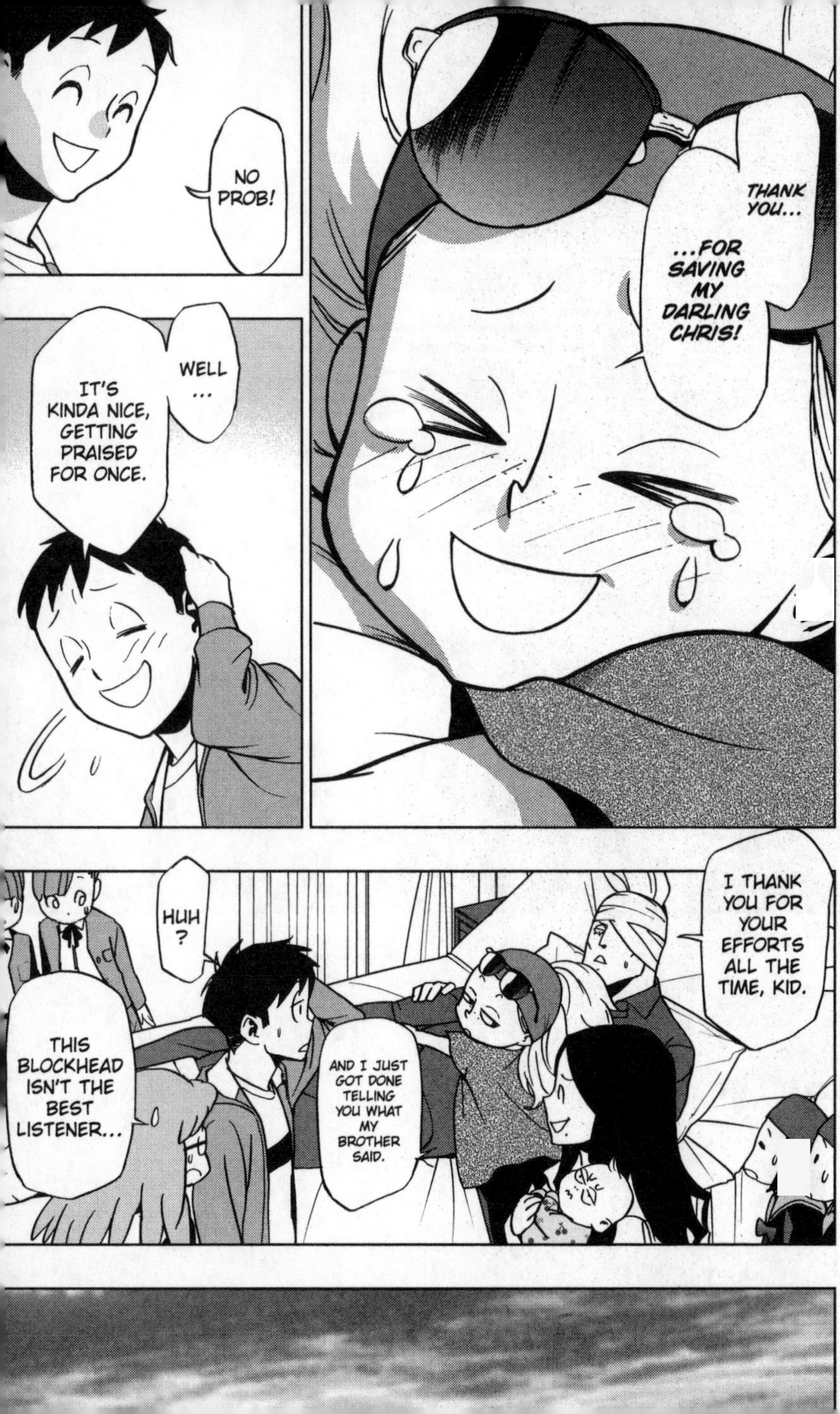
THANK YOU...
...FOR SAVING MY DARLING CHRIS!
NO PROB!
WELL...
IT'S KINDA NICE, GETTING PRAISED FOR ONCE.
I THANK YOU FOR YOUR EFFORTS ALL THE TIME, KID.
HUH?
AND I JUST GOT DONE TELLING YOU WHAT MY BROTHER SAID.
THIS BLOCKHEAD ISN'T THE BEST LISTENER...

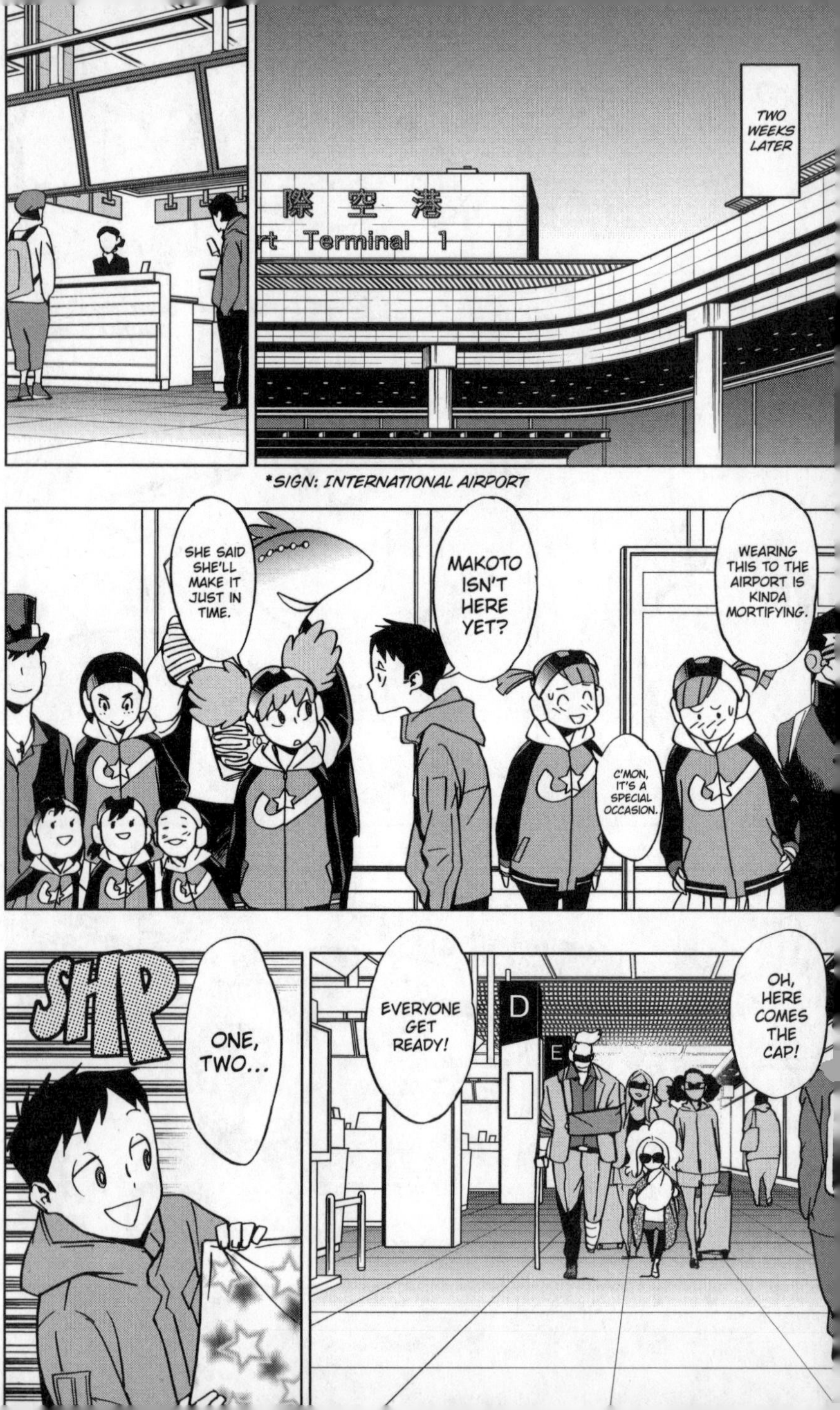
TWO WEEKS LATER
際空港
rt Terminal 1
*SIGN: INTERNATIONAL AIRPORT
WEARING THIS TO THE AIRPORT IS KINDA MORTIFYING.
C'MON, IT'S A SPECIAL OCCASION.
MAKOTO ISN'T HERE YET?
SHE SAID SHE'LL MAKE IT JUST IN TIME.
OH, HERE COMES THE CAP!
D
E
EVERYONE GET READY!
ONE, TWO...
SHR

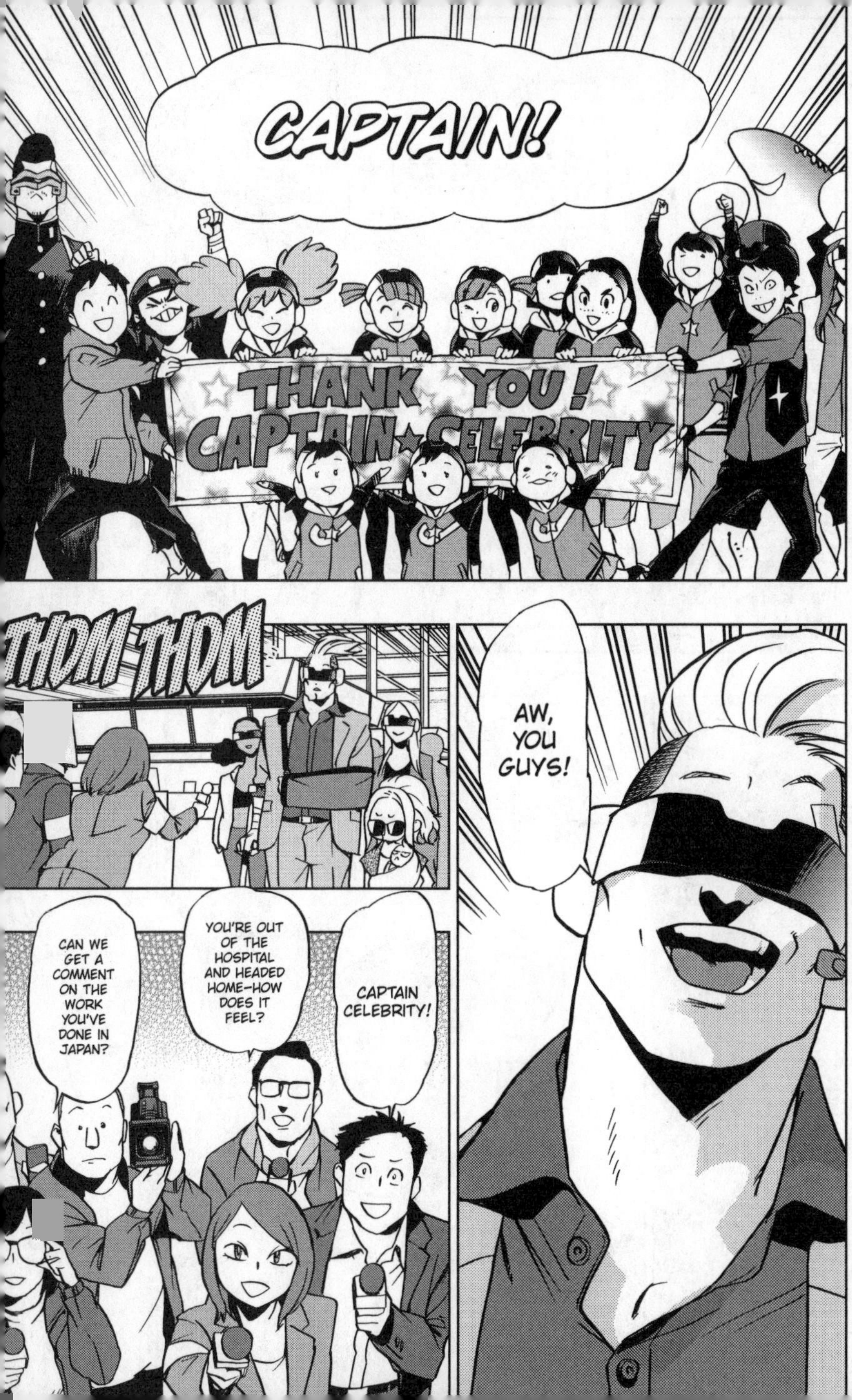
CAPTAIN!
THANK YOU! CAPTAIN★CELEBRITY
AW, YOU GUYS!
THOM THOM
CAPTAIN CELEBRITY!
YOU'RE OUT OF THE HOSPITAL AND HEADED HOME–HOW DOES IT FEEL?
CAN WE GET A COMMENT ON THE WORK YOU'VE DONE IN JAPAN?

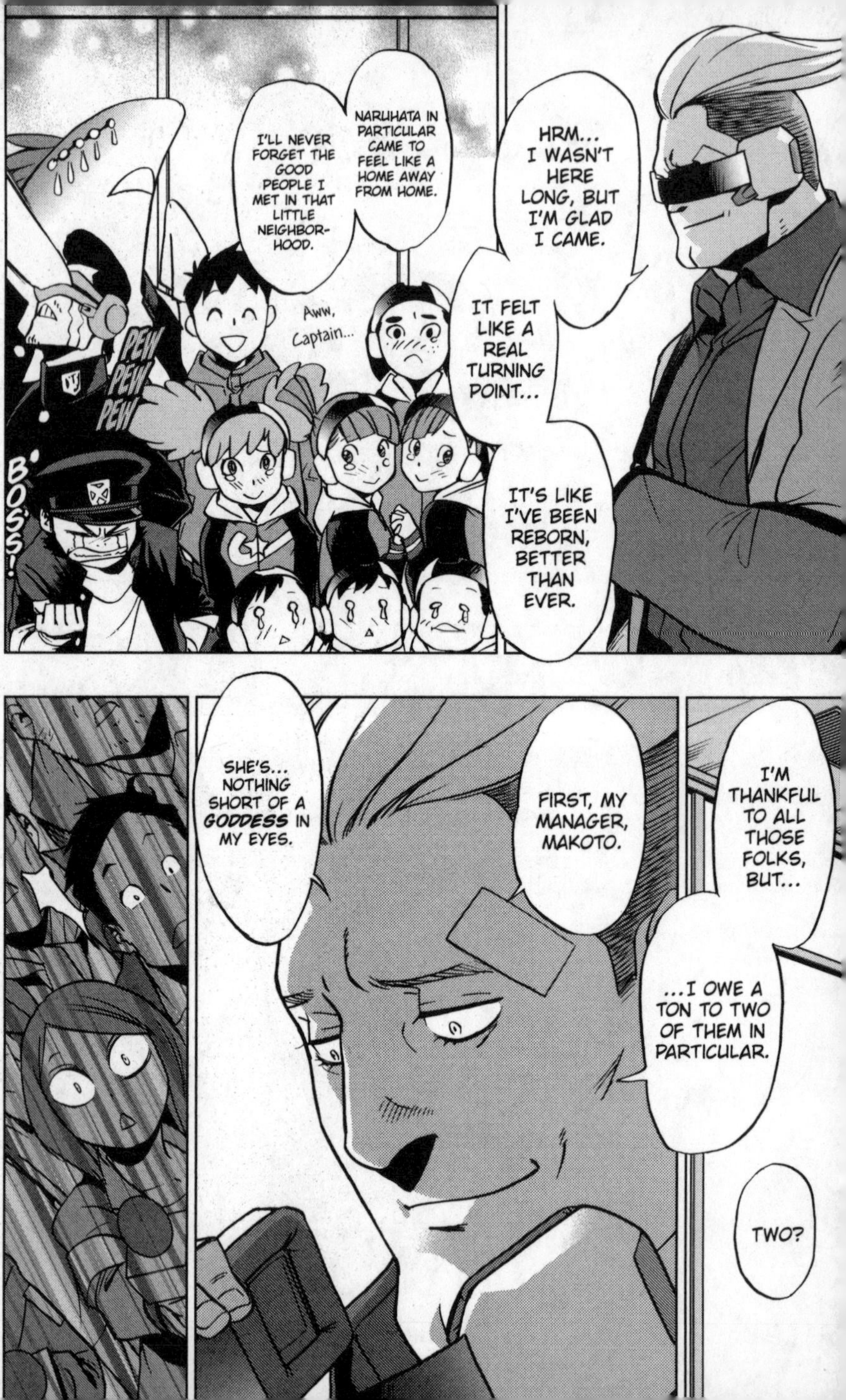
HRM... I WASN'T HERE LONG, BUT I'M GLAD I CAME.
IT FELT LIKE A REAL TURNING POINT...
IT'S LIKE I'VE BEEN REBORN, BETTER THAN EVER.
NARUHATA IN PARTICULAR CAME TO FEEL LIKE A HOME AWAY FROM HOME.
I'LL NEVER FORGET THE GOOD PEOPLE I MET IN THAT LITTLE NEIGHBOR-HOOD.
Aww, Captain...
PEW PEW PEW
BOSS!
I'M THANKFUL TO ALL THOSE FOLKS, BUT...
...I OWE A TON TO TWO OF THEM IN PARTICULAR.
TWO?
FIRST, MY MANAGER, MAKOTO.
SHE'S... NOTHING SHORT OF A **GODDESS** IN MY EYES.

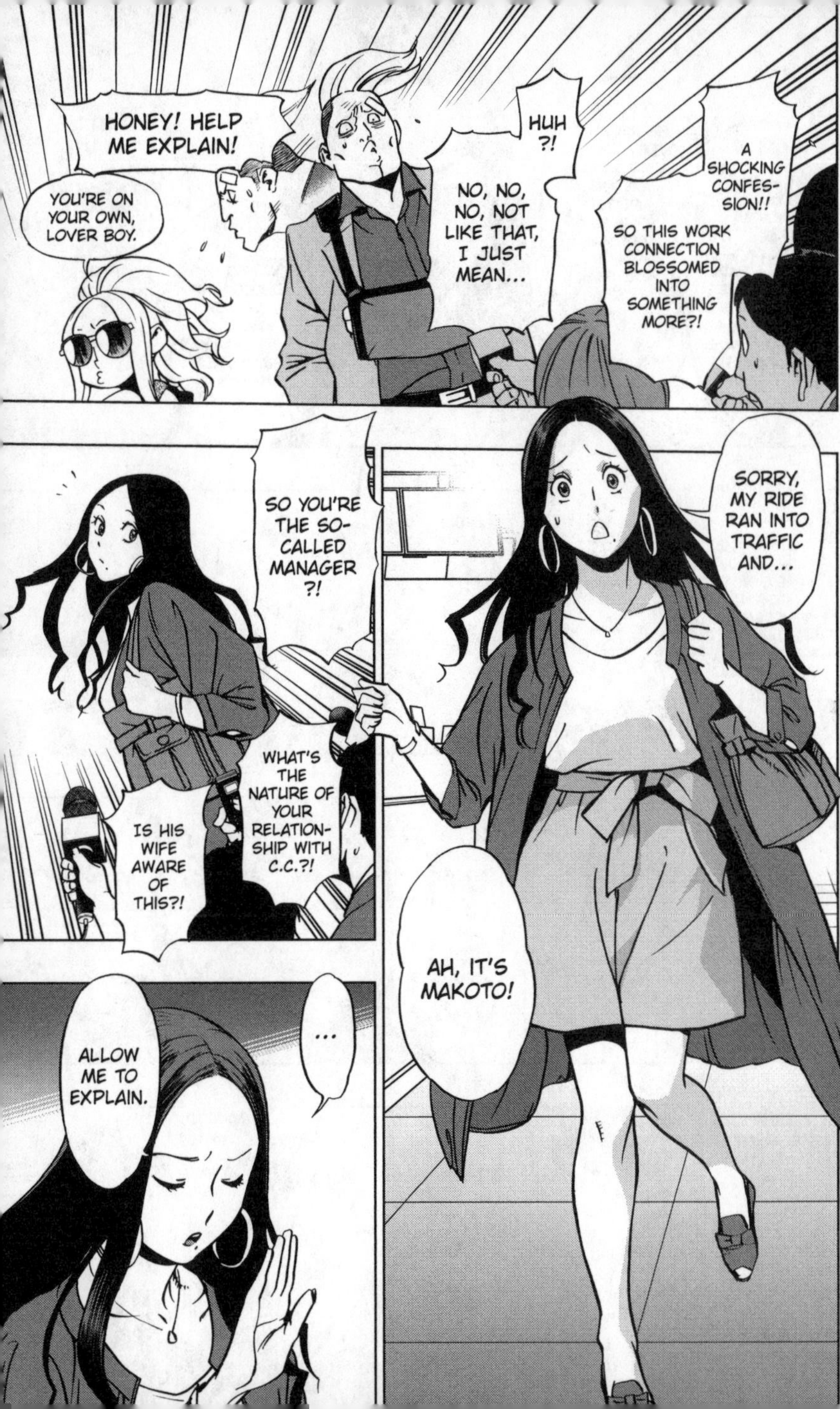
A SHOCKING CONFESSION!!
SO THIS WORK CONNECTION BLOSSOMED INTO SOMETHING MORE?!
HUH ?!
NO, NO, NO, NOT LIKE THAT, I JUST MEAN...
HONEY! HELP ME EXPLAIN!
YOU'RE ON YOUR OWN, LOVER BOY.
SORRY, MY RIDE RAN INTO TRAFFIC AND...
AH, IT'S MAKOTO!
SO YOU'RE THE SO-CALLED MANAGER ?!
WHAT'S THE NATURE OF YOUR RELATIONSHIP WITH C.C.?!
IS HIS WIFE AWARE OF THIS?!
...
ALLOW ME TO EXPLAIN.

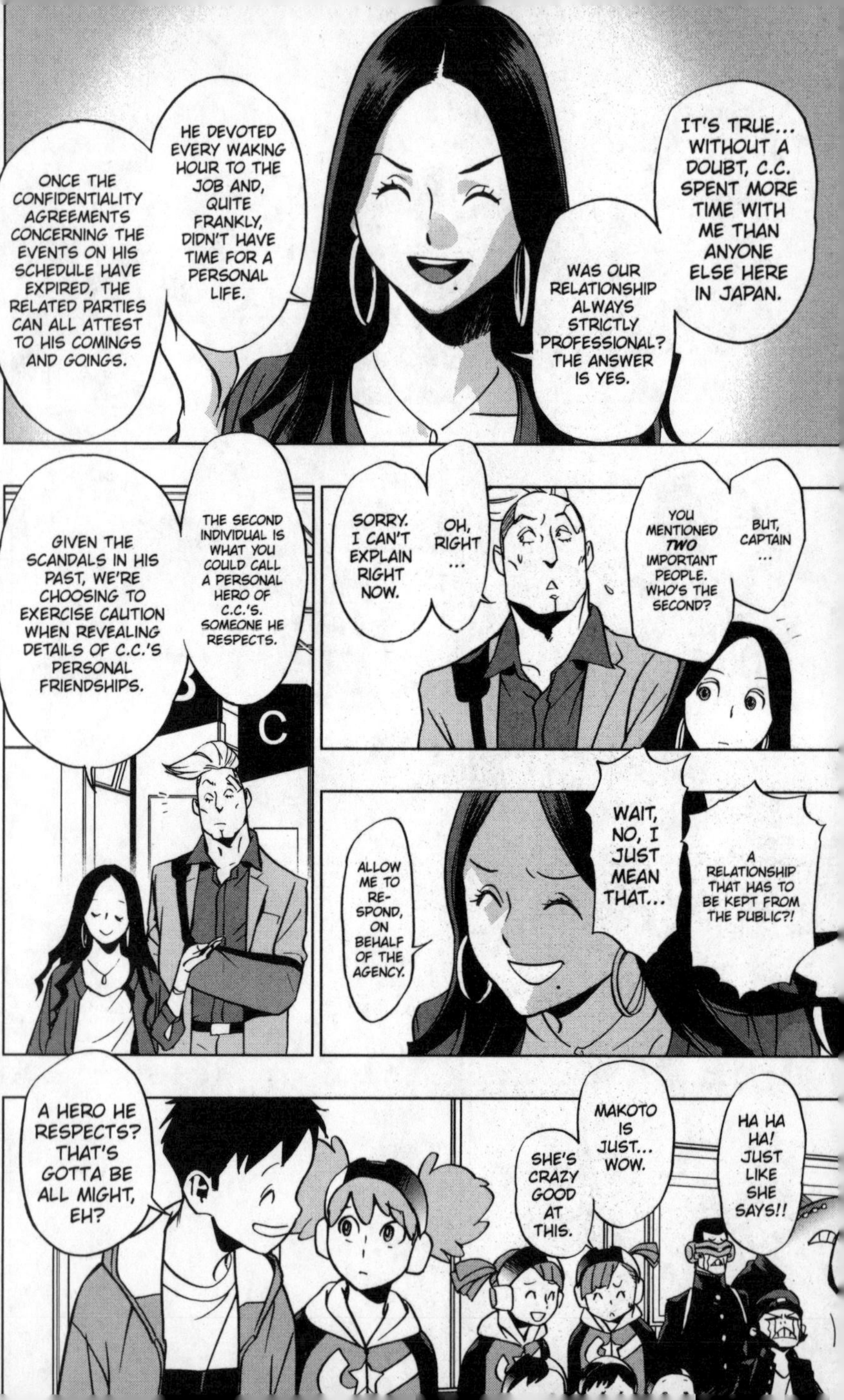
IT'S TRUE... WITHOUT A DOUBT, C.C. SPENT MORE TIME WITH ME THAN ANYONE ELSE HERE IN JAPAN.
WAS OUR RELATIONSHIP ALWAYS STRICTLY PROFESSIONAL? THE ANSWER IS YES.
HE DEVOTED EVERY WAKING HOUR TO THE JOB AND, QUITE FRANKLY, DIDN'T HAVE TIME FOR A PERSONAL LIFE.
ONCE THE CONFIDENTIALITY AGREEMENTS CONCERNING THE EVENTS ON HIS SCHEDULE HAVE EXPIRED, THE RELATED PARTIES CAN ALL ATTEST TO HIS COMINGS AND GOINGS.
BUT, CAPTAIN...
YOU MENTIONED TWO IMPORTANT PEOPLE. WHO'S THE SECOND?
OH, RIGHT...
SORRY. I CAN'T EXPLAIN RIGHT NOW.
A RELATIONSHIP THAT HAS TO BE KEPT FROM THE PUBLIC?!
WAIT, NO, I JUST MEAN THAT...
ALLOW ME TO RE-SPOND, ON BEHALF OF THE AGENCY.
THE SECOND INDIVIDUAL IS WHAT YOU COULD CALL A PERSONAL HERO OF C.C.'S. SOMEONE HE RESPECTS.
GIVEN THE SCANDALS IN HIS PAST, WE'RE CHOOSING TO EXERCISE CAUTION WHEN REVEALING DETAILS OF C.C.'S PERSONAL FRIENDSHIPS.
C
HA HA HA! JUST LIKE SHE SAYS!!
MAKOTO IS JUST... WOW.
SHE'S CRAZY GOOD AT THIS.
A HERO HE RESPECTS? THAT'S GOTTA BE ALL MIGHT, EH?

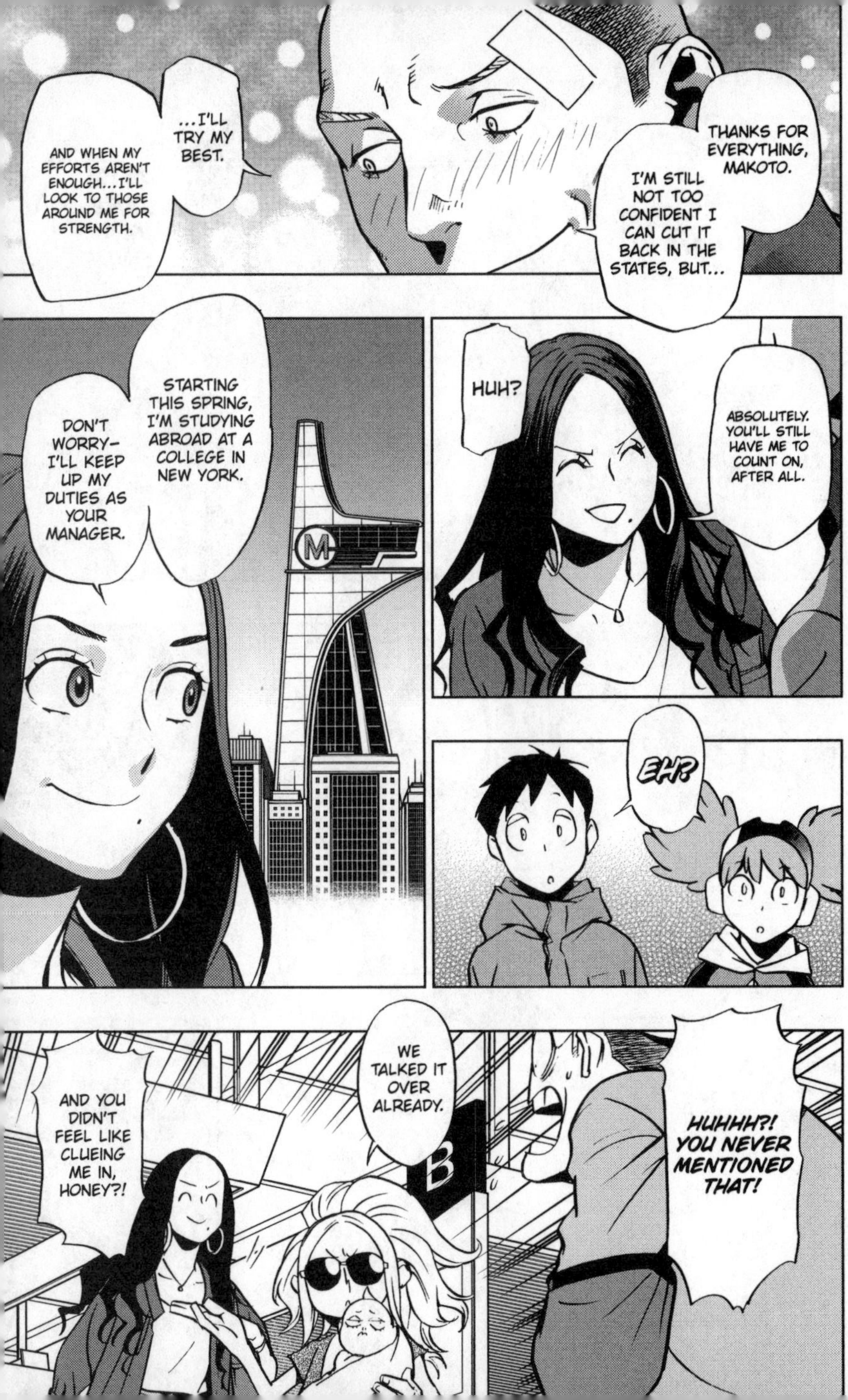
THANKS FOR EVERYTHING, MAKOTO.
I'M STILL NOT TOO CONFIDENT I CAN CUT IT BACK IN THE STATES, BUT...
...I'LL TRY MY BEST.
AND WHEN MY EFFORTS AREN'T ENOUGH...I'LL LOOK TO THOSE AROUND ME FOR STRENGTH.
ABSOLUTELY. YOU'LL STILL HAVE ME TO COUNT ON, AFTER ALL.
HUH?
EH?
STARTING THIS SPRING, I'M STUDYING ABROAD AT A COLLEGE IN NEW YORK.
DON'T WORRY—I'LL KEEP UP MY DUTIES AS YOUR MANAGER.
HUHHH?! YOU NEVER MENTIONED THAT!
WE TALKED IT OVER ALREADY.
AND YOU DIDN'T FEEL LIKE CLUEING ME IN, HONEY?!

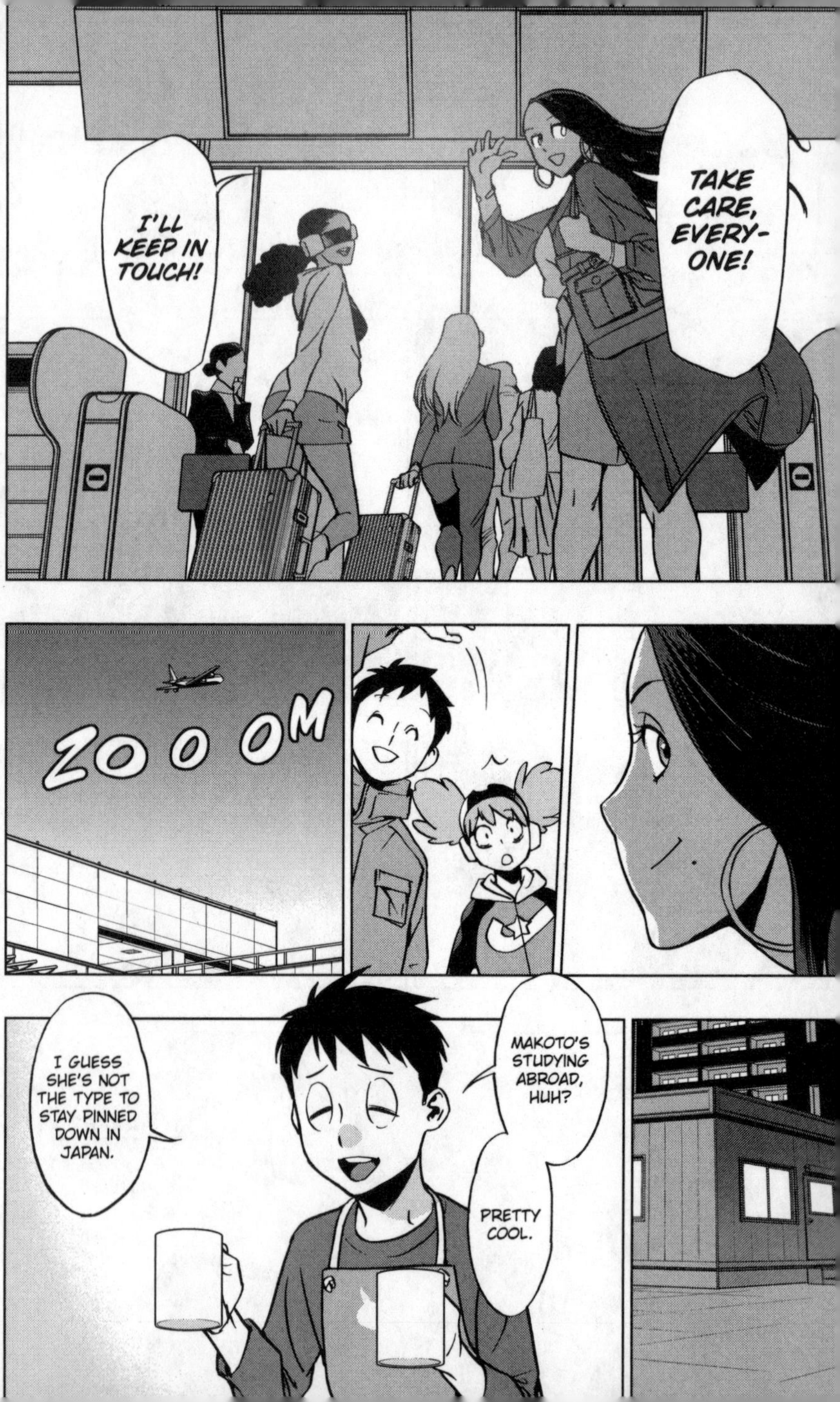
TAKE CARE, EVERYONE!
I'LL KEEP IN TOUCH!
ZOOOM
MAKOTO'S STUDYING ABROAD, HUH?
PRETTY COOL.
I GUESS SHE'S NOT THE TYPE TO STAY PINNED DOWN IN JAPAN.

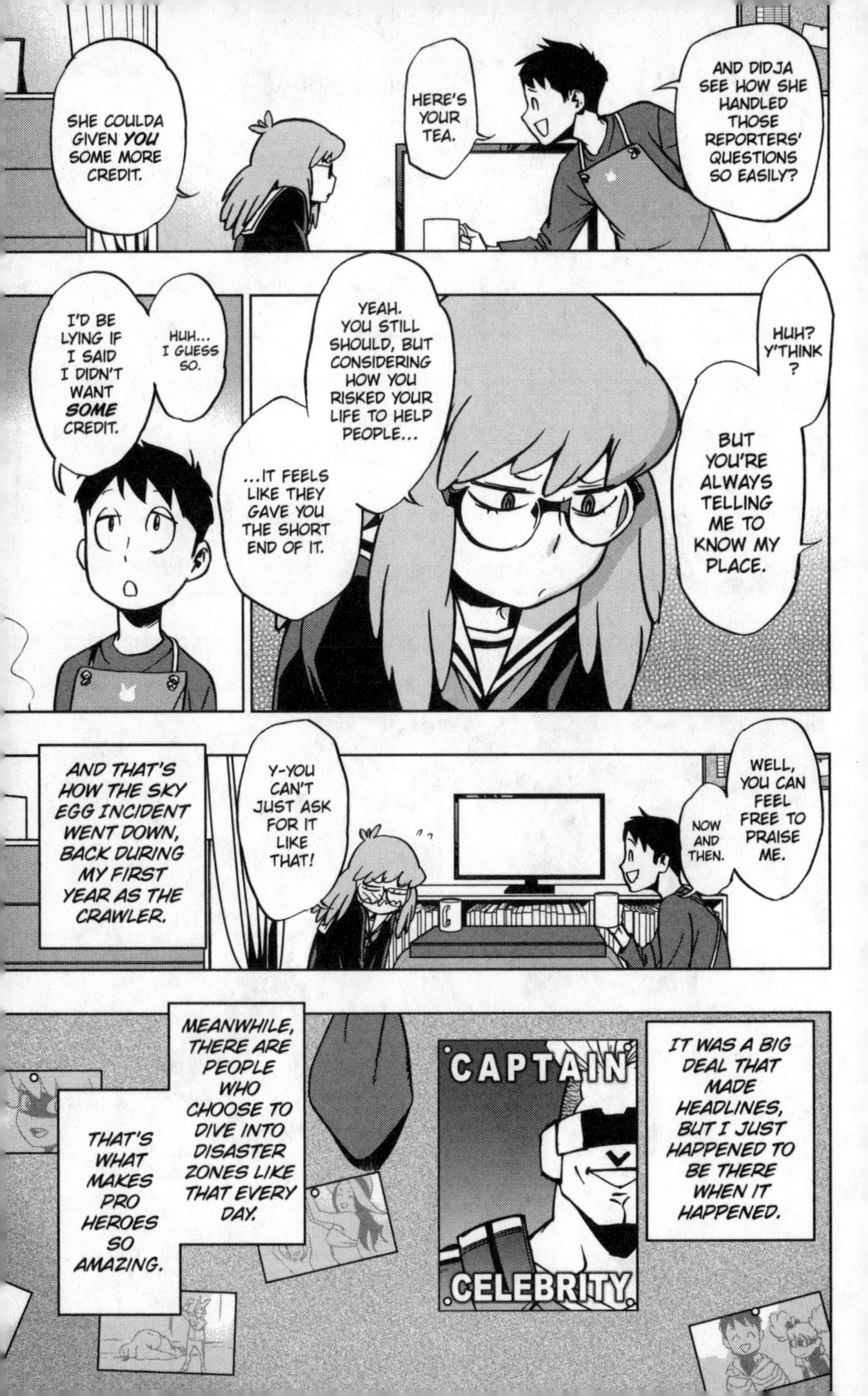
AND DIDJA SEE HOW SHE HANDLED THOSE REPORTERS' QUESTIONS SO EASILY?
HERE'S YOUR TEA.
SHE COULDA GIVEN *YOU* SOME MORE CREDIT.
HUH? Y'THINK ?
BUT YOU'RE ALWAYS TELLING ME TO KNOW MY PLACE.
YEAH. YOU STILL SHOULD, BUT CONSIDERING HOW YOU RISKED YOUR LIFE TO HELP PEOPLE...
...IT FEELS LIKE THEY GAVE YOU THE SHORT END OF IT.
HUH... I GUESS SO.
I'D BE LYING IF I SAID I DIDN'T WANT *SOME* CREDIT.
WELL, YOU CAN FEEL FREE TO PRAISE ME.
NOW AND THEN.
Y-YOU CAN'T JUST ASK FOR IT LIKE THAT!
AND THAT'S HOW THE SKY EGG INCIDENT WENT DOWN, BACK DURING MY FIRST YEAR AS THE CRAWLER.
IT WAS A BIG DEAL THAT MADE HEADLINES, BUT I JUST HAPPENED TO BE THERE WHEN IT HAPPENED.
CAPTAIN
CELEBRITY
MEANWHILE, THERE ARE PEOPLE WHO CHOOSE TO DIVE INTO DISASTER ZONES LIKE THAT EVERY DAY.
THAT'S WHAT MAKES PRO HEROES SO AMAZING.

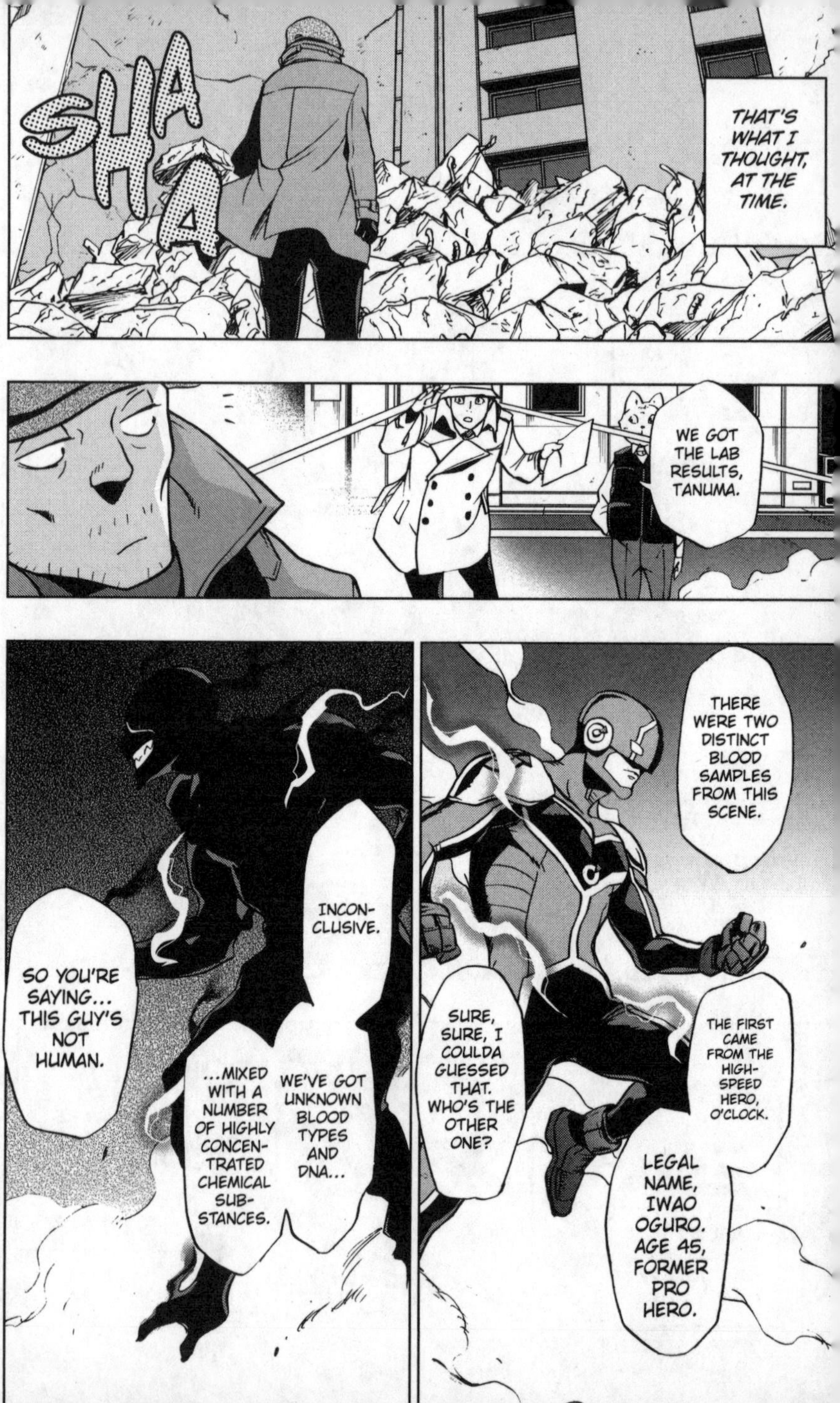
THAT'S WHAT I THOUGHT, AT THE TIME.
SHA SHA
WE GOT THE LAB RESULTS, TANUMA.
THERE WERE TWO DISTINCT BLOOD SAMPLES FROM THIS SCENE.
THE FIRST CAME FROM THE HIGH-SPEED HERO, O'CLOCK.
LEGAL NAME, IWAO OGURO. AGE 45, FORMER PRO HERO.
SURE, SURE, I COULDA GUESSED THAT. WHO'S THE OTHER ONE?
INCON-CLUSIVE.
WE'VE GOT UNKNOWN BLOOD TYPES AND DNA...
...MIXED WITH A NUMBER OF HIGHLY CONCEN-TRATED CHEMICAL SUB-STANCES.
SO YOU'RE SAYING... THIS GUY'S NOT HUMAN.

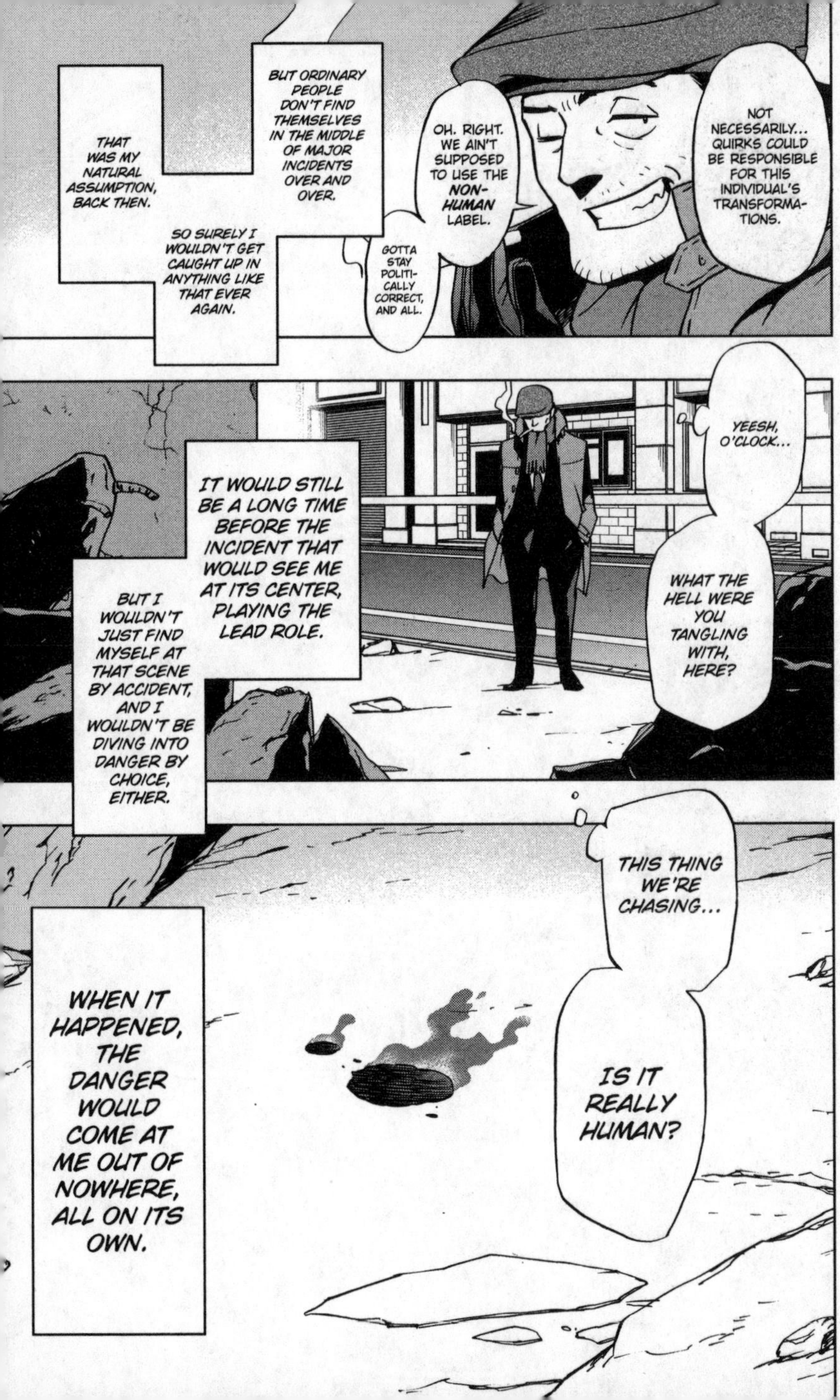
NOT NECESSARILY... QUIRKS COULD BE RESPONSIBLE FOR THIS INDIVIDUAL'S TRANSFORMATIONS.
OH. RIGHT. WE AIN'T SUPPOSED TO USE THE NON-HUMAN LABEL.
GOTTA STAY POLITICALLY CORRECT, AND ALL.
BUT ORDINARY PEOPLE DON'T FIND THEMSELVES IN THE MIDDLE OF MAJOR INCIDENTS OVER AND OVER.
THAT WAS MY NATURAL ASSUMPTION, BACK THEN.
SO SURELY I WOULDN'T GET CAUGHT UP IN ANYTHING LIKE THAT EVER AGAIN.
YEESH, O'CLOCK...
WHAT THE HELL WERE YOU TANGLING WITH, HERE?
IT WOULD STILL BE A LONG TIME BEFORE THE INCIDENT THAT WOULD SEE ME AT ITS CENTER, PLAYING THE LEAD ROLE.
BUT I WOULDN'T JUST FIND MYSELF AT THAT SCENE BY ACCIDENT, AND I WOULDN'T BE DIVING INTO DANGER BY CHOICE, EITHER.
THIS THING WE'RE CHASING...
IS IT REALLY HUMAN?
WHEN IT HAPPENED, THE DANGER WOULD COME AT ME OUT OF NOWHERE, ALL ON ITS OWN.

THE COMMENTARY

Vigilantes has always incorporated cameos of characters from the main series, and though the whole Young Aizawa arc is an example of that, we got a much more intense reaction from readers than usual, and I feel like we even managed to reach outside the usual demographic.

—Furuhashi

The only snippet of Aizawa's and Mic's school days provided by Horikoshi himself came in "The Digression" page of volume 6 of the main series. When I realized that, I was at something of a loss. "Oh crap…" I thought.

—Betten

PRACTICE SKETCH

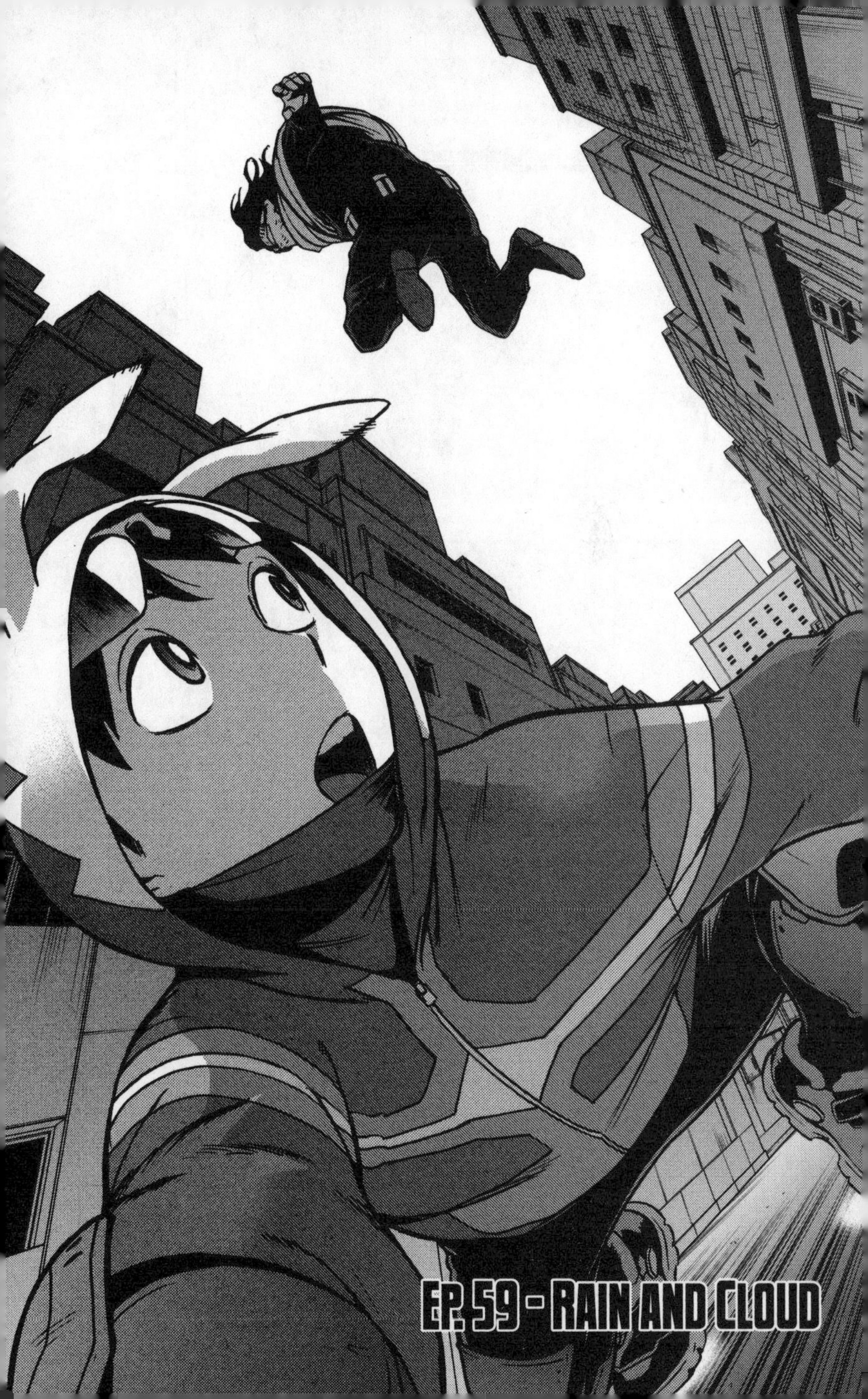
EP. 59 - RAIN AND CLOUD

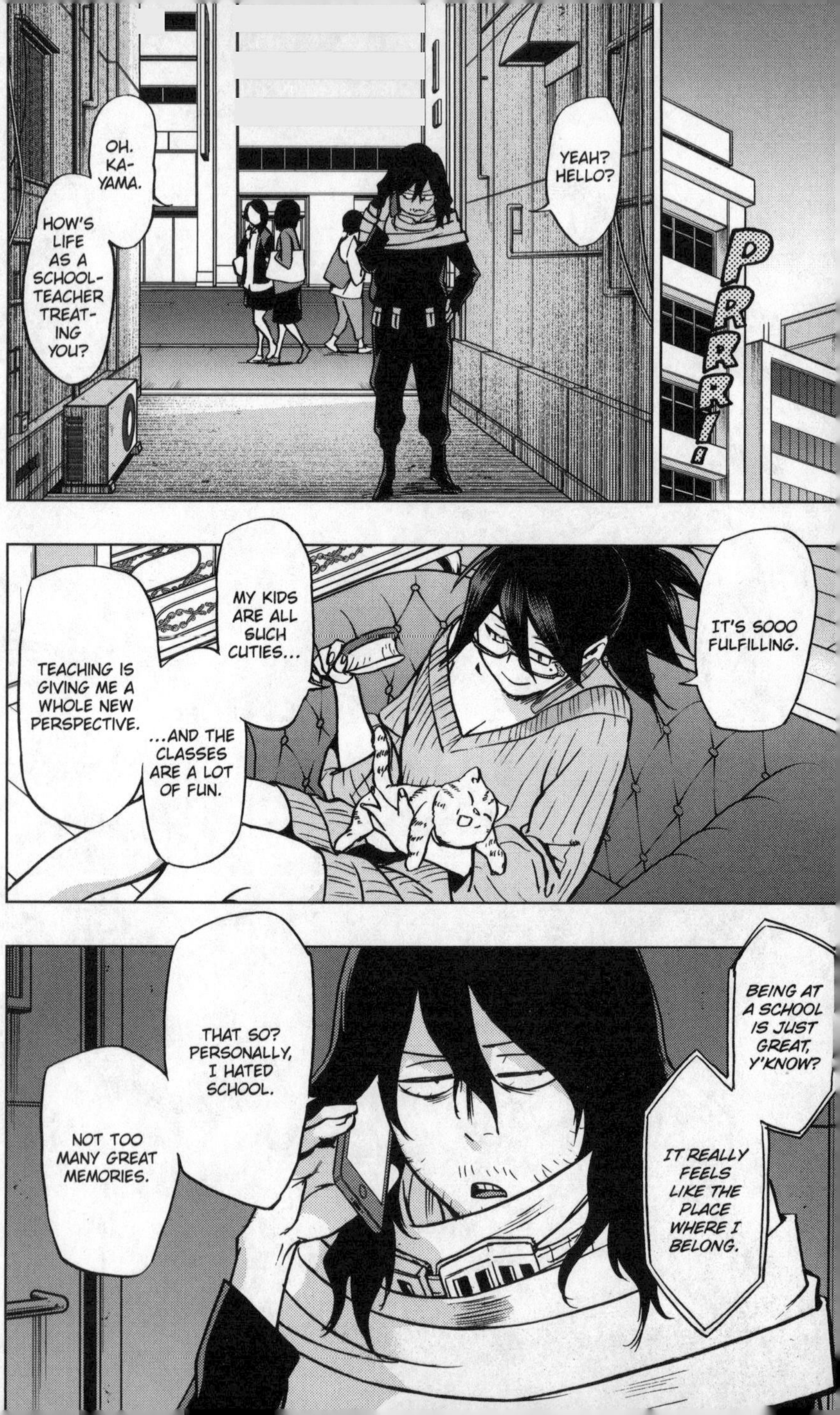
PRRRI!!
YEAH? HELLO?
OH. KA-YAMA.
HOW'S LIFE AS A SCHOOL-TEACHER TREAT-ING YOU?
IT'S SOOO FULFILLING.
MY KIDS ARE ALL SUCH CUTIES...
...AND THE CLASSES ARE A LOT OF FUN.
TEACHING IS GIVING ME A WHOLE NEW PERSPECTIVE.
BEING AT A SCHOOL IS JUST GREAT, Y'KNOW?
IT REALLY FEELS LIKE THE PLACE WHERE I BELONG.
THAT SO? PERSONALLY, I HATED SCHOOL.
NOT TOO MANY GREAT MEMORIES.

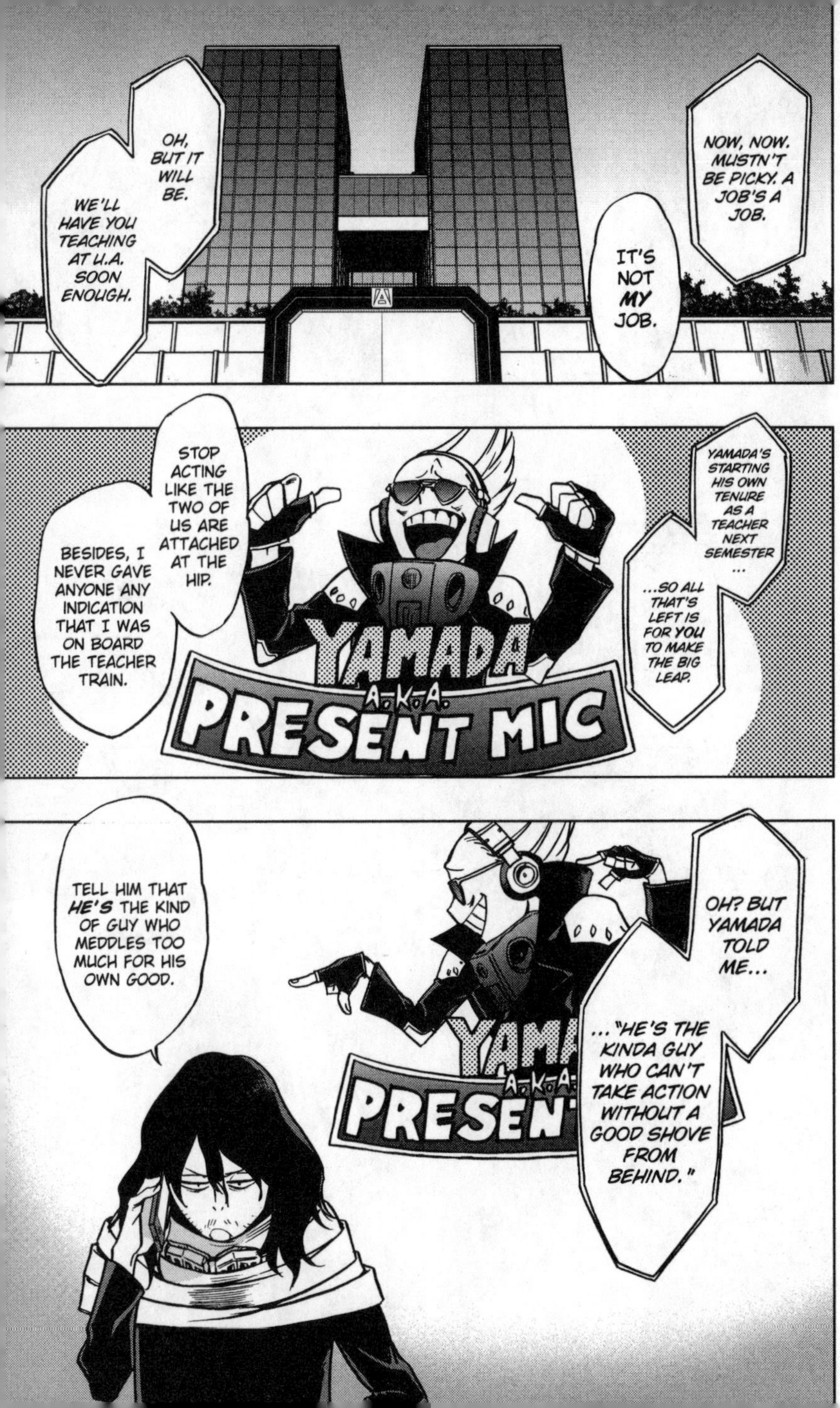
NOW, NOW. MUSTN'T BE PICKY. A JOB'S A JOB.
IT'S NOT MY JOB.
OH, BUT IT WILL BE.
WE'LL HAVE YOU TEACHING AT U.A. SOON ENOUGH.
YAMADA'S STARTING HIS OWN TENURE AS A TEACHER NEXT SEMESTER...
...SO ALL THAT'S LEFT IS FOR YOU TO MAKE THE BIG LEAP.
YAMADA A.K.A. PRESENT MIC
STOP ACTING LIKE THE TWO OF US ARE ATTACHED AT THE HIP.
BESIDES, I NEVER GAVE ANYONE ANY INDICATION THAT I WAS ON BOARD THE TEACHER TRAIN.
OH? BUT YAMADA TOLD ME...
..."HE'S THE KINDA GUY WHO CAN'T TAKE ACTION WITHOUT A GOOD SHOVE FROM BEHIND."
TELL HIM THAT HE'S THE KIND OF GUY WHO MEDDLES TOO MUCH FOR HIS OWN GOOD.

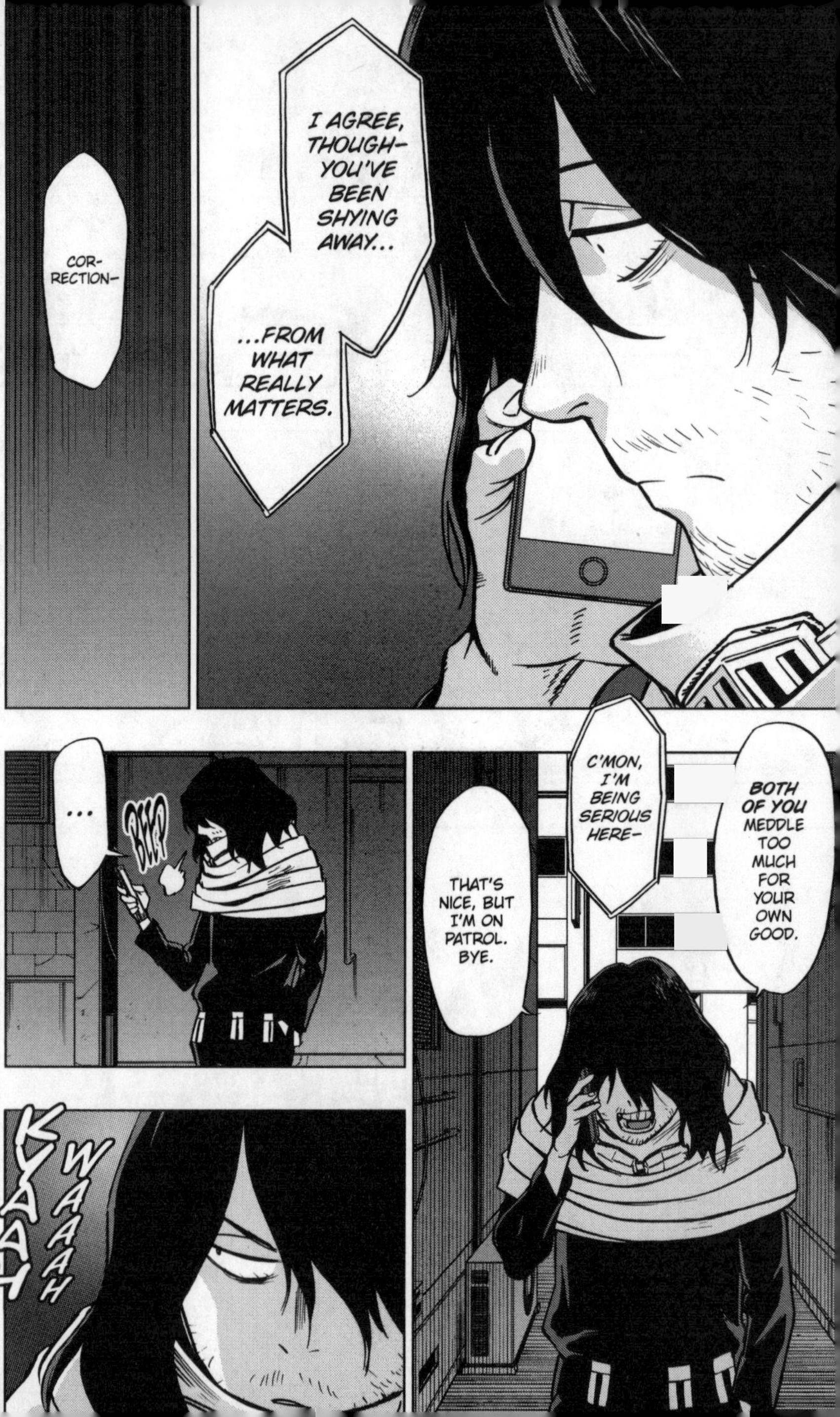
I AGREE, THOUGH—YOU'VE BEEN SHYING AWAY...
...FROM WHAT REALLY MATTERS.
COR-RECTION—
BOTH OF YOU MEDDLE TOO MUCH FOR YOUR OWN GOOD.
C'MON, I'M BEING SERIOUS HERE—
THAT'S NICE, BUT I'M ON PATROL. BYE.
BEEP
...
WAAAAH
KYAAAH

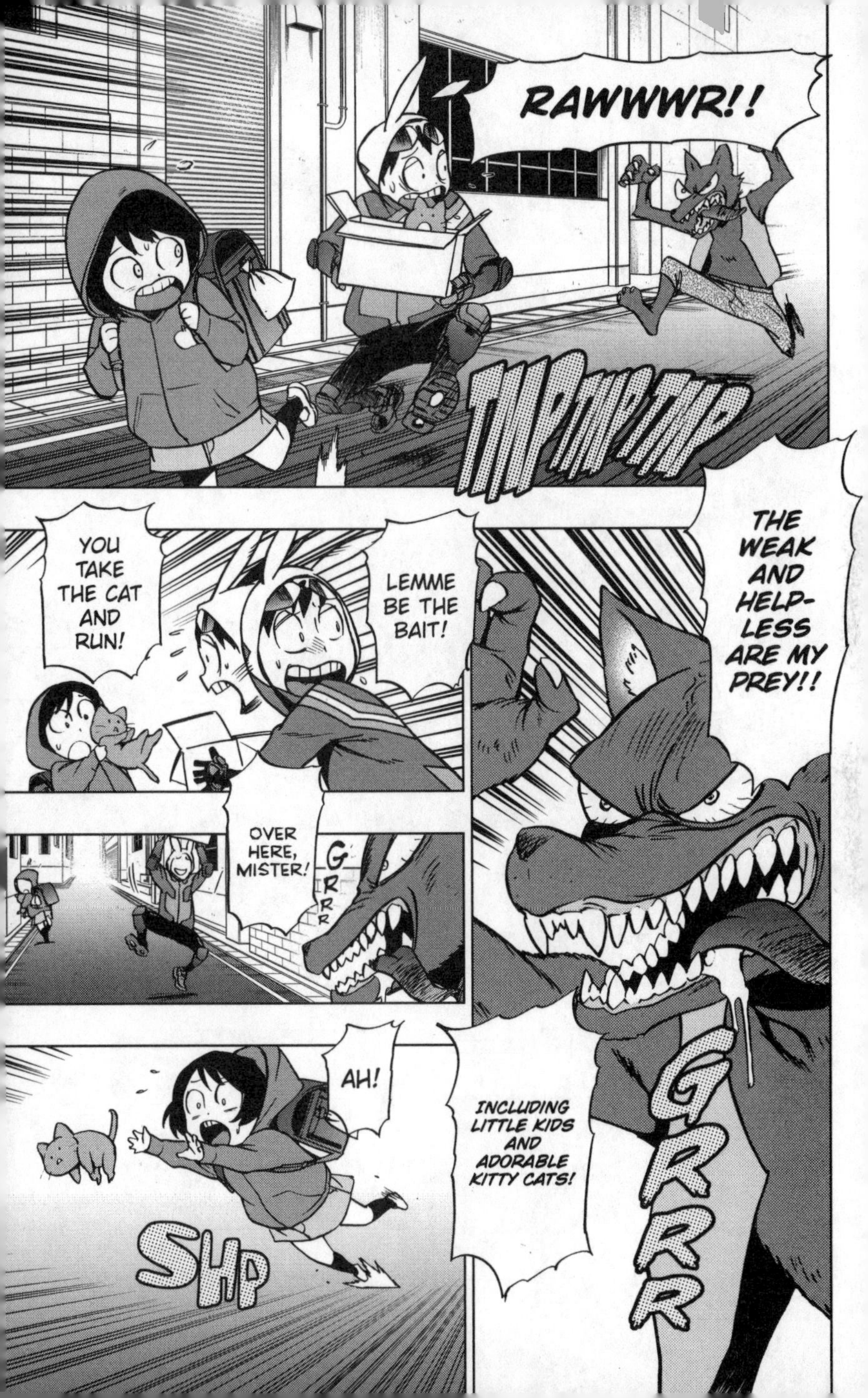

RAWWWR!!
TMP TMP TMP
THE WEAK AND HELP-LESS ARE MY PREY!!
INCLUDING LITTLE KIDS AND ADORABLE KITTY CATS!
GRRRR
LEMME BE THE BAIT!
YOU TAKE THE CAT AND RUN!
OVER HERE, MISTER!
GRRR
AH!
SHP

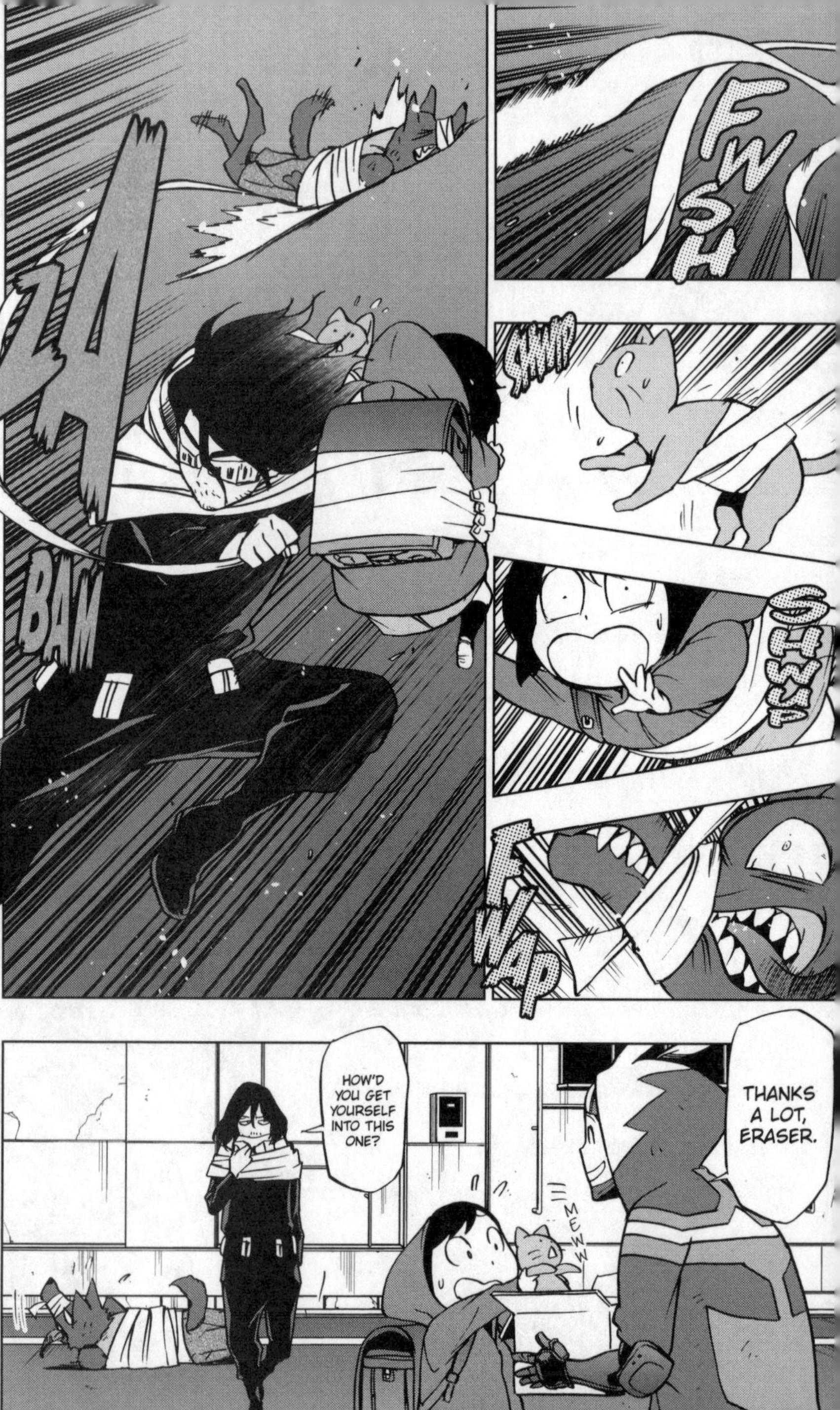
FWSH
SHWIP
SHWIP
FWAP
ZA
BAM
THANKS A LOT, ERASER.
MEWW
HOW'D YOU GET YOURSELF INTO THIS ONE?

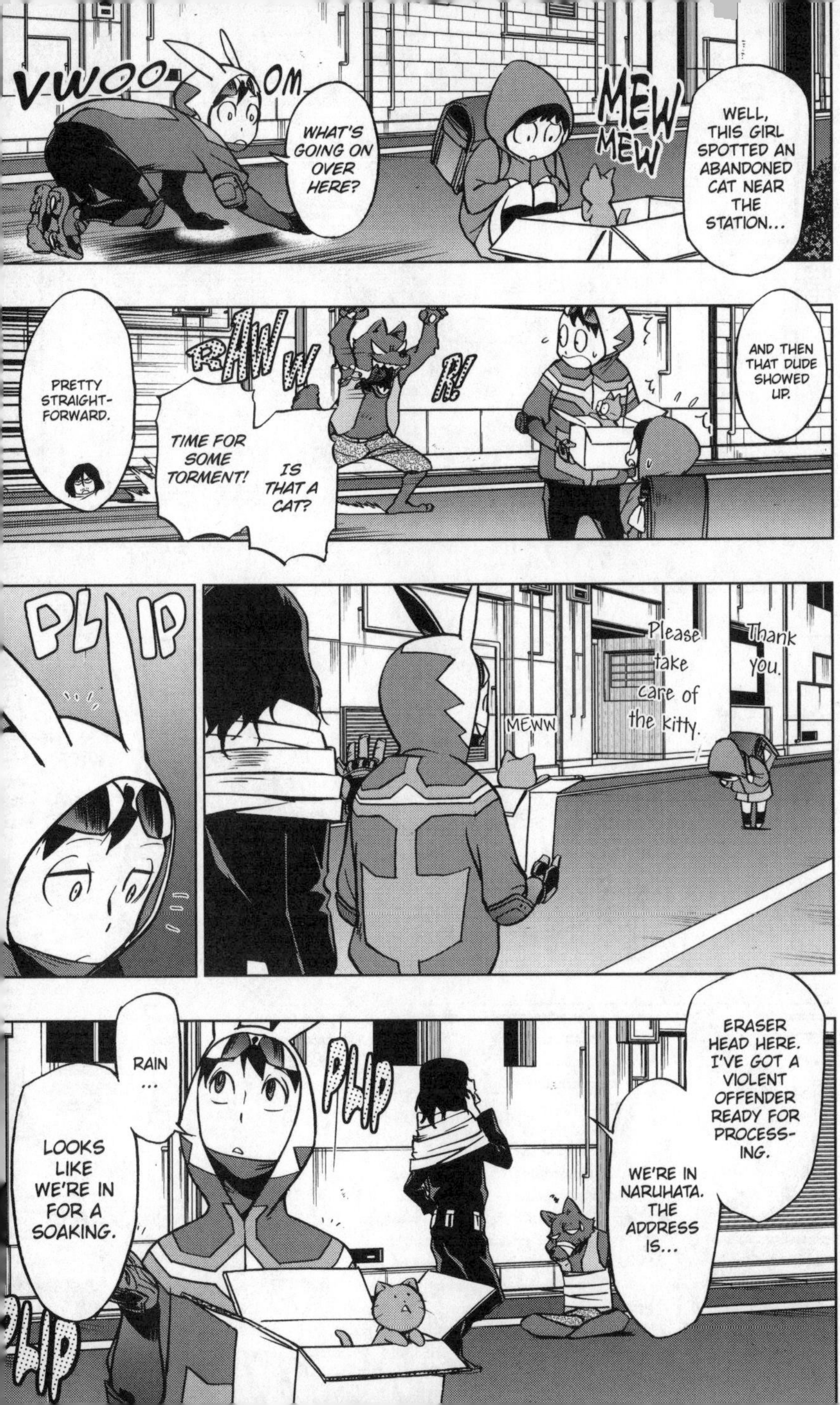
MEW
MEW
WELL, THIS GIRL SPOTTED AN ABANDONED CAT NEAR THE STATION...
WHAT'S GOING ON OVER HERE?
VWOO-OM
AND THEN THAT DUDE SHOWED UP.
RAWWR!
IS THAT A CAT?
TIME FOR SOME TORMENT!
PRETTY STRAIGHT-FORWARD.
Thank you.
Please take care of the kitty.
MEWW
PLIP
ERASER HEAD HERE. I'VE GOT A VIOLENT OFFENDER READY FOR PROCESS-ING.
WE'RE IN NARUHATA. THE ADDRESS IS...
PLIP
RAIN...
LOOKS LIKE WE'RE IN FOR A SOAKING.
PLIP

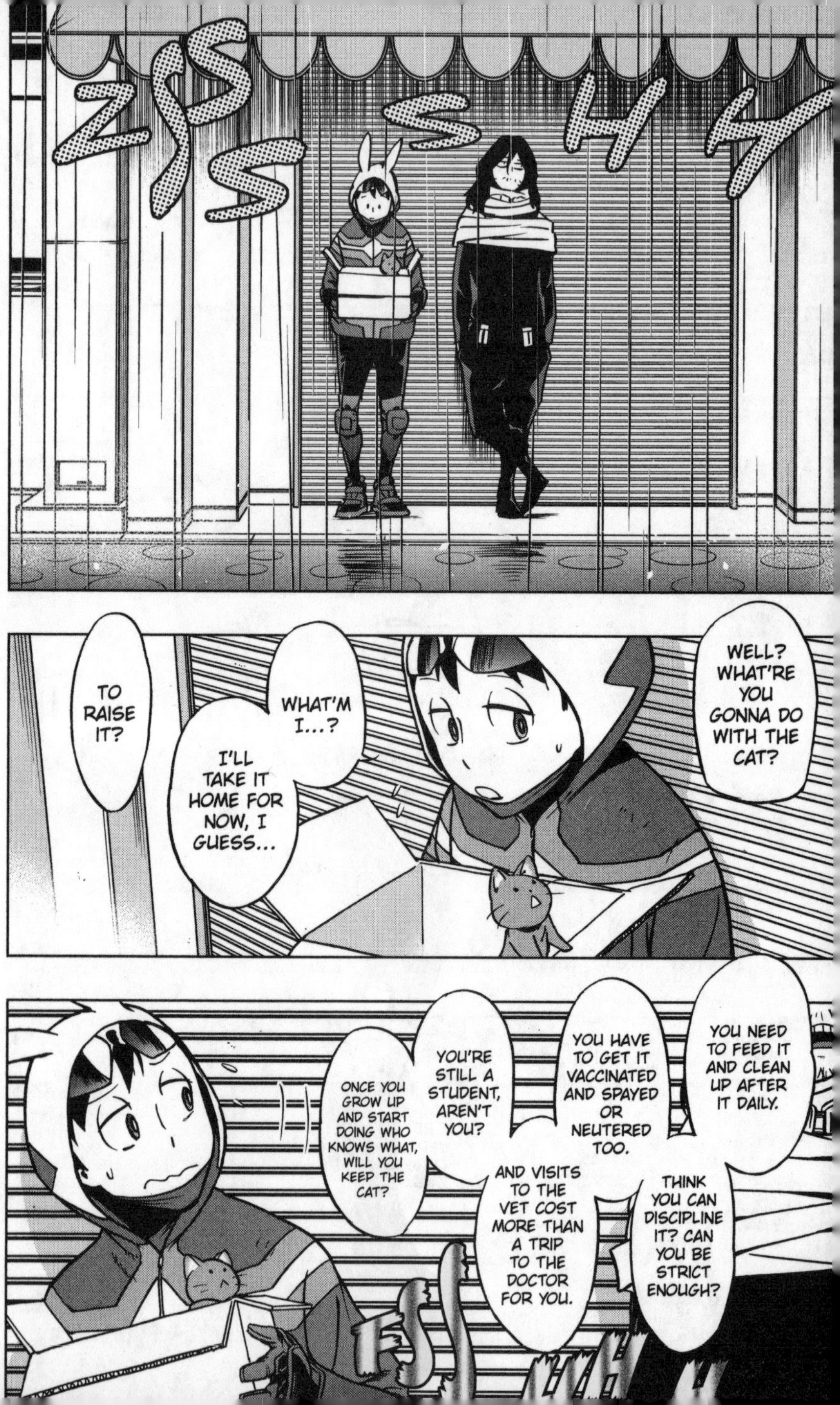
ZSSSHH
WELL? WHAT'RE YOU GONNA DO WITH THE CAT?
WHAT'M I...?
I'LL TAKE IT HOME FOR NOW, I GUESS...
TO RAISE IT?
YOU NEED TO FEED IT AND CLEAN UP AFTER IT DAILY.
YOU HAVE TO GET IT VACCINATED AND SPAYED OR NEUTERED TOO.
THINK YOU CAN DISCIPLINE IT? CAN YOU BE STRICT ENOUGH?
AND VISITS TO THE VET COST MORE THAN A TRIP TO THE DOCTOR FOR YOU.
YOU'RE STILL A STUDENT, AREN'T YOU?
ONCE YOU GROW UP AND START DOING WHO KNOWS WHAT, WILL YOU KEEP THE CAT?

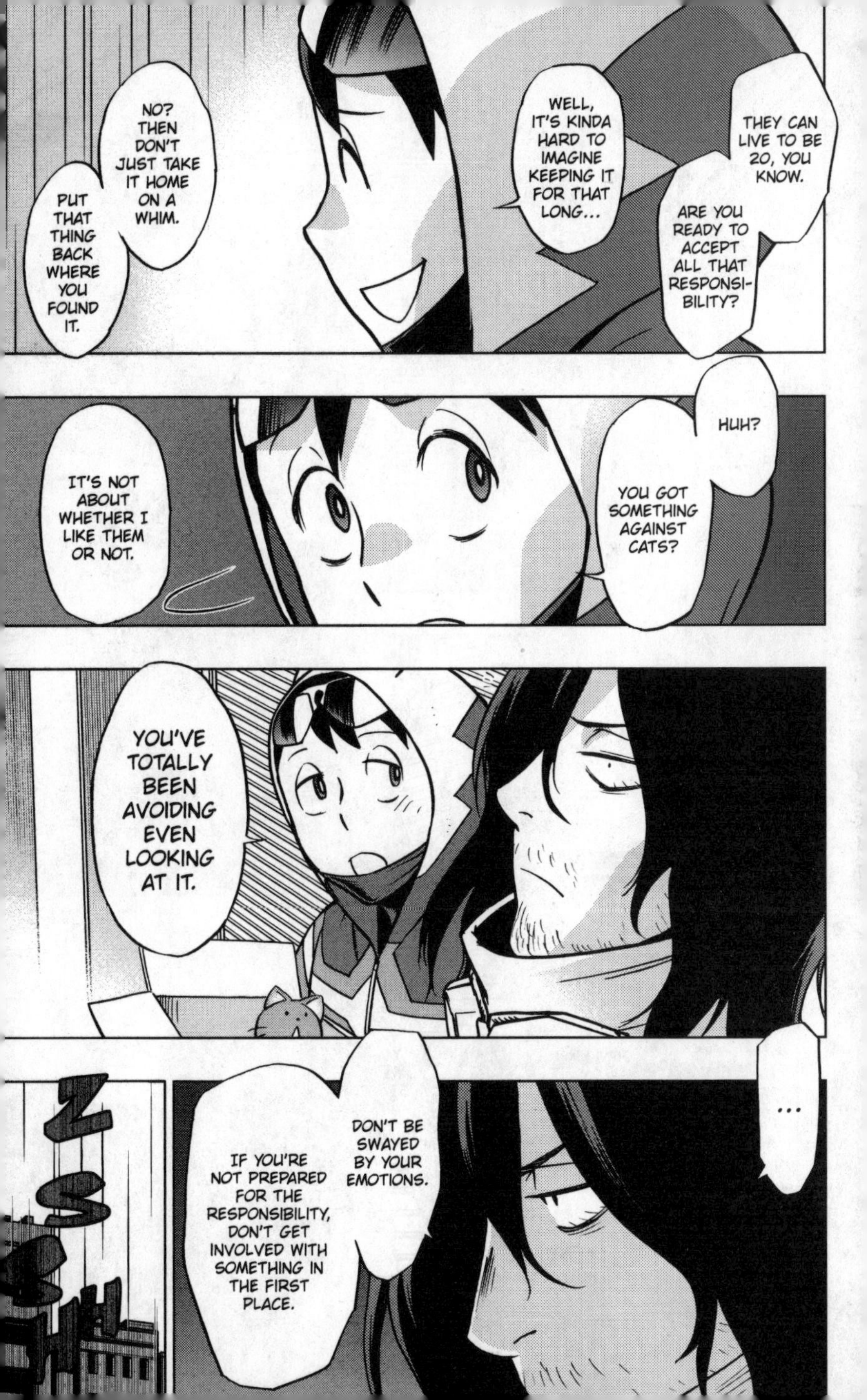
THEY CAN LIVE TO BE 20, YOU KNOW.
ARE YOU READY TO ACCEPT ALL THAT RESPONSIBILITY?
WELL, IT'S KINDA HARD TO IMAGINE KEEPING IT FOR THAT LONG...
NO? THEN DON'T JUST TAKE IT HOME ON A WHIM.
PUT THAT THING BACK WHERE YOU FOUND IT.
HUH?
YOU GOT SOMETHING AGAINST CATS?
IT'S NOT ABOUT WHETHER I LIKE THEM OR NOT.
YOU'VE TOTALLY BEEN AVOIDING EVEN LOOKING AT IT.
...
DON'T BE SWAYED BY YOUR EMOTIONS.
IF YOU'RE NOT PREPARED FOR THE RESPONSIBILITY, DON'T GET INVOLVED WITH SOMETHING IN THE FIRST PLACE.

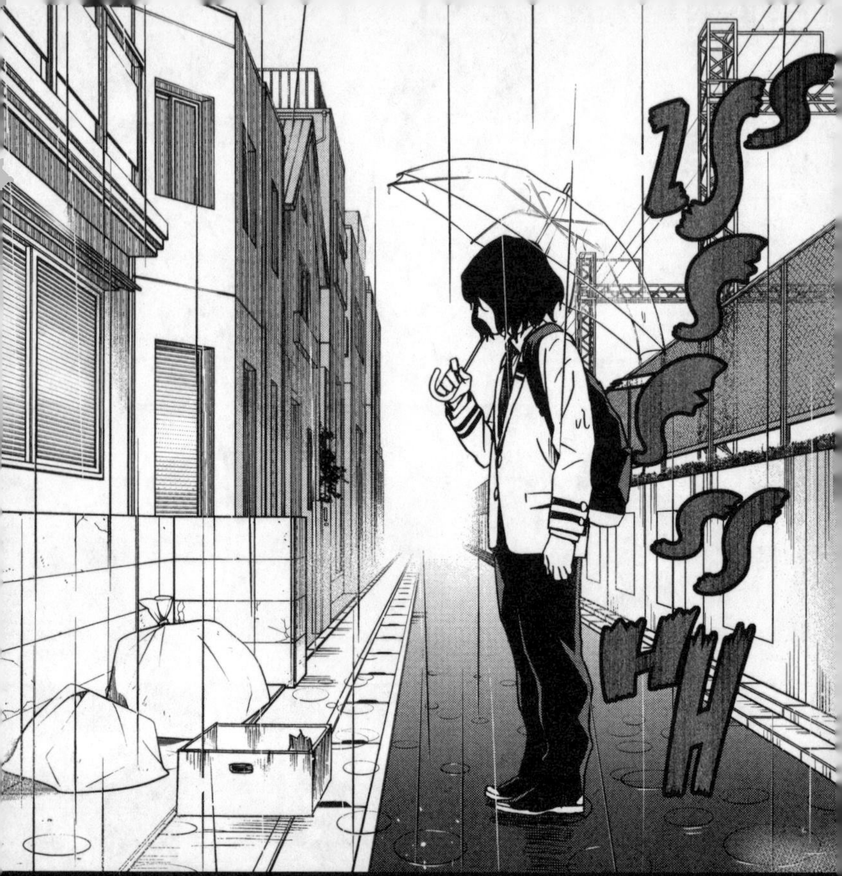

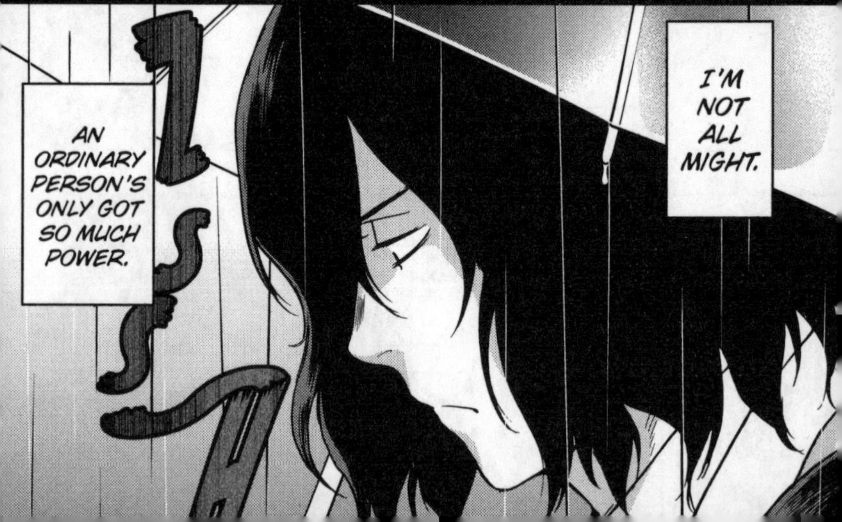
I'M NOT ALL MIGHT.
AN ORDINARY PERSON'S ONLY GOT SO MUCH POWER.

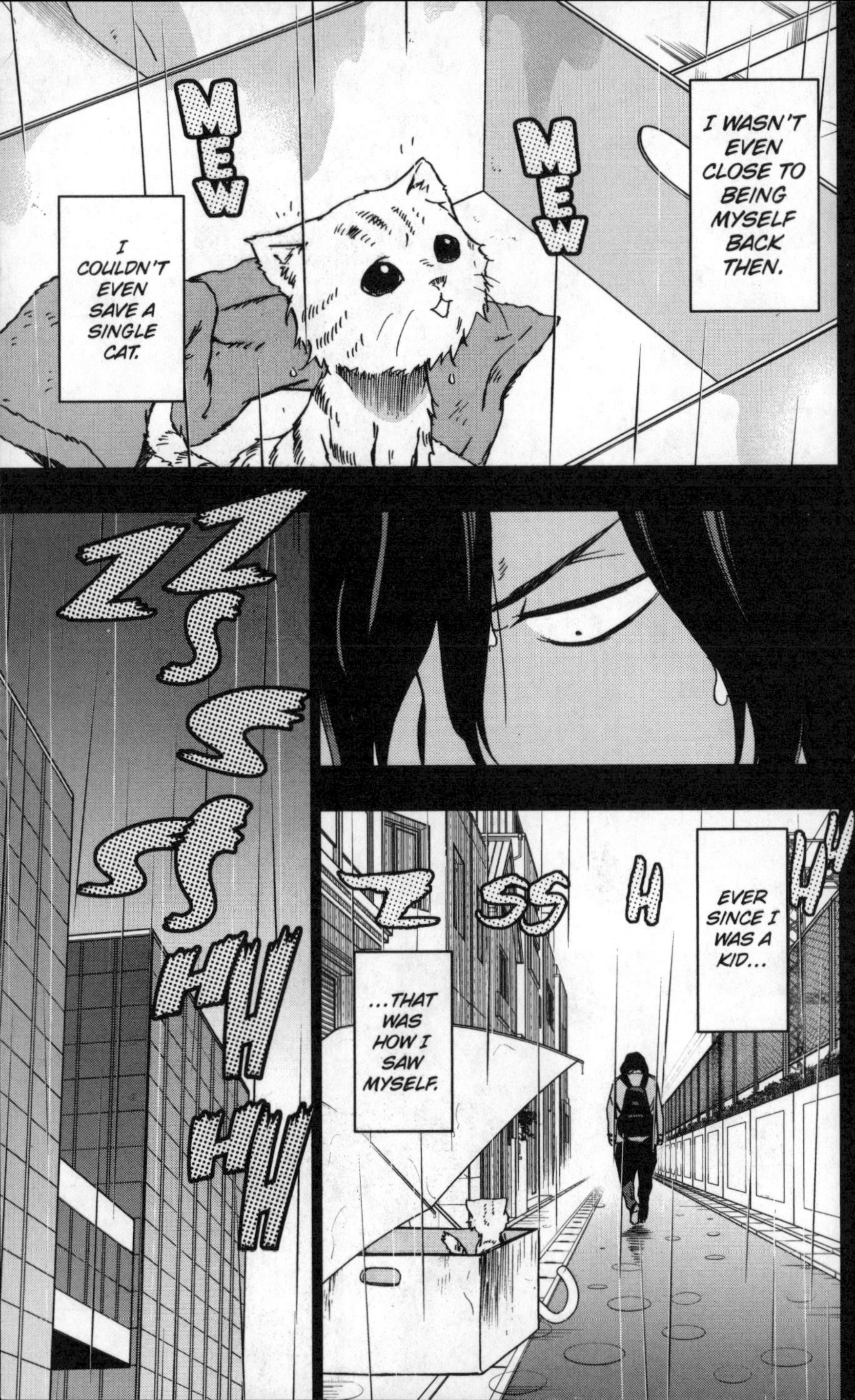
I WASN'T EVEN CLOSE TO BEING MYSELF BACK THEN.
MEW
MEW
I COULDN'T EVEN SAVE A SINGLE CAT.
ZSSHHH
EVER SINCE I WAS A KID...
...THAT WAS HOW I SAW MYSELF.
ZZSSSHHHHH

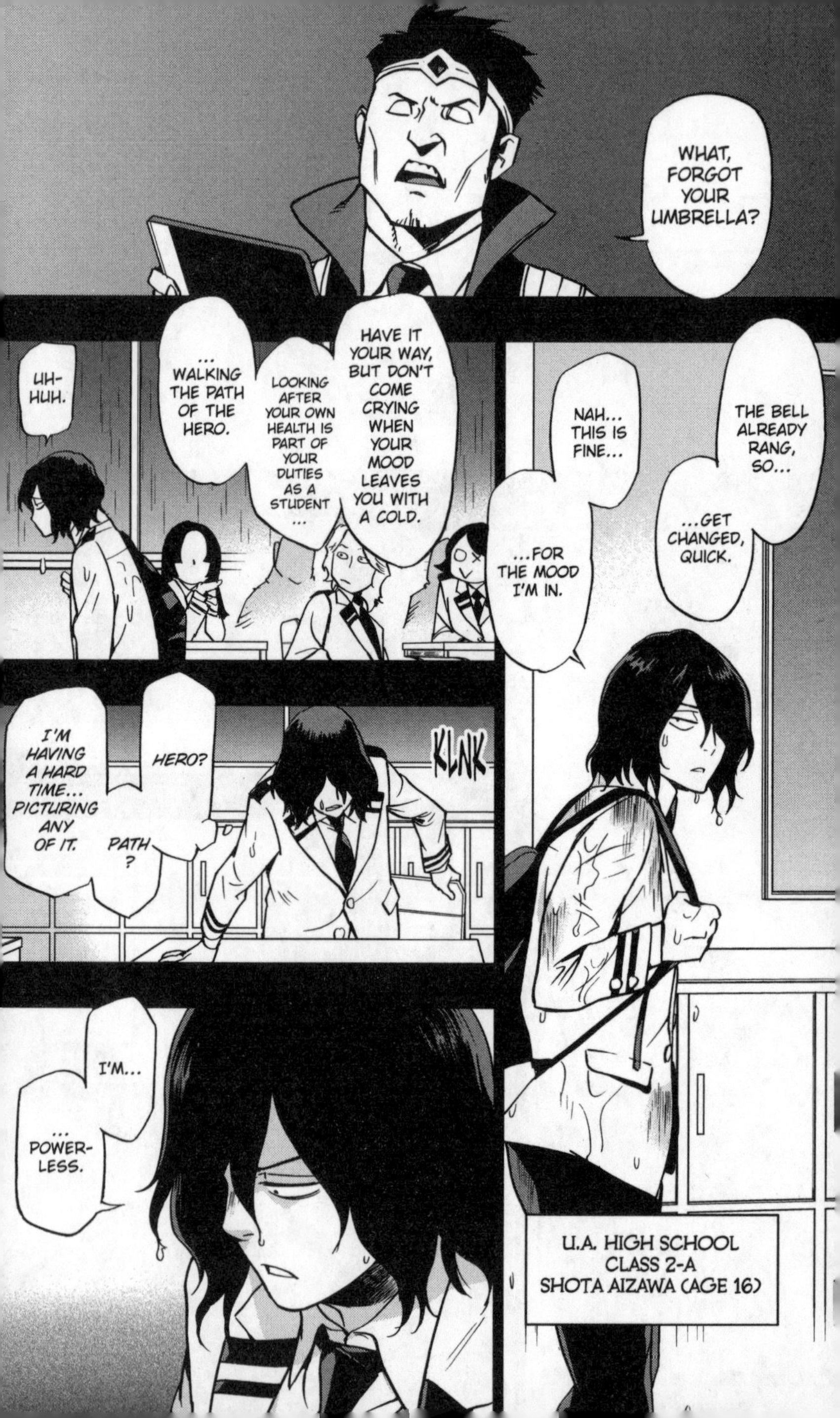
WHAT, FORGOT YOUR UMBRELLA?
THE BELL ALREADY RANG, SO...
...GET CHANGED, QUICK.
NAH... THIS IS FINE...
...FOR THE MOOD I'M IN.
U.A. HIGH SCHOOL CLASS 2-A SHOTA AIZAWA (AGE 16)
HAVE IT YOUR WAY, BUT DON'T COME CRYING WHEN YOUR MOOD LEAVES YOU WITH A COLD.
LOOKING AFTER YOUR OWN HEALTH IS PART OF YOUR DUTIES AS A STUDENT...
...WALKING THE PATH OF THE HERO.
UH-HUH.
KLNK
HERO?
PATH?
I'M HAVING A HARD TIME... PICTURING ANY OF IT.
I'M...
...POWERLESS.

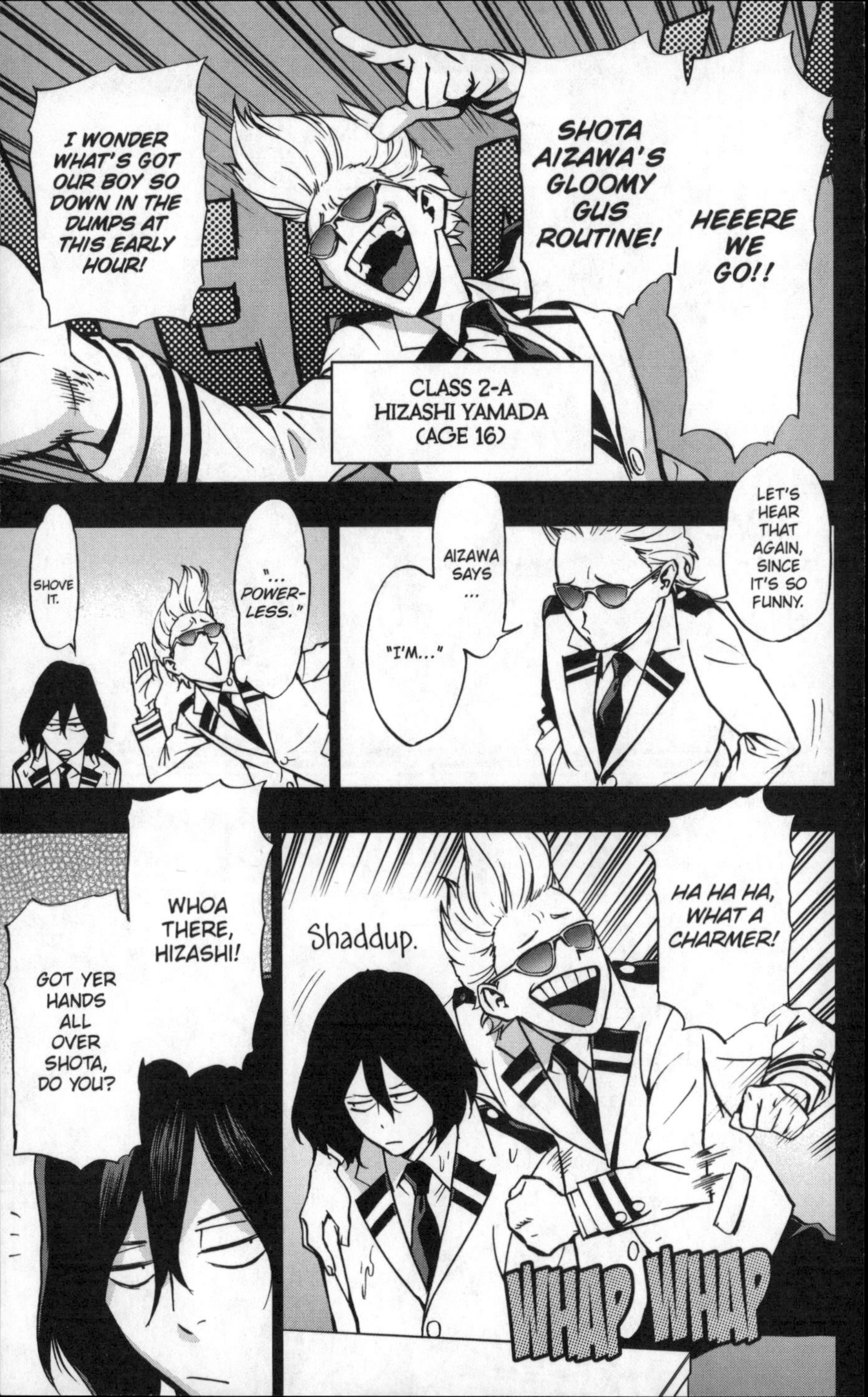
HEEERE WE GO!!
SHOTA AIZAWA'S GLOOMY GUS ROUTINE!
I WONDER WHAT'S GOT OUR BOY SO DOWN IN THE DUMPS AT THIS EARLY HOUR!
CLASS 2-A HIZASHI YAMADA (AGE 16)
LET'S HEAR THAT AGAIN, SINCE IT'S SO FUNNY.
AIZAWA SAYS ...
"I'M..."
"... POWERLESS."
SHOVE IT.
HA HA HA, WHAT A CHARMER!
Shaddup.
WHAP WHAP
WHOA THERE, HIZASHI!
GOT YER HANDS ALL OVER SHOTA, DO YOU?

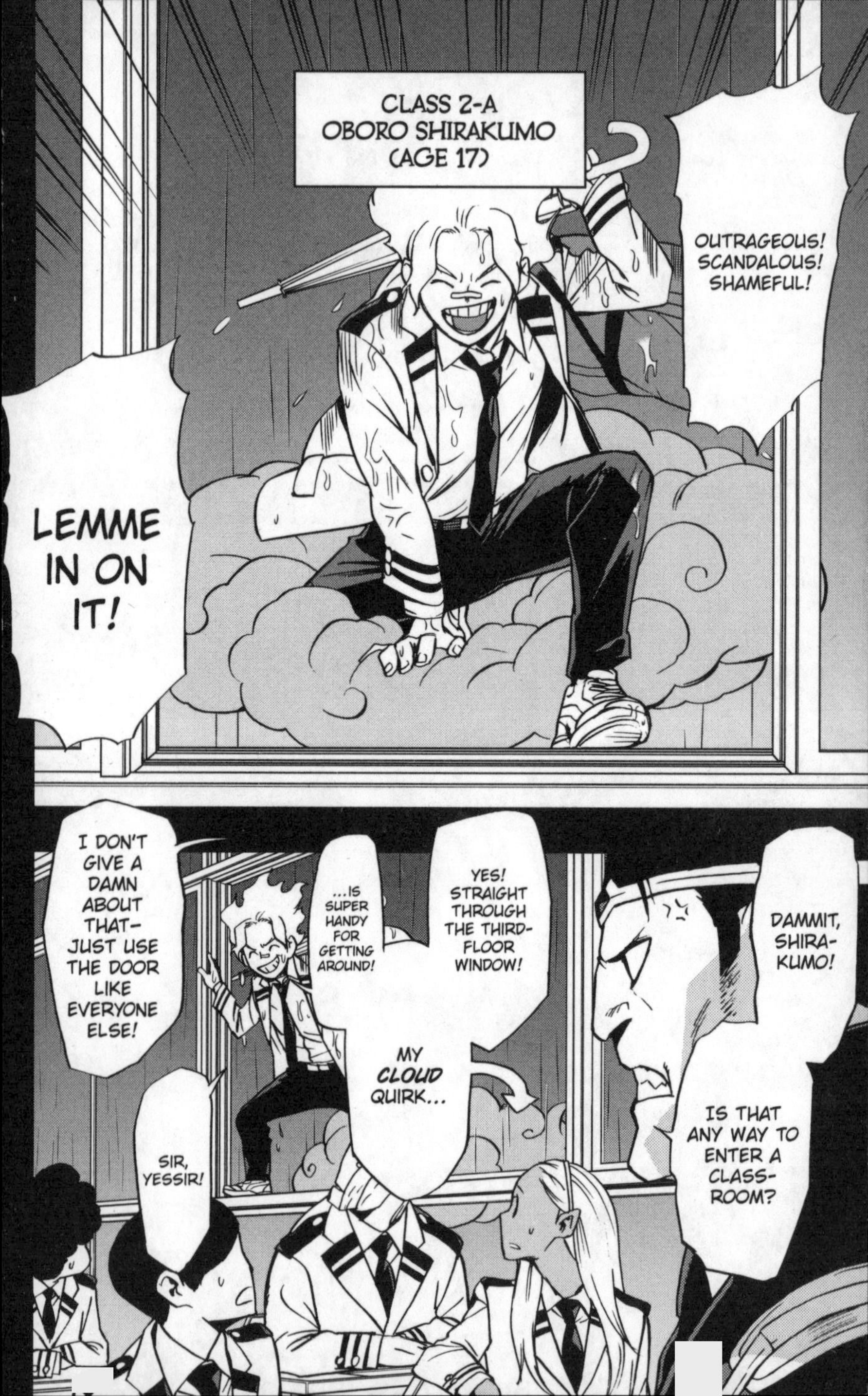
OUTRAGEOUS! SCANDALOUS! SHAMEFUL!
CLASS 2-A OBORO SHIRAKUMO (AGE 17)
LEMME IN ON IT!
DAMMIT, SHIRAKUMO!
IS THAT ANY WAY TO ENTER A CLASSROOM?
YES! STRAIGHT THROUGH THE THIRD-FLOOR WINDOW!
MY ***CLOUD*** QUIRK...
...IS SUPER HANDY FOR GETTING AROUND!
I DON'T GIVE A DAMN ABOUT THAT–JUST USE THE DOOR LIKE EVERYONE ELSE!
SIR, YESSIR!

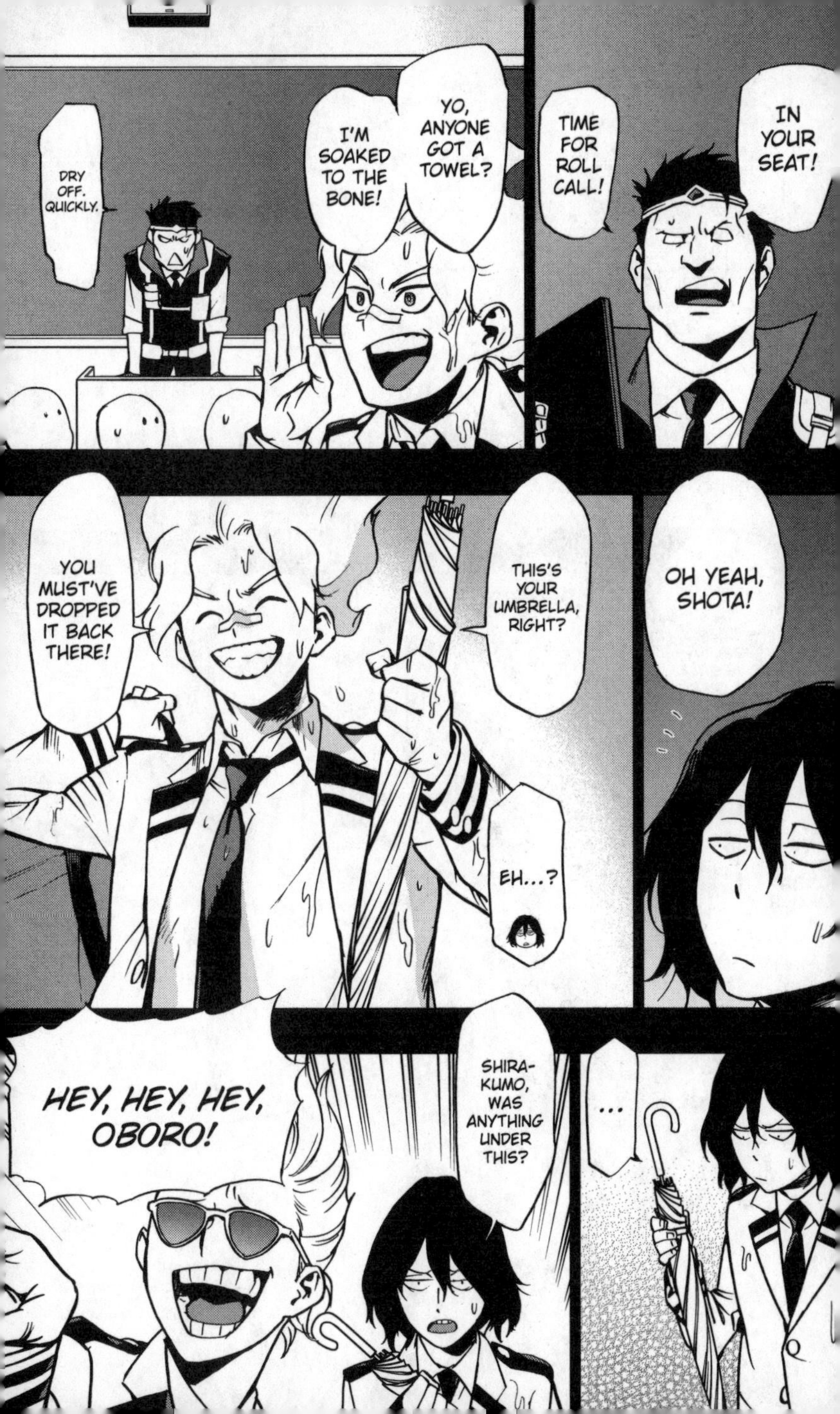
IN YOUR SEAT!
TIME FOR ROLL CALL!
YO, ANYONE GOT A TOWEL?
I'M SOAKED TO THE BONE!
DRY OFF. QUICKLY.
OH YEAH, SHOTA!
THIS'S YOUR UMBRELLA, RIGHT?
YOU MUST'VE DROPPED IT BACK THERE!
EH...?
...
SHIRAKUMO, WAS ANYTHING UNDER THIS?
HEY, HEY, HEY, OBORO!

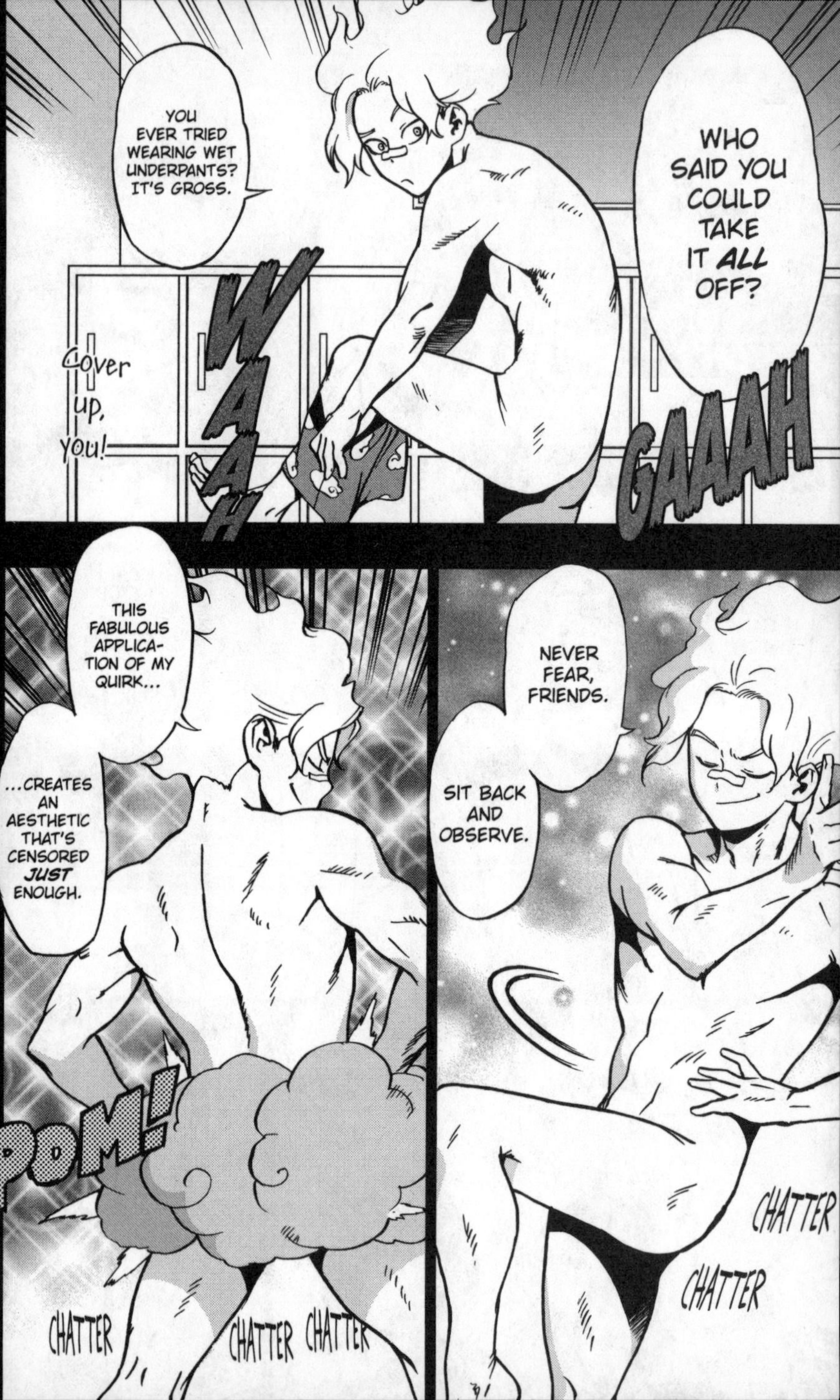
WHO SAID YOU COULD TAKE IT ALL OFF?
GAAAH
YOU EVER TRIED WEARING WET UNDERPANTS? IT'S GROSS.
WAAH
Cover up, you!
NEVER FEAR, FRIENDS.
SIT BACK AND OBSERVE.
CHATTER
CHATTER
THIS FABULOUS APPLICATION OF MY QUIRK...
...CREATES AN AESTHETIC THAT'S CENSORED JUST ENOUGH.
POM!
CHATTER
CHATTER
CHATTER

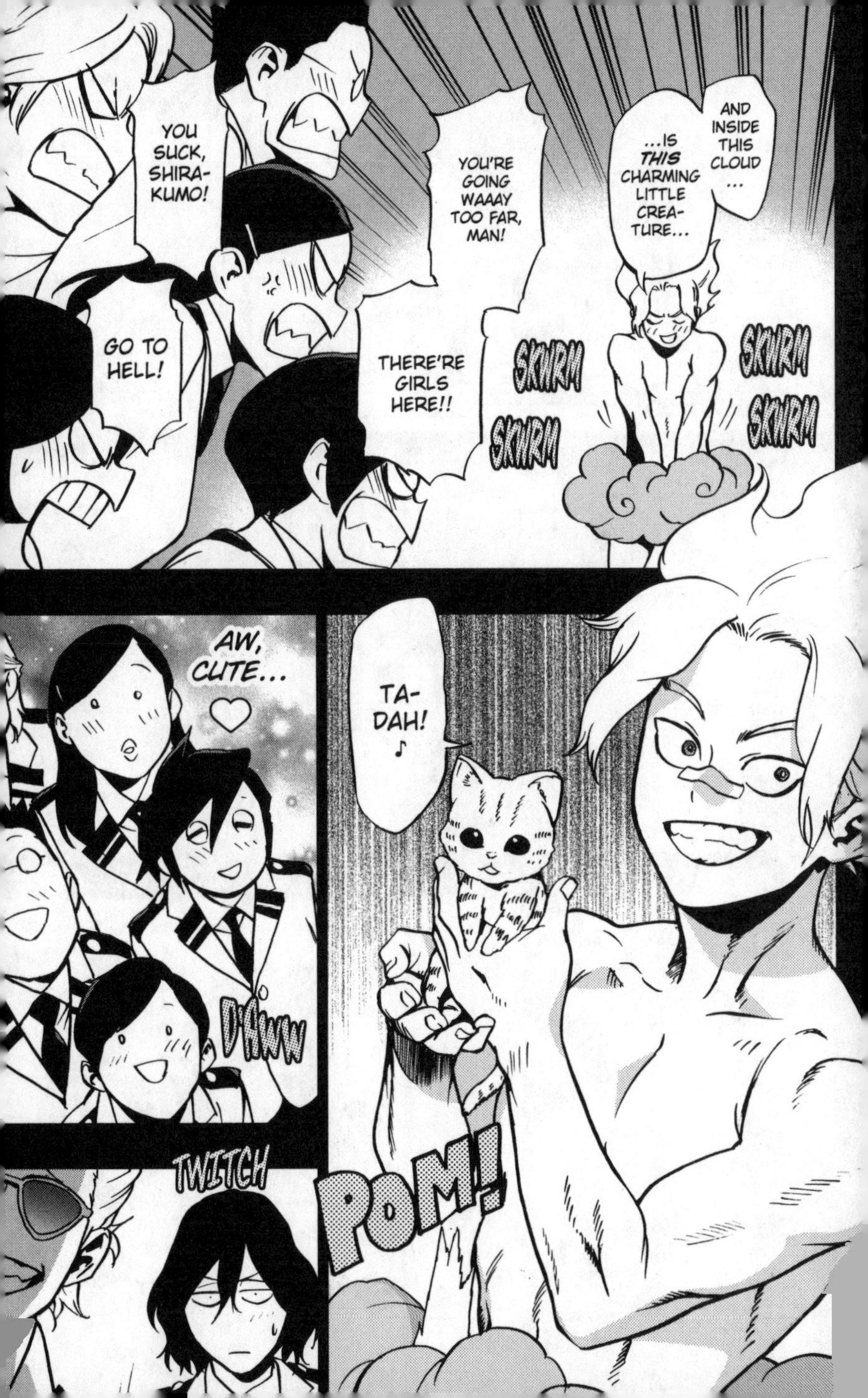

AND INSIDE THIS CLOUD...
...IS *THIS* CHARMING LITTLE CREA-TURE...
SKWRM
SKWRM
SKWRM
SKWRM
YOU'RE GOING WAAAY TOO FAR, MAN!
YOU SUCK, SHIRA-KUMO!
THERE'RE GIRLS HERE!!
GO TO HELL!
TA-DAH! ♪
POM!
AW, CUTE...
D'AWW
TWITCH

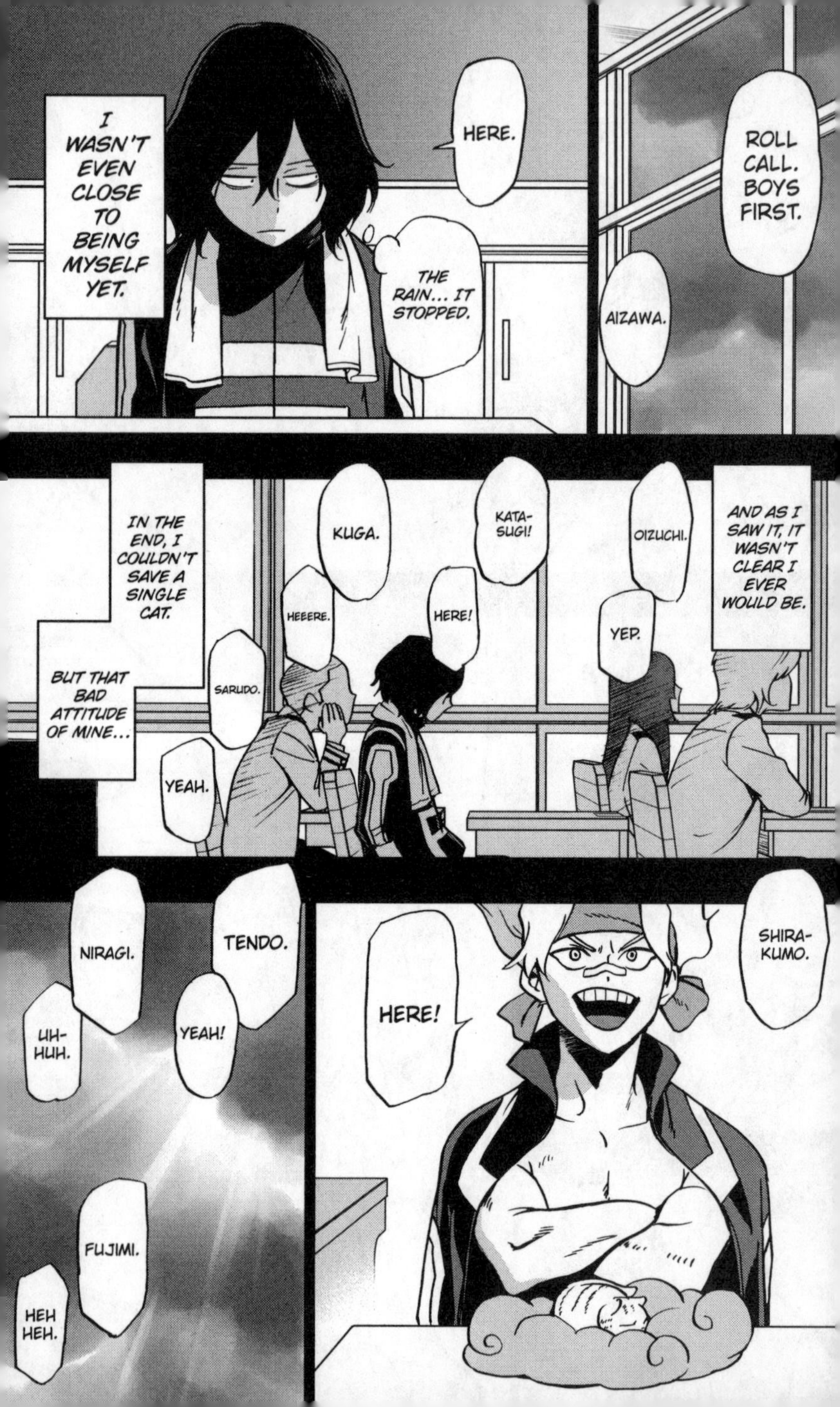

ROLL CALL. BOYS FIRST.
AIZAWA.
HERE.
THE RAIN... IT STOPPED.
I WASN'T EVEN CLOSE TO BEING MYSELF YET.
AND AS I SAW IT, IT WASN'T CLEAR I EVER WOULD BE.
OIZUCHI.
YEP.
KATA-SUGI!
HERE!
KUGA.
HEEERE.
IN THE END, I COULDN'T SAVE A SINGLE CAT.
SARUDO.
YEAH.
BUT THAT BAD ATTITUDE OF MINE...
SHIRA-KUMO.
HERE!
TENDO.
YEAH!
NIRAGI.
UH-HUH.
FUJIMI.
HEH HEH.

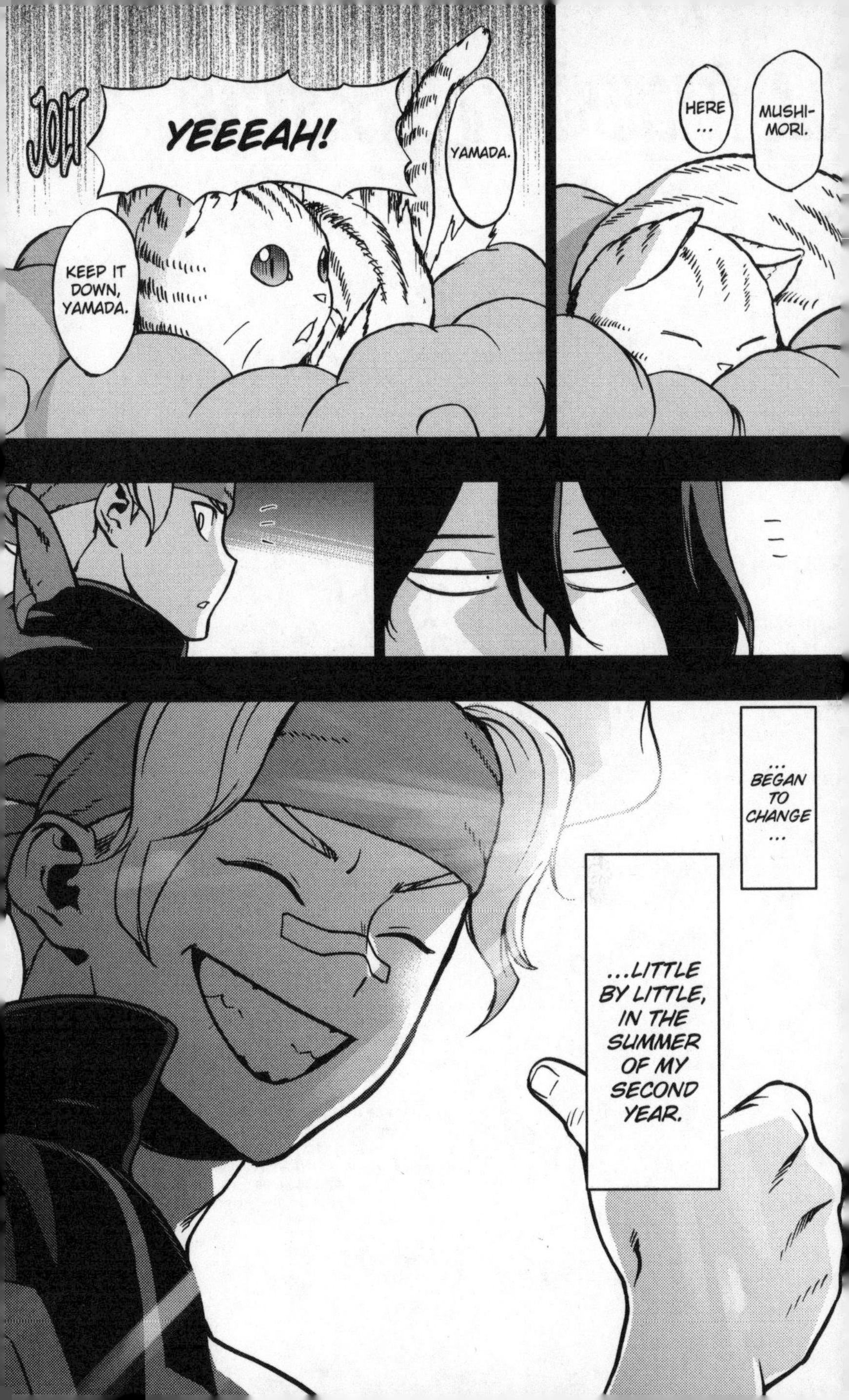
MUSHI-MORI.
HERE ...
YAMADA.
YEEEAH!
JOLT
KEEP IT DOWN, YAMADA.
... BEGAN TO CHANGE ...
...LITTLE BY LITTLE, IN THE SUMMER OF MY SECOND YEAR.

U.A. TEACHERS AND CLASSMATES

THE ROUGH DESIGN

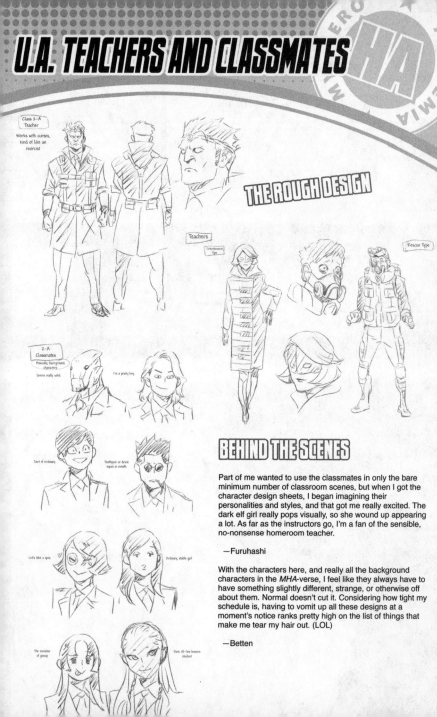

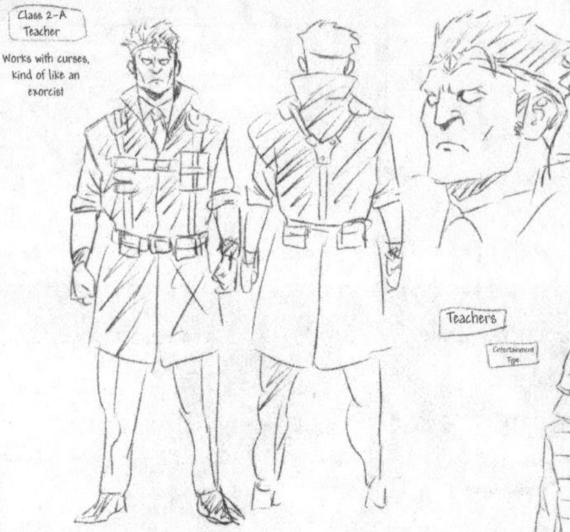
Class 2-A Teacher
Works with curses, kind of like an exorcist

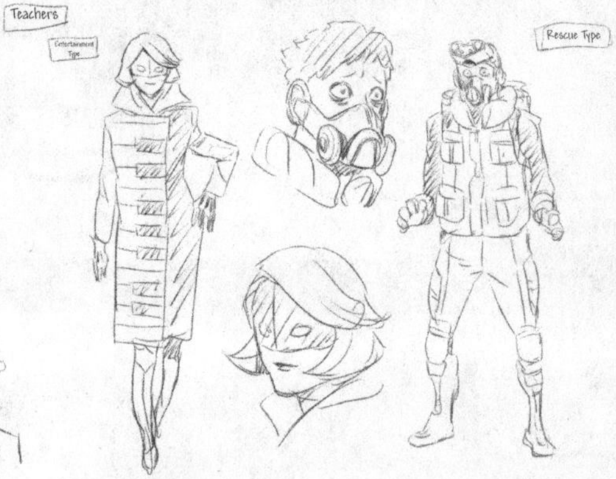
Teachers
Entertainment Type
Rescue Type

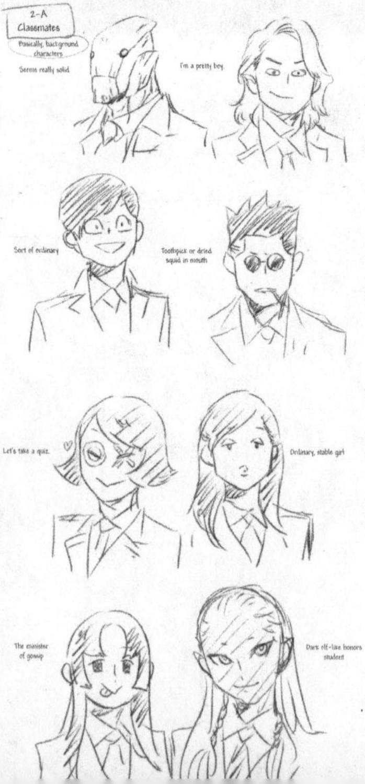
2-A Classmates
Basically, background characters
Seems really solid
I'm a pretty boy.
Sort of ordinary
Toothpick or dried squid in mouth
Let's take a quiz.
Ordinary, stable girl
The minister of gossip
Dark elf-like honors student

BEHIND THE SCENES

Part of me wanted to use the classmates in only the bare minimum number of classroom scenes, but when I got the character design sheets, I began imagining their personalities and styles, and that got me really excited. The dark elf girl really pops visually, so she wound up appearing a lot. As far as the instructors go, I'm a fan of the sensible, no-nonsense homeroom teacher.

—Furuhashi

With the characters here, and really all the background characters in the *MHA*-verse, I feel like they always have to have something slightly different, strange, or otherwise off about them. Normal doesn't cut it. Considering how tight my schedule is, having to vomit up all these designs at a moment's notice ranks pretty high on the list of things that make me tear my hair out. (LOL)

—Betten

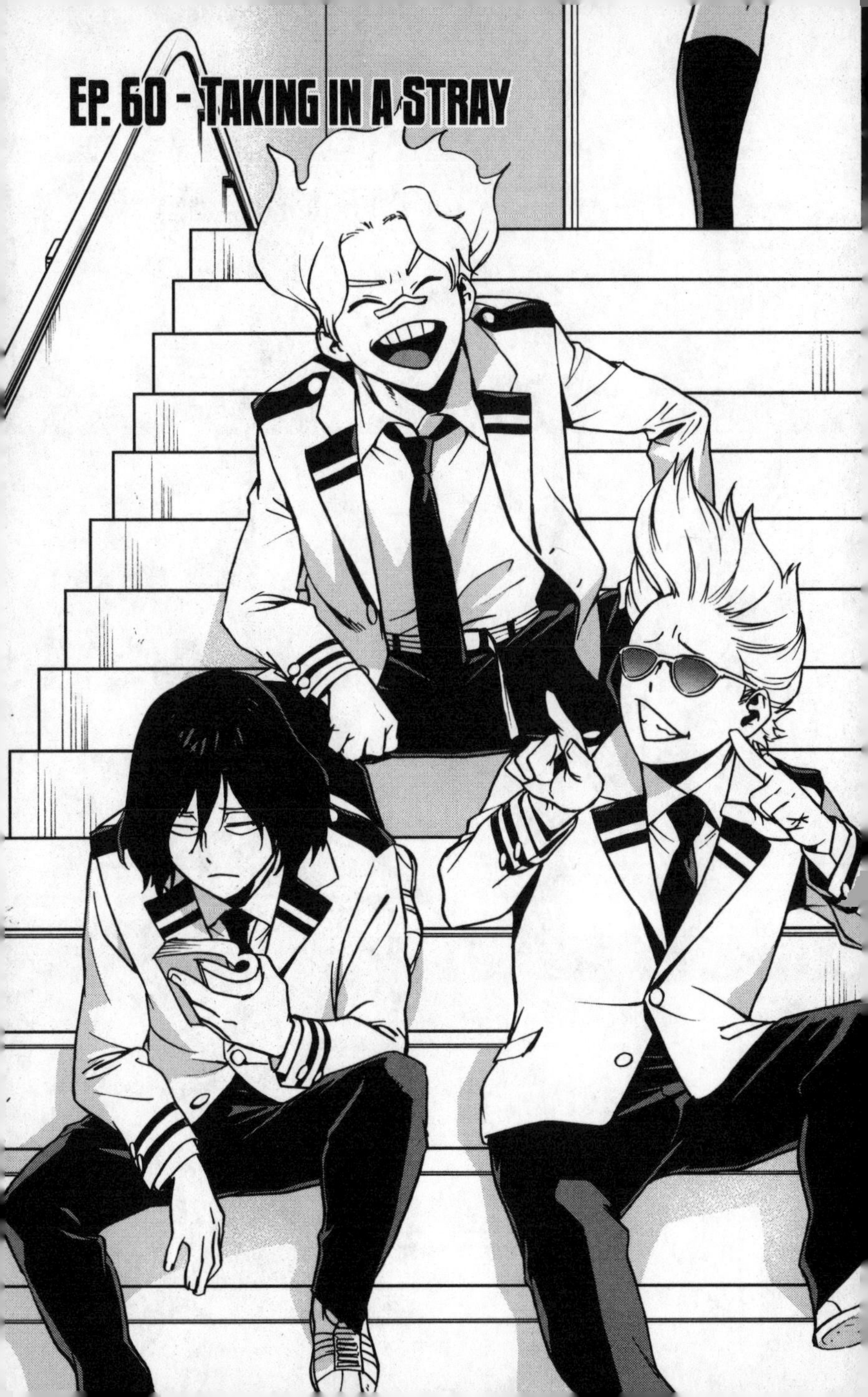
EP. 60 - TAKING IN A STRAY

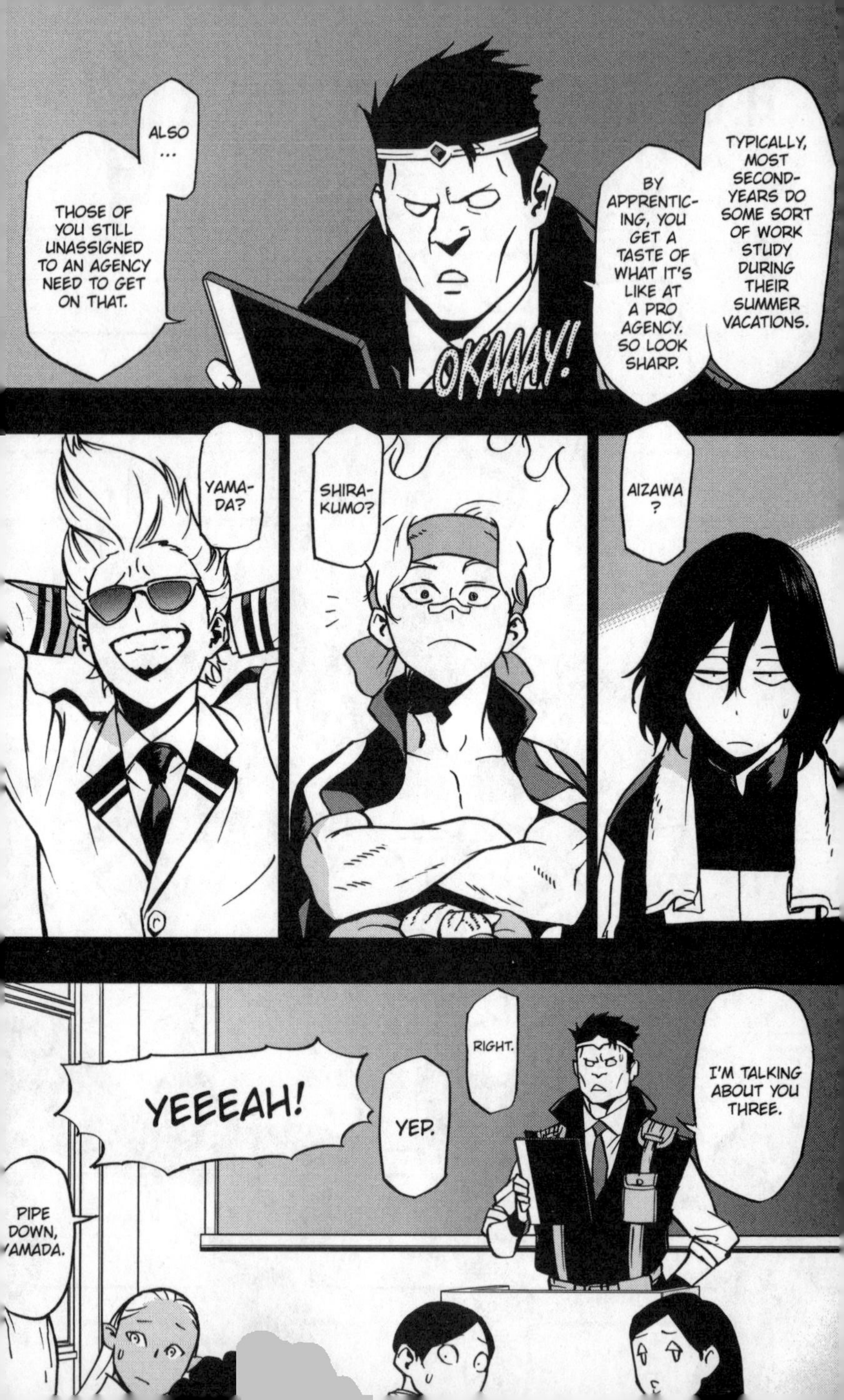
TYPICALLY, MOST SECOND-YEARS DO SOME SORT OF WORK STUDY DURING THEIR SUMMER VACATIONS.
BY APPRENTICING, YOU GET A TASTE OF WHAT IT'S LIKE AT A PRO AGENCY. SO LOOK SHARP.
OKAAAY!
ALSO ...
THOSE OF YOU STILL UNASSIGNED TO AN AGENCY NEED TO GET ON THAT.
AIZAWA ?
SHIRAKUMO?
YAMADA?
I'M TALKING ABOUT YOU THREE.
RIGHT.
YEP.
YEEEAH!
PIPE DOWN, YAMADA.

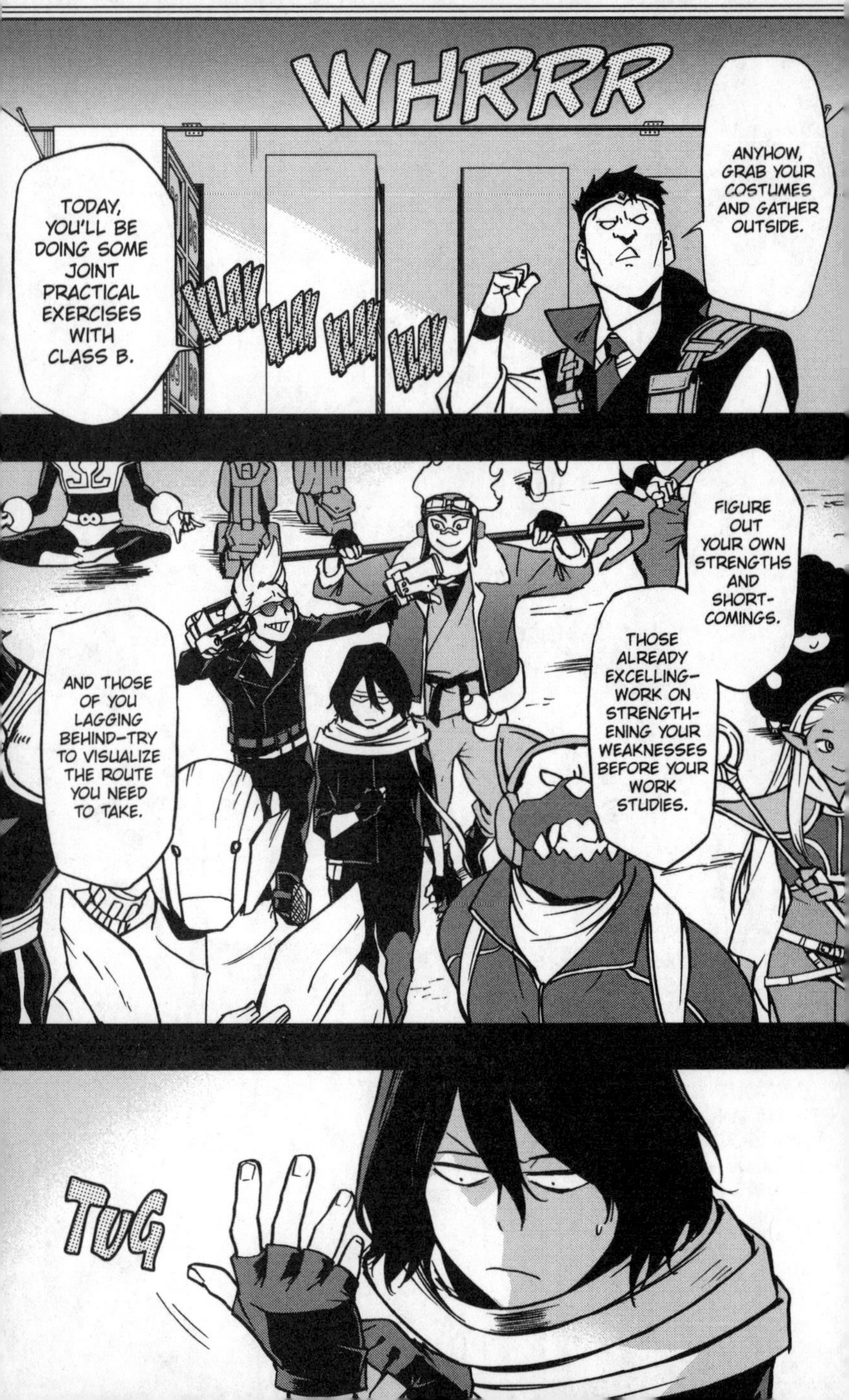
WHRRR
ANYHOW, GRAB YOUR COSTUMES AND GATHER OUTSIDE.
TODAY, YOU'LL BE DOING SOME JOINT PRACTICAL EXERCISES WITH CLASS B.
KLAK KLAK KLAK KLAK
FIGURE OUT YOUR OWN STRENGTHS AND SHORT-COMINGS.
THOSE ALREADY EXCELLING—WORK ON STRENGTH-ENING YOUR WEAKNESSES BEFORE YOUR WORK STUDIES.
AND THOSE OF YOU LAGGING BEHIND—TRY TO VISUALIZE THE ROUTE YOU NEED TO TAKE.
TUG

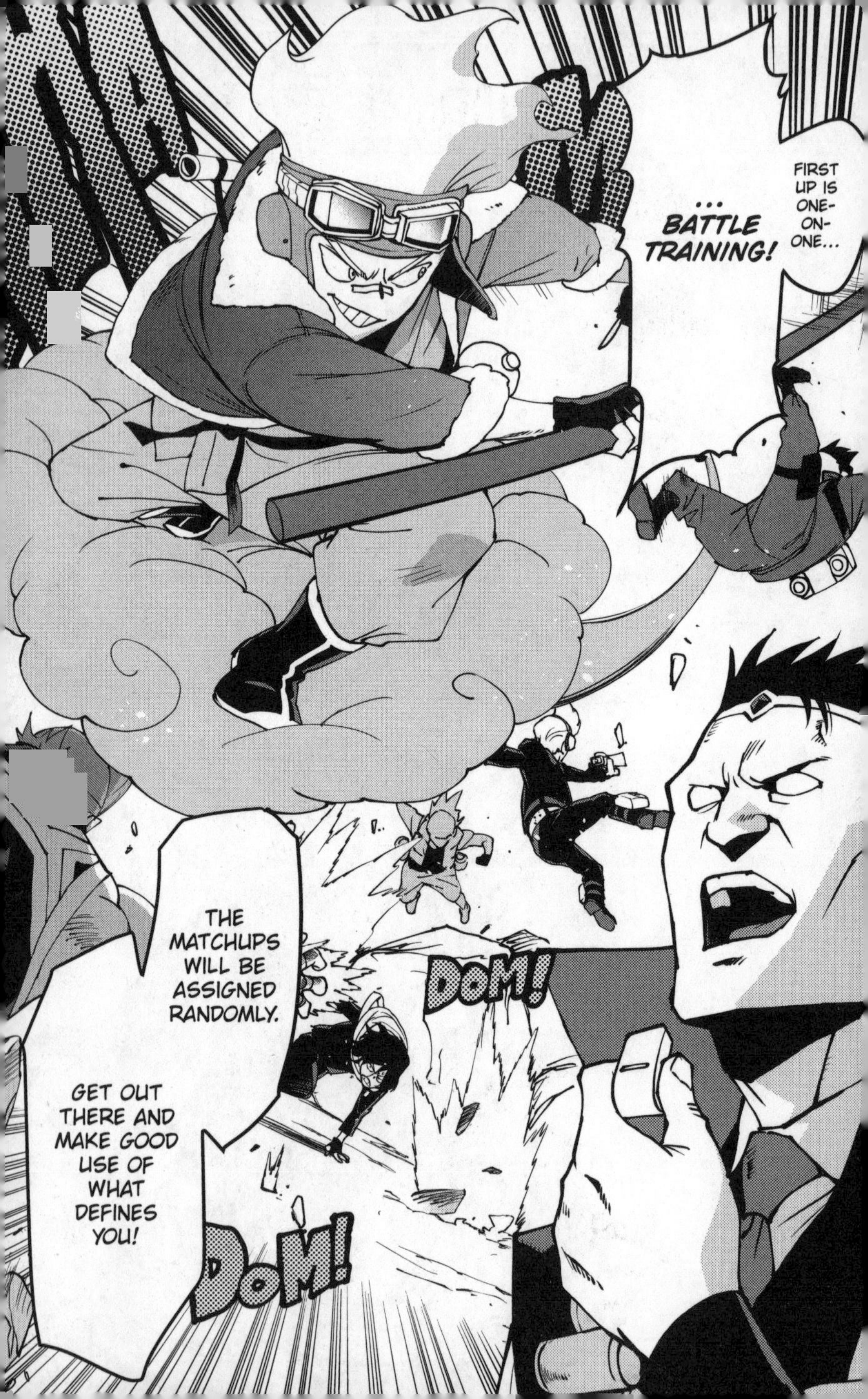
FIRST UP IS ONE-ON-ONE...
... BATTLE TRAINING!
DOM!
THE MATCHUPS WILL BE ASSIGNED RANDOMLY.
GET OUT THERE AND MAKE GOOD USE OF WHAT DEFINES YOU!
DOM!

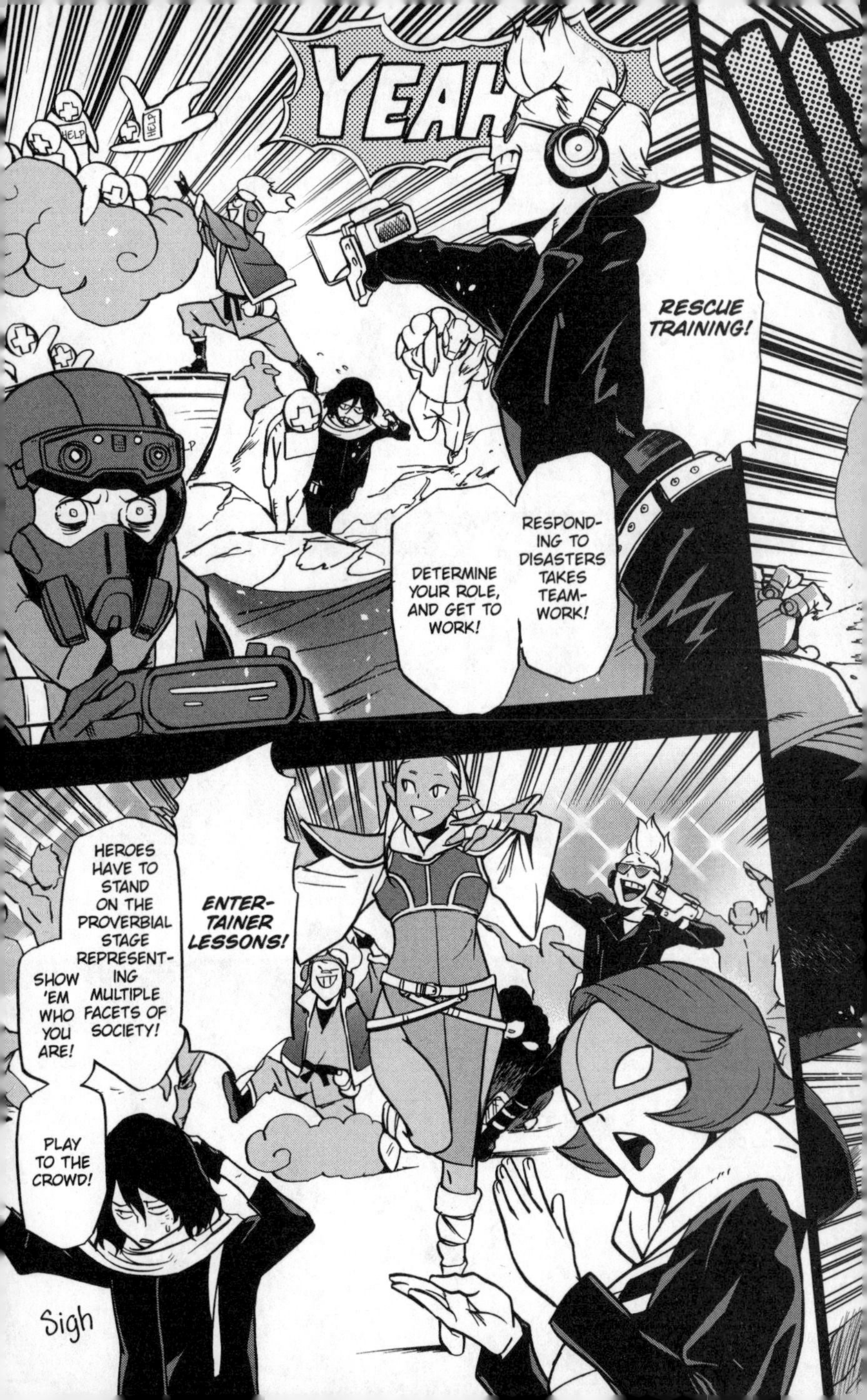
YEAH
RESCUE TRAINING!
RESPONDING TO DISASTERS TAKES TEAMWORK!
DETERMINE YOUR ROLE, AND GET TO WORK!
ENTERTAINER LESSONS!
HEROES HAVE TO STAND ON THE PROVERBIAL STAGE REPRESENTING MULTIPLE FACETS OF SOCIETY!
SHOW 'EM WHO YOU ARE!
PLAY TO THE CROWD!
Sigh

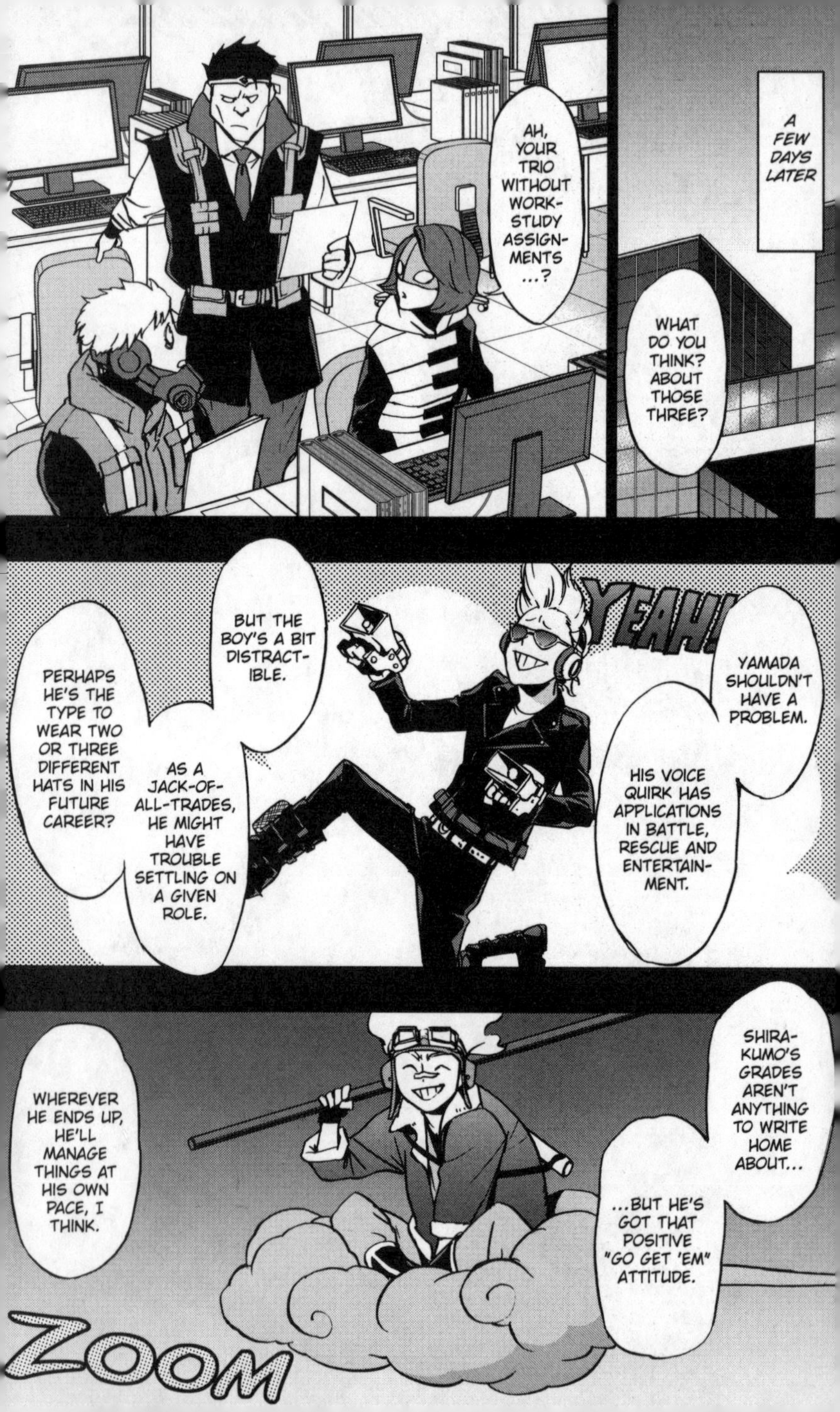
A FEW DAYS LATER
WHAT DO YOU THINK? ABOUT THOSE THREE?
AH, YOUR TRIO WITHOUT WORK-STUDY ASSIGNMENTS...?
YEAH!
YAMADA SHOULDN'T HAVE A PROBLEM.
HIS VOICE QUIRK HAS APPLICATIONS IN BATTLE, RESCUE AND ENTERTAINMENT.
BUT THE BOY'S A BIT DISTRACTIBLE.
AS A JACK-OF-ALL-TRADES, HE MIGHT HAVE TROUBLE SETTLING ON A GIVEN ROLE.
PERHAPS HE'S THE TYPE TO WEAR TWO OR THREE DIFFERENT HATS IN HIS FUTURE CAREER?
SHIRAKUMO'S GRADES AREN'T ANYTHING TO WRITE HOME ABOUT...
...BUT HE'S GOT THAT POSITIVE "GO GET 'EM" ATTITUDE.
WHEREVER HE ENDS UP, HE'LL MANAGE THINGS AT HIS OWN PACE, I THINK.
ZOOM

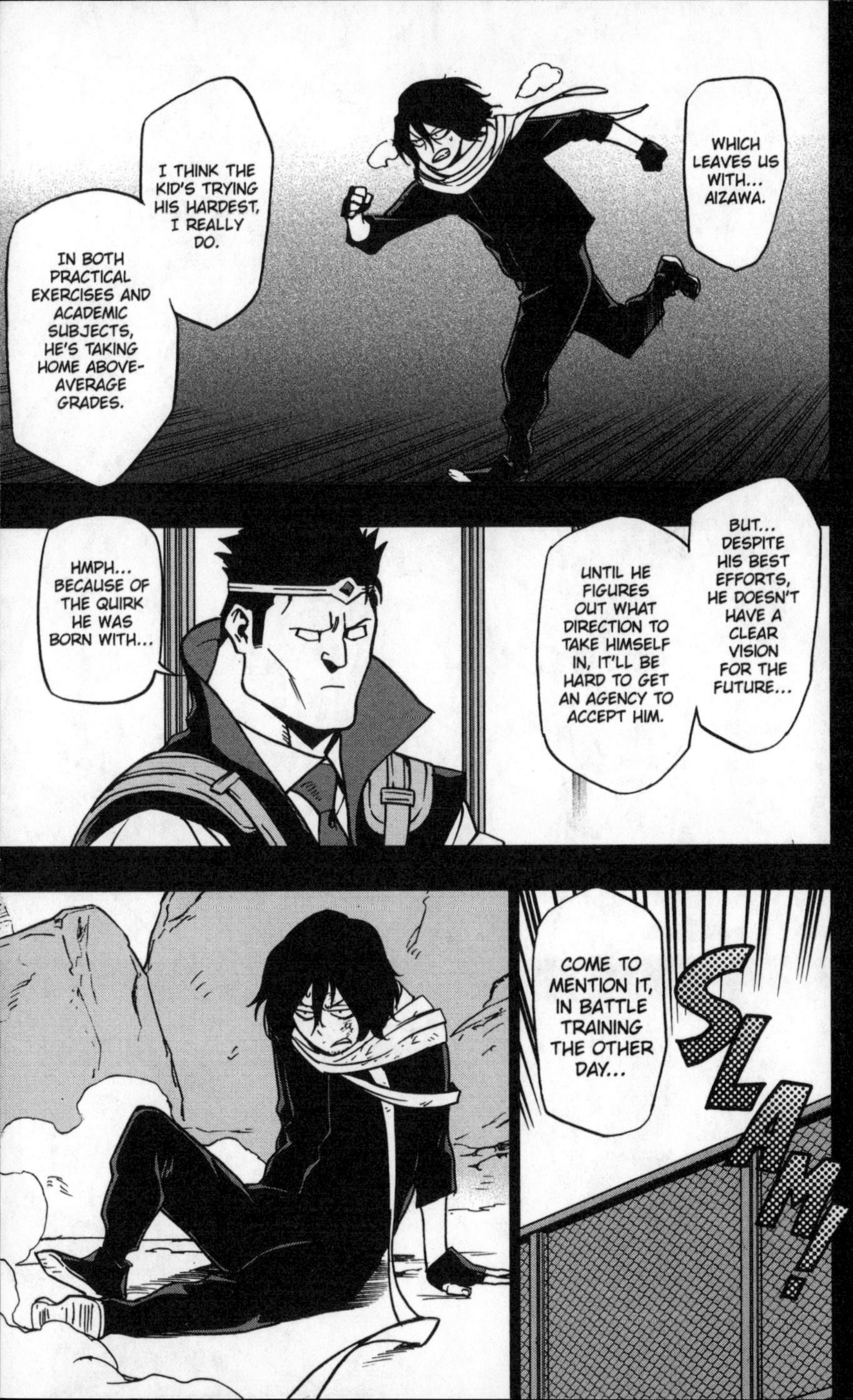
WHICH LEAVES US WITH... AIZAWA.
I THINK THE KID'S TRYING HIS HARDEST, I REALLY DO.
IN BOTH PRACTICAL EXERCISES AND ACADEMIC SUBJECTS, HE'S TAKING HOME ABOVE-AVERAGE GRADES.
BUT... DESPITE HIS BEST EFFORTS, HE DOESN'T HAVE A CLEAR VISION FOR THE FUTURE...
UNTIL HE FIGURES OUT WHAT DIRECTION TO TAKE HIMSELF IN, IT'LL BE HARD TO GET AN AGENCY TO ACCEPT HIM.
HMPH... BECAUSE OF THE QUIRK HE WAS BORN WITH...
COME TO MENTION IT, IN BATTLE TRAINING THE OTHER DAY...
SLAM!!

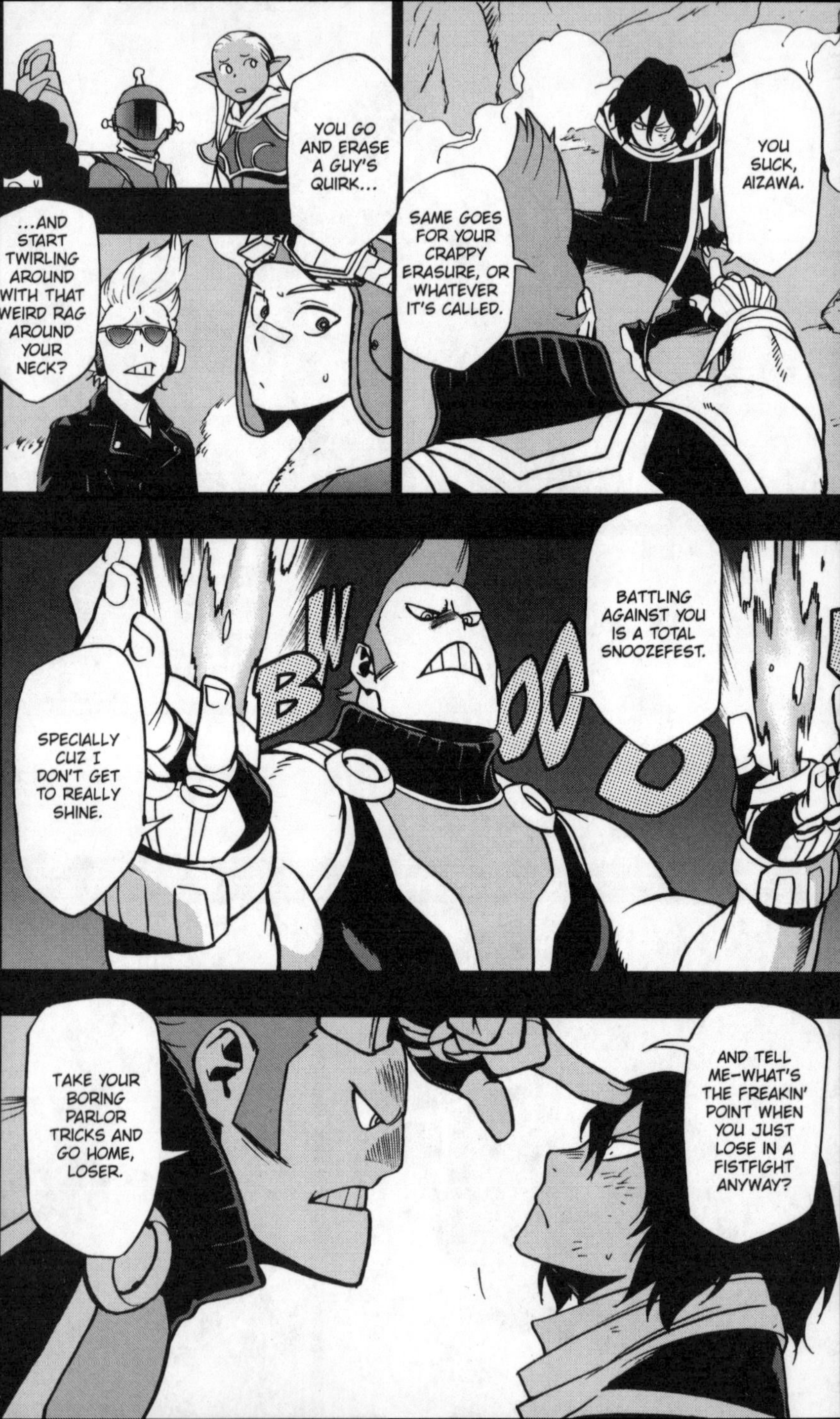
YOU SUCK, AIZAWA.
SAME GOES FOR YOUR CRAPPY ERASURE, OR WHATEVER IT'S CALLED.
YOU GO AND ERASE A GUY'S QUIRK...
...AND START TWIRLING AROUND WITH THAT WEIRD RAG AROUND YOUR NECK?
BATTLING AGAINST YOU IS A TOTAL SNOOZEFEST.
BOOOD
SPECIALLY CUZ I DON'T GET TO REALLY SHINE.
AND TELL ME—WHAT'S THE FREAKIN' POINT WHEN YOU JUST LOSE IN A FISTFIGHT ANYWAY?
TAKE YOUR BORING PARLOR TRICKS AND GO HOME, LOSER.

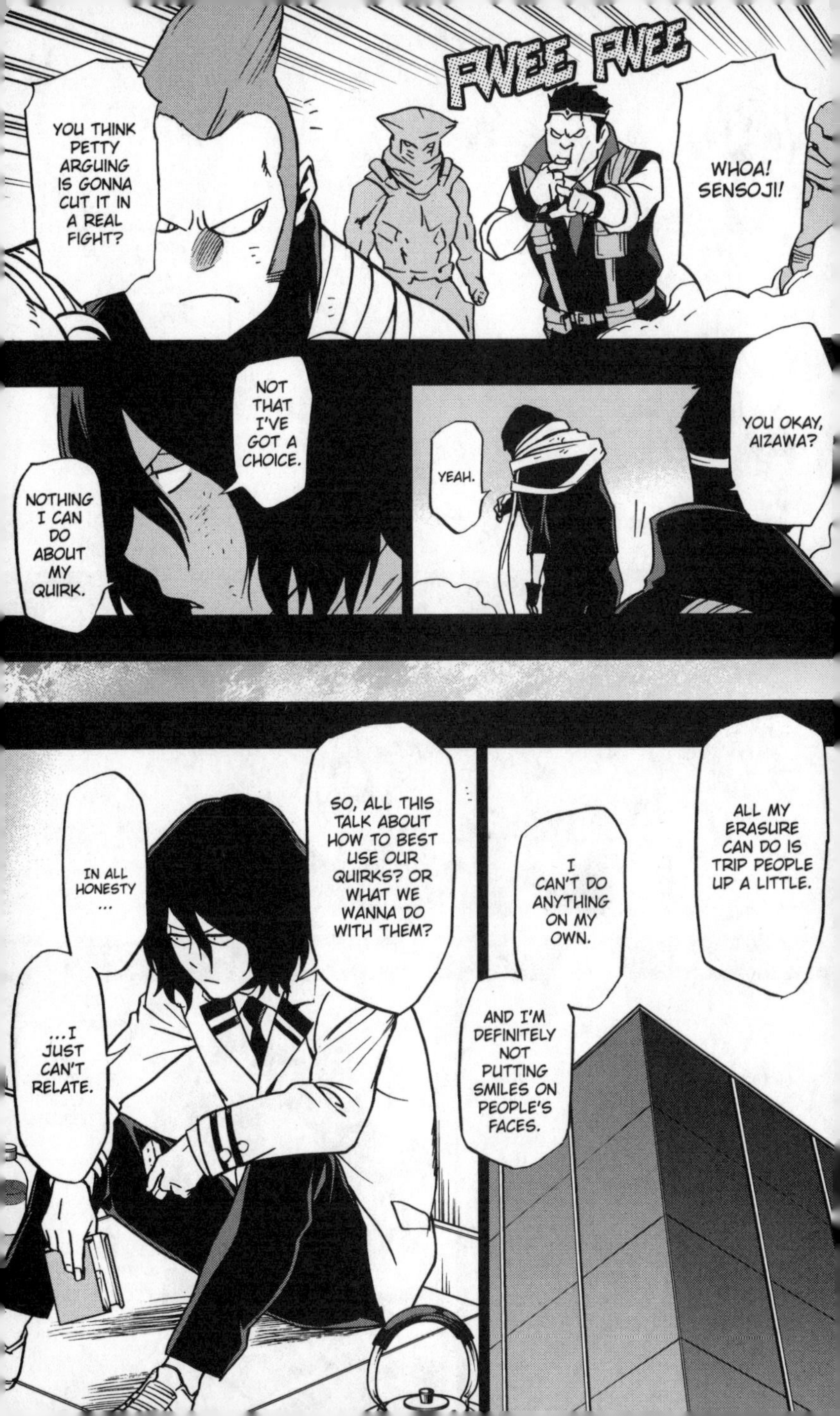
FWEE FWEE
WHOA! SENSOJI!
YOU THINK PETTY ARGUING IS GONNA CUT IT IN A REAL FIGHT?
YOU OKAY, AIZAWA?
YEAH.
NOT THAT I'VE GOT A CHOICE.
NOTHING I CAN DO ABOUT MY QUIRK.
ALL MY ERASURE CAN DO IS TRIP PEOPLE UP A LITTLE.
I CAN'T DO ANYTHING ON MY OWN.
AND I'M DEFINITELY NOT PUTTING SMILES ON PEOPLE'S FACES.
SO, ALL THIS TALK ABOUT HOW TO BEST USE OUR QUIRKS? OR WHAT WE WANNA DO WITH THEM?
IN ALL HONESTY ...
...I JUST CAN'T RELATE.

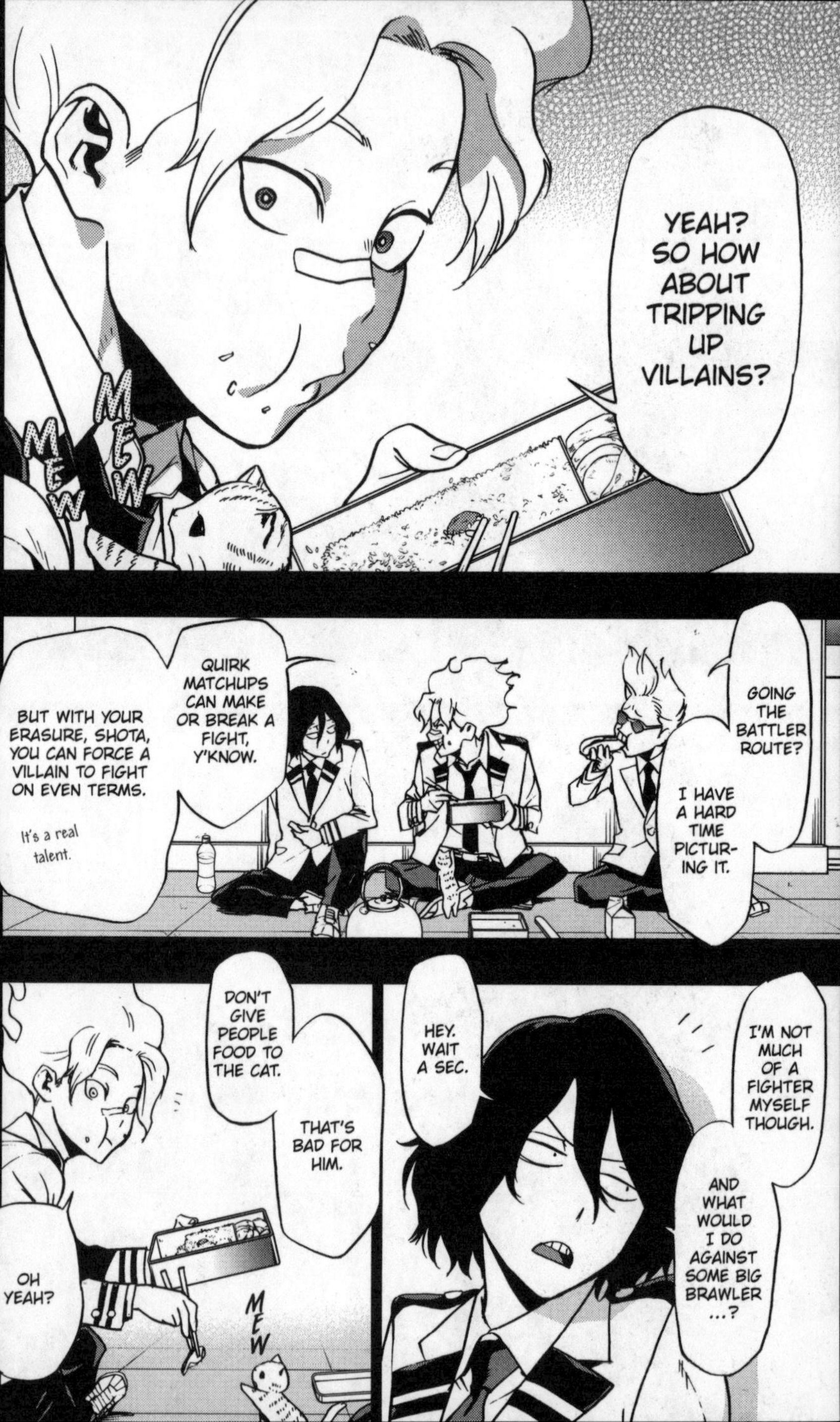
YEAH? SO HOW ABOUT TRIPPING UP VILLAINS?
MEW MEW
MEW MEW
GOING THE BATTLER ROUTE?
I HAVE A HARD TIME PICTURING IT.
QUIRK MATCHUPS CAN MAKE OR BREAK A FIGHT, Y'KNOW.
BUT WITH YOUR ERASURE, SHOTA, YOU CAN FORCE A VILLAIN TO FIGHT ON EVEN TERMS.
It's a real talent.
I'M NOT MUCH OF A FIGHTER MYSELF THOUGH.
HEY. WAIT A SEC.
AND WHAT WOULD I DO AGAINST SOME BIG BRAWLER ...?
DON'T GIVE PEOPLE FOOD TO THE CAT.
THAT'S BAD FOR HIM.
OH YEAH?
MEW

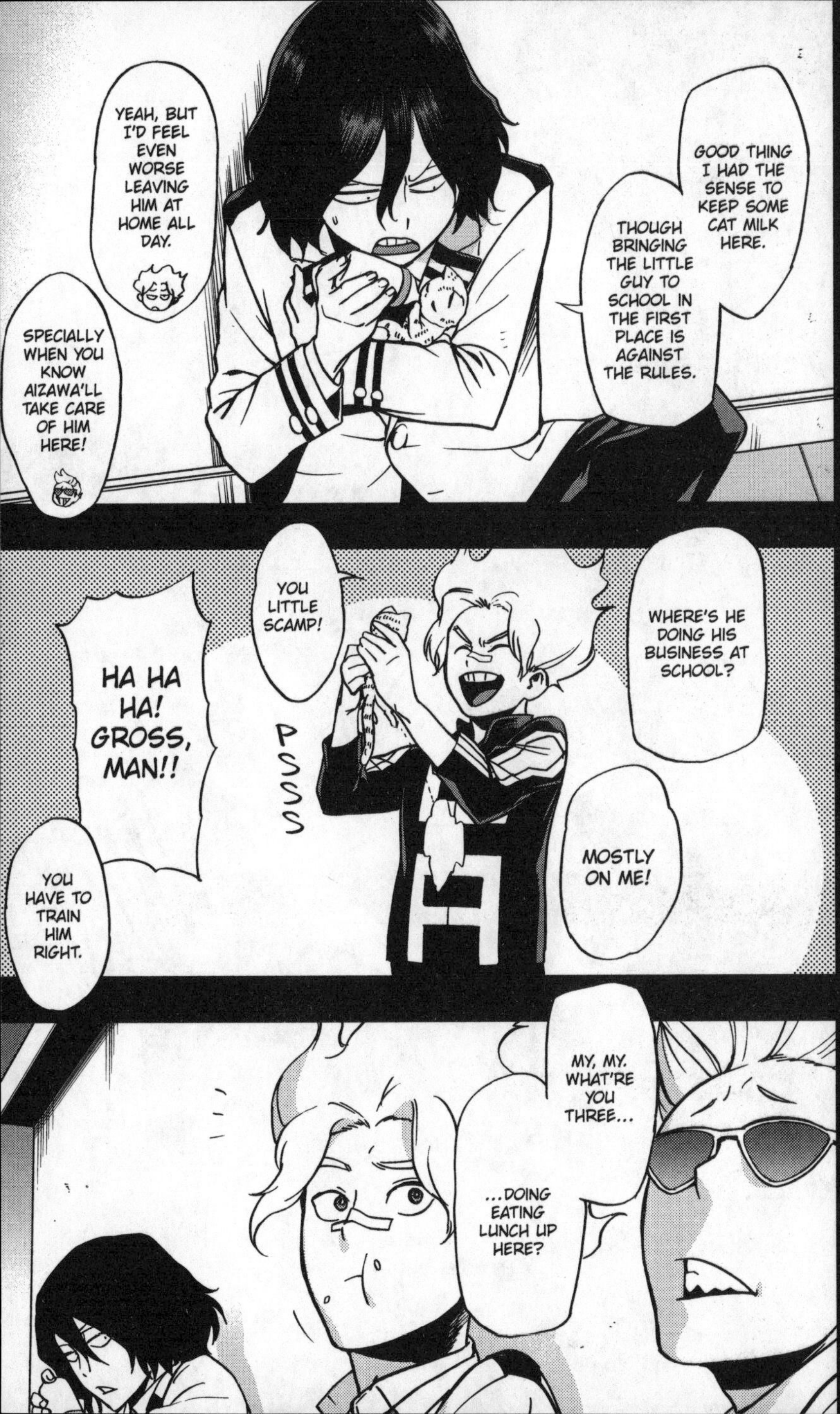
GOOD THING I HAD THE SENSE TO KEEP SOME CAT MILK HERE.
THOUGH BRINGING THE LITTLE GUY TO SCHOOL IN THE FIRST PLACE IS AGAINST THE RULES.
YEAH, BUT I'D FEEL EVEN WORSE LEAVING HIM AT HOME ALL DAY.
SPECIALLY WHEN YOU KNOW AIZAWA'LL TAKE CARE OF HIM HERE!
WHERE'S HE DOING HIS BUSINESS AT SCHOOL?
MOSTLY ON ME!
YOU LITTLE SCAMP!
PSSS
HA HA HA! GROSS, MAN!!
YOU HAVE TO TRAIN HIM RIGHT.
MY, MY. WHAT'RE YOU THREE...
...DOING EATING LUNCH UP HERE?

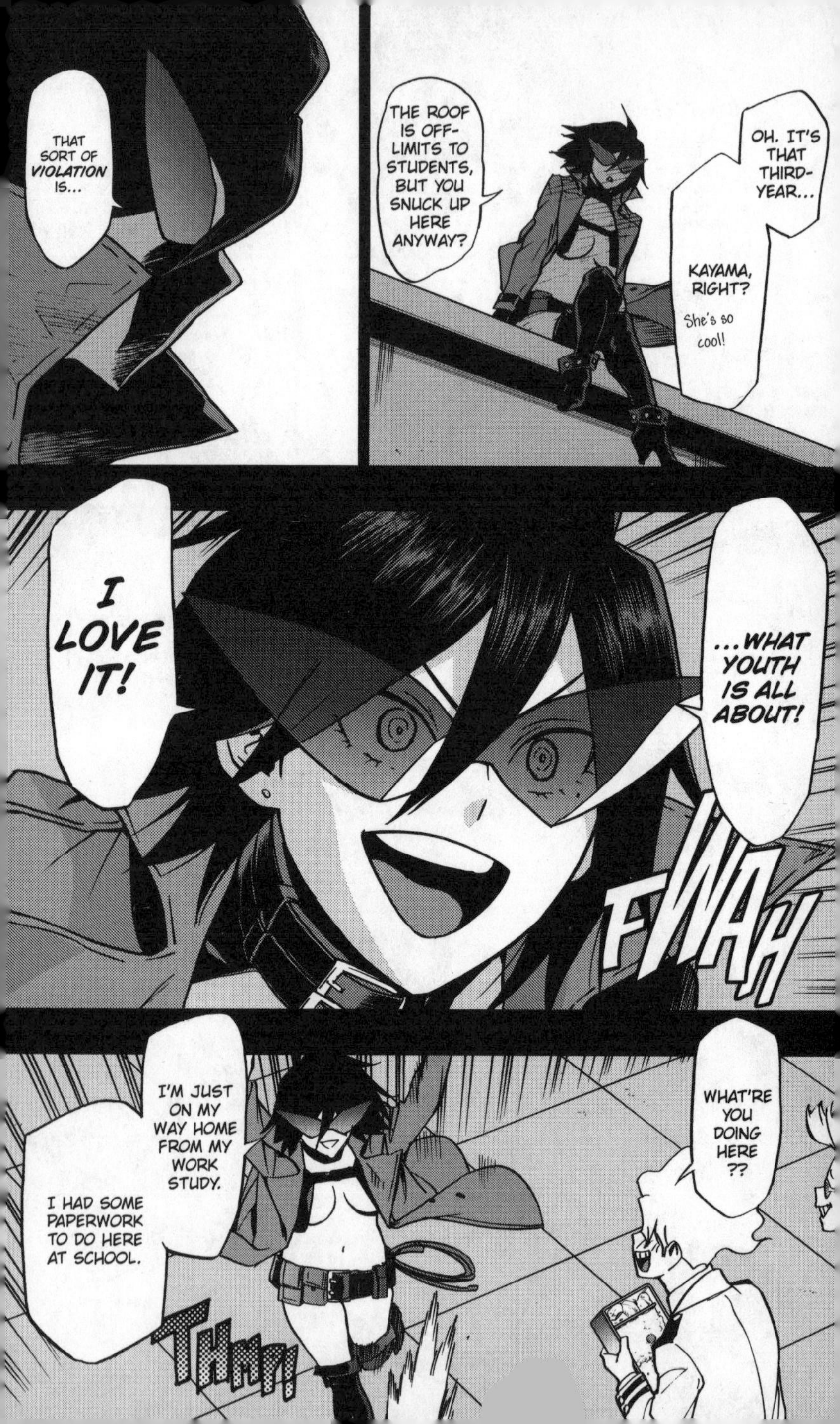
OH. IT'S THAT THIRD-YEAR...
KAYAMA, RIGHT?
She's so cool!
THE ROOF IS OFF-LIMITS TO STUDENTS, BUT YOU SNUCK UP HERE ANYWAY?
THAT SORT OF *VIOLATION* IS...
...WHAT YOUTH IS ALL ABOUT!
I LOVE IT!
FWAH
WHAT'RE YOU DOING HERE??
I'M JUST ON MY WAY HOME FROM MY WORK STUDY.
I HAD SOME PAPERWORK TO DO HERE AT SCHOOL.
THMP!

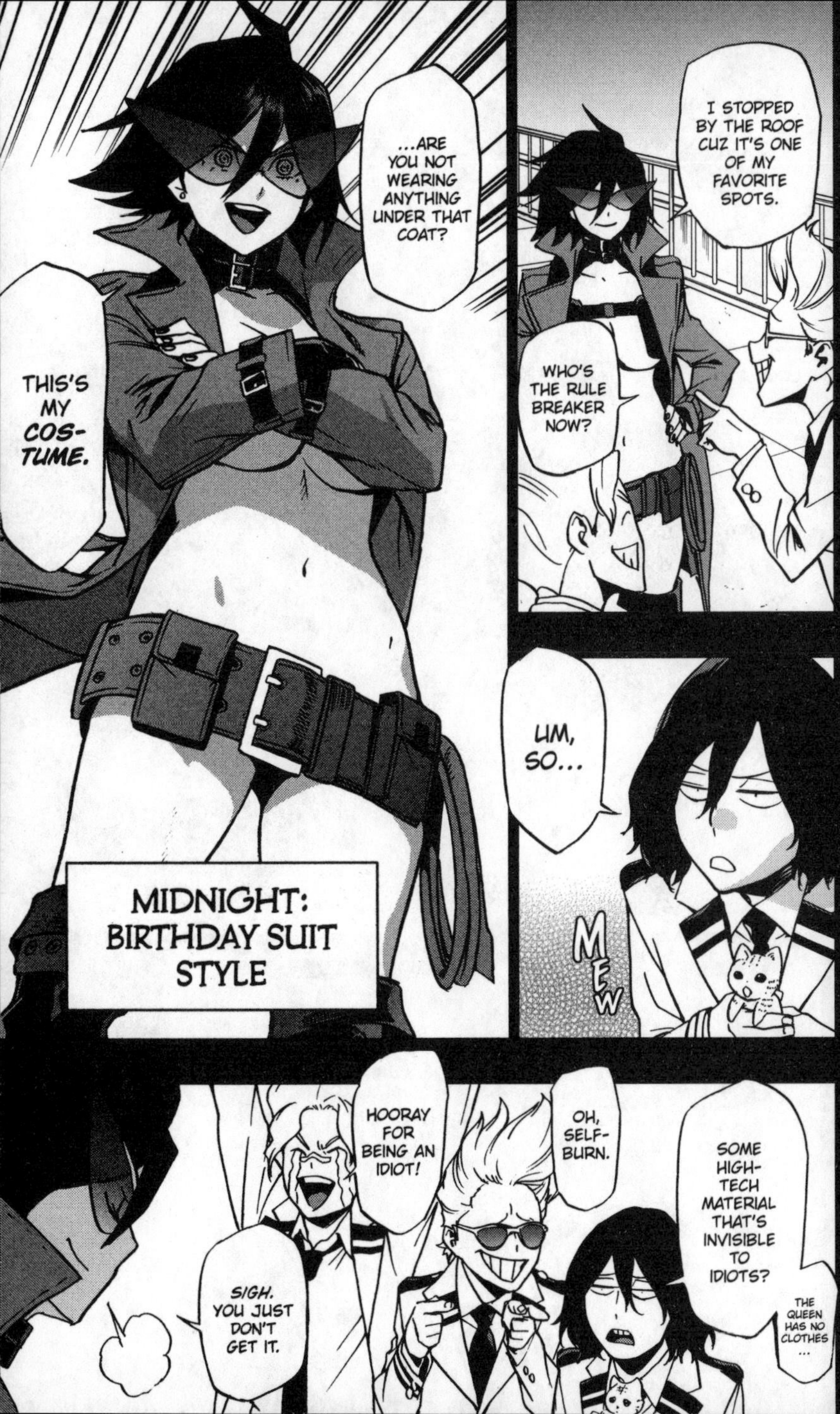
I STOPPED BY THE ROOF CUZ IT'S ONE OF MY FAVORITE SPOTS.
WHO'S THE RULE BREAKER NOW?
UM, SO...
MEW
...ARE YOU NOT WEARING ANYTHING UNDER THAT COAT?
THIS'S MY COSTUME.
MIDNIGHT: BIRTHDAY SUIT STYLE
SOME HIGH-TECH MATERIAL THAT'S INVISIBLE TO IDIOTS?
THE QUEEN HAS NO CLOTHES ...
OH, SELF-BURN.
HOORAY FOR BEING AN IDIOT!
SIGH. YOU JUST DON'T GET IT.

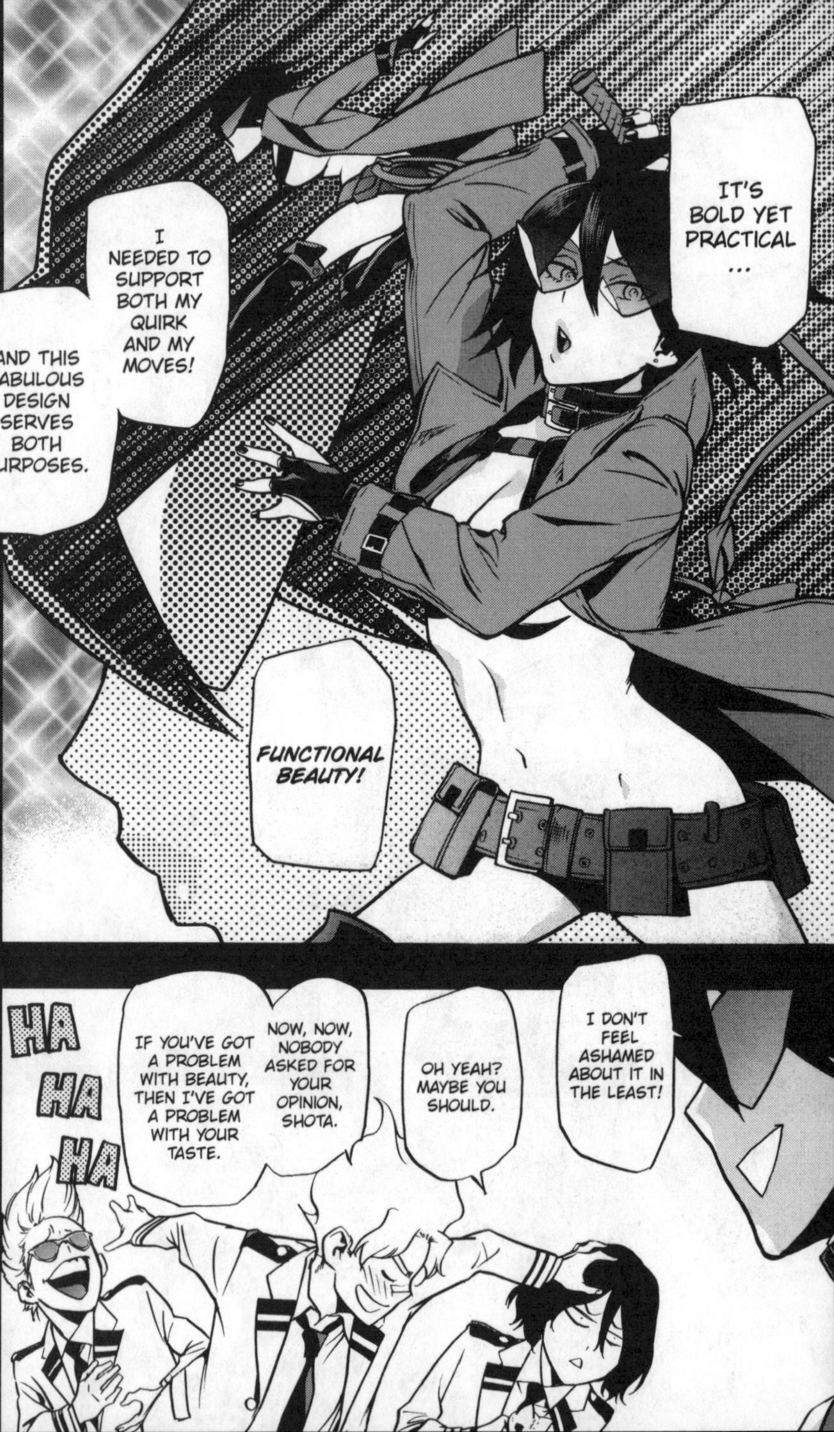
IT'S BOLD YET PRACTICAL...
I NEEDED TO SUPPORT BOTH MY QUIRK AND MY MOVES!
AND THIS FABULOUS DESIGN SERVES BOTH PURPOSES.
FUNCTIONAL BEAUTY!
I DON'T FEEL ASHAMED ABOUT IT IN THE LEAST!
OH YEAH? MAYBE YOU SHOULD.
NOW, NOW, NOBODY ASKED FOR YOUR OPINION, SHOTA.
IF YOU'VE GOT A PROBLEM WITH BEAUTY, THEN I'VE GOT A PROBLEM WITH YOUR TASTE.
HA HA HA

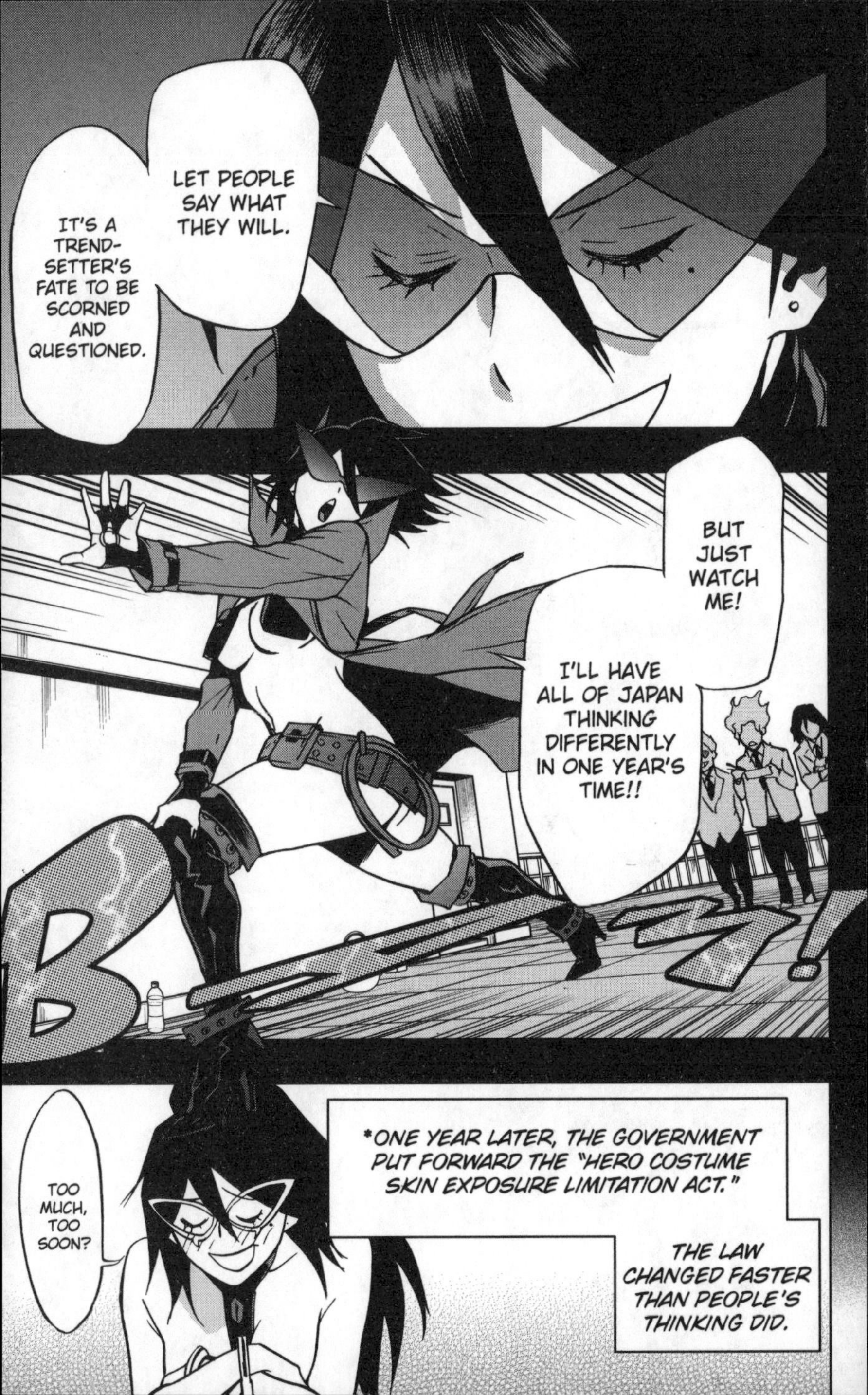
LET PEOPLE SAY WHAT THEY WILL.
IT'S A TREND-SETTER'S FATE TO BE SCORNED AND QUESTIONED.
BUT JUST WATCH ME!
I'LL HAVE ALL OF JAPAN THINKING DIFFERENTLY IN ONE YEAR'S TIME!!
*ONE YEAR LATER, THE GOVERNMENT PUT FORWARD THE "HERO COSTUME SKIN EXPOSURE LIMITATION ACT."
THE LAW CHANGED FASTER THAN PEOPLE'S THINKING DID.
TOO MUCH, TOO SOON?

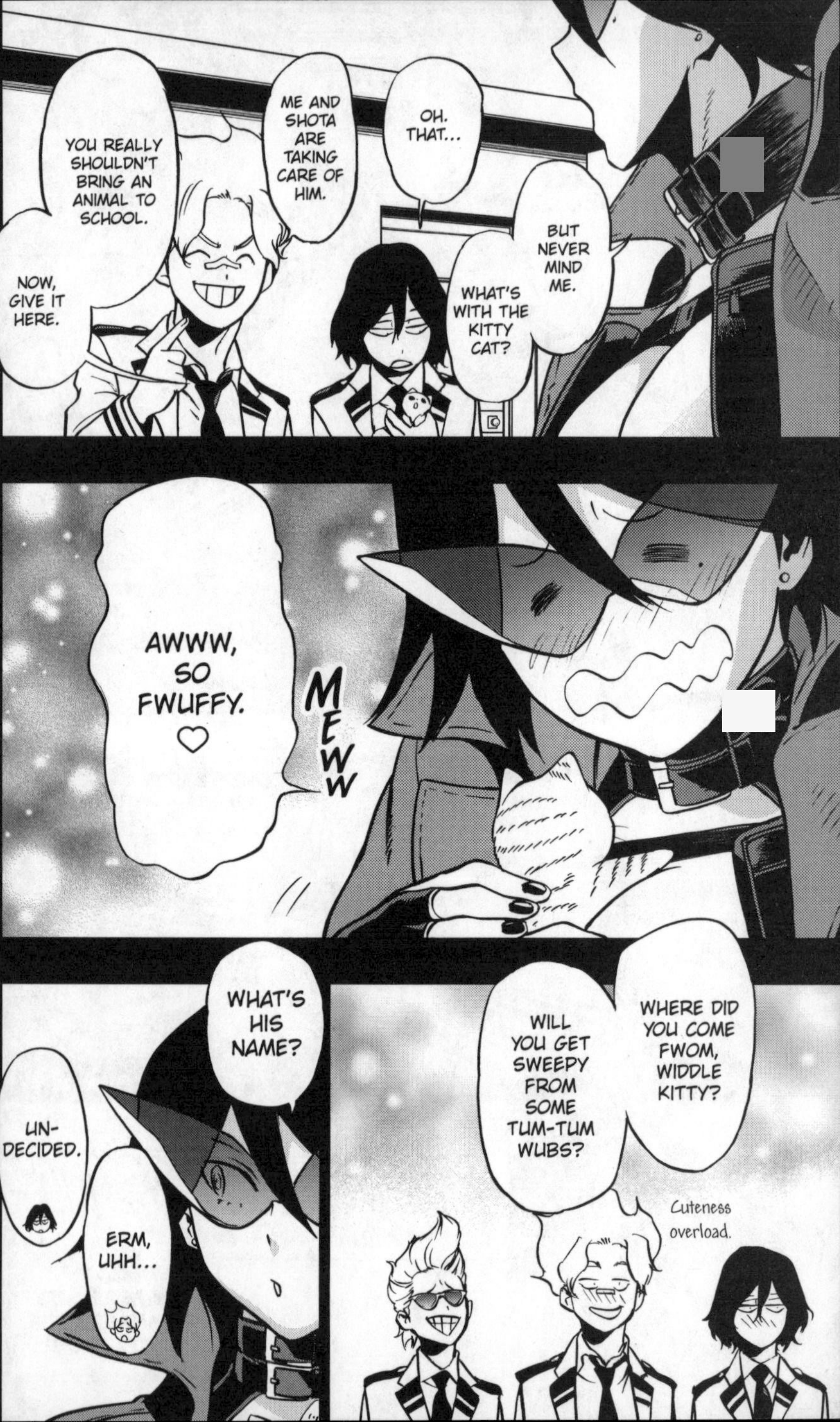
BUT NEVER MIND ME.
WHAT'S WITH THE KITTY CAT?
OH. THAT...
ME AND SHOTA ARE TAKING CARE OF HIM.
YOU REALLY SHOULDN'T BRING AN ANIMAL TO SCHOOL.
NOW, GIVE IT HERE.
MEWW
AWWW, SO FWUFFY. ♡
WHERE DID YOU COME FWOM, WIDDLE KITTY?
WILL YOU GET SWEEPY FROM SOME TUM-TUM WUBS?
Cuteness overload.
WHAT'S HIS NAME?
UN-DECIDED.
ERM, UHH...

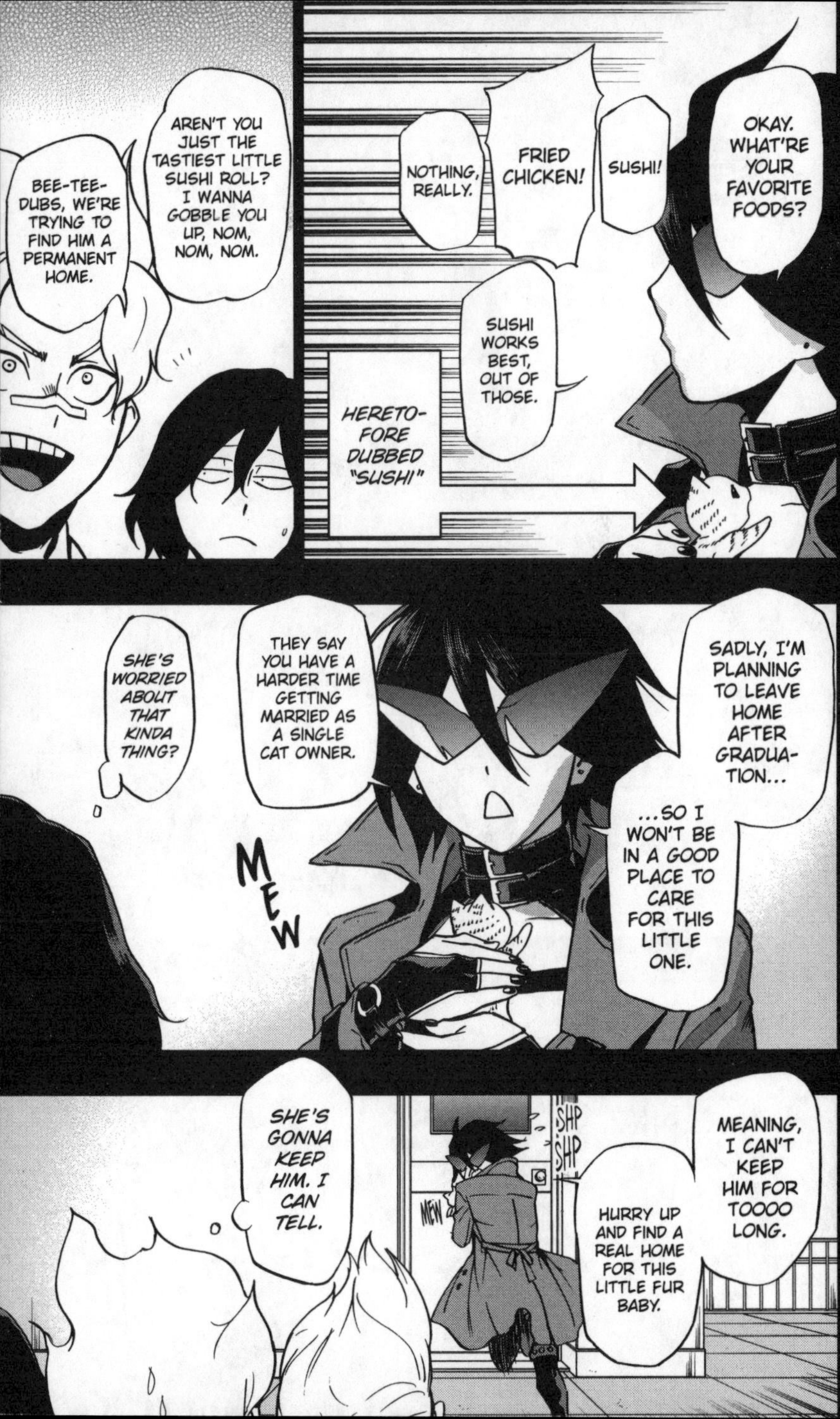
OKAY. WHAT'RE YOUR FAVORITE FOODS?
SUSHI!
FRIED CHICKEN!
NOTHING, REALLY.
SUSHI WORKS BEST, OUT OF THOSE.
HERETO-FORE DUBBED "SUSHI"
AREN'T YOU JUST THE TASTIEST LITTLE SUSHI ROLL? I WANNA GOBBLE YOU UP, NOM, NOM, NOM.
BEE-TEE-DUBS, WE'RE TRYING TO FIND HIM A PERMANENT HOME.
SADLY, I'M PLANNING TO LEAVE HOME AFTER GRADUA-TION...
...SO I WON'T BE IN A GOOD PLACE TO CARE FOR THIS LITTLE ONE.
MEW
THEY SAY YOU HAVE A HARDER TIME GETTING MARRIED AS A SINGLE CAT OWNER.
SHE'S WORRIED ABOUT THAT KINDA THING?
MEANING, I CAN'T KEEP HIM FOR TOOOO LONG.
HURRY UP AND FIND A REAL HOME FOR THIS LITTLE FUR BABY.
SHP SHP
MEW
SHE'S GONNA KEEP HIM. I CAN TELL.

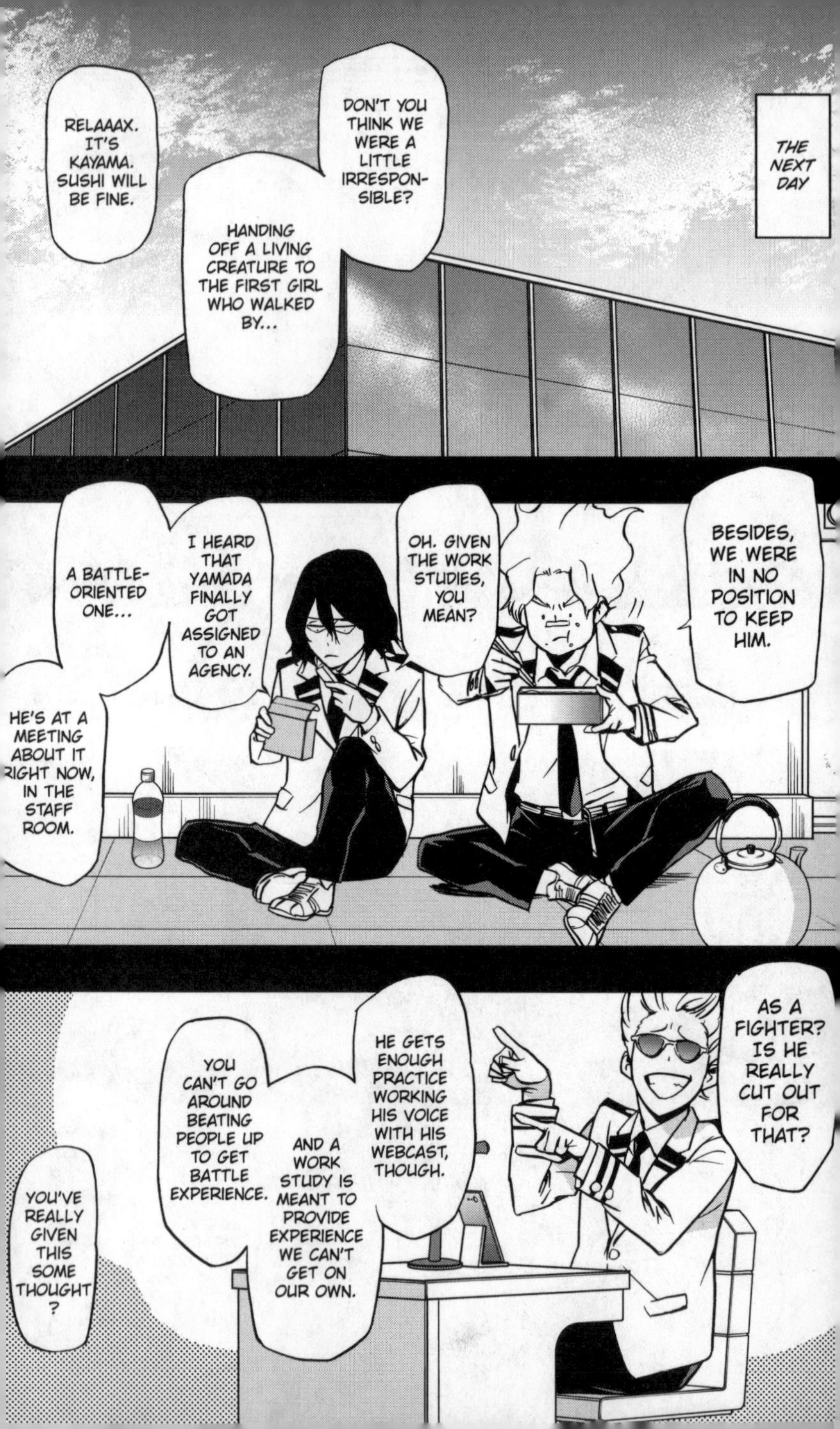
THE NEXT DAY
DON'T YOU THINK WE WERE A LITTLE IRRESPON-SIBLE?
HANDING OFF A LIVING CREATURE TO THE FIRST GIRL WHO WALKED BY...
RELAAAX. IT'S KAYAMA. SUSHI WILL BE FINE.
BESIDES, WE WERE IN NO POSITION TO KEEP HIM.
OH. GIVEN THE WORK STUDIES, YOU MEAN?
I HEARD THAT YAMADA FINALLY GOT ASSIGNED TO AN AGENCY.
A BATTLE-ORIENTED ONE...
HE'S AT A MEETING ABOUT IT RIGHT NOW, IN THE STAFF ROOM.
AS A FIGHTER? IS HE REALLY CUT OUT FOR THAT?
HE GETS ENOUGH PRACTICE WORKING HIS VOICE WITH HIS WEBCAST, THOUGH.
YOU CAN'T GO AROUND BEATING PEOPLE UP TO GET BATTLE EXPERIENCE.
AND A WORK STUDY IS MEANT TO PROVIDE EXPERIENCE WE CAN'T GET ON OUR OWN.
YOU'VE REALLY GIVEN THIS SOME THOUGHT?

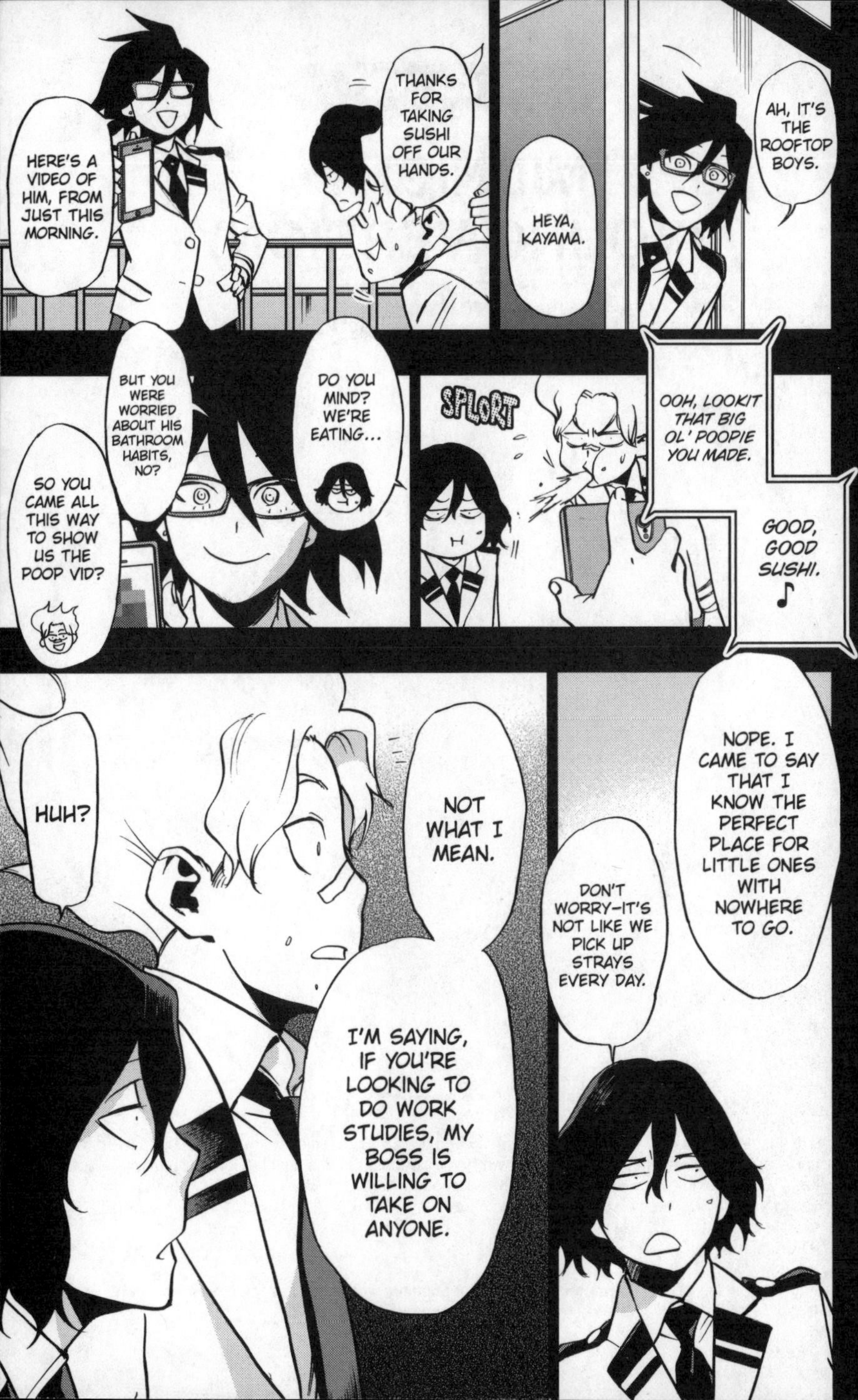
AH, IT'S THE ROOFTOP BOYS.
HEYA, KAYAMA.
THANKS FOR TAKING SUSHI OFF OUR HANDS.
HERE'S A VIDEO OF HIM, FROM JUST THIS MORNING.
OOH, LOOKIT THAT BIG OL' POOPIE YOU MADE.
GOOD, GOOD SUSHI. ♪
SPLORT
DO YOU MIND? WE'RE EATING...
BUT YOU WERE WORRIED ABOUT HIS BATHROOM HABITS, NO?
SO YOU CAME ALL THIS WAY TO SHOW US THE POOP VID?
NOPE. I CAME TO SAY THAT I KNOW THE PERFECT PLACE FOR LITTLE ONES WITH NOWHERE TO GO.
DON'T WORRY—IT'S NOT LIKE WE PICK UP STRAYS EVERY DAY.
NOT WHAT I MEAN.
HUH?
I'M SAYING, IF YOU'RE LOOKING TO DO WORK STUDIES, MY BOSS IS WILLING TO TAKE ON ANYONE.

MIDNIGHT
(YOUNG VERSION)

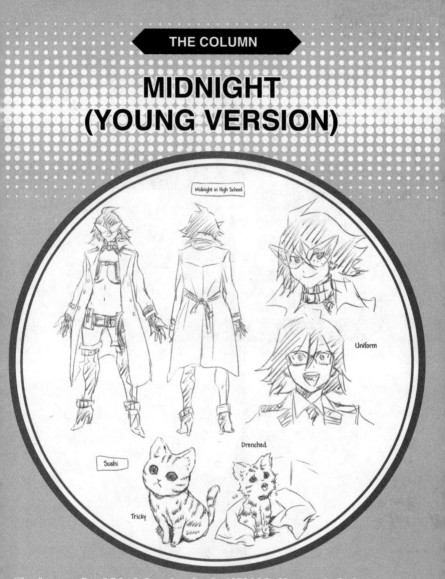

Midnight in High School

Uniform

Sushi

Tricky

Drenched

There's a canon line of dialog in the main series about Midnight's old costume having been even more scandalous in the past, so that was a point we had to touch on in this flashback arc. So many people asked if Sushi the cat was a parody of Sushi the dog in Tite Kubo's *Burn the Witch* one-shot, but actually, it was more of a play on the series, *Shota no Sushi*...

—Furuhashi

I received specifications and reference images for Midnight's costume from Furuhashi-san, and upon reflection, I think I stuck a little too closely to that reference material.

—Betten

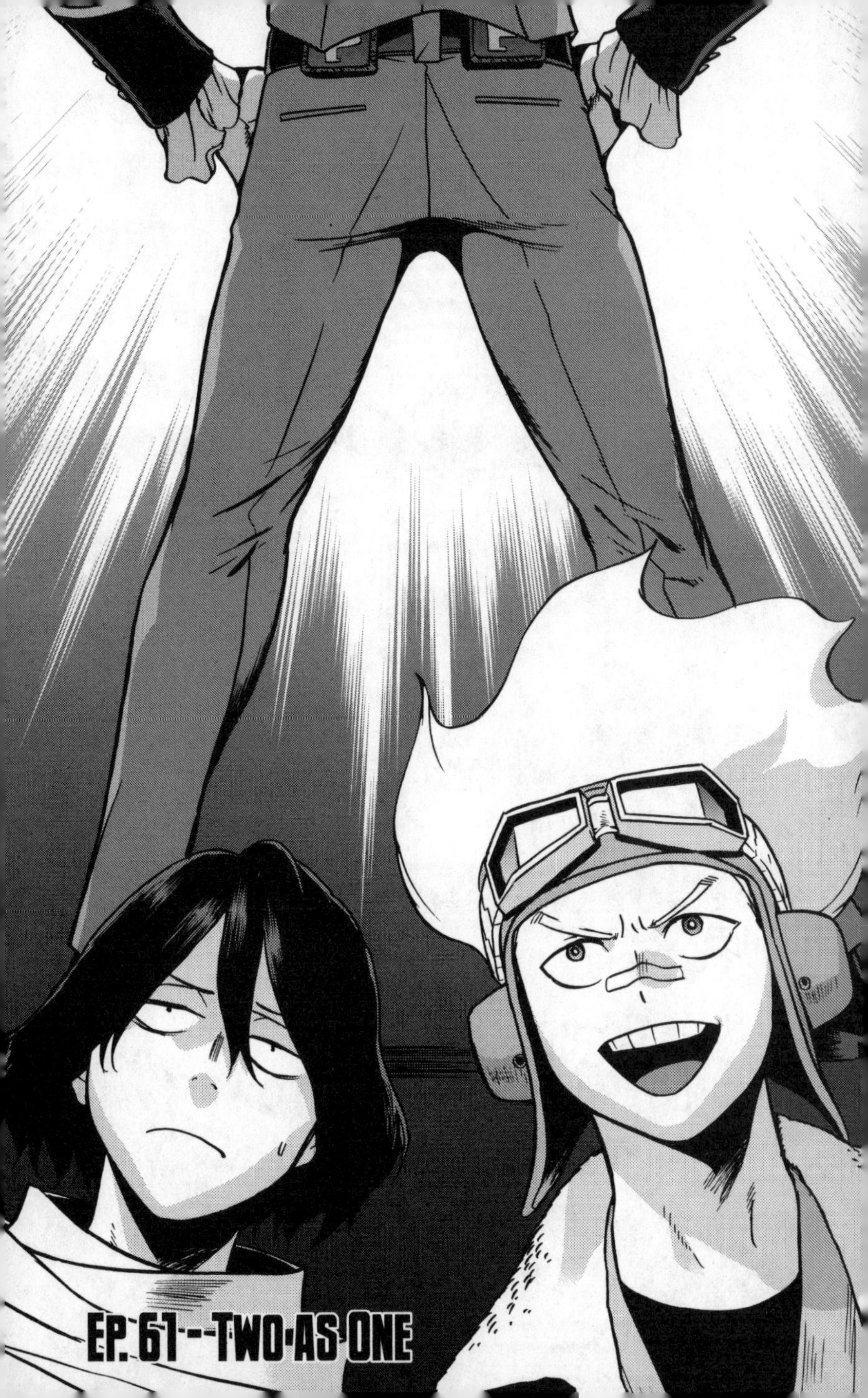
EP. 61 - - TWO AS ONE

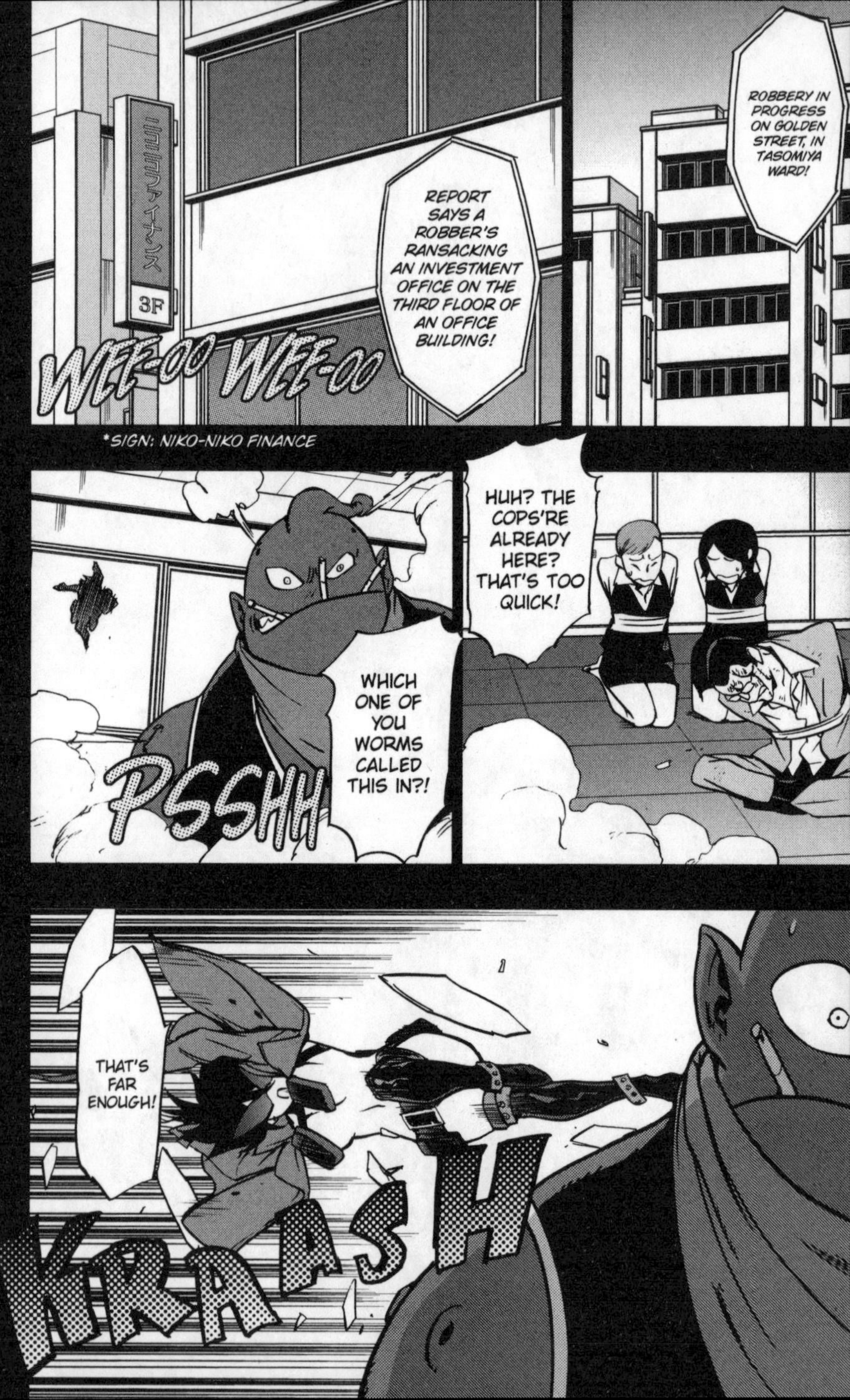
ROBBERY IN PROGRESS ON GOLDEN STREET, IN TASOMIYA WARD!
REPORT SAYS A ROBBER'S RANSACKING AN INVESTMENT OFFICE ON THE THIRD FLOOR OF AN OFFICE BUILDING!
ニコニコファイナンス
3F
WEE-OO WEE-OO
HUH? THE COPS'RE ALREADY HERE? THAT'S TOO QUICK!
WHICH ONE OF YOU WORMS CALLED THIS IN?!
PSSHH
THAT'S FAR ENOUGH!
KRAASH
*SIGN: NIKO-NIKO FINANCE

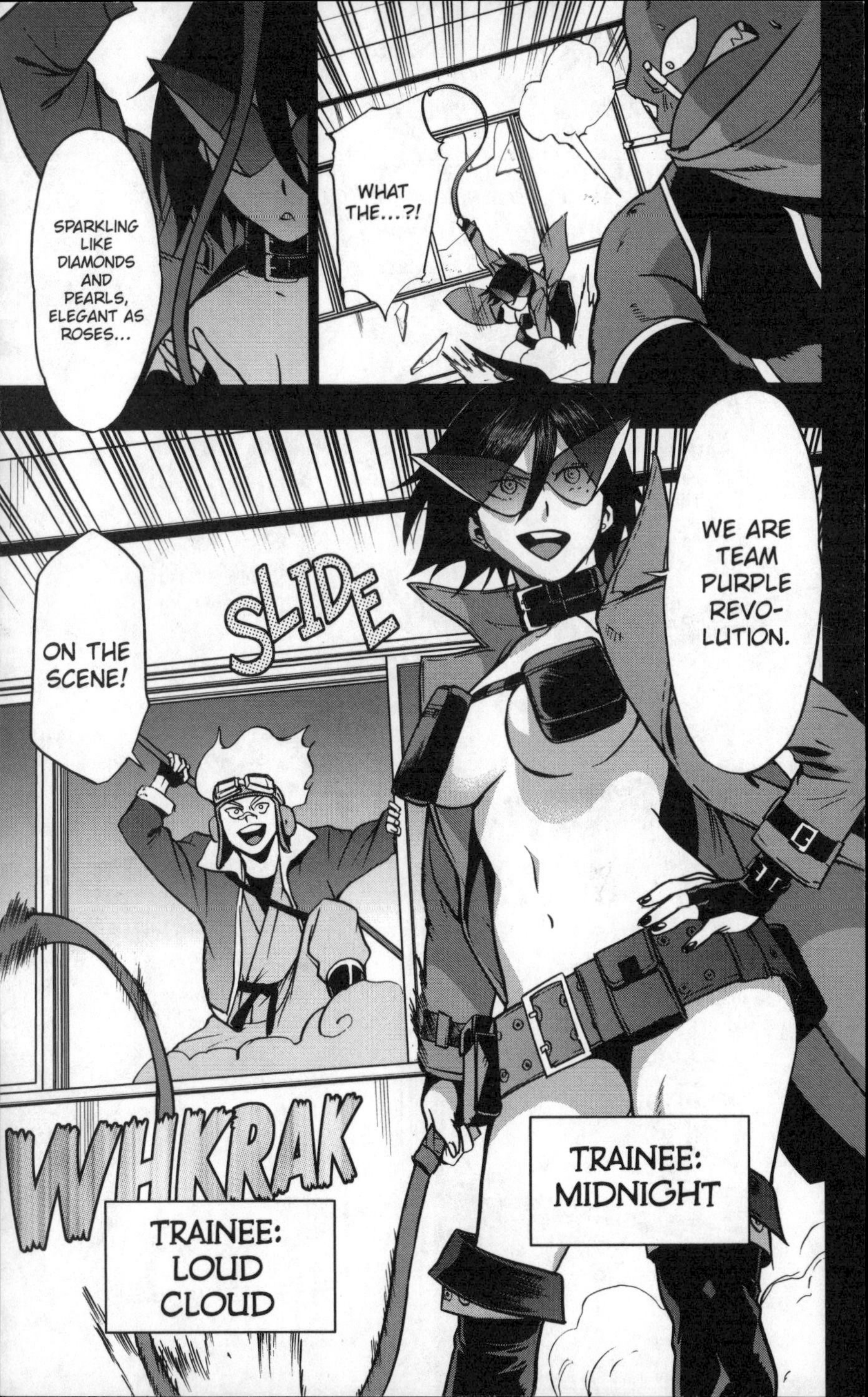
WHAT THE...?!
SPARKLING LIKE DIAMONDS AND PEARLS, ELEGANT AS ROSES...
WE ARE TEAM PURPLE REVOLUTION.
ON THE SCENE!
SLIDE
WHKRAK
TRAINEE: MIDNIGHT
TRAINEE: LOUD CLOUD

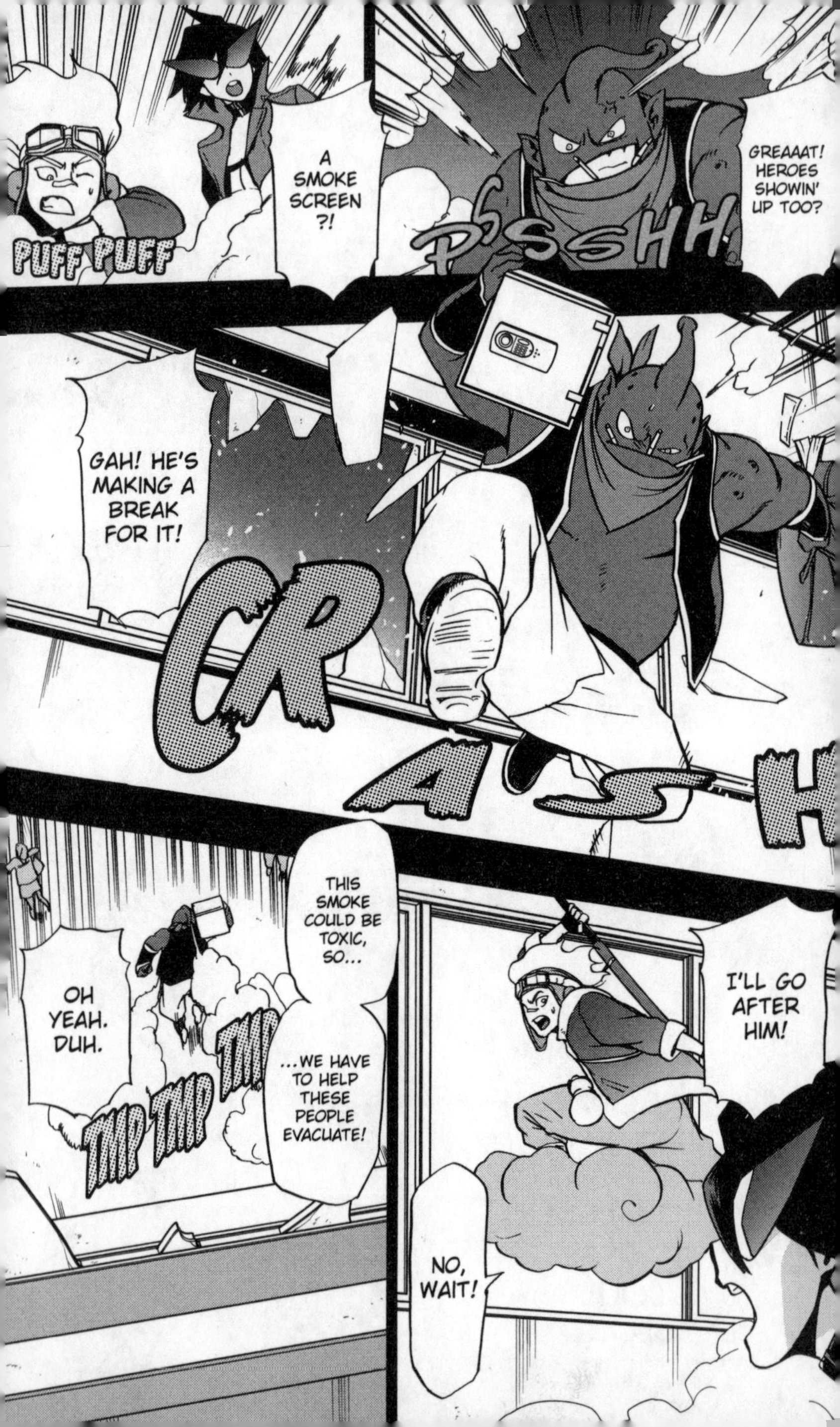
GREAAAT! HEROES SHOWIN' UP TOO?
PSSHH
A SMOKE SCREEN ?!
PUFF PUFF
GAH! HE'S MAKING A BREAK FOR IT!
CRASH
I'LL GO AFTER HIM!
NO, WAIT!
THIS SMOKE COULD BE TOXIC, SO...
...WE HAVE TO HELP THESE PEOPLE EVACUATE!
OH YEAH. DUH.
TMP TMP TMP

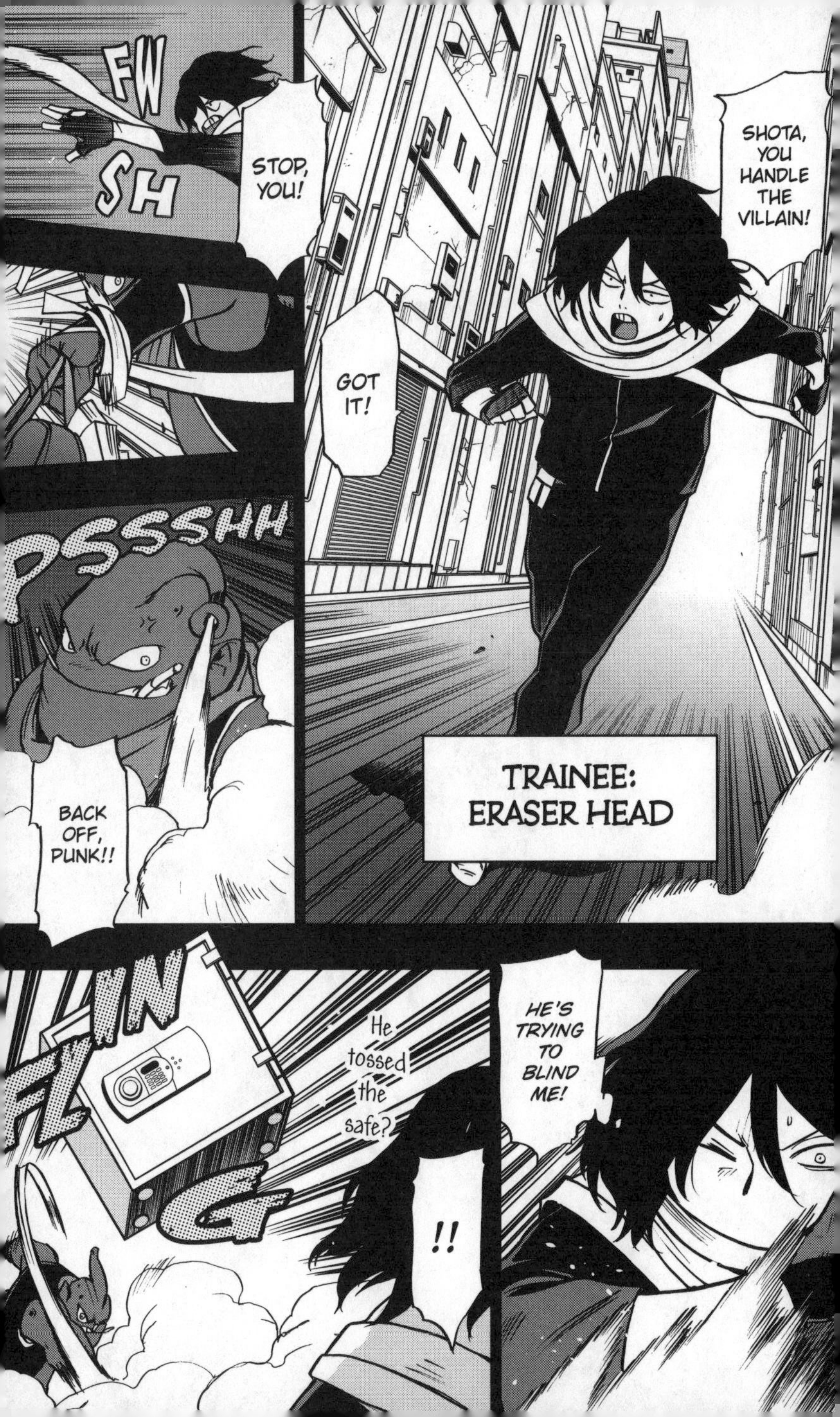
SHOTA, YOU HANDLE THE VILLAIN!
GOT IT!
TRAINEE: ERASER HEAD
FWSH
STOP, YOU!
PSSSHH
BACK OFF, PUNK!!
HE'S TRYING TO BLIND ME!
He tossed the safe?
FLING
!!

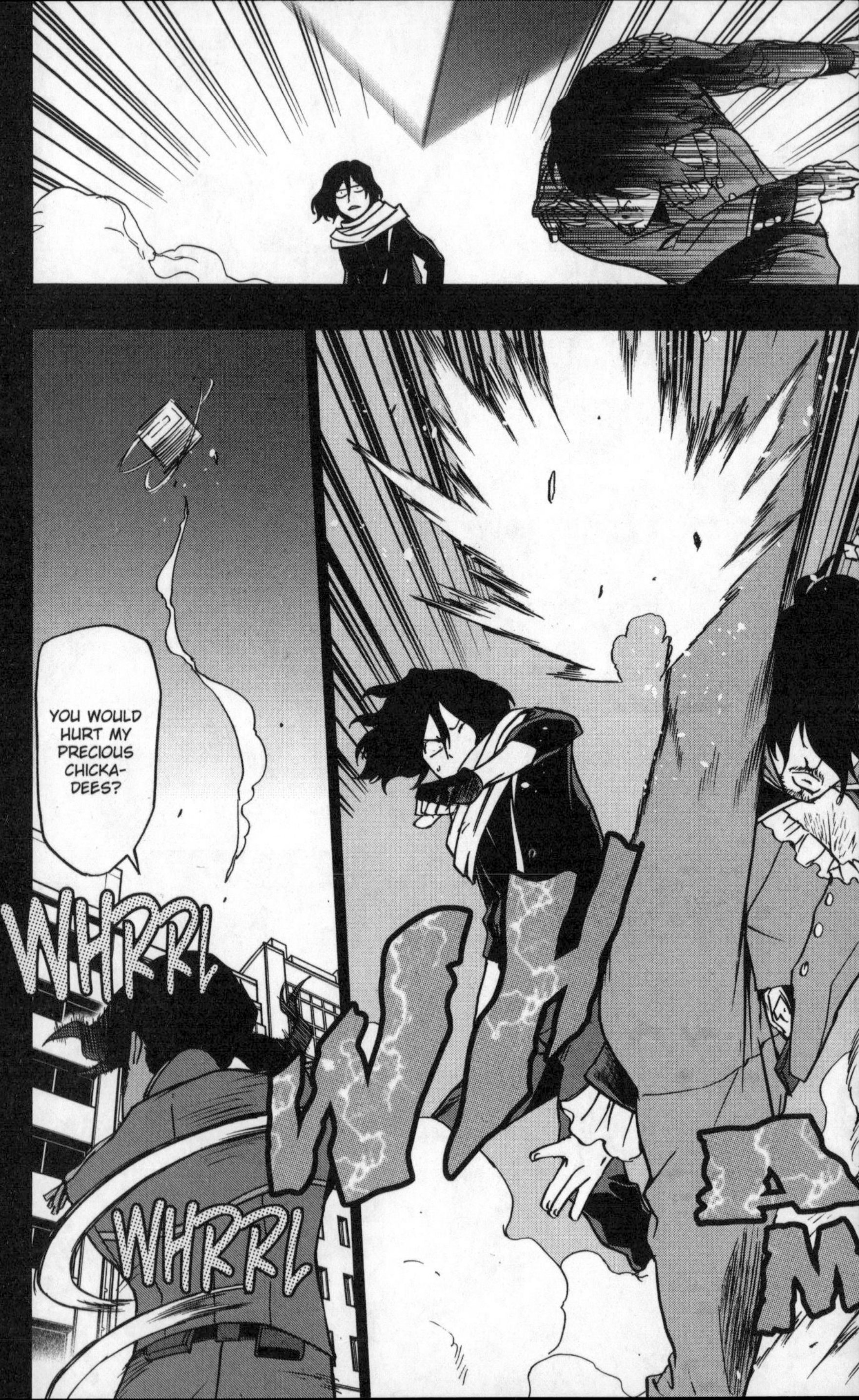
YOU WOULD HURT MY PRECIOUS CHICKA-DEES?
WHRRL
WHRRL

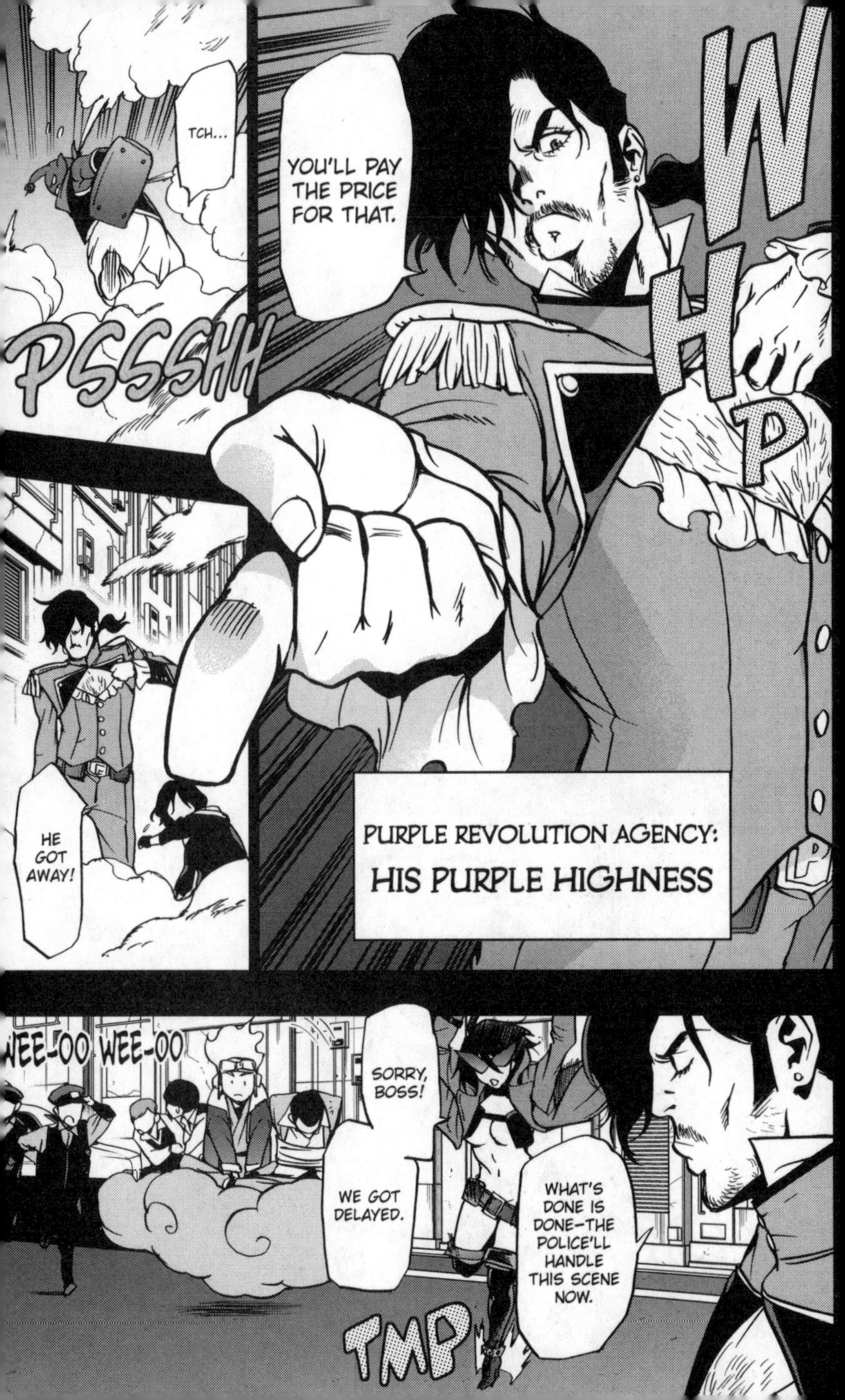
WHIP
YOU'LL PAY THE PRICE FOR THAT.
PURPLE REVOLUTION AGENCY:
HIS PURPLE HIGHNESS
TCH...
PSSSHH
HE GOT AWAY!
SORRY, BOSS!
WE GOT DELAYED.
WHAT'S DONE IS DONE—THE POLICE'LL HANDLE THIS SCENE NOW.
WEE-OO WEE-OO
TMP

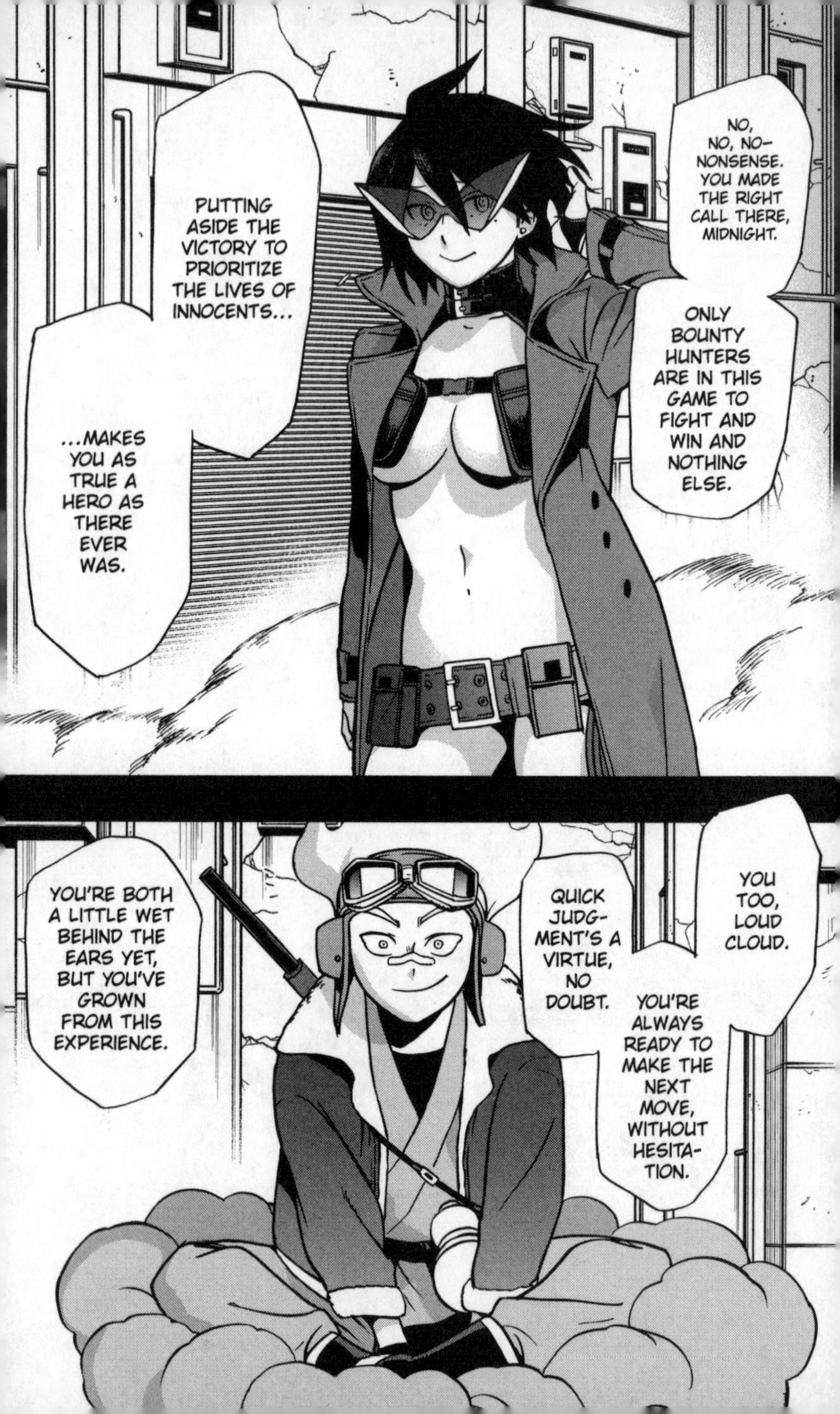
NO, NO, NO— NONSENSE. YOU MADE THE RIGHT CALL THERE, MIDNIGHT.
ONLY BOUNTY HUNTERS ARE IN THIS GAME TO FIGHT AND WIN AND NOTHING ELSE.
PUTTING ASIDE THE VICTORY TO PRIORITIZE THE LIVES OF INNOCENTS...
...MAKES YOU AS TRUE A HERO AS THERE EVER WAS.
YOU TOO, LOUD CLOUD.
QUICK JUDG-MENT'S A VIRTUE, NO DOUBT.
YOU'RE ALWAYS READY TO MAKE THE NEXT MOVE, WITHOUT HESITA-TION.
YOU'RE BOTH A LITTLE WET BEHIND THE EARS YET, BUT YOU'VE GROWN FROM THIS EXPERIENCE.

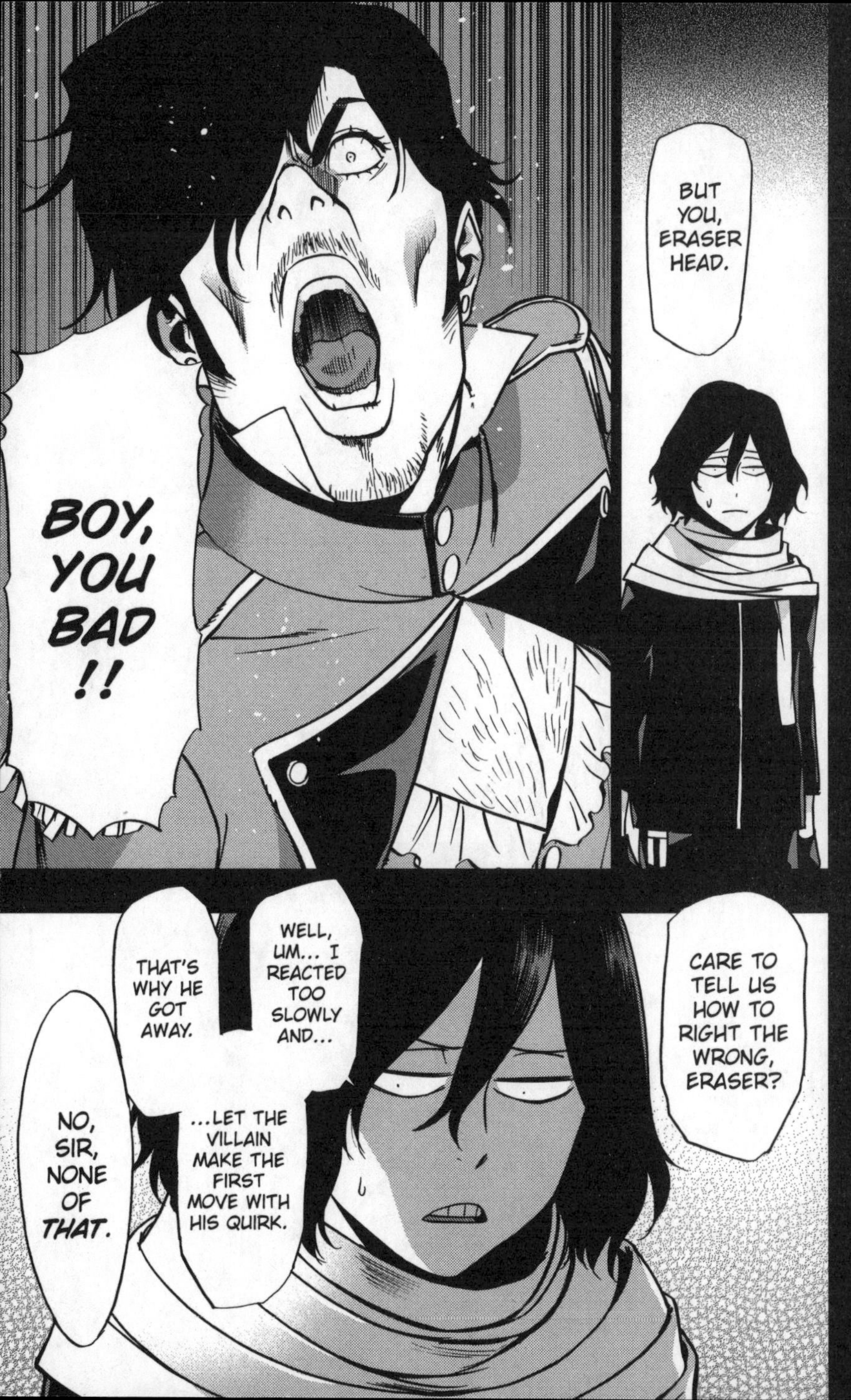
BUT YOU, ERASER HEAD.
BOY, YOU BAD!!
CARE TO TELL US HOW TO RIGHT THE WRONG, ERASER?
WELL, UM... I REACTED TOO SLOWLY AND...
THAT'S WHY HE GOT AWAY.
...LET THE VILLAIN MAKE THE FIRST MOVE WITH HIS QUIRK.
NO, SIR, NONE OF THAT.

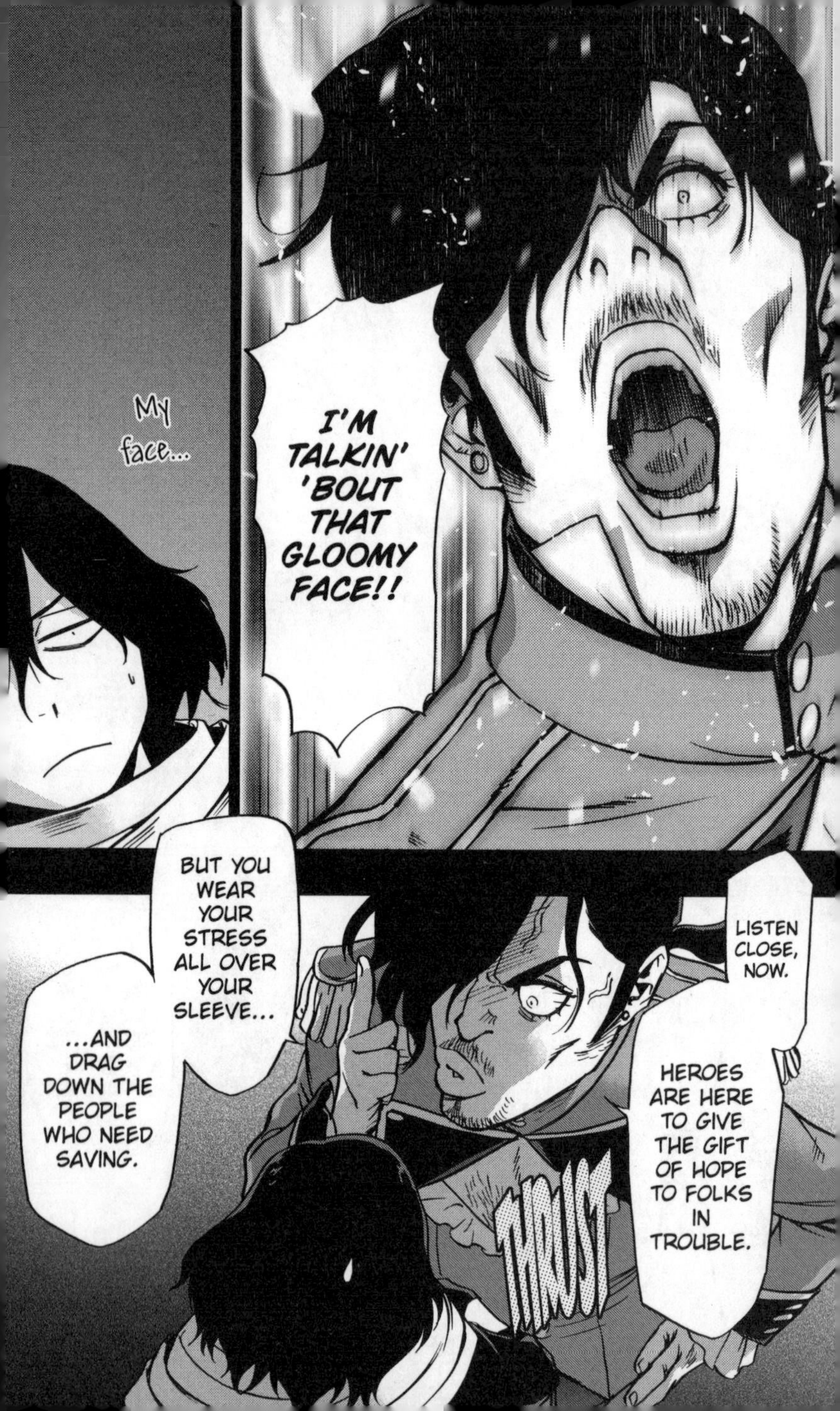
I'M TALKIN' 'BOUT THAT GLOOMY FACE!!
My face...
LISTEN CLOSE, NOW.
HEROES ARE HERE TO GIVE THE GIFT OF HOPE TO FOLKS IN TROUBLE.
THRUST
BUT YOU WEAR YOUR STRESS ALL OVER YOUR SLEEVE...
...AND DRAG DOWN THE PEOPLE WHO NEED SAVING.

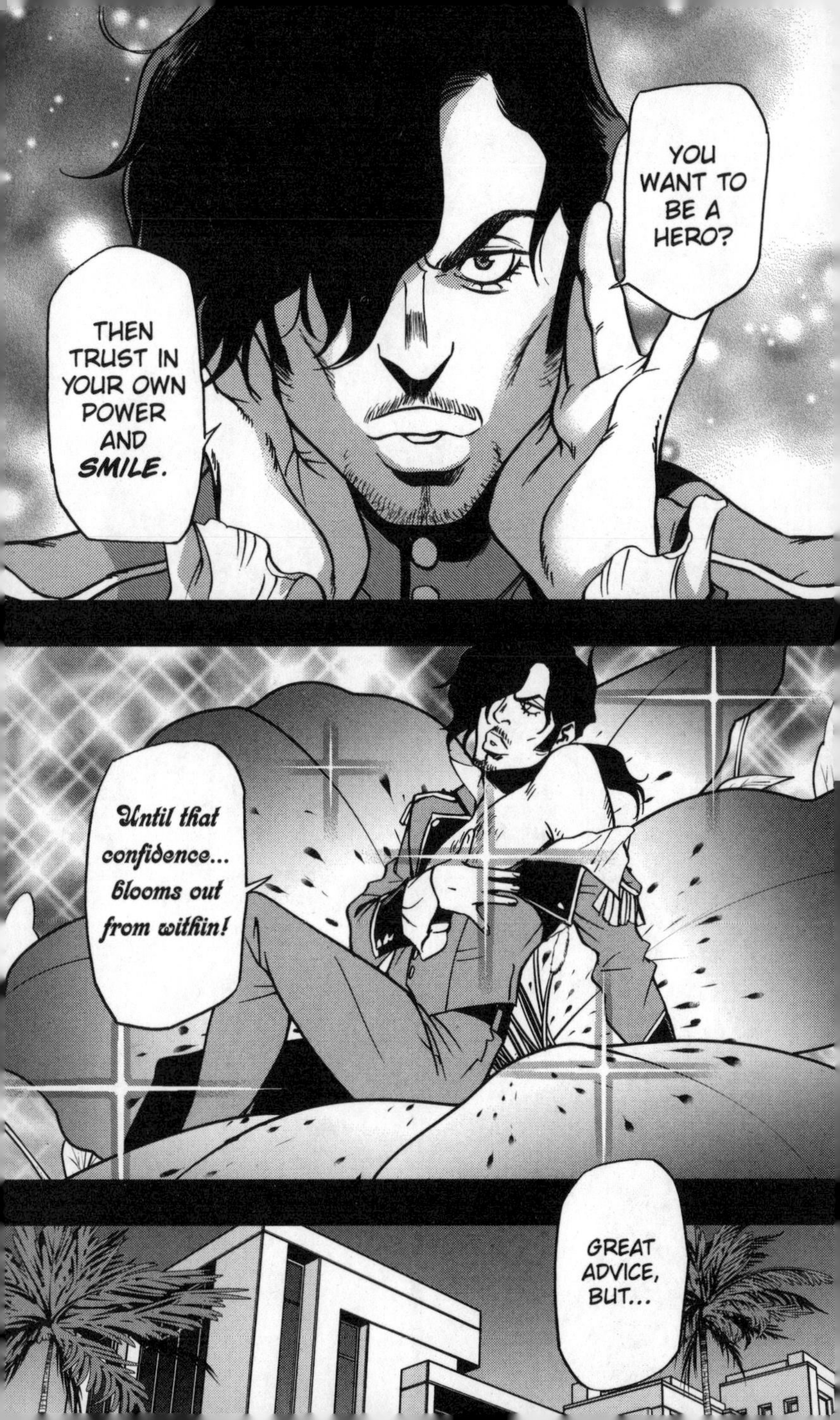
YOU WANT TO BE A HERO?
THEN TRUST IN YOUR OWN POWER AND SMILE.
Until that confidence... blooms out from within!
GREAT ADVICE, BUT...

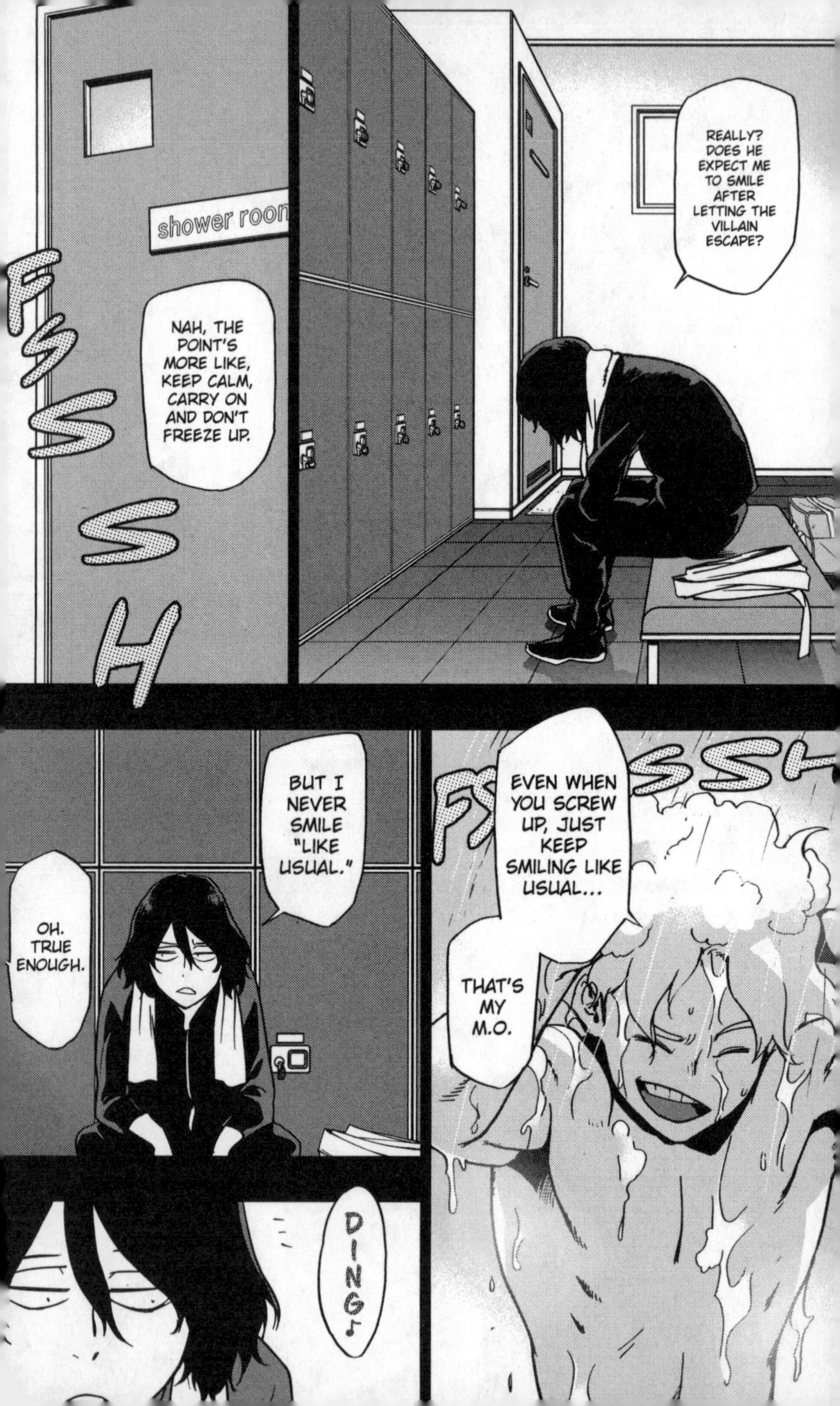

REALLY? DOES HE EXPECT ME TO SMILE AFTER LETTING THE VILLAIN ESCAPE?
shower room
FSSSH
NAH, THE POINT'S MORE LIKE, KEEP CALM, CARRY ON AND DON'T FREEZE UP.
FSSSH
EVEN WHEN YOU SCREW UP, JUST KEEP SMILING LIKE USUAL...
THAT'S MY M.O.
BUT I NEVER SMILE "LIKE USUAL."
OH. TRUE ENOUGH.
DING♪

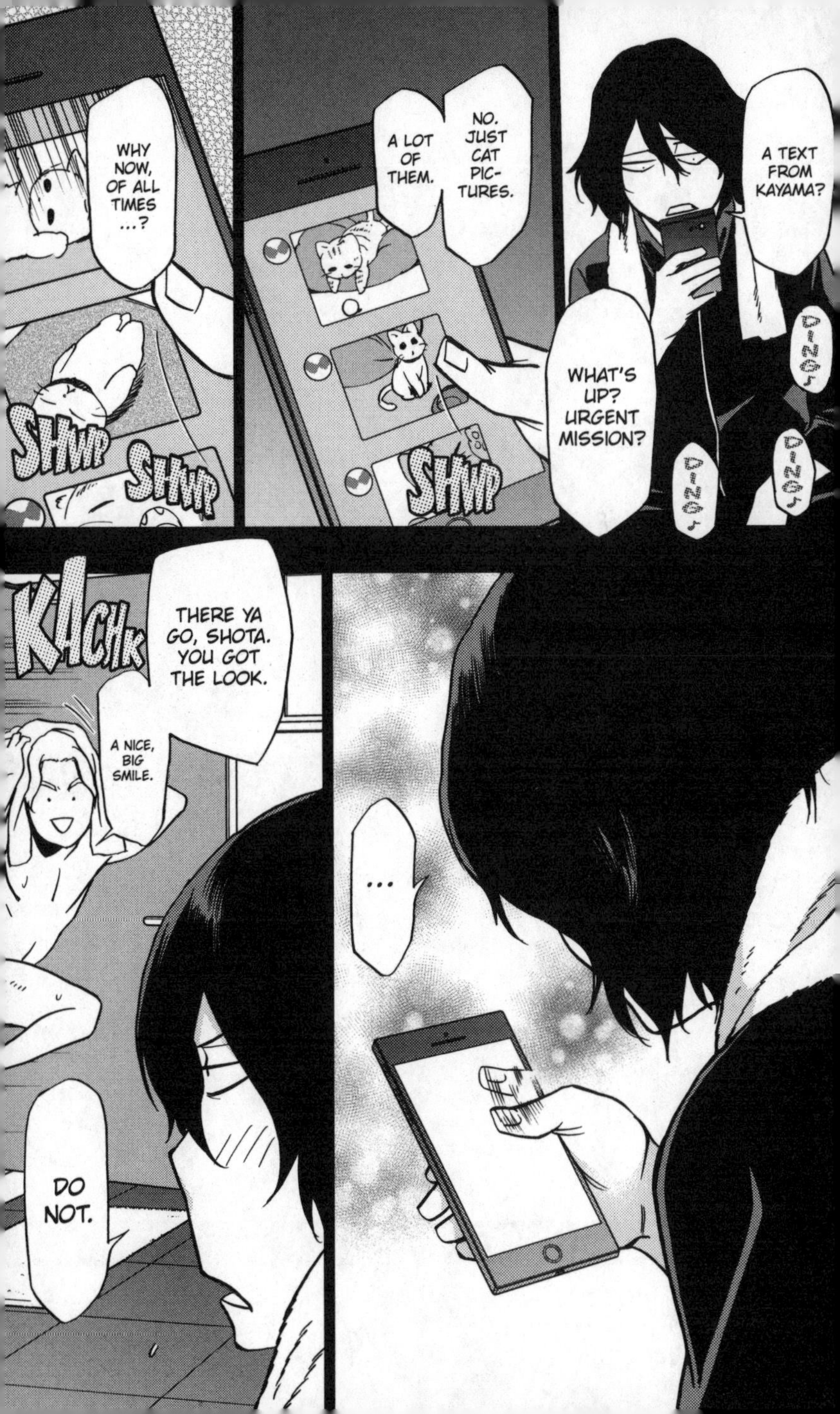
A TEXT FROM KAYAMA?
WHAT'S UP? URGENT MISSION?
DING♪
DING♪
DING♪
NO. JUST CAT PIC-TURES.
A LOT OF THEM.
SHWP
WHY NOW, OF ALL TIMES ...?
SHWP
SHWP
...
KACHK
THERE YA GO, SHOTA. YOU GOT THE LOOK.
A NICE, BIG SMILE.
DO NOT.

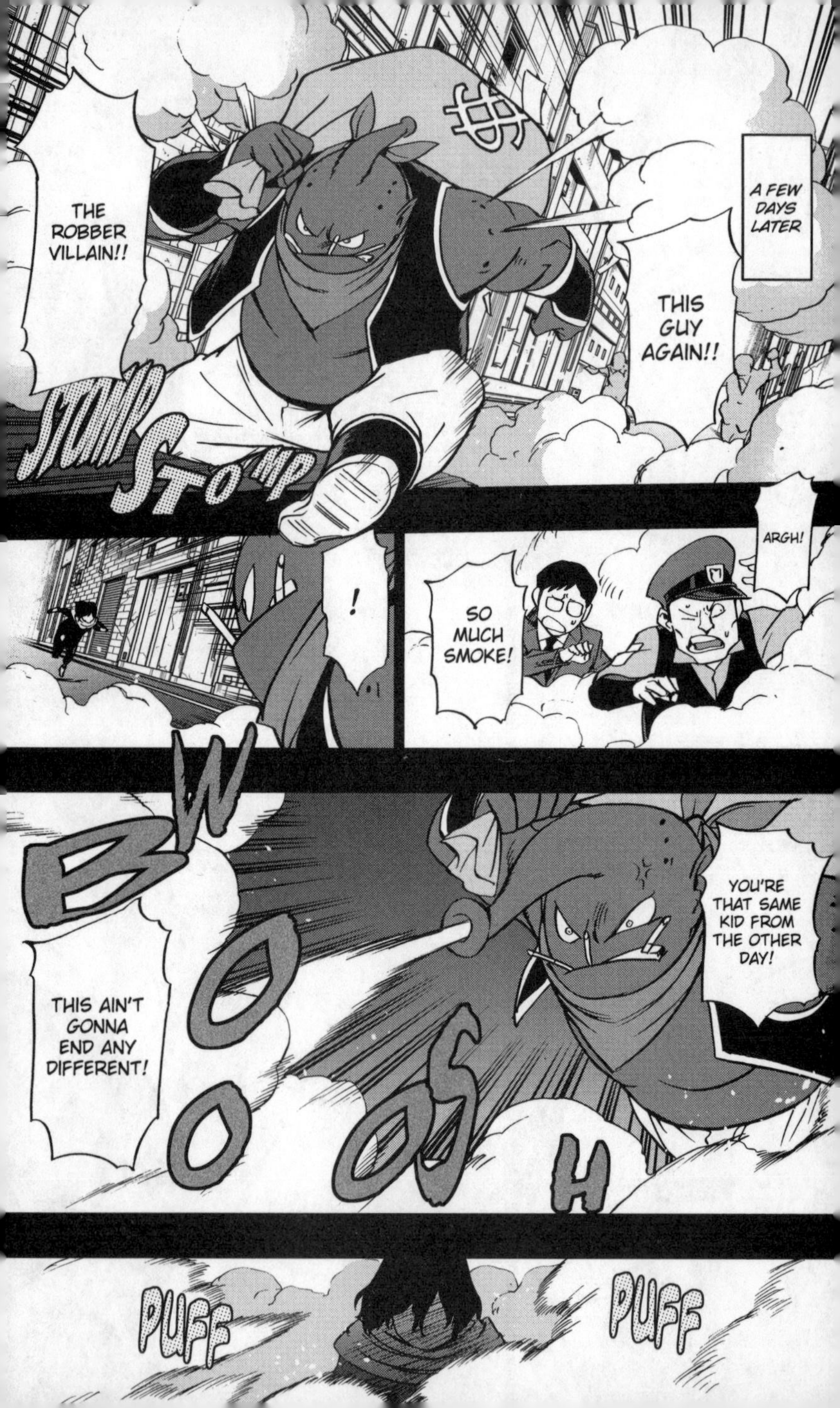
A FEW DAYS LATER
THIS GUY AGAIN!!
THE ROBBER VILLAIN!!
STOMP
STOMP
ARGH!
SO MUCH SMOKE!
!
YOU'RE THAT SAME KID FROM THE OTHER DAY!
THIS AIN'T GONNA END ANY DIFFERENT!
BWOOOSH
PUFF
PUFF

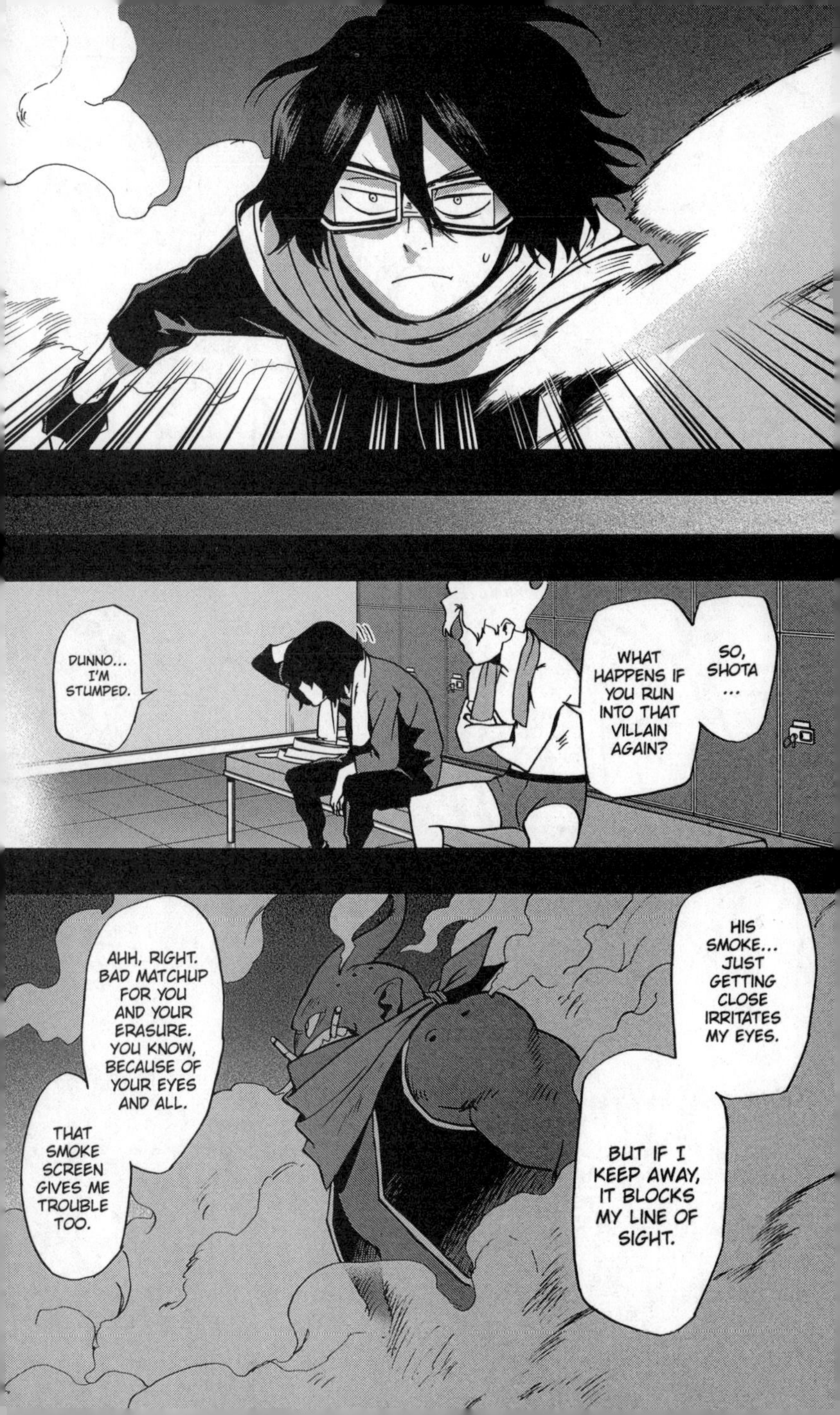
SO, SHOTA ...
WHAT HAPPENS IF YOU RUN INTO THAT VILLAIN AGAIN?
DUNNO... I'M STUMPED.
HIS SMOKE... JUST GETTING CLOSE IRRITATES MY EYES.
BUT IF I KEEP AWAY, IT BLOCKS MY LINE OF SIGHT.
AHH, RIGHT. BAD MATCHUP FOR YOU AND YOUR ERASURE. YOU KNOW, BECAUSE OF YOUR EYES AND ALL.
THAT SMOKE SCREEN GIVES ME TROUBLE TOO.

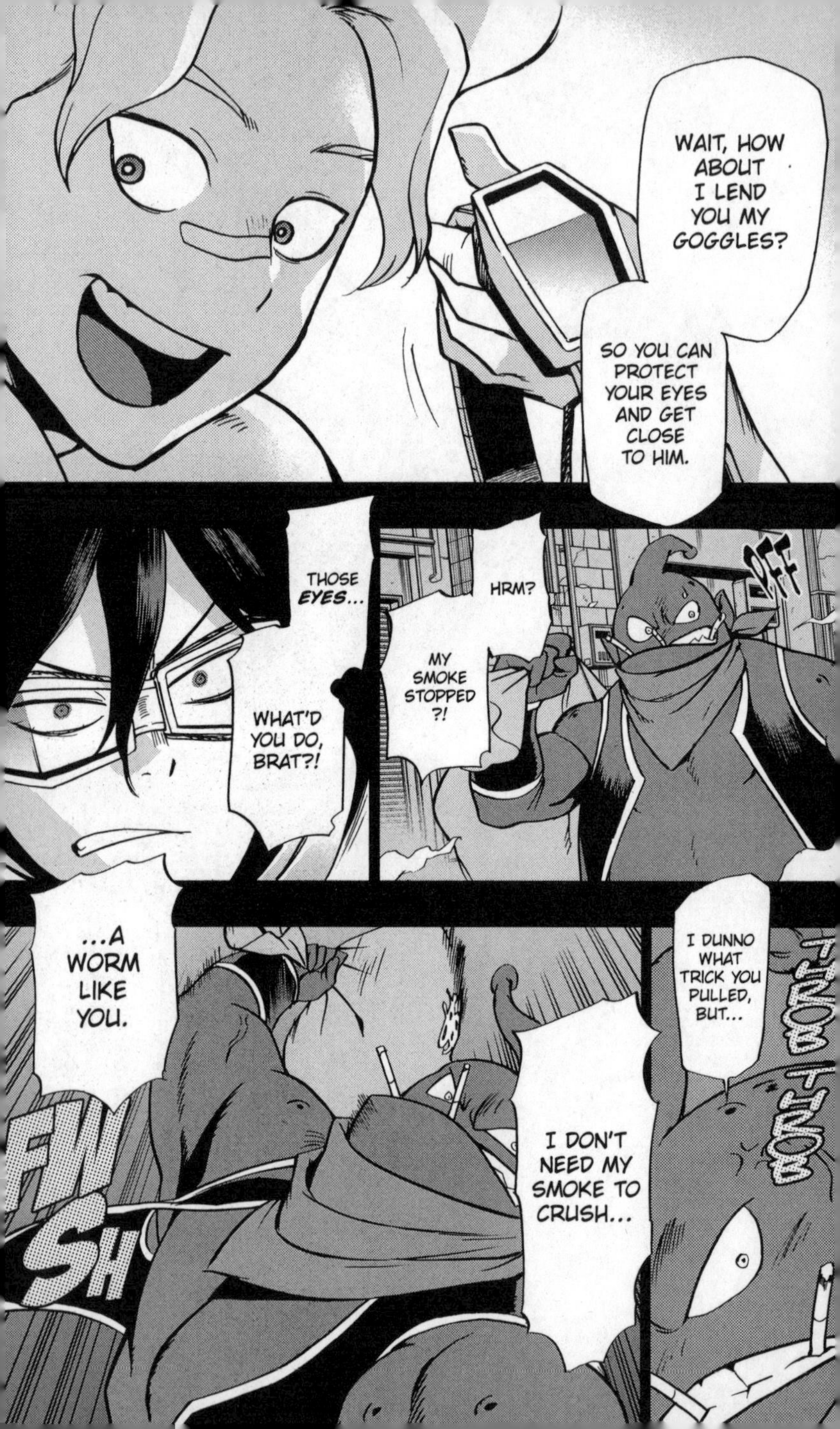
WAIT, HOW ABOUT I LEND YOU MY GOGGLES?
SO YOU CAN PROTECT YOUR EYES AND GET CLOSE TO HIM.
HRM?
MY SMOKE STOPPED?!
THOSE *EYES*...
WHAT'D YOU DO, BRAT?!
I DUNNO WHAT TRICK YOU PULLED, BUT...
THROB THROB
I DON'T NEED MY SMOKE TO CRUSH...
...A WORM LIKE YOU.
FWSH

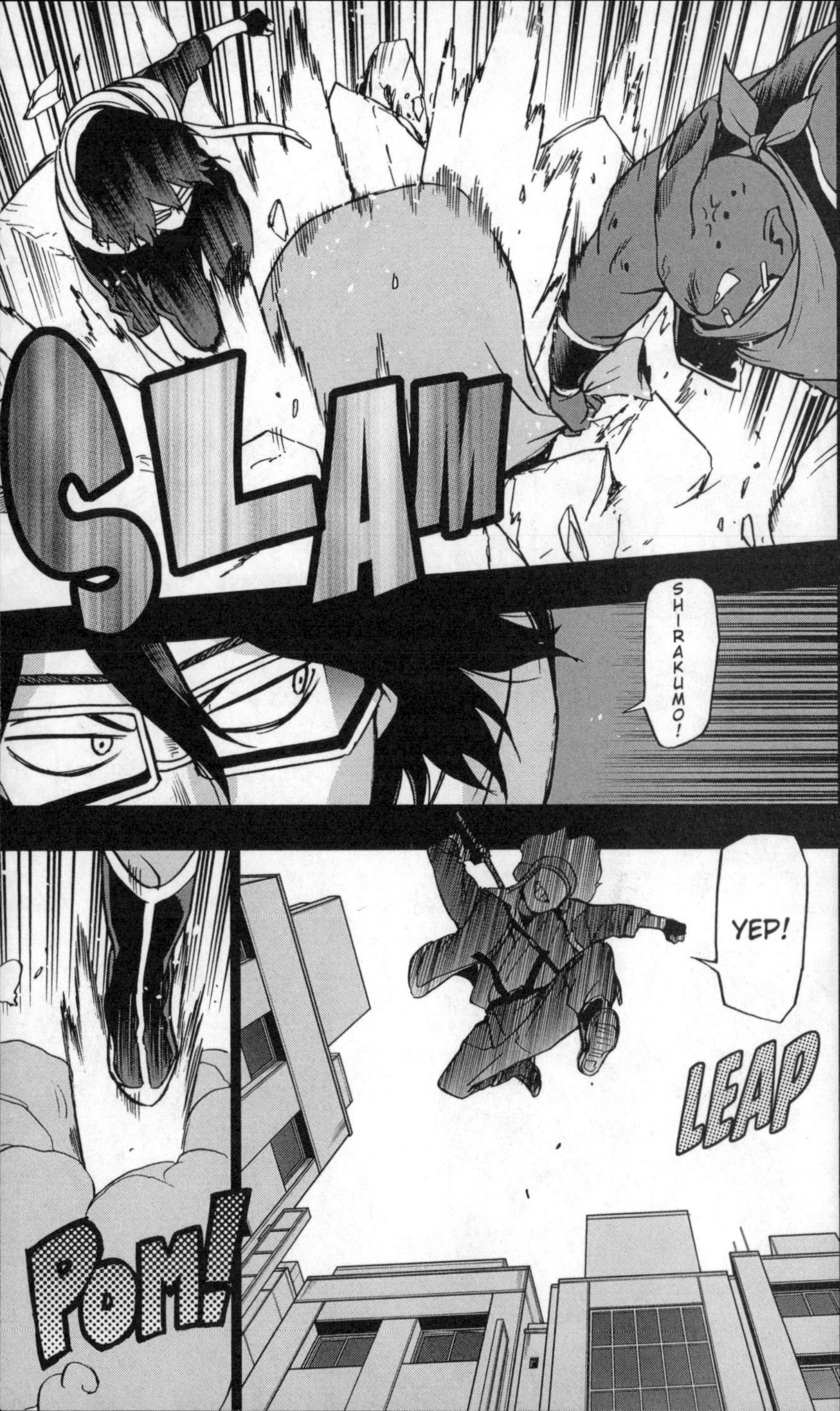
SLAM
SHIRAKUMO!
YEP!
LEAP
POM!

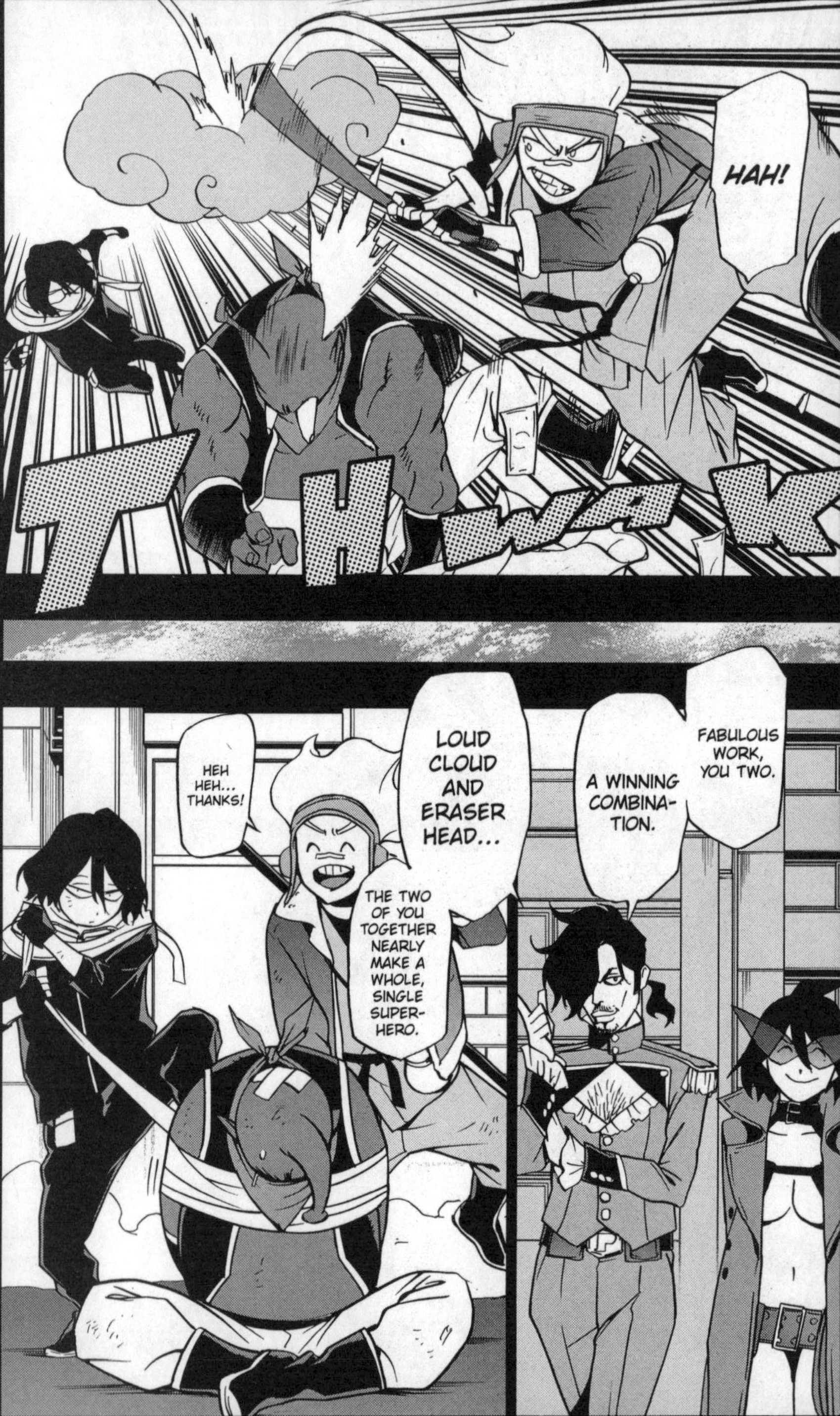
HAH!
THWAK
FABULOUS WORK, YOU TWO.
A WINNING COMBINATION.
LOUD CLOUD AND ERASER HEAD...
THE TWO OF YOU TOGETHER NEARLY MAKE A WHOLE, SINGLE SUPER-HERO.
HEH HEH... THANKS!

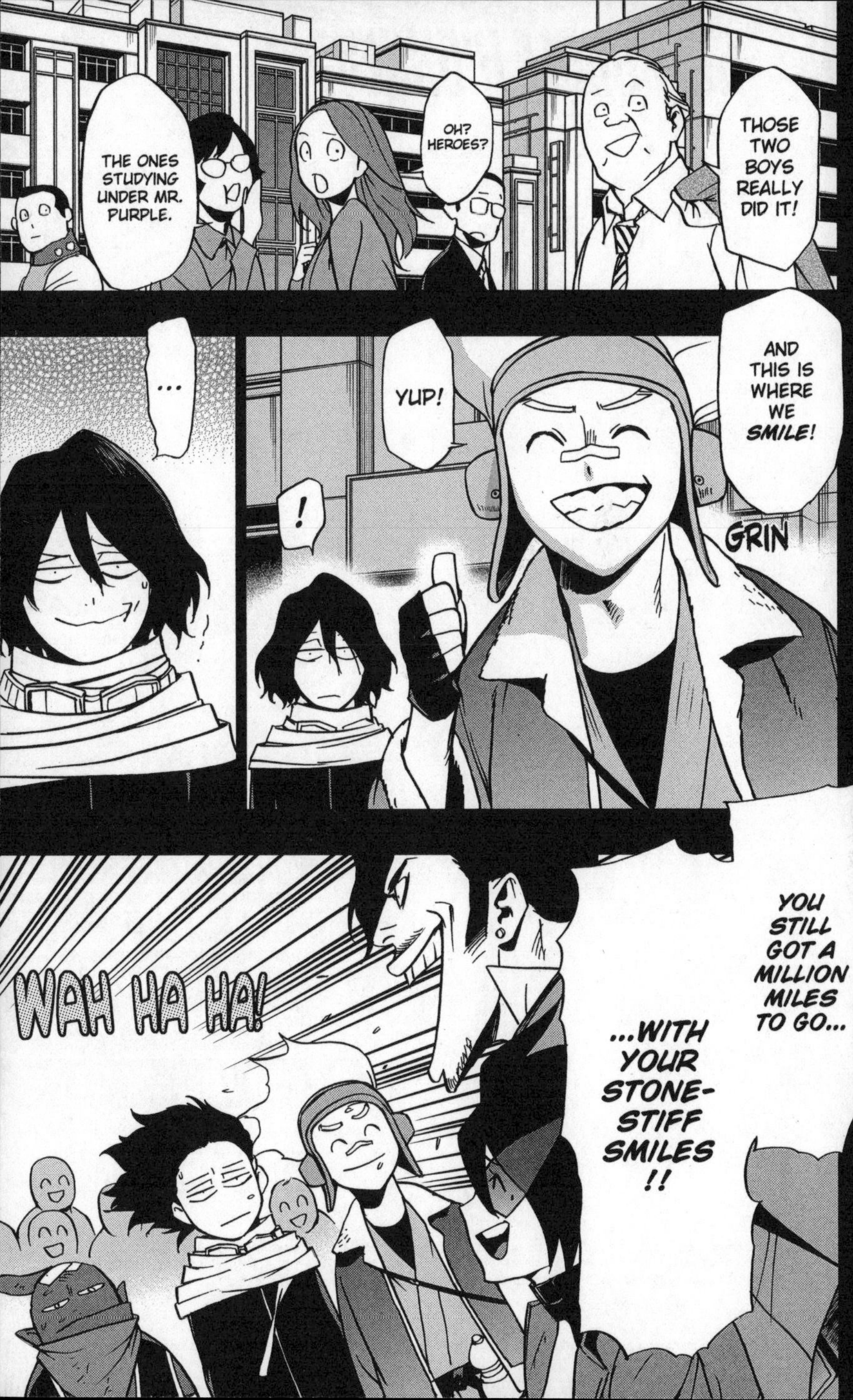
THOSE TWO BOYS REALLY DID IT!
OH? HEROES?
THE ONES STUDYING UNDER MR. PURPLE.
AND THIS IS WHERE WE SMILE!
GRIN
YUP!
!
...
YOU STILL GOT A MILLION MILES TO GO...
...WITH YOUR STONE-STIFF SMILES!!
WAH HA HA!

HIS PURPLE HIGHNESS

THE ROUGH DESIGN

His Purple Highness

Mole on cheek was too similar to Midnight's, so I cut it

NAME: TENMA NAKAOJI

BIRTHDAY: 6/7

HEIGHT: 185 CM

FAVORITE THINGS: SPAGHETTI AND ORANGE JUICE

QUIRK: CHEST HAIR

BEHIND THE SCENES

This guy is Midnight's mentor, so he had to be at least as intense as her. I was a little worried about whether or not readers would appreciate that intensity, but it seems like he was well received in the end. Disclaimer: I'm not suggesting that The Artist Formerly Known as Prince was quite this flamboyant.

—Furuhashi

A fusion of Giorno Giovanna and Prince! Danger—don't mix! That's basically the concept behind this design. (LOL)

—Betten

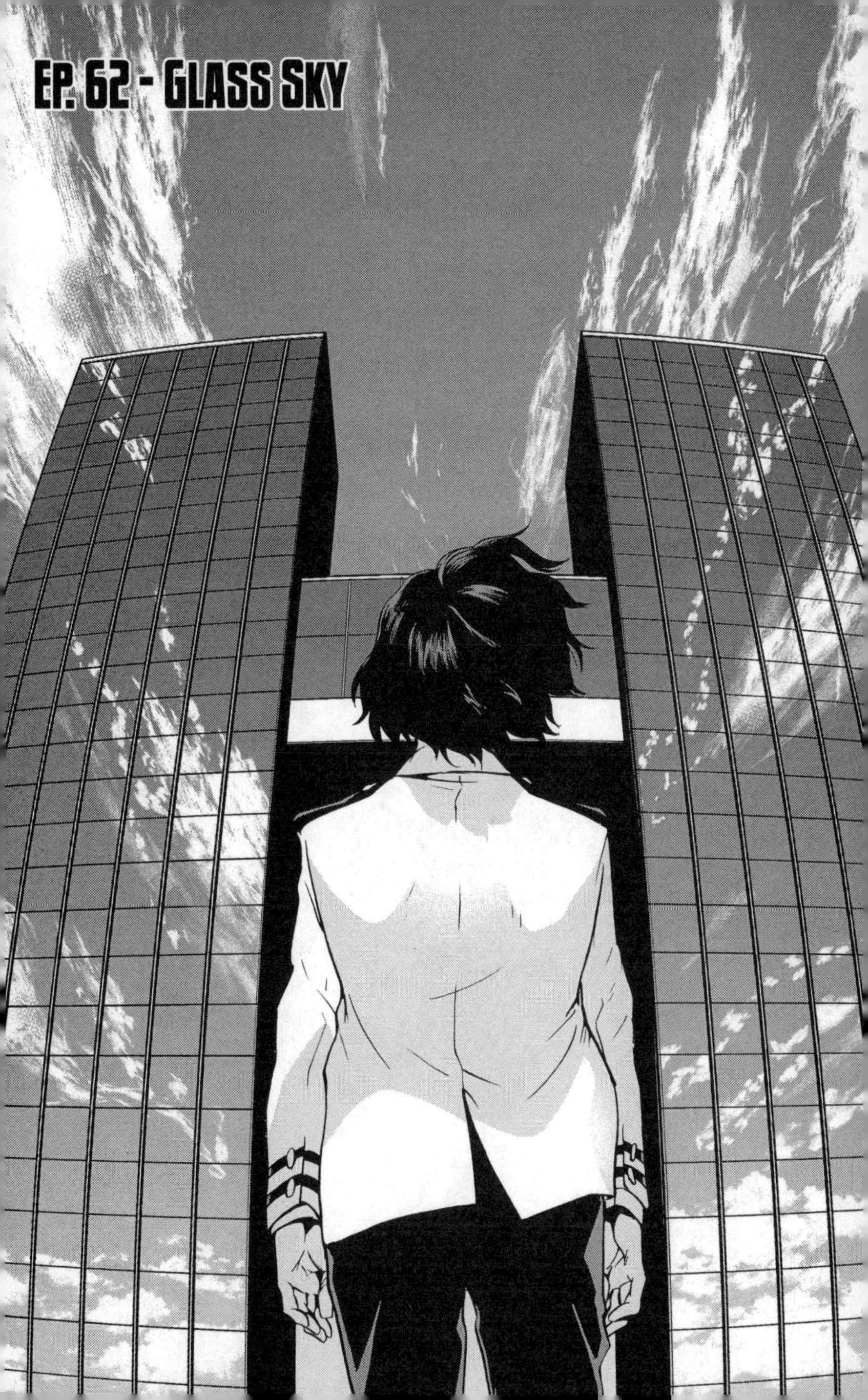
EP. 62 - GLASS SKY

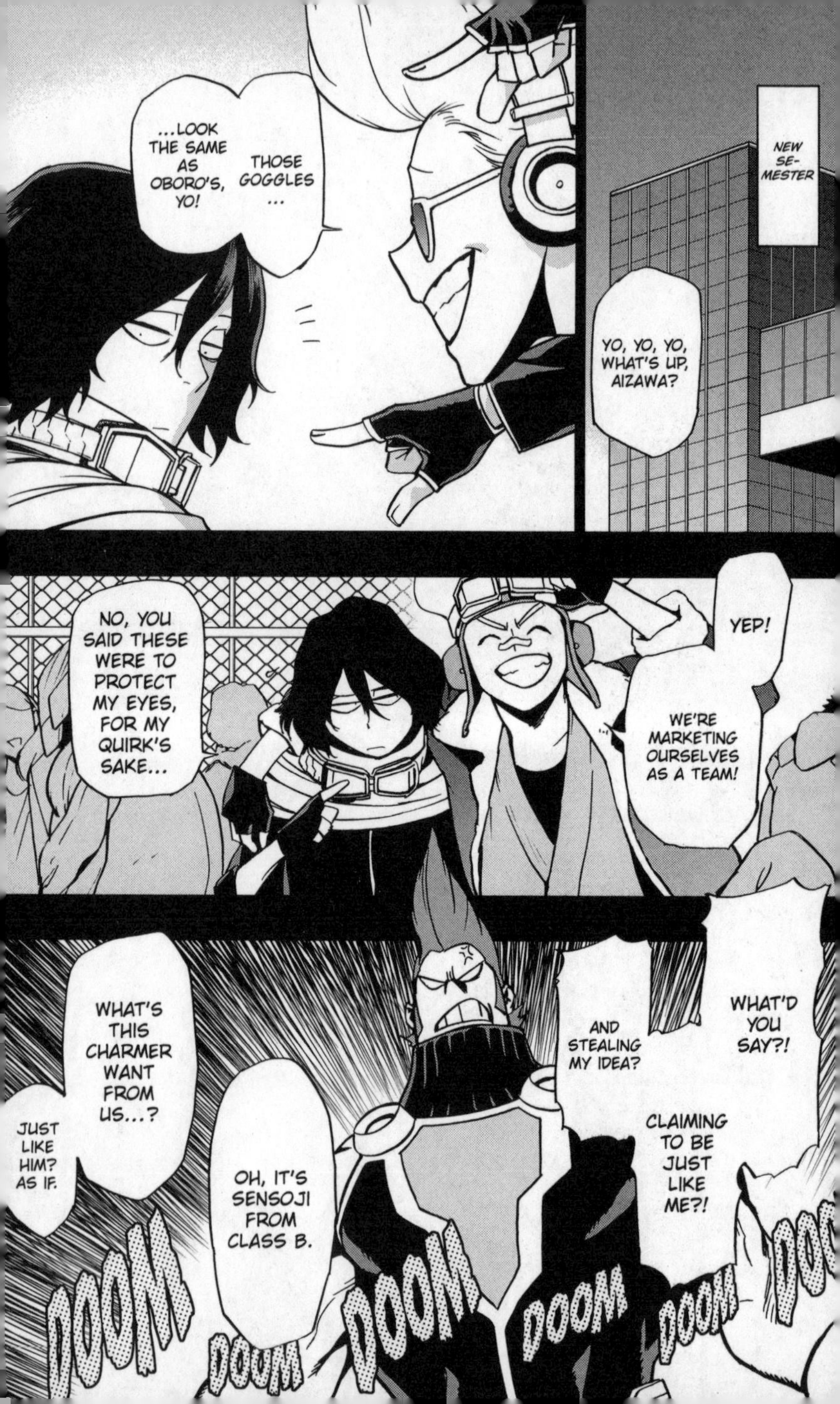
NEW SE-MESTER
YO, YO, YO, WHAT'S UP, AIZAWA?
THOSE GOGGLES... ...LOOK THE SAME AS OBORO'S, YO!
YEP!
WE'RE MARKETING OURSELVES AS A TEAM!
NO, YOU SAID THESE WERE TO PROTECT MY EYES, FOR MY QUIRK'S SAKE...
WHAT'D YOU SAY?!
CLAIMING TO BE JUST LIKE ME?!
AND STEALING MY IDEA?
OH, IT'S SENSOJI FROM CLASS B.
WHAT'S THIS CHARMER WANT FROM US...?
JUST LIKE HIM? AS IF.
DOOM DOOM DOOM DOOM DOOM DOOM DOOM

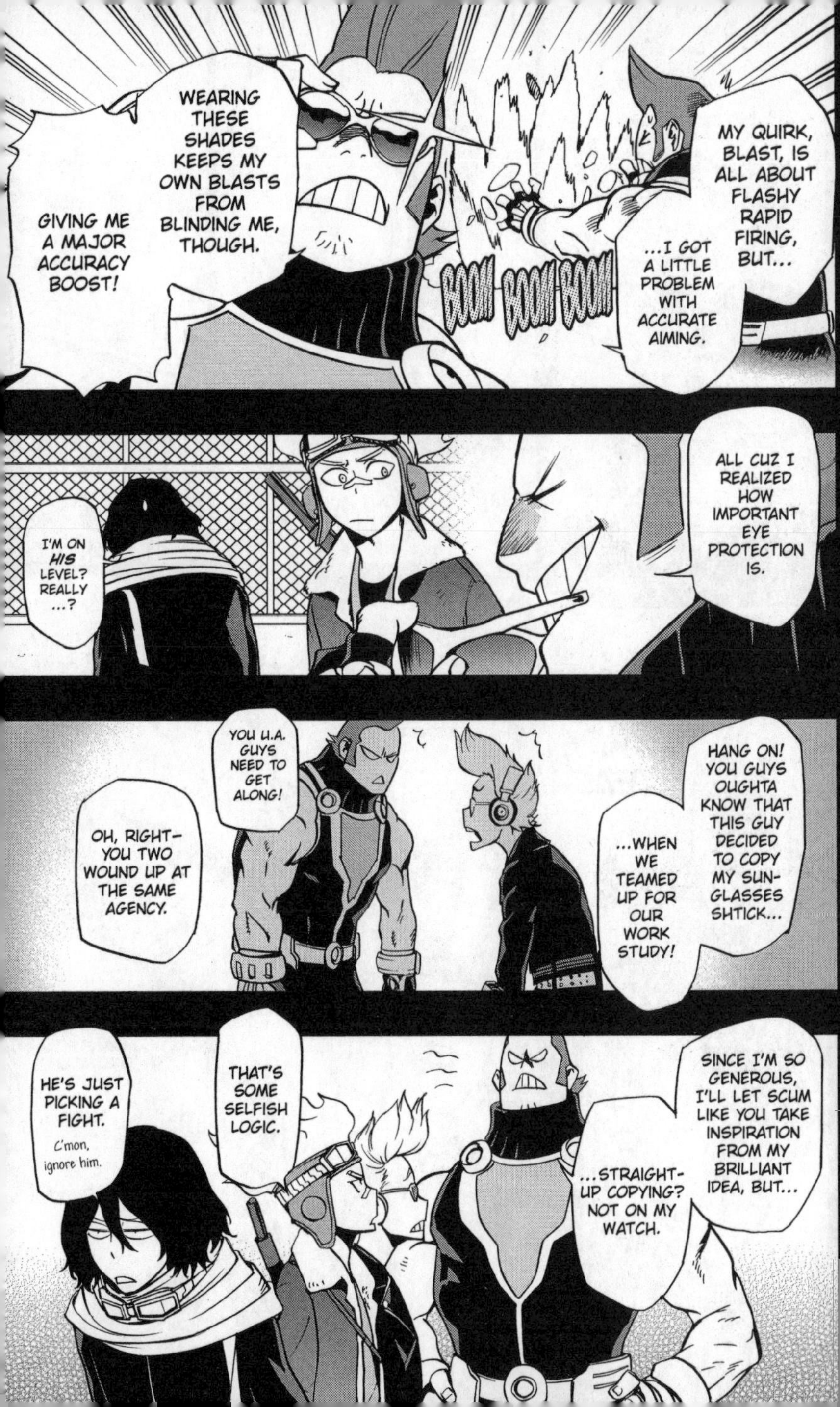
MY QUIRK, BLAST, IS ALL ABOUT FLASHY RAPID FIRING, BUT...
...I GOT A LITTLE PROBLEM WITH ACCURATE AIMING.
BOOM BOOM BOOM
WEARING THESE SHADES KEEPS MY OWN BLASTS FROM BLINDING ME, THOUGH.
GIVING ME A MAJOR ACCURACY BOOST!
ALL CUZ I REALIZED HOW IMPORTANT EYE PROTECTION IS.
I'M ON HIS LEVEL? REALLY ...?
HANG ON! YOU GUYS OUGHTA KNOW THAT THIS GUY DECIDED TO COPY MY SUN-GLASSES SHTICK...
...WHEN WE TEAMED UP FOR OUR WORK STUDY!
YOU U.A. GUYS NEED TO GET ALONG!
OH, RIGHT— YOU TWO WOUND UP AT THE SAME AGENCY.
SINCE I'M SO GENEROUS, I'LL LET SCUM LIKE YOU TAKE INSPIRATION FROM MY BRILLIANT IDEA, BUT...
...STRAIGHT-UP COPYING? NOT ON MY WATCH.
THAT'S SOME SELFISH LOGIC.
HE'S JUST PICKING A FIGHT.
C'mon, ignore him.

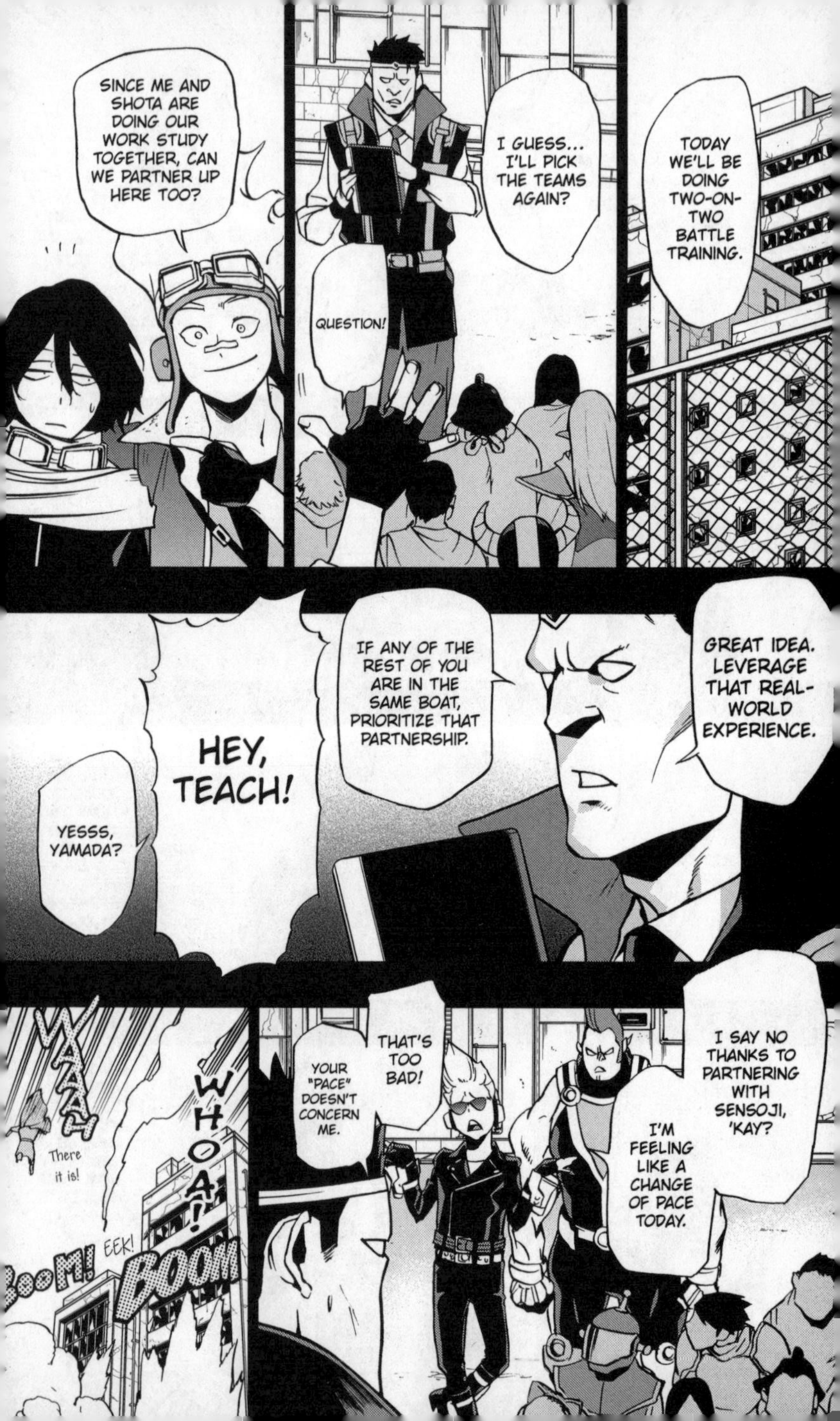
TODAY WE'LL BE DOING TWO-ON-TWO BATTLE TRAINING.
I GUESS... I'LL PICK THE TEAMS AGAIN?
QUESTION!
SINCE ME AND SHOTA ARE DOING OUR WORK STUDY TOGETHER, CAN WE PARTNER UP HERE TOO?
GREAT IDEA. LEVERAGE THAT REAL-WORLD EXPERIENCE.
IF ANY OF THE REST OF YOU ARE IN THE SAME BOAT, PRIORITIZE THAT PARTNERSHIP.
HEY, TEACH!
YESSS, YAMADA?
I SAY NO THANKS TO PARTNERING WITH SENSOJI, 'KAY?
I'M FEELING LIKE A CHANGE OF PACE TODAY.
THAT'S TOO BAD!
YOUR "PACE" DOESN'T CONCERN ME.
WHOA!
BOOM
EEK!
BOOM!
WAAAH
There it is!

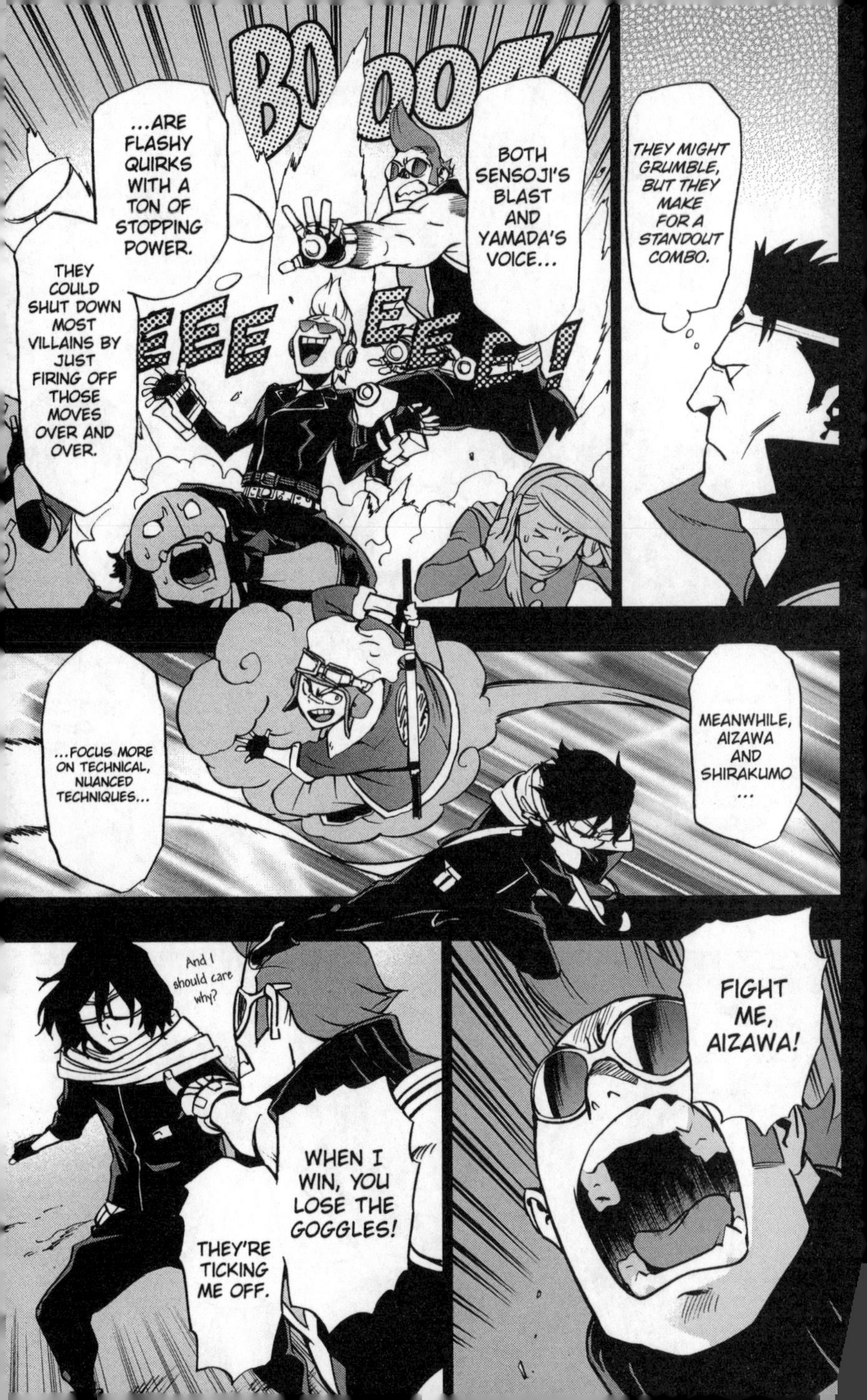
THEY MIGHT GRUMBLE, BUT THEY MAKE FOR A STANDOUT COMBO.
BOOOM
BOTH SENSOJI'S BLAST AND YAMADA'S VOICE...
...ARE FLASHY QUIRKS WITH A TON OF STOPPING POWER.
EEEEEEE!
THEY COULD SHUT DOWN MOST VILLAINS BY JUST FIRING OFF THOSE MOVES OVER AND OVER.
MEANWHILE, AIZAWA AND SHIRAKUMO ...
...FOCUS MORE ON TECHNICAL, NUANCED TECHNIQUES...
FIGHT ME, AIZAWA!
WHEN I WIN, YOU LOSE THE GOGGLES!
And I should care why?
THEY'RE TICKING ME OFF.

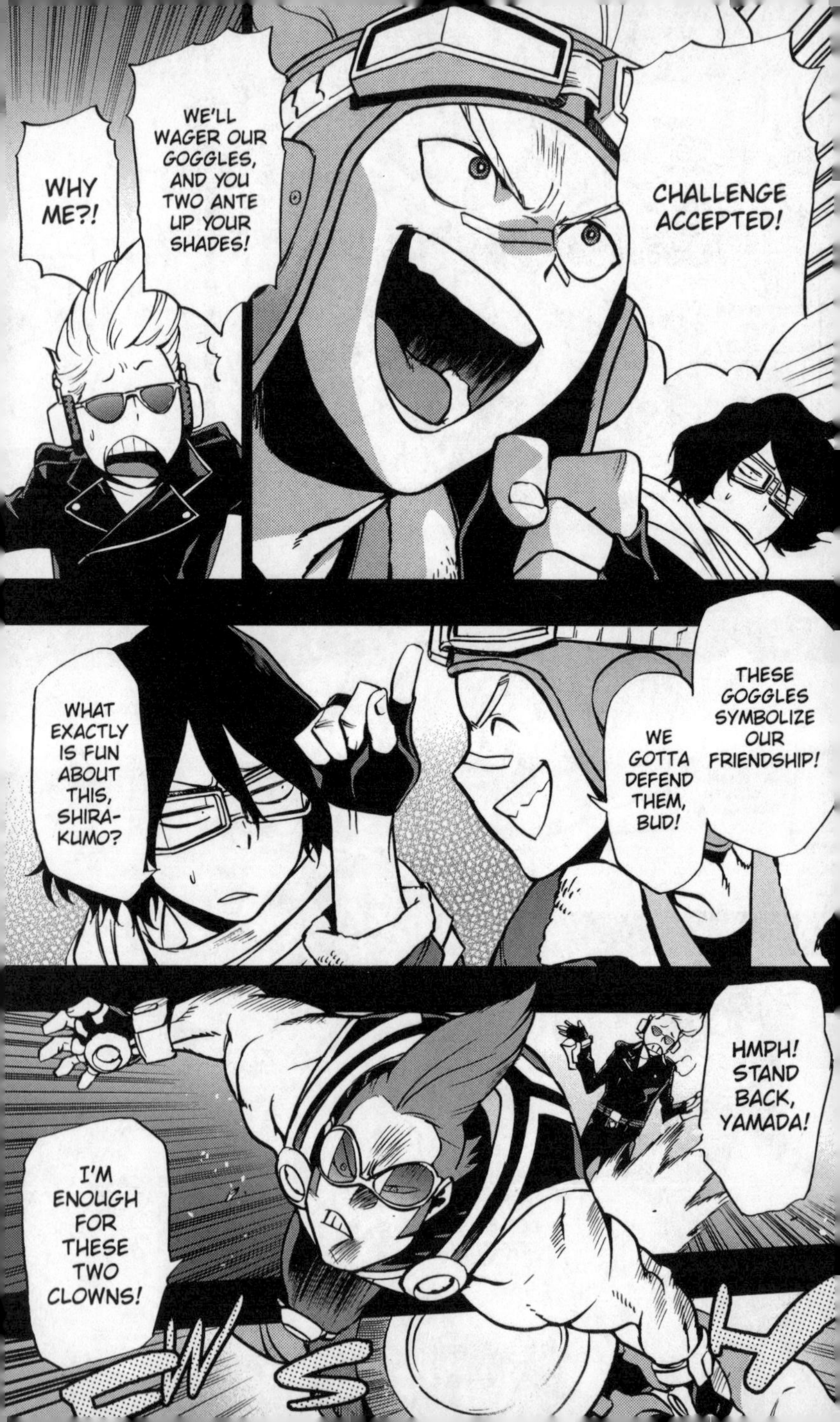
CHALLENGE ACCEPTED!
WE'LL WAGER OUR GOGGLES, AND YOU TWO ANTE UP YOUR SHADES!
WHY ME?!
THESE GOGGLES SYMBOLIZE OUR FRIENDSHIP!
WE GOTTA DEFEND THEM, BUD!
WHAT EXACTLY IS FUN ABOUT THIS, SHIRA-KUMO?
HMPH! STAND BACK, YAMADA!
I'M ENOUGH FOR THESE TWO CLOWNS!

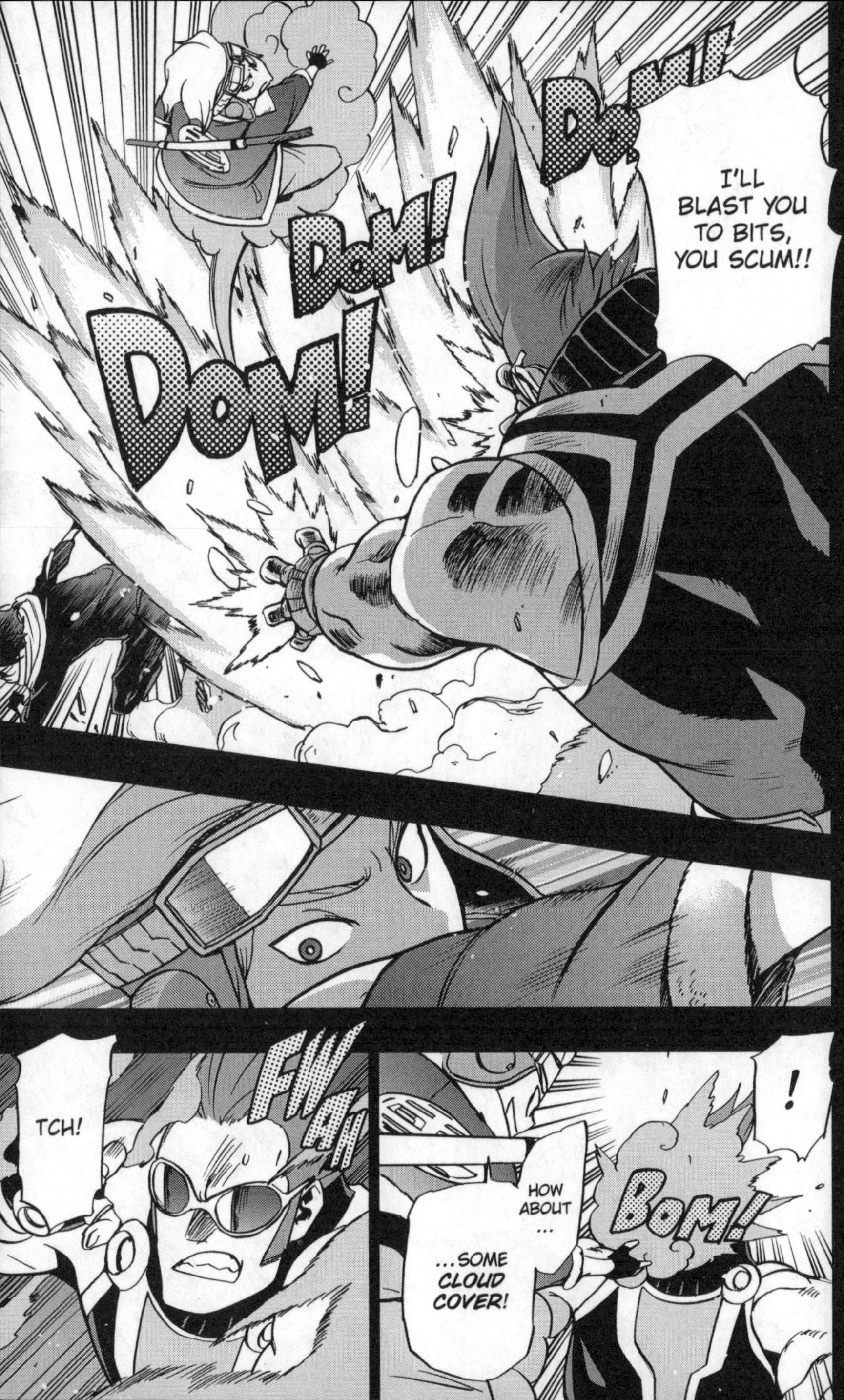
I'LL BLAST YOU TO BITS, YOU SCUM!!
DOM!
DOM!
!
BOM!
HOW ABOUT ...
...SOME CLOUD COVER!
FWAH
TCH!

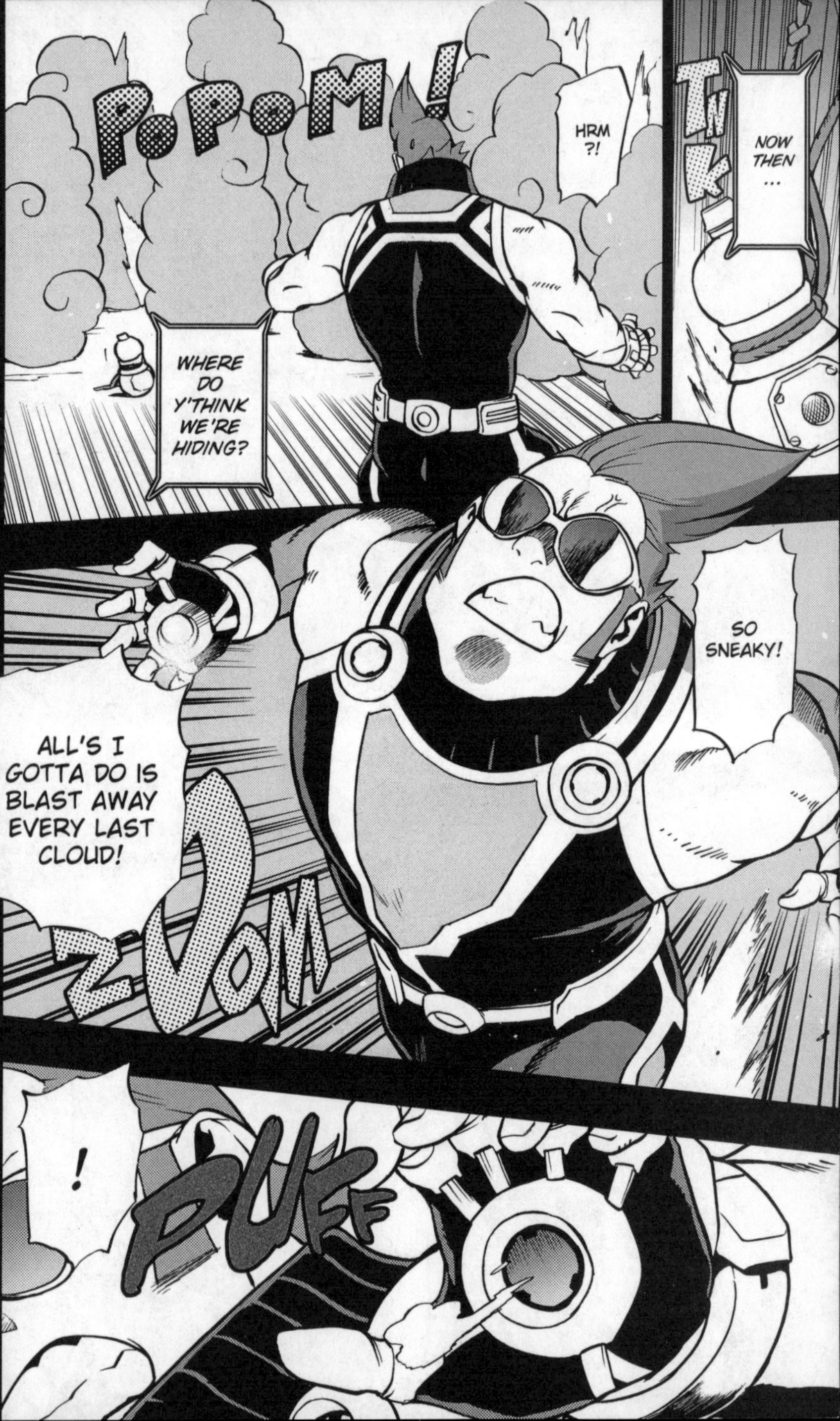
TNK
NOW THEN ...
HRM ?!
POPOM!
WHERE DO Y'THINK WE'RE HIDING?
SO SNEAKY!
ALL'S I GOTTA DO IS BLAST AWAY EVERY LAST CLOUD!
ZOOM
DUFF
!

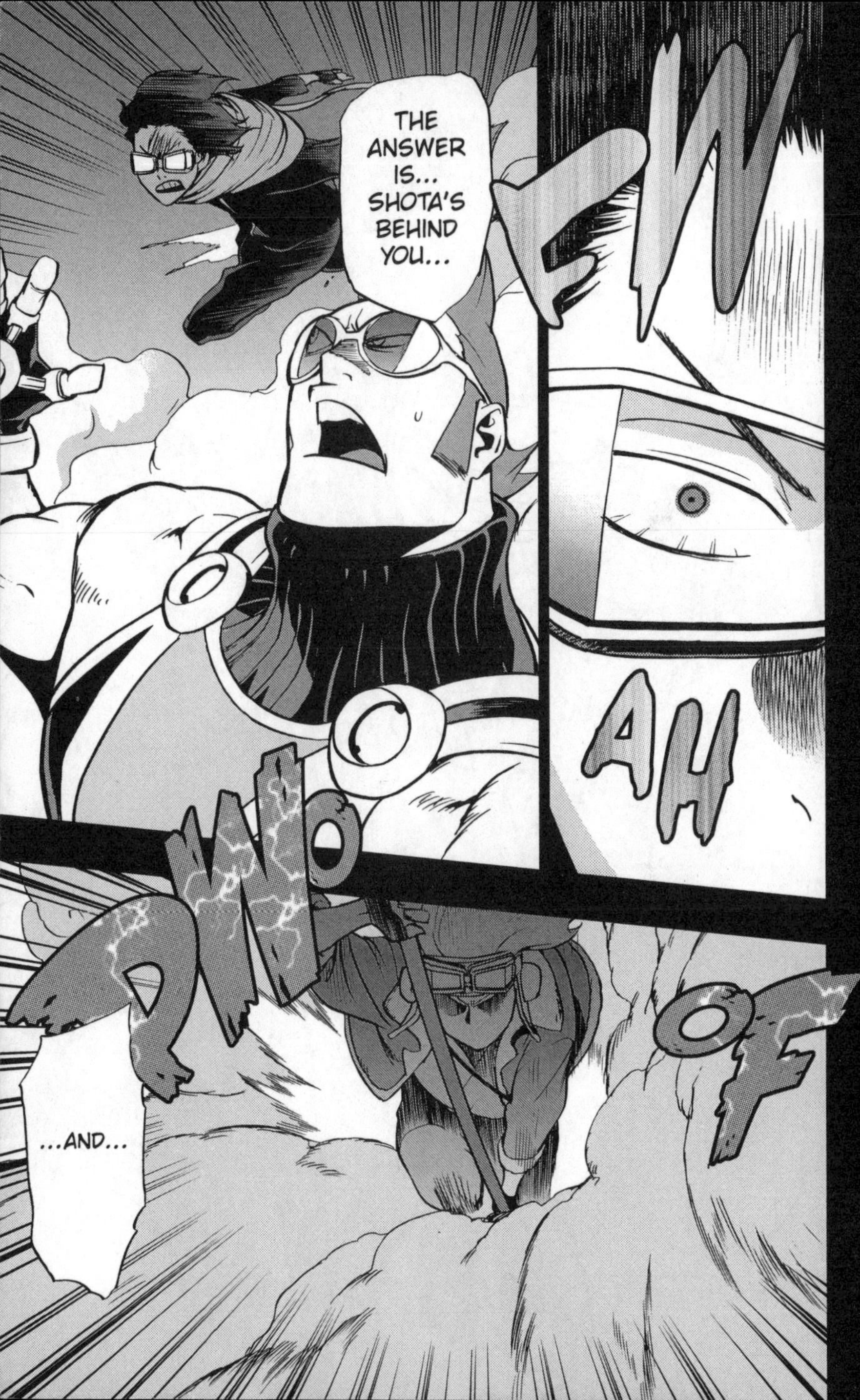
FW
AH
THE ANSWER IS... SHOTA'S BEHIND YOU...
DWO
OF
...AND...

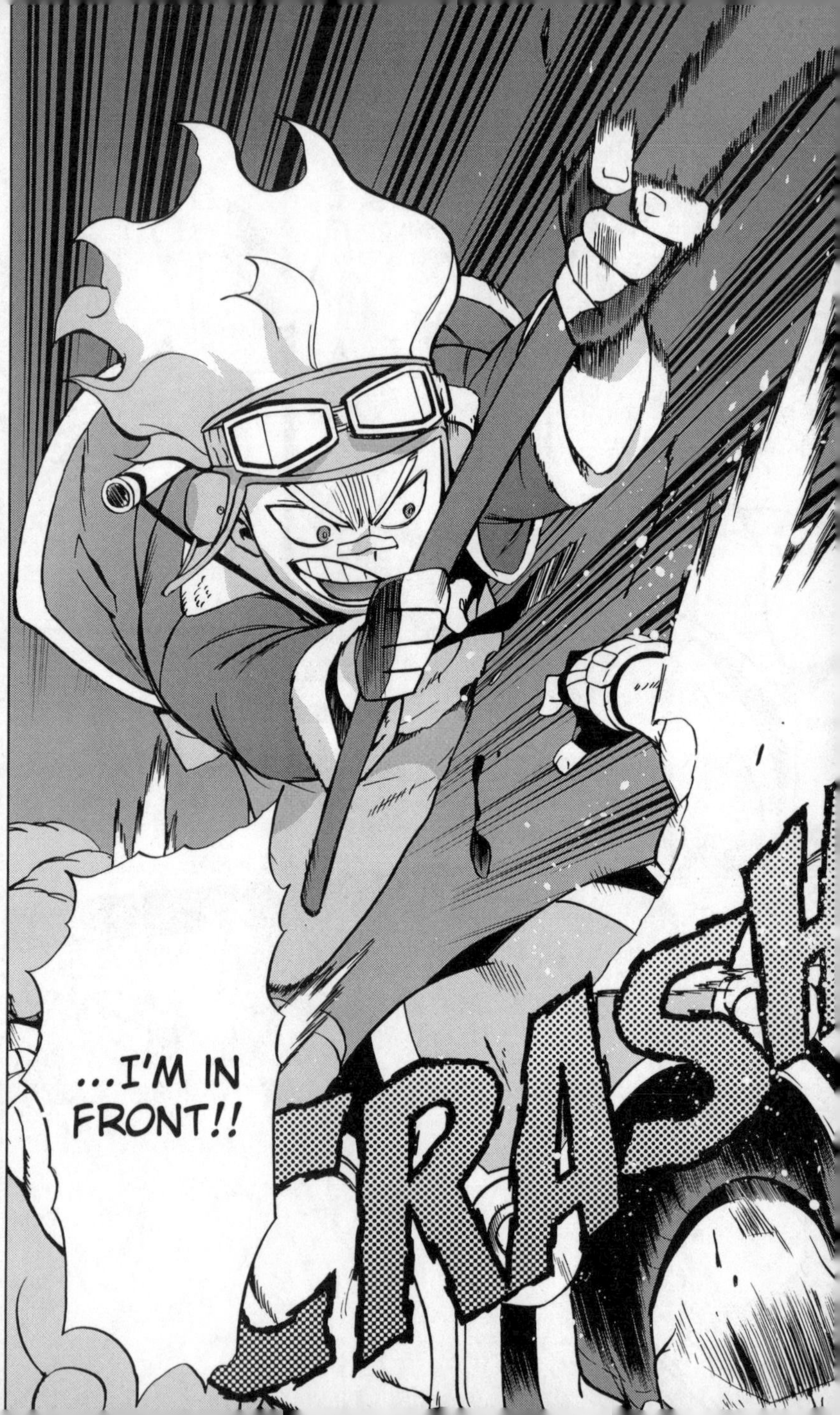
...I'M IN FRONT!!
CRASH

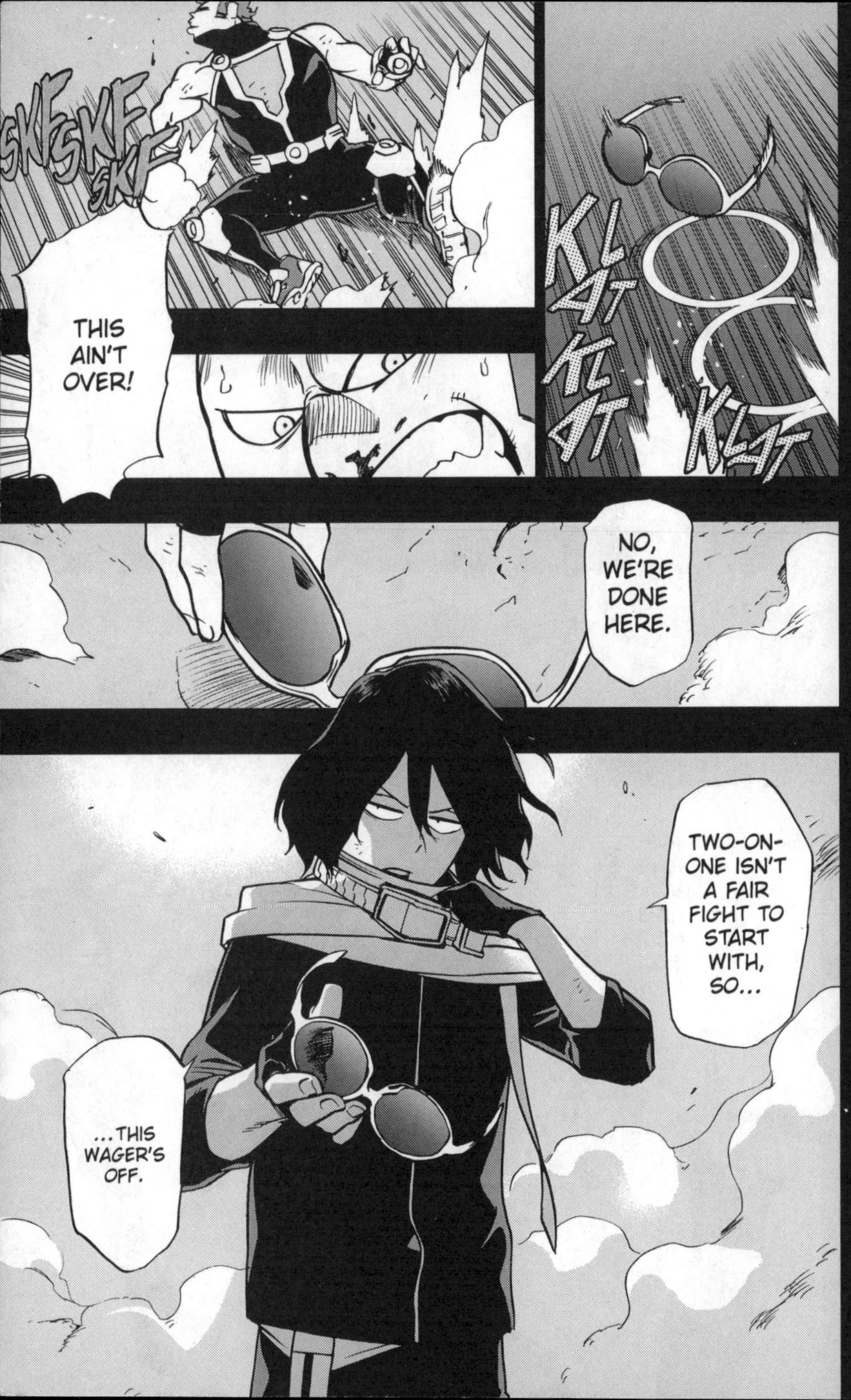
KLAT
KLAT
KLAT
SKF SKF
SKF
THIS AIN'T OVER!
NO, WE'RE DONE HERE.
TWO-ON-ONE ISN'T A FAIR FIGHT TO START WITH, SO...
...THIS WAGER'S OFF.

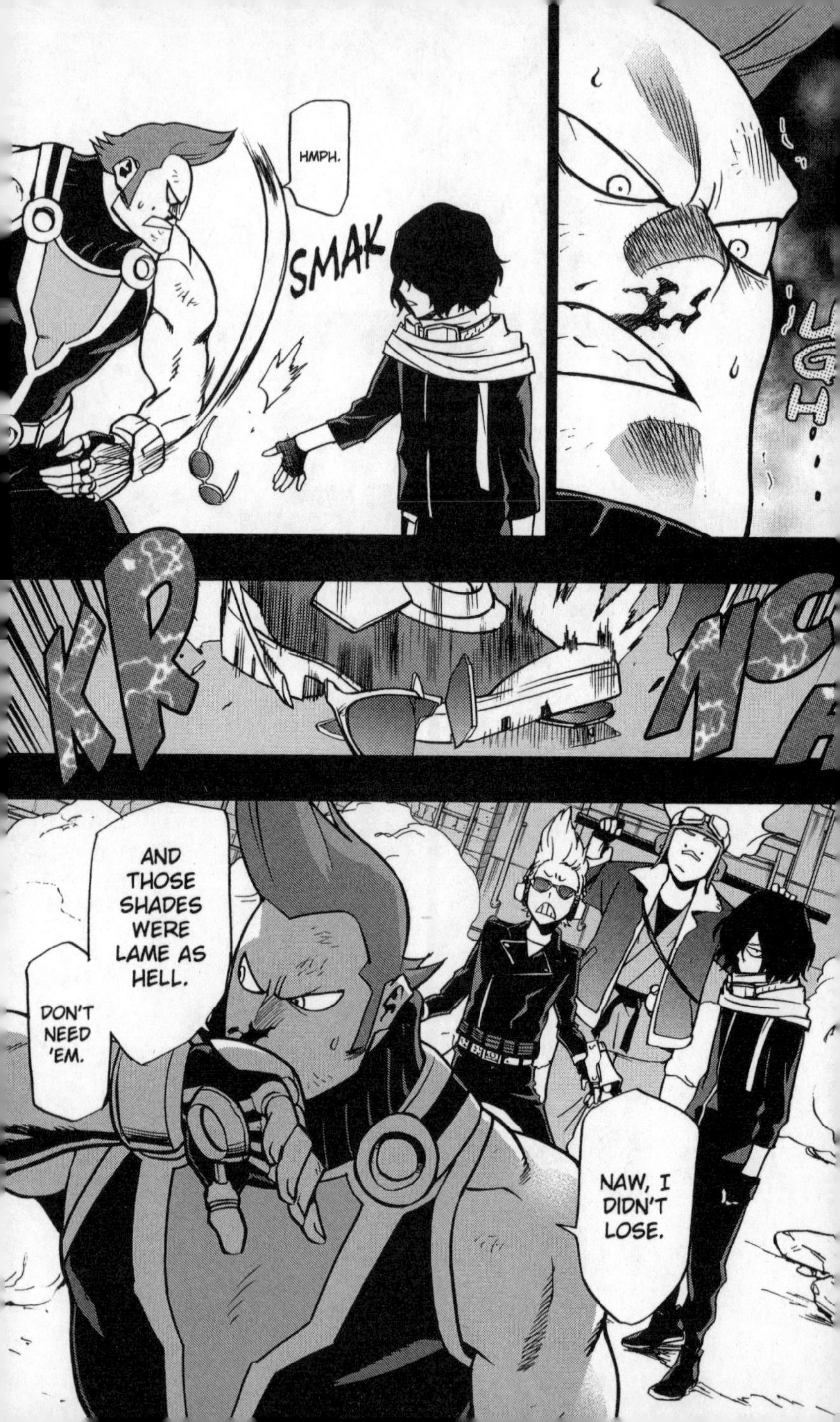
UGH...
HMPH.
SMAK
KRNCH
NAW, I DIDN'T LOSE.
AND THOSE SHADES WERE LAME AS HELL.
DON'T NEED 'EM.

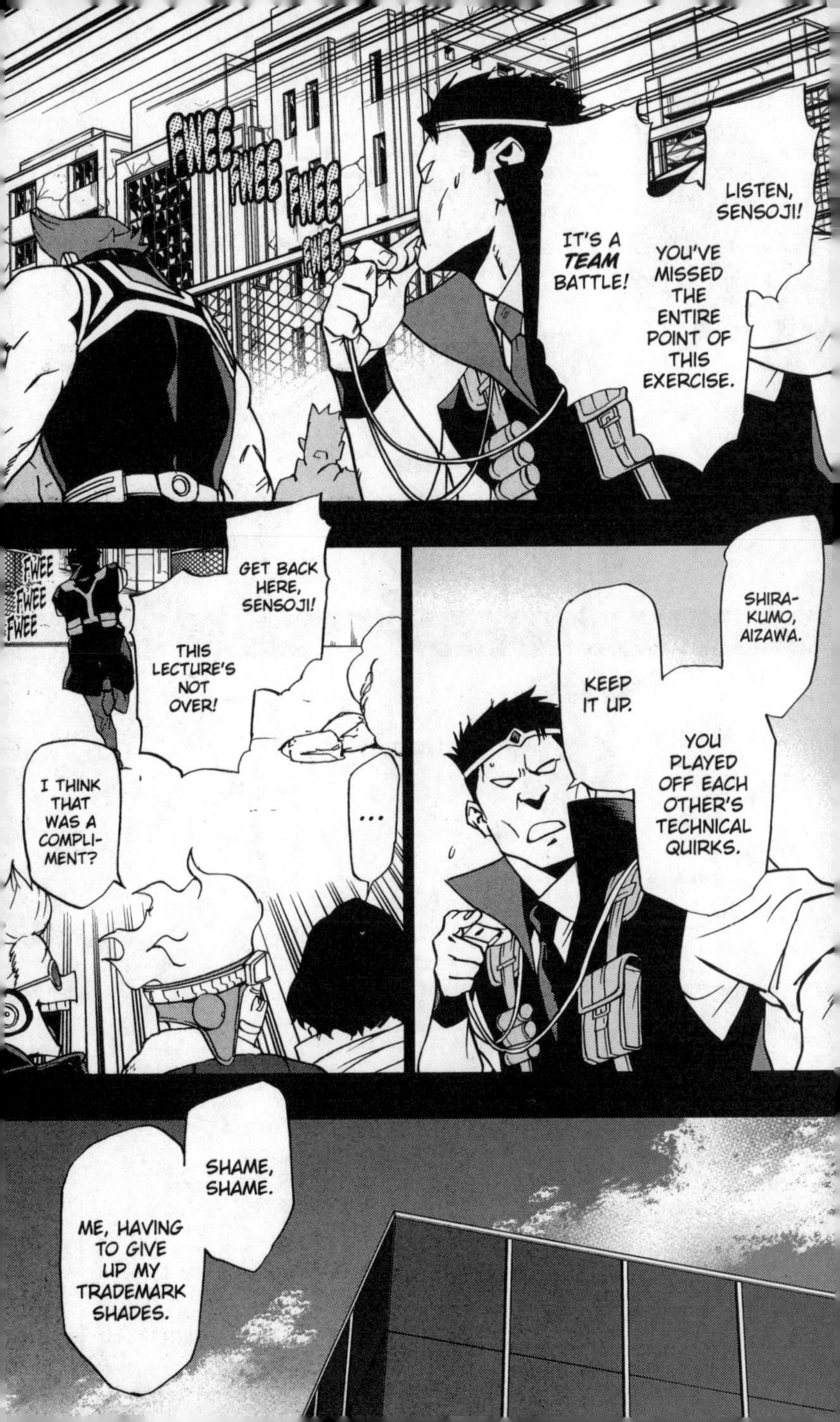
LISTEN, SENSOJI!
YOU'VE MISSED THE ENTIRE POINT OF THIS EXERCISE.
IT'S A *TEAM* BATTLE!
FWEE FWEE FWEE FWEE
SHIRA-KUMO, AIZAWA.
KEEP IT UP.
YOU PLAYED OFF EACH OTHER'S TECHNICAL QUIRKS.
GET BACK HERE, SENSOJI!
THIS LECTURE'S NOT OVER!
FWEE FWEE FWEE
...
I THINK THAT WAS A COMPLI-MENT?
SHAME, SHAME.
ME, HAVING TO GIVE UP MY TRADEMARK SHADES.

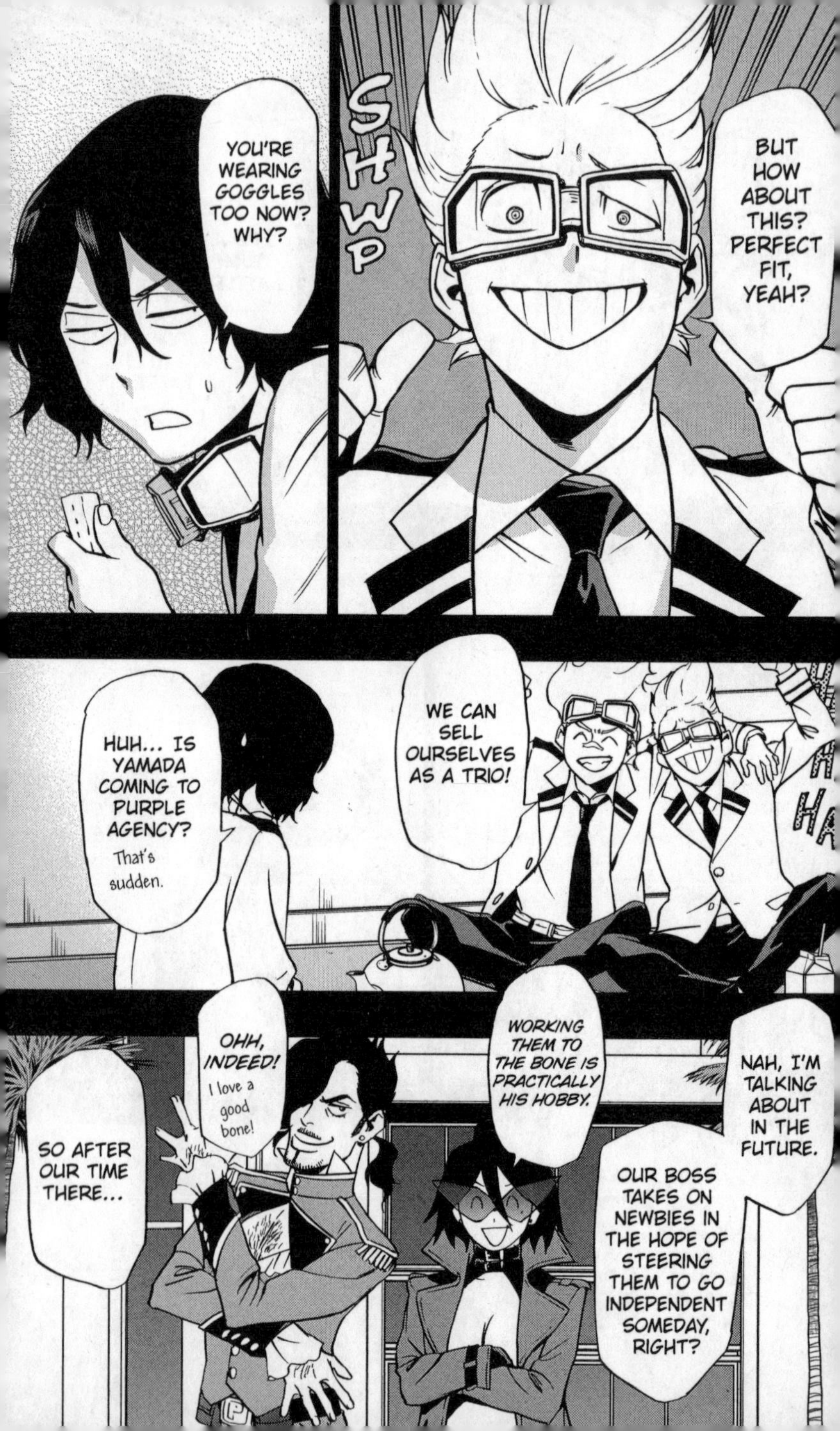
BUT HOW ABOUT THIS? PERFECT FIT, YEAH?
SHWP
YOU'RE WEARING GOGGLES TOO NOW? WHY?
HA
WE CAN SELL OURSELVES AS A TRIO!
HUH... IS YAMADA COMING TO PURPLE AGENCY? That's sudden.
NAH, I'M TALKING ABOUT IN THE FUTURE.
OUR BOSS TAKES ON NEWBIES IN THE HOPE OF STEERING THEM TO GO INDEPENDENT SOMEDAY, RIGHT?
WORKING THEM TO THE BONE IS PRACTICALLY HIS HOBBY.
OHH, INDEED! I love a good bone!
SO AFTER OUR TIME THERE...

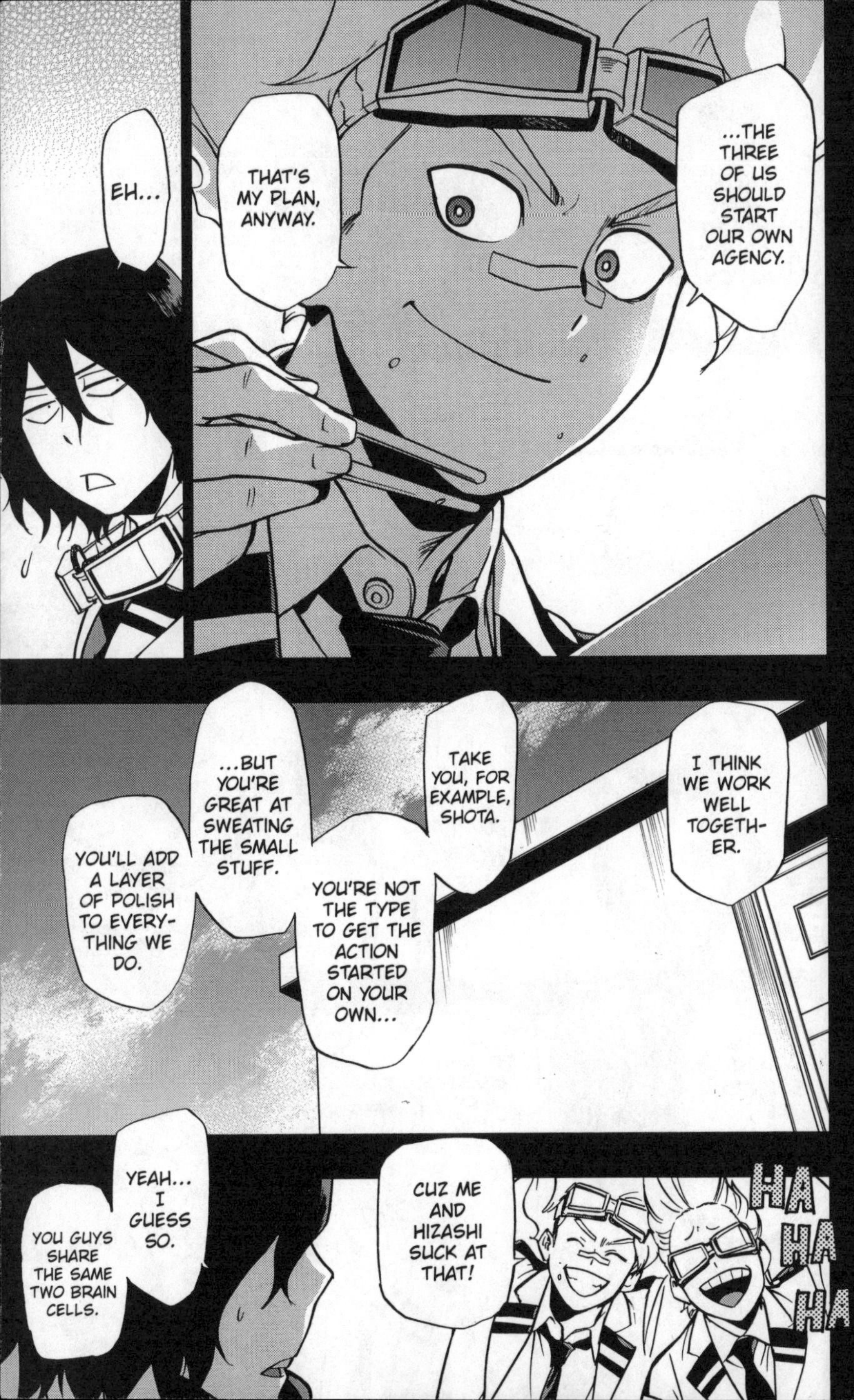
...THE THREE OF US SHOULD START OUR OWN AGENCY.
THAT'S MY PLAN, ANYWAY.
EH...
I THINK WE WORK WELL TOGETH-ER.
TAKE YOU, FOR EXAMPLE, SHOTA.
YOU'RE NOT THE TYPE TO GET THE ACTION STARTED ON YOUR OWN...
...BUT YOU'RE GREAT AT SWEATING THE SMALL STUFF.
YOU'LL ADD A LAYER OF POLISH TO EVERY-THING WE DO.
HA HA HA
CUZ ME AND HIZASHI SUCK AT THAT!
YEAH... I GUESS SO.
YOU GUYS SHARE THE SAME TWO BRAIN CELLS.

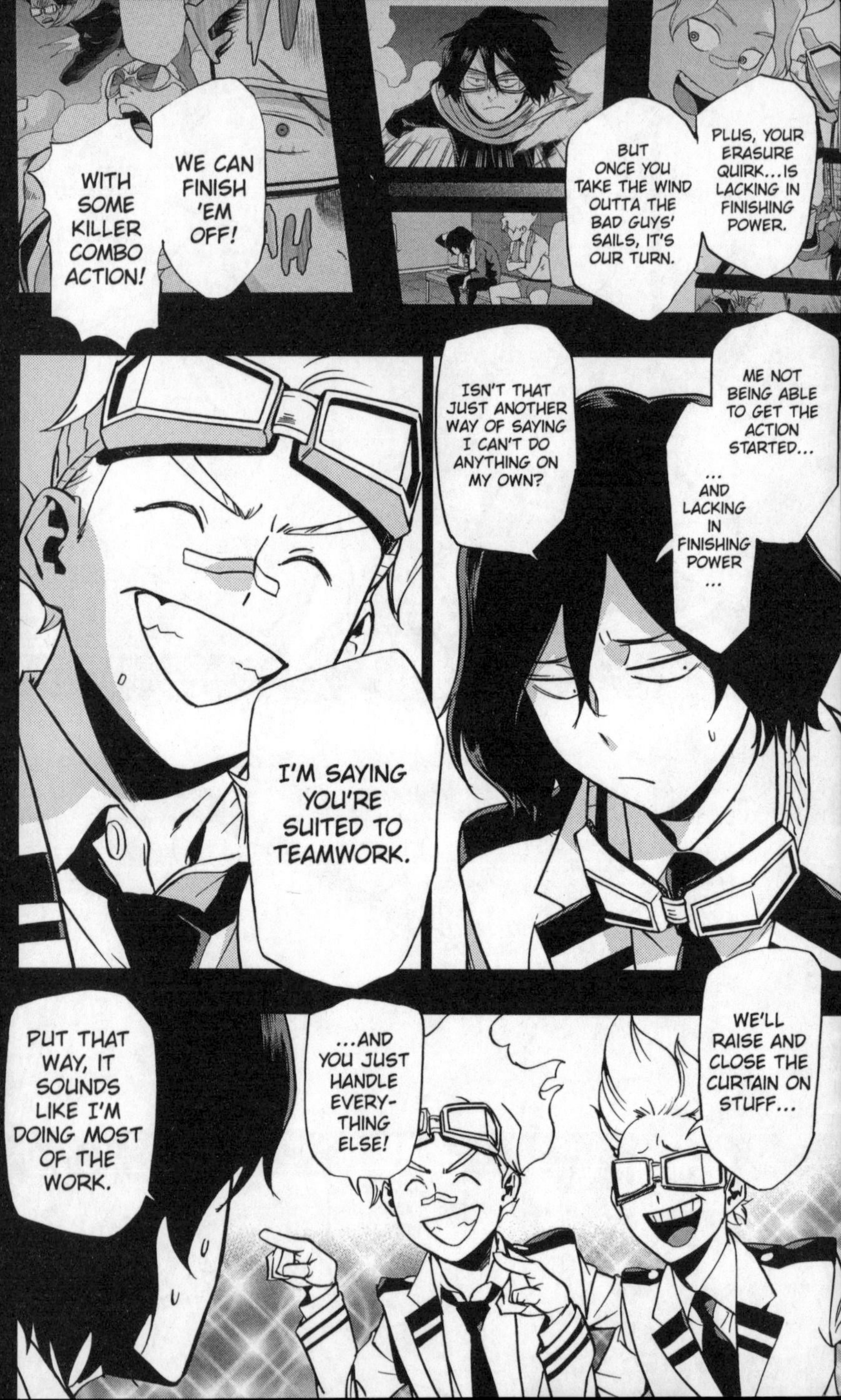
PLUS, YOUR ERASURE QUIRK...IS LACKING IN FINISHING POWER.
BUT ONCE YOU TAKE THE WIND OUTTA THE BAD GUYS' SAILS, IT'S OUR TURN.
WE CAN FINISH 'EM OFF!
WITH SOME KILLER COMBO ACTION!
ME NOT BEING ABLE TO GET THE ACTION STARTED...
...AND LACKING IN FINISHING POWER...
ISN'T THAT JUST ANOTHER WAY OF SAYING I CAN'T DO ANYTHING ON MY OWN?
I'M SAYING YOU'RE SUITED TO TEAMWORK.
WE'LL RAISE AND CLOSE THE CURTAIN ON STUFF...
...AND YOU JUST HANDLE EVERY-THING ELSE!
PUT THAT WAY, IT SOUNDS LIKE I'M DOING MOST OF THE WORK.

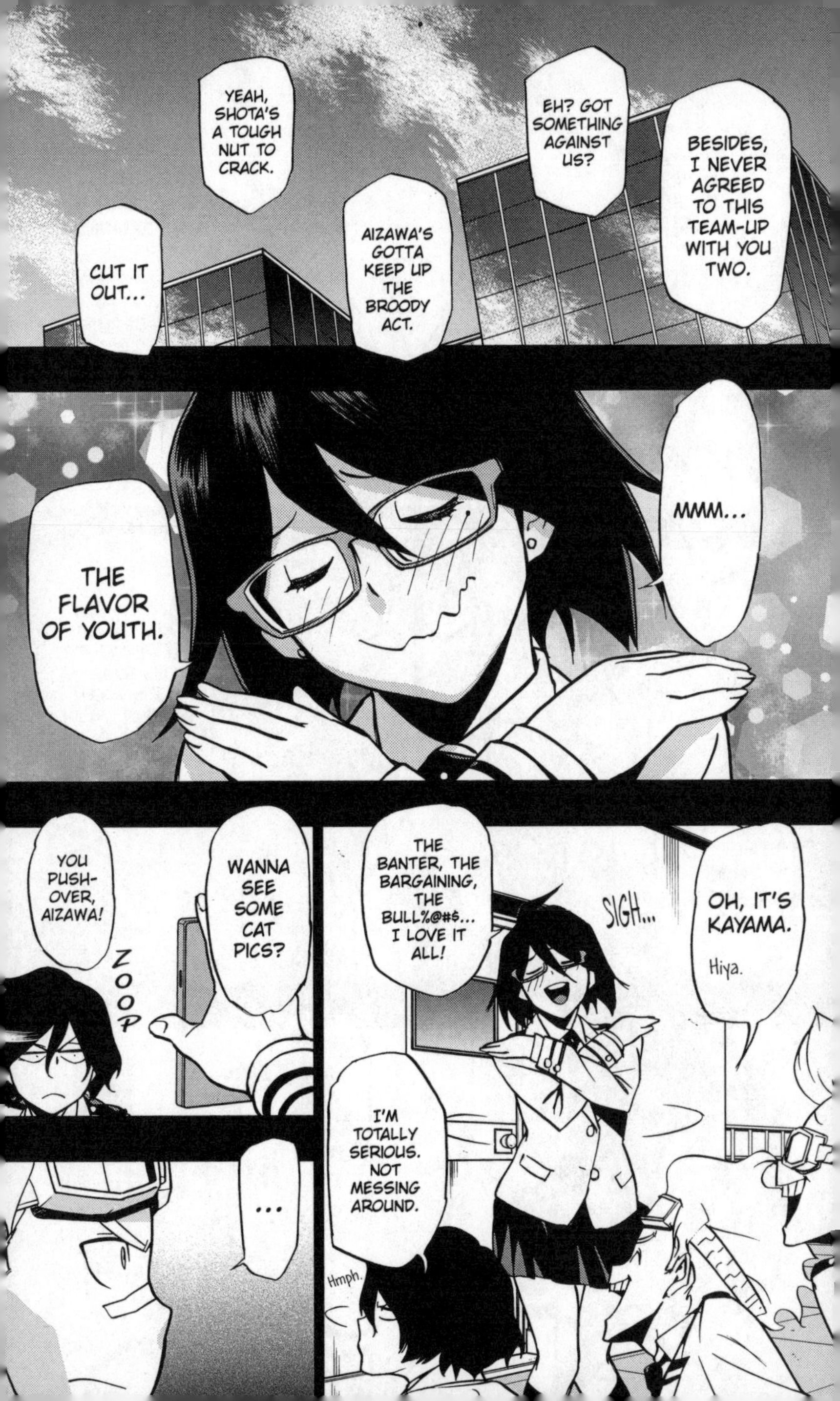
BESIDES, I NEVER AGREED TO THIS TEAM-UP WITH YOU TWO.
EH? GOT SOMETHING AGAINST US?
YEAH, SHOTA'S A TOUGH NUT TO CRACK.
AIZAWA'S GOTTA KEEP UP THE BROODY ACT.
CUT IT OUT...
MMM...
THE FLAVOR OF YOUTH.
OH, IT'S KAYAMA.
Hiya.
SIGH...
THE BANTER, THE BARGAINING, THE BULL%@#$... I LOVE IT ALL!
I'M TOTALLY SERIOUS. NOT MESSING AROUND.
Hmph.
WANNA SEE SOME CAT PICS?
YOU PUSHOVER, AIZAWA!
ZOOOP
...

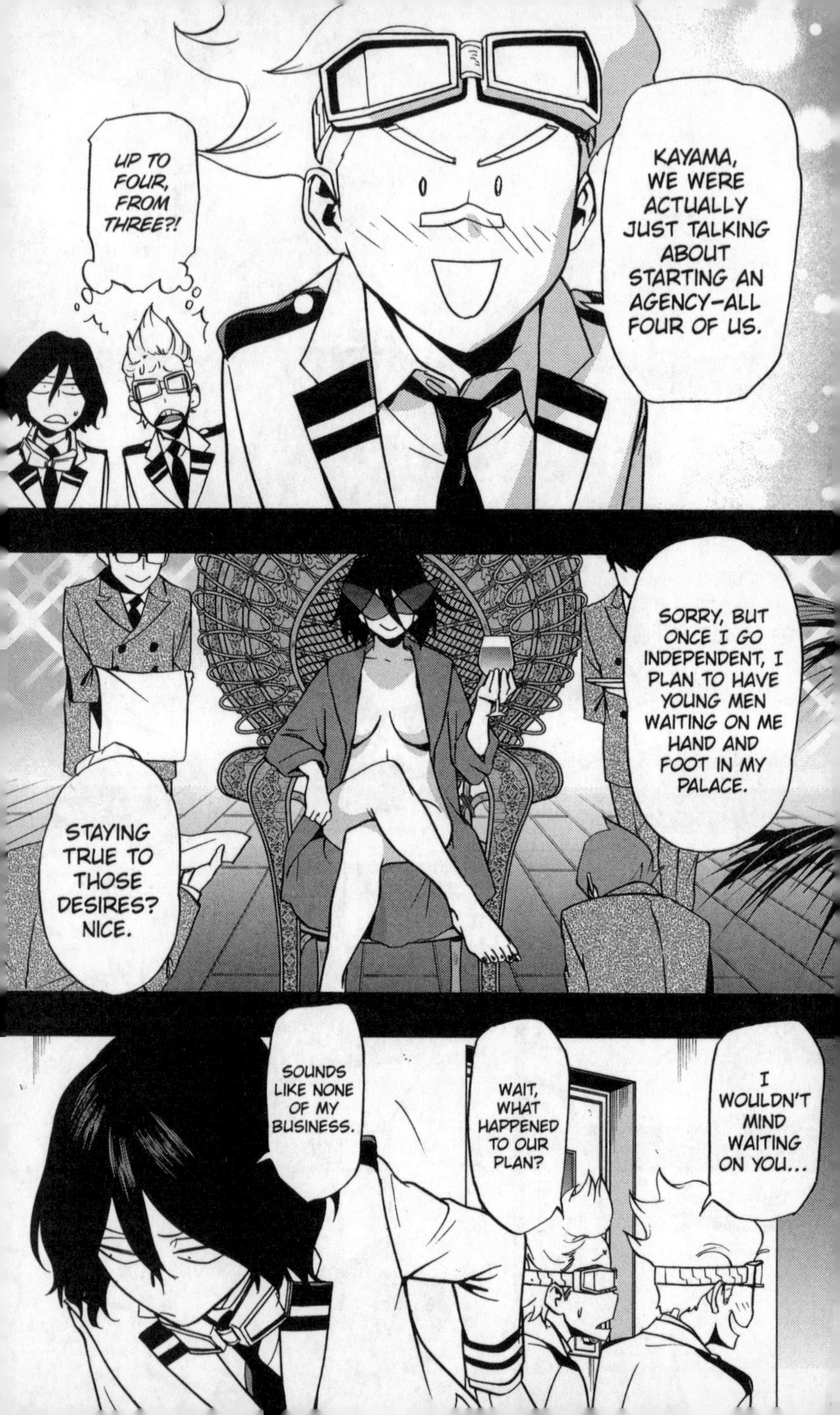
KAYAMA, WE WERE ACTUALLY JUST TALKING ABOUT STARTING AN AGENCY—ALL FOUR OF US.
UP TO FOUR, FROM THREE?!
SORRY, BUT ONCE I GO INDEPENDENT, I PLAN TO HAVE YOUNG MEN WAITING ON ME HAND AND FOOT IN MY PALACE.
STAYING TRUE TO THOSE DESIRES? NICE.
I WOULDN'T MIND WAITING ON YOU...
WAIT, WHAT HAPPENED TO OUR PLAN?
SOUNDS LIKE NONE OF MY BUSINESS.

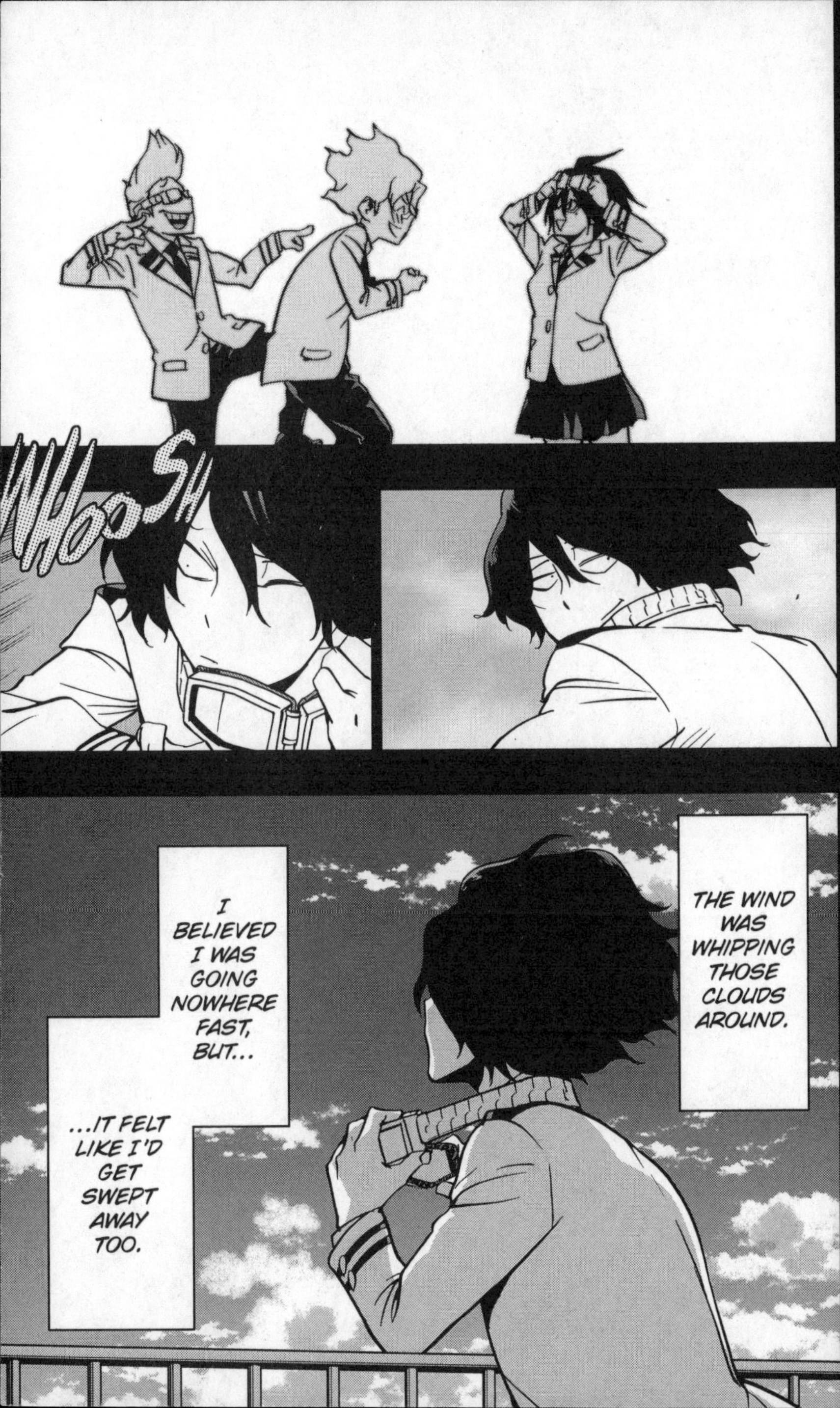
WHOOSH
THE WIND WAS WHIPPING THOSE CLOUDS AROUND.
I BELIEVED I WAS GOING NOWHERE FAST, BUT...
...IT FELT LIKE I'D GET SWEPT AWAY TOO.

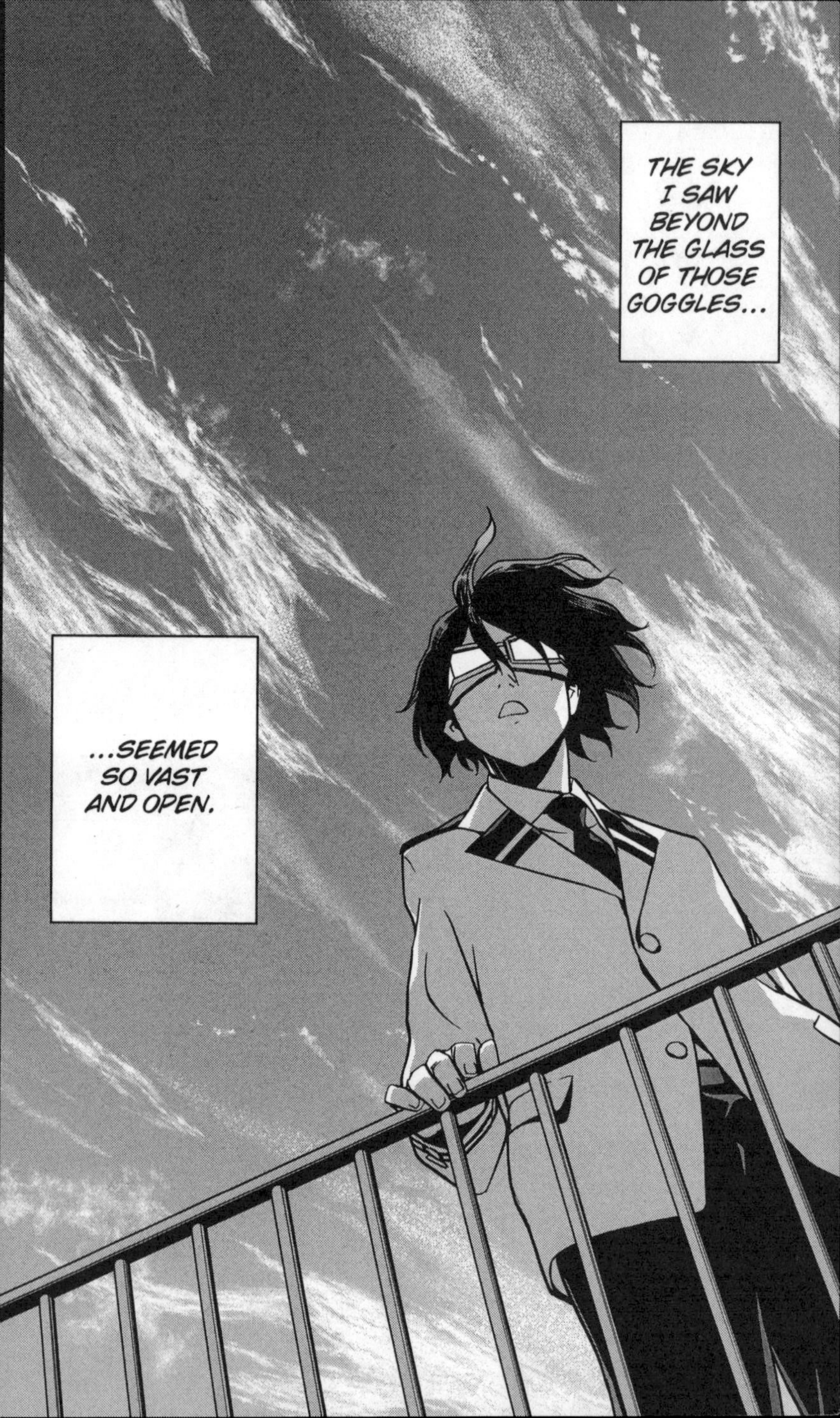
THE SKY I SAW BEYOND THE GLASS OF THOSE GOGGLES...
...SEEMED SO VAST AND OPEN.

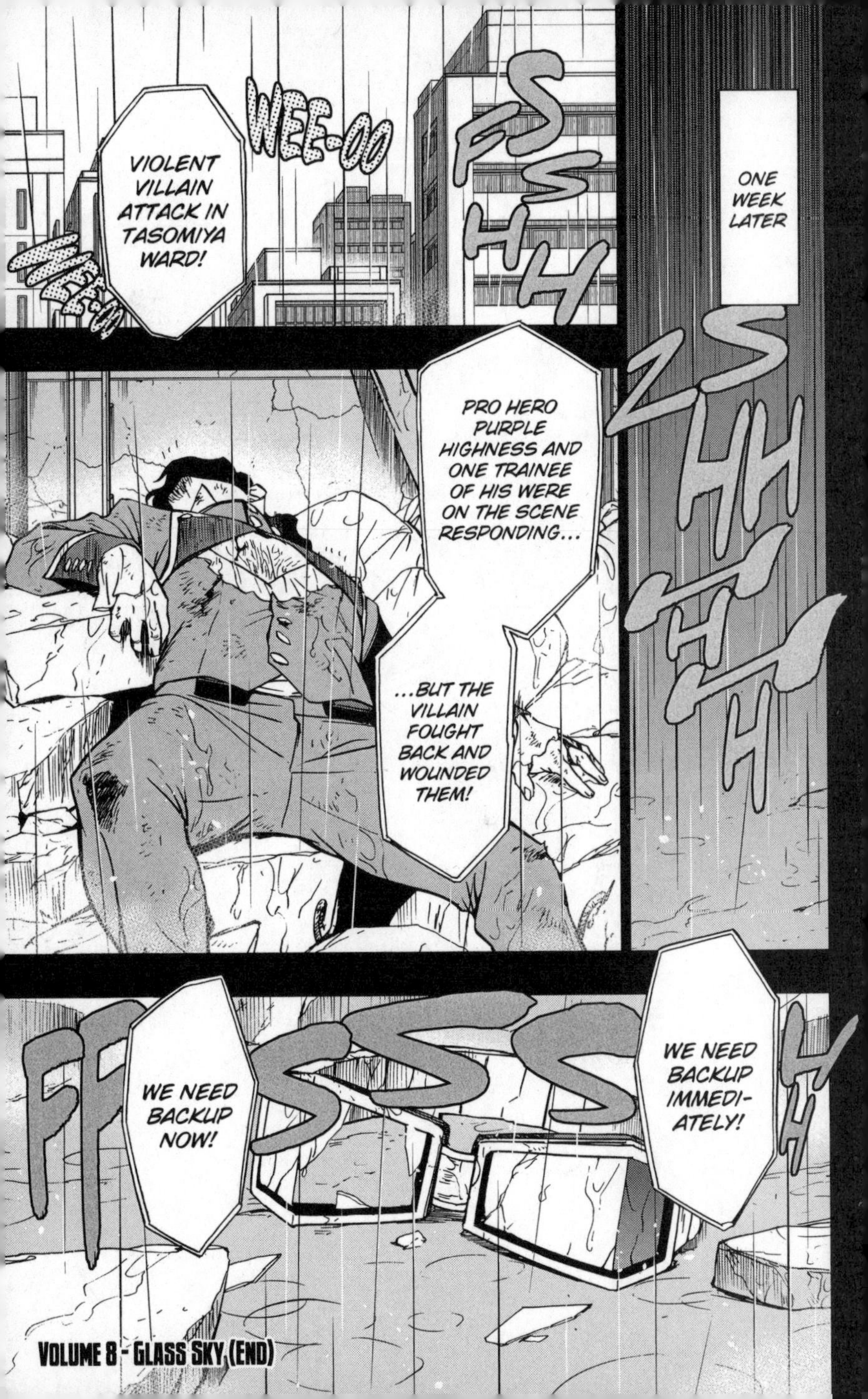
ONE WEEK LATER
ZSHHHHH
FSSHH
WEE-OO
VIOLENT VILLAIN ATTACK IN TASOMIYA WARD!
WEE-OO
PRO HERO PURPLE HIGHNESS AND ONE TRAINEE OF HIS WERE ON THE SCENE RESPONDING...
...BUT THE VILLAIN FOUGHT BACK AND WOUNDED THEM!
FFSSSHHH
WE NEED BACKUP IMMEDI-ATELY!
WE NEED BACKUP NOW!

VOLUME 8 - GLASS SKY (END)

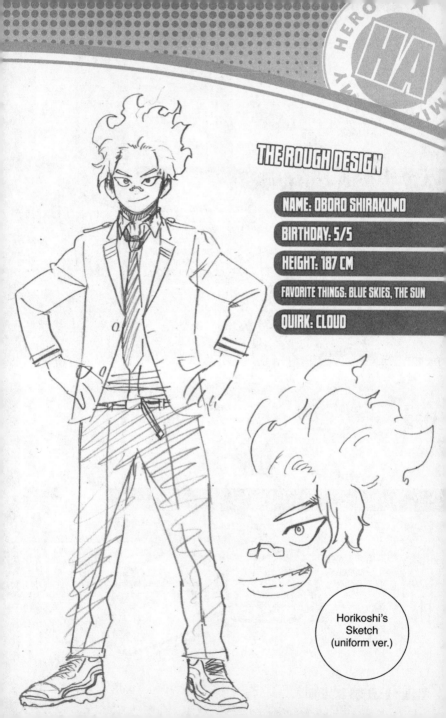

THE ROUGH DESIGN

NAME: OBORO SHIRAKUMO

BIRTHDAY: 5/5

HEIGHT: 187 CM

FAVORITE THINGS: BLUE SKIES, THE SUN

QUIRK: CLOUD

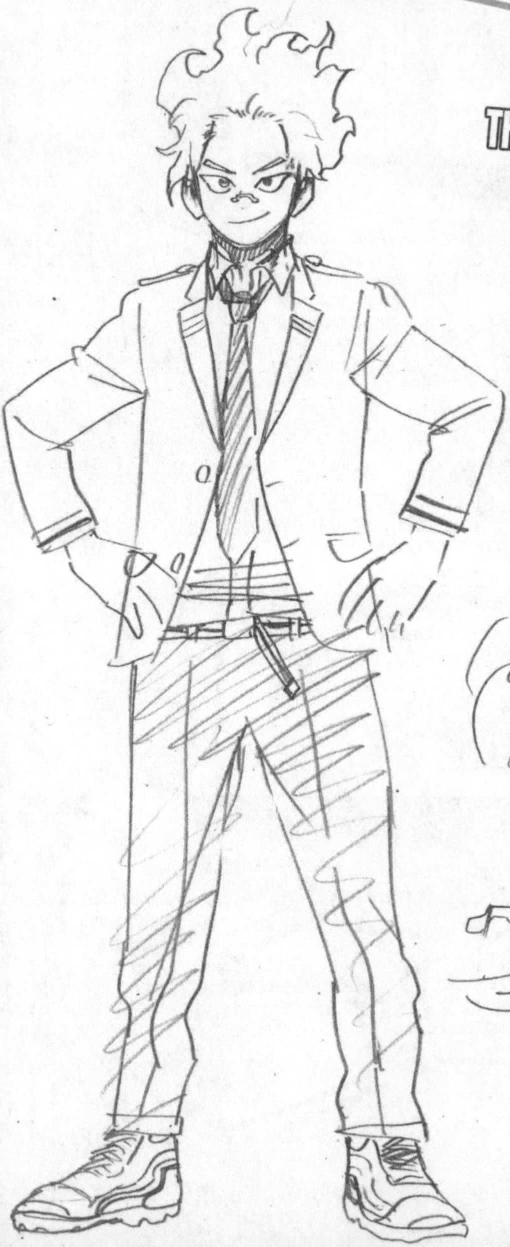

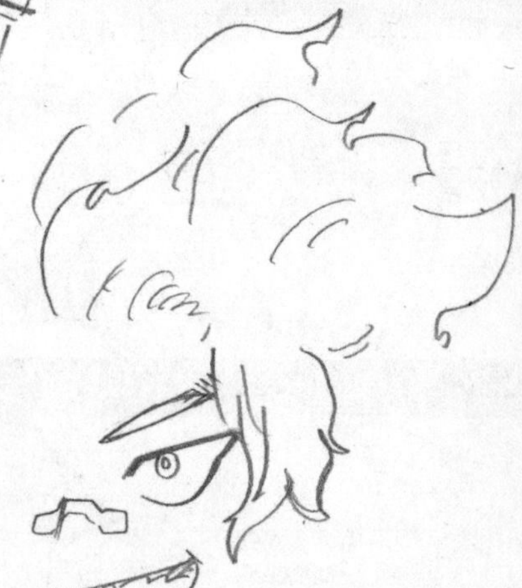

Horikoshi's Sketch (uniform ver.)

LOUD CLOUD

BEHIND THE SCENES

Shirakumo's whole concept started with Horikoshi Sensei describing him as "a Mirio-like friend of Aizawa's during his school days." Then, through a lot of back-and-forth conversations between Horikoshi Sensei and the *Vigilantes* team, we came up with a more detailed profile, visual design and so on, until the character really took form. Shirakumo's presence meant that Aizawa's and Mic's personalities and roles had to be a little different in the past. That necessitated including that altered portrayal, as well as showing the way they changed moving towards the present day, so the Young Aizawa arc turned into a pretty extended affair. It'll keep going for several more chapters.

—Furuhashi

Shirakumo's U.A. uniform design came from Horikoshi-san. The goggles I designed as part of his costume just happened to look like Aizawa's, and I'm grateful that Furuhashi-san picked up on that and made a whole point of it.

—Betten

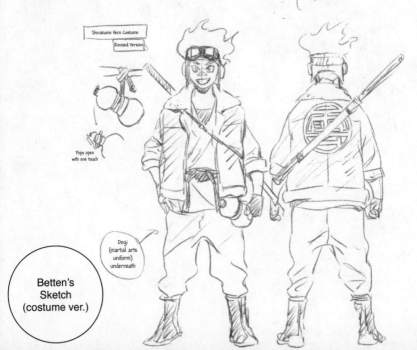

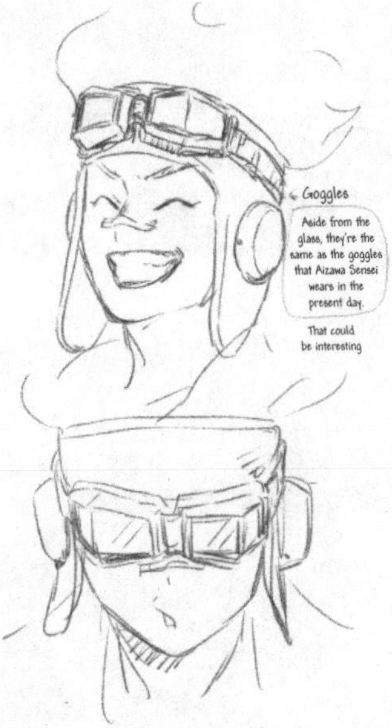
Goggles
Aside from the glass, they're the same as the goggles that Aizawa Sensei wears in the present day.
That could be interesting

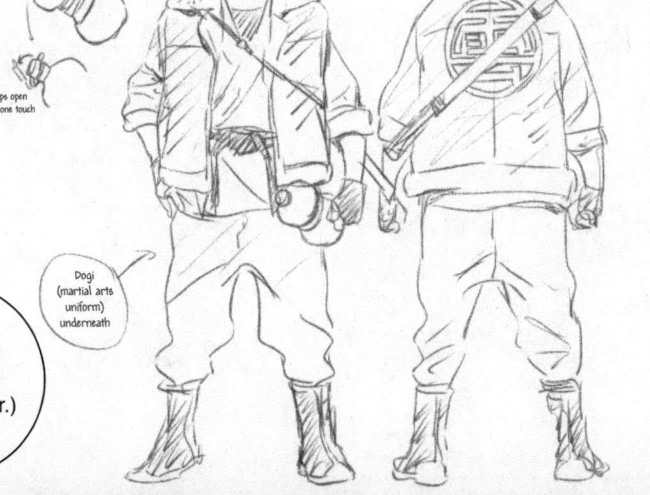
Shirakumo Hero Costume
Revised Version
Pops open with one touch
Dogi (martial arts uniform) underneath

Betten's Sketch (costume ver.)

MY HERO ACADEMIA

SCHOOL BRIEFS

ORIGINAL STORY BY
KOHEI HORIKOSHI

WRITTEN BY
ANRI YOSHI

Prose short stories featuring the everyday school lives of My Hero Academia's fan-favorite characters!

VIZ

MY HERO ACADEMIA SMASH!!

Story and Art by Hirofumi Neda
Original Concept by Kohei Horikoshi

HILARIOUS HIJINKS
featuring the characters
and story lines of
MY HERO ACADEMIA!

The superpowered society of *My Hero Academia* takes a hilarious turn in this reimagining of the best-selling series! Join Midoriya, All Might and all the aspiring heroes of U.A. High, plus memorable villains, in an irreverent take on the main events of the series, complete with funny gags, ridiculous jokes and superpowered humor!

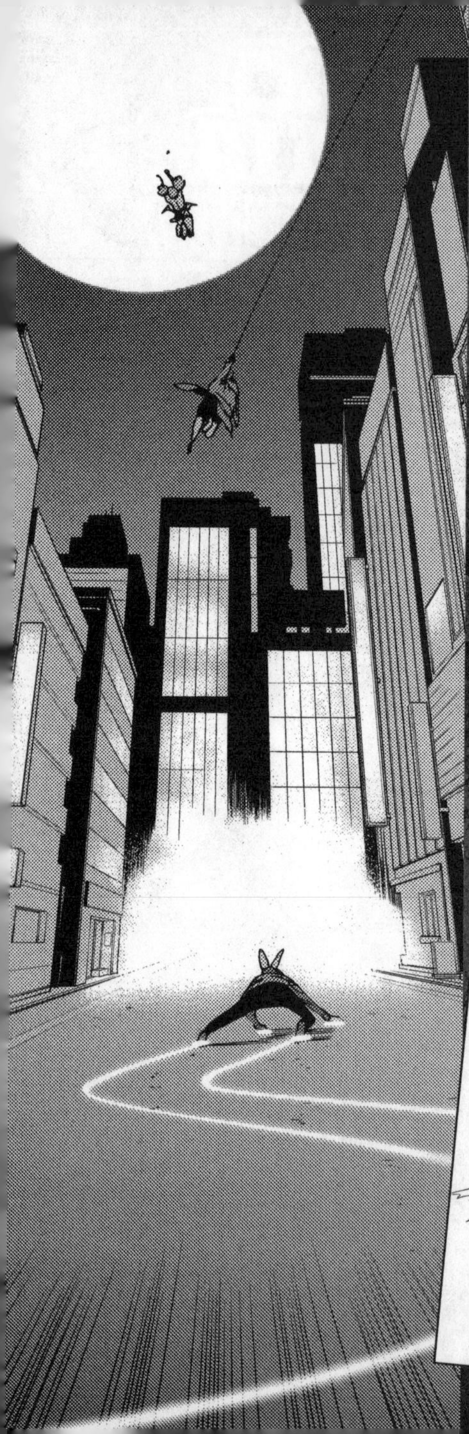

YOU'RE READING THE WRONG WAY!!

MY HERO ACADEMIA VIGILANTES

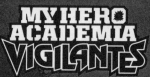

reads from right to left, starting in the upper-right corner. Japanese is read from right to left, meaning that action, sound effects and word-balloon order are completely reversed from English order.

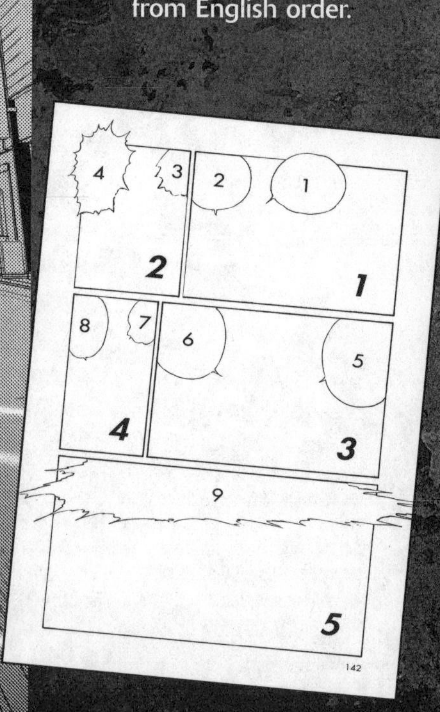

1
2
3
4
1
2
5
6
7
8
3
4
9
5
142